# A Journey From Prince of Wales's Fort, in Hudson's Bay, to the Northern Ocean. Undertaken ... for the Discovery of Copper Mines, a North West Passage, &c. in the Years 1769, ... 1772

A

# JOURNEY

FROM

PRINCE OF WALES'S FORT.

A MA[P]

exhibiting M.R HEARN[E]

two Journies for t[he]

COPPER MI[NE]

in the Years 177[0]

under the [direction of]

HUDSON'S B[AY]

P A R [T]

Arctic Circle

ATHAPUSCOW [LAKE]

Coppermine R.

Coppermine Hill

Copper mine Hill

White Lake

Stoney Mount.

Cong. or Bar who shot.

Thleweyaza Yeth

Large white fish Lake

Thleweyaza Lake

Thlewiaza Lake

Lake

Island Lake

Cath Lake

Partridge Lake

Snowy Lake

Snared Lake

Tittmeg Lake

Wholdiah Lake

Doo Round R.

Doo Round Lake

Hawk Hill

Pachubby L.

Island Lake

Buckmaster's

Hill Island Lake

Garnished Lake

Large White Lake

N O R T H   A M E R [I C A]

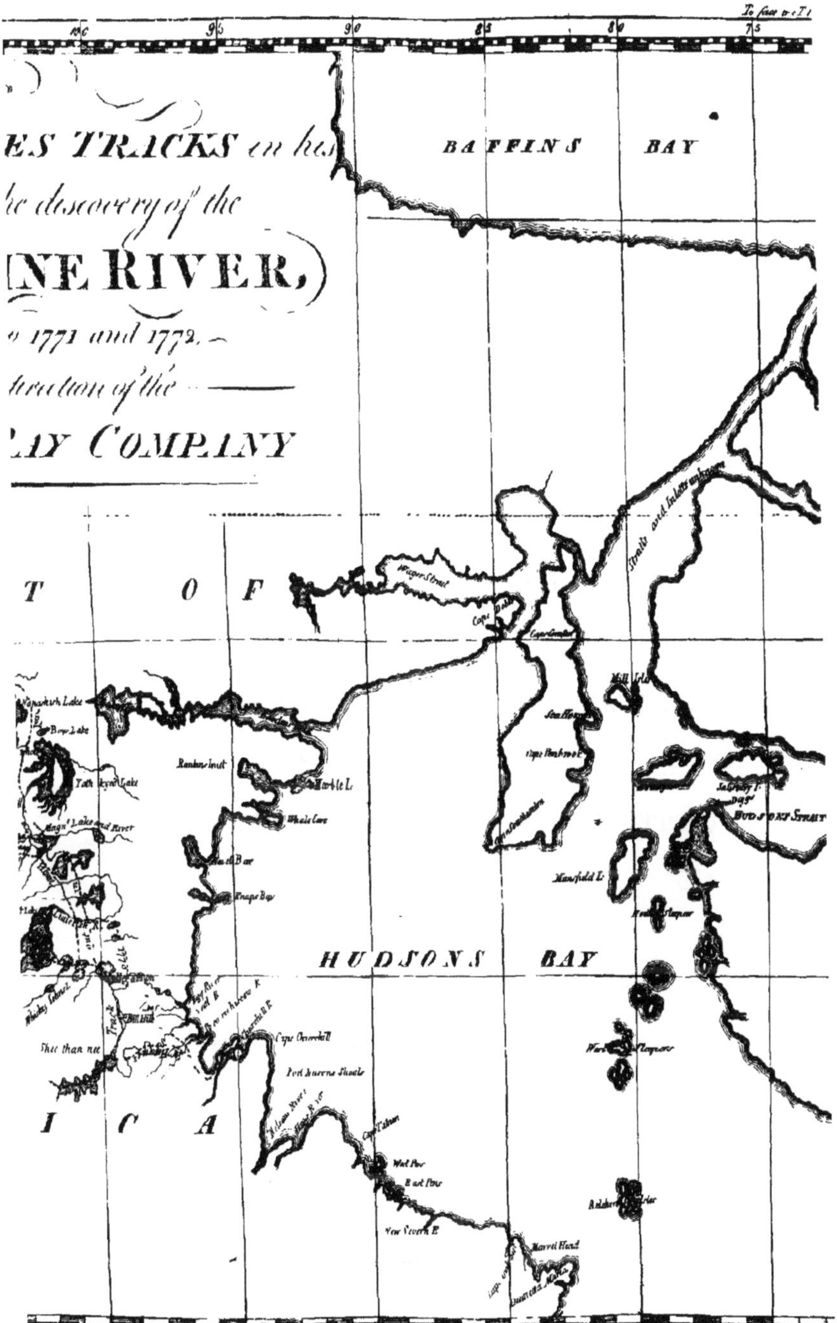

ES TRACKS in his
he discovery of the
NE RIVER,
1771 and 1772.
tion of the
AY COMPANY
BAFFINS BAY
T O F
I C A
HUDSONS BAY
Wager Strait
Cape Dobbs
Rankins Inlet
Marble I.
Whale Cove
Knaps Bay
Cape Churchill
Mansfield I.
Hudsons Strait
New Severn R.
Bow Lake
Straits and Inlets unknown
100
95
90
85
80
75

A

JOURNEY

FROM

PRINCE OF WALES'S FORT,

*IN HUDSON'S BAY,*

TO

THE NORTHERN OCEAN.

UNDERTAKEN

*BY ORDER OF THE HUDSON'S BAY COMPANY*

FOR THE DISCOVERY OF

COPPER MINES, A NORTH WEST PASSAGE, &c

In the Years 1769, 1770, 1771, & 1772.

———————

By SAMUEL HEARNE.

———————

DUBLIN.

PRINTED FOR P BYRNE, No 108, AND J. RICE, No. 111,
GRAFTON-STREET.

1796.

TO

SAMUEL WEGG, Efq     Governor,

Sir JAMES WINTER LAKE, Deputy Governor,

A N D

'THE REST OF THE COMMITTEE

OF THE HONOURABLE

*HUDSON'S BAY COMPANY,*

———————————

HONOURABLE SIRS,

AS the following Journey, was undertaken at your Requeſt and Expence, I feel it no leſs my Duty than my Inclination to ad-dreſs it to you ; hoping that my humble En-deavours to relate, in a plain and unadorned Style, the various Circumſtances and Remarks

a            which

which occurred during that Journey, will
meet with your Approbation.

I am, with much Efteem and Gratitude,

HONOURABLE SIRS,

Your moft obedient, and

moft obliged humble Servant,

SAMUEL HEARNE.

# PREFACE.

MR. DALRYMPLE, in one of his Pamphlets relating to Hudfon's Bay, has been fo very particular in his obfervations on my Journey, as to remark, that I have not explained the conftruction of the Quadrant which I had the misfortune to break in my fecond Journey to the North. It was a Hadley's Quadrant, with a bubble attached to it for an horizon, and made by Daniel Scatlif of Wapping. But as no inftrument on the fame principle could be procured when I was fetting out on my laft Journey, an old Elton's Quadrant, which had been upwards of thirty years at the Fort, was the only inftrument I could then be provided with, in any refpect proper for making obfervations with on the land.

Mr. Dalrymple alfo obferves, that I only inferted in my laft Journal to the Company, one obfervation for the latitude, which may be true; but I had, neverthelefs, feveral others during that journey, particularly at Snow-bird Lake, Thelwey-aza-yeth, and Clowey, exclufive of that mentioned in the Journal taken at Conge-cathawhachaga. But when I was on that Journey,

and

and for feveral years after, I little thought that
any remarks made in it would ever have attract-
ed the notice of the Public: if I had, greater
pains might and would have been taken to render it more worthy of their attention than it now
is.   At that time my ideas and ambition extended no farther than to give my employers fuch an
account of my proceedings as might be fatisfactory to them, and anfwer the purpofe which they
had in view , little thinking it would ever come
under the infpection of fo ingenious and indefa-
tigable a geographer as Mr. Dalrymple muft be
allowed to be.   But as the cafe has turned out
otherwife, I have at my leifure hours recopied all
my Journals into one book, and in fome inftances added to the remarks I had before made ; not
fo much for the information of thofe who are
critics in geography, as for the amufement of can-
did and indulgent readers, who may perhaps feel
themfelves in fome meafure gratified, by having
the face of a country brought to their view,
which has hitherto been entirely unknown to
every European except myfelf.   Nor will I flatter myfelf, a defcription of the modes of living,
manners, and cuftoms of the natives, (which,
though long known, have never been defcribed.)
be lefs acceptable to the curious

I cannot help obferving, that I feel myfelf rather hurt at Mr. Dalrymple's rejecting my latitude
in fo peremptory a manner, and in fo great a proportion,

portion, as he has done, becaufe, before I arrived at Conge-cathawhachaga, the Sun did not fet during the whole night: a proof that I was then to the Northward of the Arctic Circle. I may be allowed to add, that when I was at the Copper River, on the eighteenth of July, the Sun's declination was but 21°, and yet it was certainly fome height above the horizon at midnight; how much, as I did not *then* remark, I will not *now* take upon me to fay; but it proves that the latitude was confiderably more than Mr. Dalrymple will admit of. His affertion, that no grafs is to be found on the (rocky) coaft of Greenland farther North than the latitude of 65°, is no proof there fhould not be any in a much higher latitude in the interior parts of North America. For, in the firft place, I think it is more than probable, that the Copper River empties itfelf into a fort of inland Sea, or extenfive Bay, fomewhat like that of Hudfon's: and it is well known that no part of the coaft of Hudfon's Straits, nor thofe of Labradore, at leaft for fome degrees South of them, any more than the Eaft coaft of Hudfon's Bay, till we arrive near Whale River, have any trees on them, while the Weft coaft of the Bay in the fame latitudes, is well clothed with timber. Where then is the ground for fuch an affertion? Had Mr. Dalrymple confidered this circumftance only, I flatter myfelf he would not fo haftily have objected to woods and grafs being feen in fimilar fituations, though in a much higher latitude. Neither can the reafon-

ing

ing which Mr. Dalrymple derives from the error I committed in estimating the distance to Cumberland House, any way affect the question under consideration; because that distance being chiefly in longitude, I had no means of correcting it by an observation, which was not the case here.

I do not by any means wish to enter into a dispute with, or incur the displeasure of Mr. Dalrymple; but thinking, as I do, that I have not been treated in so liberal a manner as I ought to have been, he will excuse me for endeavouring to convince the Public that his objections are in a great measure without foundation. And having done so, I shall quit the disagreeable subject with declaring, that if any part of the following sheets should afford amusement to Mr. Dalrymple, or any other of my readers, it will be the highest gratification I can receive, and the only recompence I desire to obtain for the hardships and fatigue which I underwent in procuring the information contained in them.

Being well assured that several learned and curious gentlemen are in possession of manuscript copies of, or extracts from, my Journals, as well as copies of the Charts, I have been induced to make this copy as correct as possible, and to publish it, especially as I observe that scarcely any two of the publications that contain extracts from my Journals, agree in the dates when I arrived at, or departed from, particular places. To rectify those disagreements I applied to the Governor and

Committee

Committee of the Hudson's Bay Company, for leave to peruse my original Journals. This was granted with the greatest affability and politenefs; as well as a fight of all my Charts relative to this Journey   With this affiftance I have been enabled to rectify fome inaccuracies that had, by trufting too much to memory, crept into this copy; and I now offer it to the Public under authentic dates and the beft authorities, however widely fome publications may differ from it.

I have taken the liberty to expunge fome paffages which were inferted in the original copy, as being no ways interefting to the Public, and feveral others have undergone great alterations; fo that, in fact, the whole may be faid to be new-modelled, by being blended with a variety of Remarks and Notes that were not inferted in the original copy, but which my long refidence in the country has enabled me to add.

The account of the principal quadrupeds and birds that frequent thofe Northern regions in Summer, as well as thofe which never migrate, though not defcribed in a fcientific manner, may not be entirely unacceptable to the moft fcientific zoologifts; and to thofe who are unacquainted with the technical terms ufed in zoology, it may perhaps be more ufeful and entertaining, than if I had defcribed them in the moft claffical manner.   But I muft not conclude this Preface, without acknowledging, in the moft ample manner, the affiftance I have received from the perufal

fal

fal of Mr. Pennant's Arctic Zoology; which has enabled me to give feveral of the birds their proper names; for thofe by which they are known in Hudfon's Bay are purely Indian, and of courfe quite unknown to every European who has not refided in that country.

To conclude, I cannot fufficiently regret the lofs of a confiderable Vocabulary of the Northern Indian Language, containing fixteen folio pages, which was lent to the late Mr. Hutchins, then Correfponding Secretary to the Company, to copy for Captain Duncan, when he went on difcoveries to Hudfon's Bay in the year one thoufand feven hundred and ninety. But Mr. Hutchins dying foon after, the Vocabulary was taken away with the reft of his effects, and cannot now be recovered; and memory, at this time, will by no means ferve to replace it.

C O N-

# CONTENTS.

---

## C H A P  II.

Transactions from our arrival at the Factory, to
my leaving it again, and during the First Part
of my Second Journey, till I had the misfortune to break the Quadrant.

**CHAP.**

## CHAP. III.

Tranſactions from the Time the Quadrant was broken, till I arrived at the Factory.

CHAP.

## C H A P. IV.

Tranfactions during our Stay at Prince of Wales's Fort, and the former Part of our third Expedition, till our Arrival at Clowey, where we built Canoes, in May 1771.

C H A P.  V.

Tranſactions at Clowey, and on our Journey, till our Arrival at the Copper-mine River.

## CHAP. VI.

Tranſactions at the Copper-mine River, and till we joined all the Women to the South of Coge-ad Lake.

*Some Copper Indians join us —Indians ſend three ſpies*
*down the river.—Begin my ſurvey —Spies return,*
*and give an account of five tents of Eſquimaux.—In-*
*dians conſult the beſt method to ſteal on them in the*
*night, and kill them while aſleep.—Croſs the river.*
*—Proceedings of the Indians as they advance to-*
*wards the Eſquimaux tents.—The Indians begin the*
*maſſacre while the poor Eſquimaux are aſleep, and*
*ſlay them all.—Much affected at the ſight of one*
*young woman killed cloſe to my feet.—The behaviour*
*of the Indians on this occaſion.—Their brutiſh treat-*
*ment of the dead bodies —Seven more tents ſeen on*
*the oppoſite ſide of the river.—The Indians haraſs*
*them, till they fly to a ſhoal in the river for ſafety.*
*—Beha-*

## C H A P.   VII.

Remarks from the Time the Women joined us
till our Arrival at the Athapufcow Lake.

## CHAP. VIII.

Tranfactions and Remarks from our Arrival on the South Side of the Athapufcow Lake, till our Arrival at Prince of Wales's Fort on Churchill River.

b  my

## C H A P. IX.

A short Description of the Northern Indians, also a farther Account of their Country, Manufactures, Customs, &c

*Some*

xxii CONTENTS.

CHAP.

## CHAP. X.

*An*

# CONTENTS.

# CONTENTS.

ry---*Eye-berry*---*Blue-Berry*,---and a *fmall fpecies*
*of Hips.*

*Burridge*---*Coltsfoot*—*Sorrel*—*Dandelion,*
*Wifh-a-capucca*—*Jackafhey-puck*—*Mofs of va-*
*rious forts*—*Grafs of feveral kinds*—*and Vetches.*

*The Trees found fo far North near the Sea, con-*
*fift only of Pines*—*Juniper*—*Small Poplar*—*Bufh-*
*willows*—*and Creeping Birch.* -

# INTRODUCTION.

FOR many years it was the opinion of all ranks of people, that the Hudſon's Bay Company were averſe to making diſcoveries of every kind; and being content with the profits of their ſmall capital, as it was then called, did not want to increaſe their trade. What might have been the ideas of former members of the Company reſpecting the firſt part of theſe charges I cannot ſay, but I am well aſſured that they, as well as the preſent members, have always been ready to embrace every plauſible plan for extending the trade. As a proof of this aſſertion, I need only mention the vaſt ſums of money which they have expended at different times in endeavouring to eſtabliſh fiſheries, though without ſucceſs: and the following Journey, together with the various attempts made by Bean, Chriſtopher, Johnſton, and Duncan, to find a North Weſt paſſage, are recent proofs that the preſent members are as deſirous of making diſcoveries, as they are of extending their trade.

That air of myſtery, and affectation of ſecrecy, perhaps, which formerly attended ſome of the
Company's

Company's proceedings in the Bay, might give rise to those conjectures; and the unfounded affertions and unjust afperfions of Dobbs, Ellis, Robfon, Dragge, and the American Traveller, the only Authors that have written on Hudfon's Bay, and w o have all, from motives of intereft or revenge, taken a particular pleafure in arraigning the conduct of the Company, without having any real knowledge of their proceedings, or any experience in their fervice, on which to found their charges, muft have contributed to confirm the public in that opinion. Moft of thofe Writers, however, advance fuch notorious abfurdities, that none except thofe who are already prejudiced againft the Company can give them credit*.

Robfon, from his fix years refidence in Hudfon's Bay and in the Company's fervice, might naturally have been fuppofed to know fomething of the climate and foil immediately round the Factories at which he refided; but the whole of his book is evidently written with prejudice, and dictated by a fpirit of revenge, becaufe his romantic and inconfiftent fchemes were rejected by the Company. Befides, it is well known that Robfon was no more than a tool in the hand of Mr. Dobbs.

The American Traveller, though a more elegant,

---

* Since the above was written, a Mr Umfreville has publifhed an account of Hudfon's Bay, with the fame ill-nature as the former Authors and for no other reafon than that of being difappointed in fucceeding to a command in the Bay, though there was no vacancy for him.

gant writer, has still lefs claim to our indulgence, as his affertions are a greater tax on our credulity. His faying that he difcovered feveral large lumps of the fineft virgin copper\*, is fuch a palpable falfehood that it needs no refutation No man, either Inglifh or Indian, ever found a bit of copper in that country to the South of the feventy-firft degree of latitude, unlefs it had been accidentally dropped by fome of the far Northern Indians in their way to the Company's Factory.

The natives who range over, rather than inhabit, the large track of land which lies to the North of Churchill River, having repeatedly brought famples of copper to the Company's Factory, many of our people conjectured that it was found not far from our fettlements; and as the Indians informed them that the mines were not very diftant from a large river, it was generally fuppofed that this river muft empty itfelf into Hudfon's Bay; as they could by no means think that any fet of people, however, wandering their manner of life might be, could ever traverfe fo large a track of country as to pafs the Northern boundary of that Bay, and particularly without the affiftance of water-carriage. The following Journal, however, will fhew how much thefe people have been miftaken, and prove alfo the improbability of putting their favourite fcheme of mining into practice.

The

---

\* American Travellers, page 23

The accounts of this grand River, which some have turned into a Strait, together with the samples of copper, were brought to the Company's Factory at Churchill River immediately after its first establishment, in the year one thousand seven hundred and fifteen, and it does not appear that any attempts were made to discover either the river or mines till the year one thousand seven hundred and nineteen, when the Company fitted out a ship, called the Albany Frigate, Captain George Barlow *, and a sloop, called the Disco-

very,

---

* Captain Barlow was Governor at Albany Fort when the French went over land from Canada to besiege it in the 1724 The Canadians and their Indian guides lurked in the neighbourhood of Albany for several days before they made the attack and killed many of the cattle that were grazing in the marshes A faithful Home-Indian, who was on a hunting excursion, discovering these strangers, and supposing them to be enemies, immediately returned to the Fort, and informed the Governor of the circumstance, who gave little credit to it. However, every measure was taken for the defence of the Fort, and orders were given to the Master of a sloop that lay at some distance, to come to the Fort with all possible expedition on hearing a gun fired

According! , in the middle of the night, or rather in the morning, the French came before the Fort, marched up to the gate, and demanded entrance M Barlow, who was then on the watch, told them, that the Governor was asleep, but he would get the keys immediately The French hearing this, expected no opposition, and flocked up to the gate as close as they could stand Barlow took the advantage of this opportunity, and instead of opening the gate only opened two port holes, where two six pounders stood loaded with grape shot, which were instantly fired This discharge killed great numbers of the French, and among them the Commander, who was an Irishman

Such an unexpected reception made the remainder retire with great precipitation, and the Master of the sloop hearing the guns, made the best of his way up to the Fort, but some of the French who lay concealed under the banks of the river killed him, and all the boat's crew

The

very, Captain David Vaughan  The sole command of this expedition, however, was given to Mr. James Knight, a man of great experience in the Company's service, who had been many years Governor at the different Factories in the Bay, and who had made the first settlement at Churchill River.  Notwithstanding the experience Mr. Knight might have had of the Company's business, and his knowledge of those parts of the Bay where he had resided, it cannot be supposed he was well acquainted with the nature of the business in which he then engaged, having nothing to direct him but the slender and imperfect accounts which he had received from the Indians, who at that time were little known, and less understood.

Those disadvantages, added to his advanced age, he being then near eighty, by no means discouraged this bold adventurer; who was so prepossessed of his success, and of the great advantage
tage

tage that would arife from his difcoveries, that
he procured, and took with him, fome large iron-
bound chefts, to hold gold duft and other valua
bles, which he fondly flattered himfelf were to be
found in thofe parts.

The firft paragraph of the Company's Order,
to Mr. Knight on this occafion appears to be as
follows:

" *To Captain* JAMES KNIGHT.

" S I R,                              4th June, 1719.
" From the experience we have had of your
" abilities in the management of our affairs, we
" have, upon your application to us, fitted out
" the Albany frigate, Captain George Barlow,
" and the Difcovery, Captain David Vaughan
" Commander, upon a difcovery, to the North
" ward; and to that end have given you power
" and authority to act and do all things relating
" to the faid voyage, the navigation of the faid
" fhip and floop only excepted; and have given
" orders and inftructions to our faid commanders
" for that purpofe.

" You are, with the firft opportunity of wind
" and weather, to depart from Gravefend on your
" intended voyage, and by God's permiffion, to
" find out the Straits of Anian, in order to difco
" ver gold and other valuable commodities to the
" Northward, &c. &c."

                                                        Mr

Mr Knight soon left Gravesend, and proceeded on his voyage, but the ship not returning to England that year, as was expected, it was judged that she had wintered in Hudson's Bay, and having on board a good stock of provisions, a house in frame, together with all necessary mechanics, and a great assortment of trading goods, little or no thoughts were entertained of their not being in safety · but as neither ship nor sloop returned to England in the following year, (one thousand seven hundred and twenty,) the Company were much alarmed for their welfare; and, by their ship which went to Churchill in the year one thousand seven hundred and twenty-one, they sent orders for a sloop called the Whale Bone, John Scroggs Master, to go in search of them; but the ship not arriving in Churchill till late in the year, those orders could not be put in execution till the summer following (one thousand seven hundred and twenty two).

The North West coast of Hudson's Bay being little known in those days, and Mr. Scroggs finding himself greatly embarrassed with shoals and rocks, returned to Prince of Wales's Fort without making any certain discovery respecting the above ship or sloop, for all the marks he saw among the Esquimaux at Whale Cove scarcely amounted to the spoils which might have been made from a trifling accident, and consequently could not be considered as signs of a total shipwreck.

The

The ftrong opinion which then prevailed in Europe refpecting the probability of a North Weft paffage by the way of Hudfon's Bay. made many conjecture that Meffrs. Knight and Barlow had found that paffage, and had gone through it into the South Sea, by the way of California. Many years elapfed without any other convincing proof occurring to the contrary, except that Middleton, Ellis, Bean, Chriftopher, and Johnfton, had not been able to find any fuch paffage. And notwithftanding a floop was annually fent to the Northward on difcovery, and to trade with the Efquimaux, it was the fummer of one thoufand feven hundred and fixty-feven, before we had pofitive proofs that poor Mr. Knight and Captain Barlow had been loft in Hudfon's Bay.

The Company were now carrying on a black whale fifhery, and Marble Ifland was made the place of rendezvous not only on account of the commodioufnefs of the harbour, but becaufe it had been obferved that the whales were more plentiful about that ifland than on any other part of the coaft. This being the cafe, the boats, when on the look-out for fifh, had frequent occafion to row clofe to the ifland, by which means they difcovered a new harbour near the Eaft end of it, at the head of which they found guns, anchors, cables, bricks, a fmith's anvil, and many other articles, which the hand of time had not defaced, and which being of no ufe to the natives, or too heavy to be removed by them, had

not

not been taken from the place in which they were originally laid. The remains of the houfe, though pulled to pieces by the Efquimaux, for the wood and iron, are yet very plain to be feen, as alfo the hulls, or more properly fpeaking, the bottoms of the fhip and floop, which he funk in about five fathoms water, toward the head of the harbour. The figure-head of the fhip, and alfo the guns, &c. were fent home to the Company, and are certain proofs that Meffrs. Knight and Barlow had been loft on that inhofpitable ifland, where neither ftick nor ftump was to be feen, and which lies near fixteen miles from the main land. Indeed the main is little better, being a jumble of barren hills and rocks, deftitute of every kind of herbage except mofs and grafs; and at that part, the woods are feveral hundreds of miles from the fea fide.

In the Summer of one thoufand feven hundred and fixty-nine, while we were profecuting the fifhery, we faw feveral Efquimaux at this new harbour; and perceiving that one or two of them were greatly advanced in years, our curiofity was excit·d to afk them fome queftions concerning the above fhip and floop, which we were the better enable to do by the affiftance of an Efquimaux, who was then in the Company's fer ice as linguift, and annually failed in one of their veffels in that character. The account which we received from them was full, clear, and unre-

c                                        ferved,

ferved, and the fum of it was to the following
purport :

When the veffels arrived at this place (Marble
Ifland) it was very late in the Fall, and in getting
them into the harbour, the largeft received much
damage; but on being fairly in, the Englifh began to build the houfe, their number at that time
feeming to be about fifty. As foon as the ice
permitted, in the following Summer, (one thoufand feven hundred and twenty,) the Efquimaux
paid them another vifit, by which time the number of the Englifh was greatly reduced, and thofe
that were living feemed very unhealthy. According to the account given by the Efquimaux they
were then very bufily employed, but about what
they could not eafily defcribe, probably in length-
ening the long boat ; for at a little diftance from
the houfe there is now lying a great quantity of
oak chips, which have been moft affuredly made
by carpenters.

Sicknefs and famine occafioned fuch havock
among the Englifh, that by the fetting in of the
fecond Winter their number was reduced to twenty. That Winter (one thoufand feven hundred
and twenty) fome of the Efquimaux took up their
abode on the oppofite fide of the harbour to that
on which the Englifh had built their houfes*, and
frequently fupplied them with fuch provifions as
they

---

* I have feen the remains of thofe houfes feveral times, they are on
the Weft fide of the harbour, and in all probability will be difcernible for
many years to come.

It

they had, which chiefly confifted of whale's blubber and feal's flefh and train oil. When the Spring advanced, the Efquimaux went to the continent, and on their vifiting Marble Ifland again, in the Summer of one thoufand feven hundred and twenty-one, they only found five of the Englifh alive, and thofe were in fuch diftrefs for provifions that they eagerly eat the feal's flefh and whale's blubber quite raw, as they purchafed it from the natives. This difordered them fo much, that three of them died in a few days, and the other two, though very weak, made a fhift to bury them. Thofe two furvived many days after the reft, and frequently went to the top of an adjacent rock, and earneftly looked to the South and Eaft, as if in expectation of fome veffels coming to their relief. After continuing there a confiderable time together, and nothing appearing in fight, they fat down clofe together, and wept bitterly. At length one of the two died, and the other's ftrength was fo far exhaufted, that he fell down and died alfo, in attempting to dig a grave for his companion. The fculls

c 2         and

---

It is rather furprifing, that neither Middleton, Ellis, Chriftopher, Johnfton, nor Garbet, who have all of them been at Marble Ifland, and fome of them often, ever difcovered this harbour, particularly the laft-mentioned gentleman, who actually failed quite round the ifland on a very fine pleafant day in the Summer of 1766. But this difcovery was referved for a Mr Jofeph Stephens, a man of the leaft merit I ever knew, though he then had the command of a veffel called the Succefs, employed in the whale fifhery, and in the year 1769, had the command of the Charlotte given to him, a fine brig of one hundred tons, when I was his mate and other large bones of thofe two men are now lying above-ground clofe to the houfe. The longeſt liver was, according to the Efquimaux account, always employed in working of iron into implements for them, probably he was the armourer, or fmith.

Some Northern Indians who came to trade at Prince of Wales's Fort in the Spring of the year one thoufand feven hundred and fixty-eight, brought farther accounts of the grand river, as it was called, and alfo feveral pieces of copper, as famples of the produce of the mine near it; which determined Mr. Norton, who was then Governor at Churchill, to reprefent it to the Company as an affair worthy of their attention; and as he went that year to England, he had an opportunity of laying all the information he had received before the Board, with his opinion thereon, and the plan which he thought moſt likely to fucceed in the difcovery of thofe mines. In confequence of Mr. Norton's reprefentations, the Committee refolved to fend an intelligent perfon by land to obferve the longitude and latitude of the river's mouth, to make a chart of the country he might walk through, with fuch remarks as occurred to him during the Journey; when I was pitched on as a proper perfon to conduct the expedition. By the fhip that went to Churchill in the Summer of one thoufand feven hundred and fixty-nine, the Company fent out fome aftronomical inſtruments, very portable, and fit for

fuch

fuch obfervations as they required me to make, and at the fame time requefted me to undertake the Journey, promifing to allow me at my return, a gratuity proportionable to the trouble and fatigue I might undergo in the expedition*.

I did

* The conditions offered me on this occafion cannot be better expreffed than in the Company's own words, which I have tranfcribed from their private letter to me, dated 25th May 1769

" From the good opinion we entertain of you, and Mr Norton's recom-
" mendation, we have agreed to raife your wages to £        per annum
" for two years, and have placed you in our Council at Prince of Wales's
" Fort, and we fhould have been ready to advance you to the command of
" the Charlotte, according to your requeft, if a matter of more immedi-
" ate confequence had not intervened.

" Mr Norton has propofed an inland Journey, far to the North of
" Churchill, to promote an extenfion of our trade, as well as for the difco-
" very of a North Weft Paffage, Copper Mines, &c, and as an undertak-
" ing of this nature requires the attention of a perfon capable of taking
" an obfervation for determining the longitude and latitude, and alfo di-
" ftances, and the courfe of rivers and their depths, we have fixed upon
" you (efpecially as it is reprefented to us to be your own inclination) to
" conduct this Journey, with proper affiftants

" We therefore hope you will fecond our expectations in readily perform-
" ing this fervice, and upon your return we fhall willingly make you any
" acknowledgment fuitable to your trouble therein

" We highly approve of your going in the Speedwell, to affift on the
" whale fifhery laft year, and heartily wifh you health and fuccefs in the
" prefent expedition

We remain your loving Friends,

" BIBYE LAKE, Dep Gov          " JAMES WINTER LAKE.
" JOHN ANTHONY MERLE            " HERMAN BERENS
" ROBERT MERRY                  " JOSEPH SPURREL
" SAMUEL WEGC                   " JAMES FITZ GERALD "

The Company had no fooner perufed my Journals and Charts, than they ordered a handfome fum to be placed to the credit of my account,

and

I did not hefitate to comply with the requeft of the Company, and in the November following, when fome Northern Indians came to trade, Mr. Norton, who was then returned to the command of Prince of Wales's Fort, engaged fuch of them for my guides as he thought were moft likely to anfwer the purpofe; but none of them had been at this grand river. I was fitted out with every thing thought neceffary, and with ammunition to ferve two years. I was to be accompanied by two of the Company's fervants, two of the Home-guard* (Southern) Indians, and a fufficient num-ber of Northern Indians to carry and haul my baggage, provide for me, &c. But for the bet-ter

and in the two firft paragraphs of their letter to me, dated 14th May 1773, they exprefs themfelves in the following words

"Mr SAMUEL HEARNE,

"SIR,

"Your letter of the 28th Auguft laft gave us the agreeable pleafure to "hear of your fafe return to our Factory Your Journal, and the two "charts you fent, fufficiently convinces us of your very judicious re-"marks

"We have maturely confidered your great affiduity in the various acci "dents which occurred in your feveral Journies We hereby return "you our grateful thanks, and to manifeft our obligation we have con "fented to allow you a gratuity of £ for thofe fervices"

As a farther proof of the Company's being perfectly fatisfied with my conduct while on that Journey, the Committee unanimoufly appointed me Chief of Prince of Wales's Fort in the Summer of 1775, and Mr Bibye Lake, who was then Governor, and feveral others of the Committee, ho-noured me with a regular correfpondence as long as they lived

* By the Home-guard Indians we are to underftand certain of the na-tives who are immediately employed under the protection of the Compa-ny's fervants, refide on the plantation, and are employed in hunting fo the Factory

ter ftating this arrangement, it will not be improper to infert my Inftructions, which, with
fome occafional remarks thereon, will throw much
light on the following Journal, and be the beft
method of proving how far thofe orders have
been complied with, as well as fhew my reafons
for neglecting fome parts as unneceffary, and the
impoffibility of putting other parts of them in
execution.

" ORDERS *and* INSTRUCTIONS *for Mr.*
" Samuel Hearne, *going on an Expedition by*
" *Land towards the Latitude* 70° *North, in*
" *order to gain a Knowledge of the Northern*
" *Indians Country,* &c. *on Behalf of the Ho-*
" *nourable Hudfon's Bay Company, in the Year*
" 1769.

" *Mr* Samuel Hearne,
" SIR,
" Whereas the Honourable Hudfon's Bay
" Company have been informed by the report
" from Indians, that there is a great probability
" of confiderable advantages to be expected from
" a better knowledge of their country by us,
" than what hitherto has been obtained ; and as
" it is the Company's earneft defire to embrace
" every circumftance that may tend to the bene-
" fit of the faid company, or the Nation at large,
" they have requefted you to conduct this Expe-
" dition ; and as you have readily confented to
" undertake the prefent Journey, you are here-
" by

" by defired to proceed as foon as poffible, with
" William Ifbefter failor, and Thomas Merriman
" landfman, as companions, they both being wil-
" ling to accompany you, alfo two of the Home-
" guard Southern Indians, who are to attend
" and affift you during the Journey; and Cap-
" tain Chawchinahaw, his Lieutenant Nabyah,
" and fix or eight of the beft Northern Indians we
" can procure, with a fmall part of their families,
" are to conduct you, provide for you, and af-
" fift you and your companions in every thing
" that lays in their power, having particular or-
" ders fo to do

" 2dly, whereas you and your companions are
" well fitted-out with every thing we think ne-
" ceffary, as alfo a fample of light trading goods;
" thefe you are to difpofe of by way of prefents
" (and not by way of trade) to fuch far-off Indi-
" ans as you may meet with, and to fmoke your
" Calimut* of Peace with their leaders, in order
" to eftablifh a friendfhip with them. You are
" alfo to perfuade them as much as poffible from
" going to war with each other, to encourage
" them to exert themfelves in procuring furis
" and other articles for trade, and to affure them
" of good payment for them at the Company's
" Factory.

" It

* The Calimut is a long ornamented ftem of a pipe, much in ufe among
all the tribes of Indians who know the ufe of tobacco   It is particularly
ufed in all cafes of ceremony, either in making war or peace, at all public
entertainments, orations &c.

" It is sincerely recommended to you and your
" companions to treat the natives with civiliry,
" so as not to give them any room for complaint
" or disgust, as they have strict orders not to give
" you the least offence, but are to aid and assist
" you in any matter you may request of them
" for the benefit of the undertaking.

" If any Indians you may meet, that are com-
" ing to the Fort, should be willing to trust you
" with either food or clothing, make your agree-
" ment for those commodities, and by them send
" me a letter, specifying the quantity of each ar-
" ticle, and they shall be paid according to your
" agreement. And, according to the Company's
" orders, you are to correspond with me, or the
" Chief at Prince of Wales's Fort for the time be-
" ing, at all opportunities : And as you have ma-
" thematical instruments with you, you are to
" send me, or the Chief for the time being, an
" account of what latitude and longitude you
" may be in at such and such periods, together
" with the heads of your proceedings ; which ac-
" counts are to be remitted to the Company by
" the return of their ships*.

" 3dly, The Indians who are now appointed
" your guides, are to conduct you to the borders
" of the Athapuscow † Indians country, where
                            " Captain

---

* No convenient opportunity offered during my last Journey, except one
on the 22d March 1771, and as nothing material had happened during that
part of my Journey, I thought there was not any necessity for sending an
extract of my Journal, I there ore only sent a Letter to the Governor, informing him of my situation with respect to latitude and longitude, and
some account of the usage which I received from the natives, &c

† By mistake in my former Journal and Draft called Arathapescow

" Captaim Matonabbee is to meet you † in the
" Spring of one thoufand feven hundred and fe-
" venty, in order to conduct you to a river re-
" prefented by the Indians to abound with cop-
" per ore, animals of the furr kind, &c. and
" which is faid to be fo far to the Northward,
" that in the middle of the Summer the Sun does
" not fet, and is fuppofed by the Indians to emp-
" ty itfelf into fome ocean. This river, which
" is called by the Northern Indians Neetha-fan-
" fan-dazey, or the Far Off Metal River, you are,
" if poffible, to trace to the mouth, and there de-
" termine the latitude and longitude as near as
" you can; but more particularly fo if you find
" it navigable, and that a fettlement can be made
" there with any degree of fafety, or benefit to
" the Company.

" Be careful to obferve what mines are near
" the river, what water there is at the river's
" mouth, how far the woods are from the fea-
" fide, the courfe of the river, the nature of the
" foil, and the productions of it; and make any
" other remarks that you may think will be ei-
" ther

---

† This was barely probable, as Matonabbee at that time had not any information of this Journey being fet on foot, much lefs had he received orders to join me at the place and time here appointed, and had we acci-
centally met, he would by no means have undertaken the Journey without firft going to the Factory, and there making his agreement with the
Governor, for no Indian is fond of performing any particular fervice for
the Englifh, without firft knowing what is to be his reward At the fame
time, had I taken that rou on my out-fet, it would have carried me fome
hundreds of miles out of my road. See my Track on the Map in the
Winter 1770, and the Spring 1771

" ther neceſſary or ſatisfactory. And if the ſaid
" river be likely to be of any utility, take poſſeſ-
" ſion of it on behalf of the Hudſon's Bay Com-
" pany, by cutting your name on ſome of the
" rocks, as alſo the date of the year, month, &c.*

" When you attempt to trace this or any other
" river, be careful that the Indians are furniſhed
" with a ſufficient number of canoes for trying
" the depth of water, the ſtrength of the current,
" &c. If by any unforeſeen accident or diſaſter
" you ſhould not be able to reach the before-men-
" tioned river, it is earneſtly recommended to you,
" if poſſible, to know the event of Wager Strait†;
" for it is repreſented by the laſt diſcoverers to ter-
" minate in ſmall rivers and lakes. See how far
" the woods are from the navigable parts of it;
" and whether a ſettlement could with any pro-
" priety be made there. If this ſhould prove un-
" worthy

* I was not provided with inſtruments for cutting on ſtone, but for form-
ſake, I cut my name, date of the year, &c on a piece of board that had
been one of the Indian's targets, and placed it in a heap of ſtones on a ſmall
eminence near the entrance of the river, on the South ſide

† There is certainly no harm in making out all Inſtructions in the fulleſt
manner, yet it muſt be allowed that thoſe two parts might have been omitted with great propriety, for as neither Middleton, Ellis, nor Chriſtopher
were able to penetrate far enough up thoſe inlets to diſcover any kind of
herbage except moſs and graſs, much leſs woods, it was not likely thoſe parts
were ſo materially altered for the better ſince their times, as to make it
worth my while to attempt a farther diſcovery of them, and eſpecially as
I had an opportunity, during my ſecond Journey, of proving that the
woods do not reach the ſea-coaſt by ſome hundreds of miles in the parallel of Cheſterfield's Inlet And as the edge of the woods to the Northward always tends to the Weſtward, the diſtance muſt be greatly increaſed
in the latitude of Wager Strait Thoſe parts have long ſince been viſited
by the Company's ſervants, and are within the known limits of their
Charter, conſequently require no other form of poſſeſſion

" worthy of notice, you are to take the fame me-
" thod with Baker's Lake, which is the head of
" Bowden's or Chefterfield's Inlet*; as alfo with
" any other rivers you may meet with; and if
" likely to be of any utility, you are to take pof-
" feffion of them, as before mentioned, on the
" behalf of the Honourable Hudfon's Bay Com-
" pany. The draft of Bowden's Inlet and Wager
" Strait I fend with you, that you may have a bet-
" ter idea of thofe places, in cafe of your vifiting
" them.

" 4thly, Another material point which is re-
" commended to you, is to find out, if you can,
" either by your own travels, or by information
" from the Indians, whether there is a paffage
" through this continent†. It will be very ufeful
" to clear up this point, if poffible, in order to
" prevent farther doubts from arifing hereafter
　　　　　　　　　　　　　　　　　　" refpect-

---

\* See the preceding Note.

† The Continent of America is much wider than many people imagine, particularly Robfon, who thought that the Pacific Ocean was but a few days journey from the Weft coaft of Hudfon s Bay This, however, is fo far from being the cafe, that when I was at my greateft Weftern dift nce, upward of five hundred miles from Prince of Wales s Fort, the natives my guides well knew that many tribes of Indians lay to the Weft of us, and they knew no end to the land in that direction, nor have I met with any Ind ans, either Northern or Southern, that ever had feen the fea to the Weftward It is, indeed, well known to the intelligent and well in- formed pa t of the Company s fervants, that an extenfive and numerous, tribe of Indians, called E-arch e-thinnews, whofe country lies far Weft of any of the Company s or Canadian fettlements, muft have traffic with the Spaniards on the Weft fide of the Continent, becaufe fome of the Indians who formerly traded to York Fort, when at war with thofe people, fre- quently found faddles, bridles, mufkets, and many other articles, in their poffeffion, which were undoubtedly of Span fh manufactory.

　　　　　　　　　　　　　　　　　　　　　I have

" refpecting a paffage out of Hudfon's Bay * into
" the Weftern Ocean, as hath lately been repre-
" fented by the American Traveller. The particu-
" lars of thofe remarks you are to infert in your
" Journal, to be remitted home to the Company.

" If you fhould want any fupplies of ammuniti-
" on, or other neceffaries, difpatch fome trufty
" Indians to the Fort with a letter, fpecifying the
" quantity of each article, and appoint a place
" for the faid Indians to meet you again.

" When on your return, if at a proper time of
" the year, and you fhould be near any of the
" harbours that are frequented by the brigantine
" Charlotte, or the floop Churchill, during their
" voyage to the Northward, and you fhould chufe
" to return in one of them, you are defired to
" make frequent fmokes as you approach thofe
" harbours, and they will endeavour to receive
" you by making fmokes in anfwer to yours ;
" and as one thoufand feven hundred and feven-
" ty one will probably be the year in which you
" will return, the Mafters of thofe veffels at that
                                                  " period

---

I have feen feveral Indians who have been fo far Weft as to crofs the top
of that immenfe chain of mountains which run from North to South of the
continent of America. Beyond thofe mountains all rivers run to the
Weftward. I muft here obferve, that all the Indians I ever heard
relate their excurfions in that country, had invariably got fo far to the
South, that they did not experience any Winter, nor the leaft appearance
of either froft or fnow, though fometimes they have been abfent eighteen
months, or two years.

* As to a paffage through the continent of America by the way of Hudfon's Bay, it has fo long been exploded, notwithstanding what Mr Ellis has
urged in its favour, and the place it has found in the visionary Map of the
American Traveller, that any comment on it would be quite unneceffary.
My latitude only will be a fufficient proof that no fuch paffage is in exiftence.

" period fhall have particular orders on that head.

" It will be pleafing to hear by the firft oppor-
" tunity, in what latitude and longitude you meet
" the Leader Matonabbee, and how far he thinks
"· it is to the Coppermine River, as alfo the pro-
" bable time it may take before you can return.
" But in cafe any thing fhould prevent the faid
" Leader from joining you, according to expecta-
" tion, you are then to procure the beft Indians
" you can for your guides, and either add to, or
" diminifh, your number, as you may from time
" to time think moft neceffary for the good of
" the expedition.

" So I conclude, wifhing you and your compa-
" nions a continuance of health, together with a
" profperous Journey, and a happy return in
" fafety. Amen.

" MOSES NORTON, Governor.

" Dated at Prince of Wales s Fort, Churchill River, Hudfon's
" Bay, North America, November 6th, 1769 "

Ifbefter and Merriman, mentioned in my Inftructions, actually accompanied me during my
firft fhort attempt; but the Indians knowing
them to be but common men, ufed them fo indifferently, particularly in fcarce times, that I was
under fome apprehenfions of their being ftarved
to death, and I thought myfelf exceedingly happy
when I got them fafe back to the Factory. This
extraordinary behaviour of the Indians made me
determine not to take any Europeans with me on
my two laft expeditions.

With regard to that part of my Inftructions
which directs me to obferve the nature of the foil,
the

the productions thereof, &c. it muſt be obſerved,
that during the whole time of my abſence from
the Fort, I was invariably confined to ſtony hills
and barren plains all the Summer, and before we
approached the woods in the Fall of the year, the
ground was always covered with ſnow to a confiderable depth; ſo that I never had an opportunity of ſeeing any of the ſmall plants and ſhrubs to
the Weſtward. But from appearances, and the
ſlow and dwarfy growth of the woods, &c. (except in the Athapuſcow country,) there is undoubtedly a greater ſcarcity of vegetable productions than at the Company's moſt Northern Settlement; and to the Eaſtward of the woods, on the
barren grounds, whether hills or vallies, there is
a total want of herbage except moſs, on which
the deer feed; a few dwarf willows creep among
the moſs; ſome wiſh-a capucca and a little graſs
may be ſeen here and there, but the latter is
ſcarcely ſufficient to ſerve the geeſe and other birds
of paſſage during their ſhort ſtay in thoſe parts,
though they are always in a ſtate of migration except when they are breeding and in a moulting ſtate.

In conſequence of my complying with the Company's requeſt, and undertaking this Journey, it
is natural to ſuppoſe that every neceſſary arrangement was made for the eaſier keeping of my reckoning, &c. under the many inconveniences I muſt
be unavoidably obliged to labour in ſuch an expedition. I drew a Map on a large ſkin of parchment, that contained twelve degrees of latitude
North, and thirty degrees of longitude Weſt,
of Churchill Factory, and ſketched all the Weſt

coaſt

coaſt of the Bay on it, but left the interior
parts blank, to be filled up during my Journey
I alſo prepared detached pieces on a much larger
ſcale for every degree of latitude and longitude
contained in the large Map. On thoſe detached
pieces I pricked off my daily courſes and diſtance,
and entered all lakes and rivers, &c. that I met
with; endeavouring, by a ſtrict enquiry of the
natives, to find out the communication of one river with another, as alſo their connections with
the many lakes with which that country abounds:
and when opportunity offered, having corrected
them by obſervations, I entered them in the general Map. Theſe and ſeveral other neceſſary preparations, for the eaſier, readier and more correctly keeping my Journal and Chart, were alſo
adopted, but as to myſelf, little was required to
be done, as the nature of travelling long journies
in thoſe countries will never admit of carrying
even the moſt common article of clothing; ſo
that the traveller is obliged to depend on the
country he paſſes through, for that article, as
well as for proviſions. Ammunition, uſeful iron-
work, ſome tobacco, a few knives, and other in-
diſpenſable articles, make a ſufficient load for any
one to carry that is going a journey likely to laſt
twenty months, or two years. As that was the
caſe, I only took the ſhirt and clothes I then had
on, one ſpare coat, a pair of drawers, and as much
cloth as would make me two or three pair of Indian ſtockings, which, together with a blanket
for bedding, compoſed the whole of my ſtock of
clothing.                                A JOUR-

A NORTH WEST VIEW OF PRINCE OF WALES'S FORT HUDSON'S BAY NORTH AMERICA By S. HEARNE 1777

# A

# JOURNEY

## TO THE

# NORTHERN OCEAN.

## CHAP I.

Transactions from my leaving Prince of Wales's Fort on my first expedition, till our arrival there again

*Set off from the Fort.—Arrive at Po-co-ree kifco River.—One of the Northern Indians desert.—Cross Seal River, and walk on the barren grounds.— Receive wrong information concerning the distance of t   oods —Weather begins to be very cold, provisions all expended and nothing to be got.—Strike to the Westward, arrive at the woods, and kill three deer.—Set forward in the North West quarter, see the tracks of musk-oxen and deer, but killed none.— Very short of provisions —Chawchinahaw wants us to return —Neither he nor his crew contribute to our maintenance.—He influences several of the Indians to desert.—Chawchinahaw and all his crew*

B                                                *leave*

*[illegible].—Begin our return to the factory, kill a few partridges, the first meal we had had for several days.—Villany of one of the home Indians and his wife, who rob a Northern Indian woman.—Arrive at Seal River, kill two deer, partridges plenty.—Meet a strange Northern Indian, accompany him to his tent, [illegible] there, [illegible] Indians assist in [illegible].—Proceed toward home, and arrive at the Fort.*

1769

HAVING made every necessary arrangement for my departure on the sixth of November, I took leave of the Governor, and my other friends, at Prince of Wales's Fort, and began my journey, under the salute of seven cannon.

The weather at that time being very mild, made it but indifferent hauling*, and all my crew being heavy laden, occasioned us to make but short days journeys, however, on the eighth, we crossed the North branch of Po-co-ree-kis-co River, and that night put up in a small tuft of woods, which is between it and Seal River. In the night, one of the Northern Indians deserted, and as all the rest of my crew were heavy laden, I was under the necessity of hauling the sledge he had left, which however was not very heavy, as it scarcely exceeded sixty pounds.

The weather still continued very fine and pleasant, we directed our course to the West North West,

* [illegible]

West, and early in the day croffed Seal River. In the course of this day's journey we met feveral northern Indians, who were going to the factory with furs and venifon, and as we had not killed any deer from our leaving the Fort, I got feveral joints of venifon from thofe ftrangers, and gave them a note on the Governor for payment, which feemed perfectly agreeable to all parties.

When on the North Weft fide of Seal River, I afked Captain Chawchinhaw the diftance, and probable time it would take, before we could reach the main woods, which he affured me could not exceed four or five days journey. This put both me and my companions in good fpirits, and we continued our courfe between the Weft by North and North Weft, in daily expectation of arriving at thofe woods, which we were told would furnifh us with every thing the country affords. Thefe accounts were fo far from being true, that after we had walked double the time here mentioned, no figns of woods were to be feen in the direction we were then fteering; but we had frequently feen the looming of woods to the South Weft.

The cold being now very intenfe, our fmall ftock of Englifh provifions all expended, and not the leaft thing to be got on the bleak hills we had for fome time been walking on, it became neceffary to ftrike more to the Weftward, which we accordingly did, and the next evening arrived at fome fmall patches of low fcrubby woods,

*leave us —Begin our return to the factory, kill a
few partridges, the first meal we had had for several
days —Villany of one of the home indians and his
wife, who was a Northern Indian woman.—Arrive at Seal River, kill two deer, partridges plenty.
—Meet a strange Northern Indian, accompany him
to his tent, usage received there; my Indians assist in
killing some beaver.—Proceed toward home, and
arrive at the Fort.*

1769.

No ember
6 1

HAVING made every necessary arrangement
for my departure on the sixth of November, I took leave of the Governor, and my other
friends, at Prince of Wales's Fort, and began
my journey, under the salute of seven cannon.

The weather at that time being very mild,
made it but indifferent hauling*, and all my
crew being heavy laden, occasioned us to make
but short days journeys; however, on the eighth,
we crossed the North branch of Po-co-ree-kis-co
River, and that night put up in a small tuft of
woods, which is between it and Seal River. In
the night, one of the Northern Indians deserted, and as all the rest of my crew were heavy
laden, I was under the necessity of hauling the
sledge he had left, which however was not very
heavy, as it scarcely exceeded sixty pounds.

The weather still continued very fine and pleasant · we directed our course to the West North
West,

8 h

* The colder the weather is, the easier the sledges slide over the snow

Weſt, and early in the day croſſed Seal River. In the courſe of this day's journey we met ſeveral Northern Indians, who were going to the factory with furs and veniſon, and as we had not killed any deer from our leaving the Fort, I got ſeveral joints of veniſon from thoſe ſtrangers, and gave them a note on the Governor for payment, which ſeemed perfectly agreeable to all parties.

*1762.*

*November 9th*

When on the North Weſt ſide of Seal River, I aſked Captain Chawchinahaw the diſtance, and probable time it would take, before we could reach the main woods, which he aſſured me would not exceed four or five days journey. This put both me and my companions in good ſpirits, and we continued our courſe between the Weſt by North and North Weſt, in daily expectation of arriving at thoſe woods, which we were told would furniſh us with every thing the country affords   Theſe accounts were ſo far from being true, that after we had walked double the time here mentioned, no ſigns of woods were to be ſeen in the direction we were then ſteering; but we had frequently ſeen the looming of woods to the South Weſt.

The cold being now very intenſe, our ſmall ſtock of Engliſh proviſions all expended, and not the leaſt thing to be got on the bleak hills we had for ſome time been walking on, it became neceſſary to ſtrike more to the Weſtward, which we accordingly did, and the next evening arrived at ſome ſmall patches of low ſcrubby woods,

*15th*

B 2                                   where

where we faw the tracks of feveral deer, and
killed a few partridges. The road we had traverfed for many days before, was in general fo
rough and ftony, that our fledges were daily
breaking; and to add to the inconveniency, the
land was fo barren, as not to afford us materials for repairing them : but the few woods we
now fell in with, amply fupplied us with neceffaries for thofe repairs, and as we were then
enabled each night to pitch proper tents, our
lodging was much more comfortable than it had
been for many nights before, while we were on
the barren grounds, where, in general, we
thought ourfelves well off if we could fcrape
together as many fhrubs as would make a fire;
but it was fcarcely ever in our power to make
any other defence againft the weather, than by
digging a hole in the fnow down to the mofs,
wrapping ourfelves up in our clothing, and lying
down in it, with our fledges fet up edgeways to
windward

On the twenty firft, we did not move; fo the
Indian men went a hunting, and the women cut
holes in the ice and caught a few fifh in a fmall
lake, by the fide of which we had pitched our
tents   At night the men returned with fome
venifon, having killed three deer, which was
without doubt very acceptable, but our number
being great, and the Indians having fuch enormous ftomachs, very little was left but fragments
after the two or three firft good meals.   Having
devoured

1769.
November

devoured the three deer, and given fome neceffary repairs to our fledges and fnow fhoes, which
only took one day, we again proceeded on toward the North Weft by Weft and Weft North
Weft, through low fcrubby pines, intermixed
with fome dwarf larch, which is commonly called
juniper in Hudfon's Bay. In our road we frequently faw the tracks of deer, and many mufk-
oxen, as they are called there, but none of my
companions were fo fortunate as to kill any
of them: fo that a few partridges were all we
could get to live on, and thofe were fo fcarce,
that we feldom could kill as many as would
amount to half a bird a day for each man, which,
confidering we had nothing elfe for the twenty-
four hours, was in reality next to nothing

By this time I found that Captain Chawchinahaw had not the profperity of the undertaking
at heart, he often painted the difficulties in the
worft colours, took every method to difhearten
me and my European companions, and feveral
times hinted his defire of our returning back to
the factory: but finding I was determined to
proceed, he took fuch methods as he thought
would be moft likely to anfwer his end, one
of which was, that of not adminiftering toward
our fupport, fo that we were a confiderable
time without any other fubfiftence, but what our
two home-guard (Southern) Indians procured,
and the little that I and the two European men
could kill; which was very difproportionate to

our

our wants, as we had to provide for several women and children who were with us.

Chawchinahaw finding that this kind of treatment was not likely to complete his defign, and
that we were not to be ftarved into compliance,
at length influenced feveral of the beft Northern
Indians to defert in the night, who took with
them feveral bags of my ammunition, fome
pieces of iron work, fuch as hatchets, ice chifels
files &c. as well as feveral other ufeful articles

When I became acquainted with this piece of
villany, I afked Chawchinahaw the reafon of fuch
behaviour.   To which he anfwered, that he
knew nothing of the affair : but as that was the
cafe, it would not be prudent, he faid, for us to
proceed any farther, adding, that he and all the
reft of his countrymen were going to ftrike off
another way, in order to join the remainder of
their wives and families, and after giving us a
fhort account which way to fteer our courfe for
the neareft part of Seal River, which he faid
would be our beft way homeward, he and his
crew delivered me moft of the things which they
had in charge, packed up their awls, and fet out
toward the South Weft, making the woods ring
with their laughter, and left us to confider of
our unhappy fituation, near two hundred miles
from Prince of Wales's Fort, all heavily laden,
and our ftrength and fpirits greatly reduced by
hunger and fatigue.

Our fituation at that time, though very alarming,

ing, would not permit us to spend much time in reflection; so we loaded our sledges to the best advantage, (but were obliged to throw away some bags of shot and ball,) and immediately set out on our return. In the course of the day's walk we were fortunate enough to kill several partridges, for which we were all very thankful, as it was the first meal we had had for several days indeed, for the five preceding days we had not killed as much as amounted to half a partridge for each man; and some days had not a single mouthful. While we were is this distress, the Northern Indians were by no means in want, for as they always walked foremost, they had ten times the chance to kill partridges, rabbits, or any other thing which was to be met with, than we had. Besides this advantage, they had great stocks of flour, oatmeal, and other English provisions, which they had embezzled out of my stock during the early part of the journey, and as one of my home Indians, called Mackachy, and his wife, who is a Northern Indian woman, always resorted to the Northern Indians tents, where they got amply supplied with provisions when neither I not my men had a single mouthful, I have great reason to suspect they had a principal hand in the embezzlement. indeed, both the man and his wife were capable of committing any crime, however diabolical.

This day we had fine pleasant weather for the season of the year. we set out early in the morning,

ning, and arrived the fame day at Seal River, along which we continued our courfe for feveral days. In our way we killed plenty of partridges, and faw many deer; but the weather was fo remarkably ferene that the Indians only killed two of the latter. By this time game was become fo plentiful, that all apprehenfions of ftarving were laid afide; and though we were heavily laden, and travelled pretty good days journeys, yet as our fpirits were good, our ftrength gradually returned.

In our courfe down Seal River we met a ftranger, a Northern Indian, on a hunting excurfion, and though he had not met with any fuccefs that day, yet he kindly invited us to his tent, faying he had plenty of venifon at my fervice; and told the Southern Indians, that as there were two or three beaver houfes near his tent, he fhould be glad of their affiftance in taking them, for there was only one man and three women at the tent.

Though we were at that time far from being in want of provifions, yet we accepted his offer, and fet off with our new guide for his tent, which, by a comparative diftance, he told us, was not above five miles from the place where we met him, but we found it to be nearer fifteen; fo that it was the middle of the night before we arrived at it. When we drew near the tent, the ufual fignal for the approach of ftrangers was given, by firing a gun or two, which was immediately
ly

ly anſwered by the man at the tent. On our

arrival at the door, the good man of the houſe came out, ſhook me by the hand, and welcomed us to his tent, but as it was too ſmall to contain us all, he ordered his women to affiſt us in pitching our tent, and in the mean time invited me and as many of my crew as his little habitation could contain, and regaled us with the beſt in the houſe. The pipe went round pretty briſkly, and the con-verſation naturally turned on the treatment we had received from Chawchinahaw and his gang; which was always anſwered by our hoſt with, " Ah ! if I had been there, it ſhould not have been " ſo !'" when, notwithſtanding his hoſpitality on the preſent occaſion, he would moſt aſſuredly have acted the ſame part as the others had done, if he had been of the party

Having refreſhed ourſelves with a plentiful ſup-per, we took leave of our hoſt for a while, and retired to our tent; but not without being made thoroughly ſenſible that many things would be expected from me, before I finally left them.

Early in the morning, my Indians aſſiſted us in taking the beaver houſes already mentioned; but the houſes being ſmall, and ſome of the beavers eſcaping, they only killed ſix, all of which were cooked the ſame night, and voraciouſly devoured under the denomination of a feaſt. I alſo receiv-ed from the Indians ſeveral joints of veniſon, to the amount of at leaſt two deer; but notwith-ſtanding I was to pay for the whole, I found that Mackachy and his wife got all the prime parts of the

6th

the meat, and on my mentioning it to them, there was fo much clanfhip among them, that they preferred making a prefent of it to Macka- chy, to felling it to me at double the price for which venifon fells in thofe parts: a fufficient proof of the fingular advantage which a native of this country has over an Englifhman, when at fuch a diftance from the Company's Factories as to depend entirely on them for fubfiftence

7th

Thinking I had made my ftay here long enough, I gave orders to prepare for our departure, and as I had purchafed plenty of meat for prefent ufe while we were at this tent, fo I likewife procured fuch a fupply to carry with us, as was likely to laft us to the Fort.

8th.

Early in the morning we took a final leave of our hoft, and proceeded on our journey home- wards. One of the ftrangers accompanied us, for which at firft I could not fee his motive; but foon after our arrival at the Factory, I found that the purport of his vifit was to be paid for the meat, faid to be given *gratis* to Mackachy while we were at his tent. The weather continued very fine, but extremely cold, and during this part of my journey nothing material happened, till we arrived fafe at Prince of Wales's Fort on the ele- venth of December, to my own great mortifica- tino, and to the no fmall furprife of the Governor, who had placed great confidence in the abilities and conduct of Chawchinahaw.

CHAP.

## C H A P. II

Tranfactions from our arrival at the Factory, to
my leaving it again, and during the firft part
of my fecond journey, till I had the misfortune
to break the quadrant.

*Tranfactions at the Factory.—Proceed on my fecond
journey.—Arrive at Seal River.—Deer plentiful
for fome time.—Method of angling fish under the ice.
—Set our fishing nets.—Method of fetting nets under the ice.—My guide propofes to ftay till the geefe
began to fly, his reafons accepted.—Pitch our tent
in the beft manner.—Method of pitching a tent in
winter.—Fifh plentiful for fome time, grow very
fcarce; in great want of provifions.—Manner of
employing my time.—My guide killed two deer.—
Move to the place they were lying at, there kill feveral more deer, and three beavers.—Soon in want
of provifions again.—Many Indians join us from the
Weftward.—We begin to move towards the barren
ground.—Arrive at She-than-nee, and there fuffer
great diftrefs for want of provifions.—Indians kill
two fwans and three geefe.—Geefe and other birds of
paffage plentiful.—Leave She-than-nee, and arrive
at Beralzone.—One of my companions guns burfts,
and fhatters his left hand.—Leave Beralzone, and
get on the barren ground, clear of all woods.—Throw
away*

*away our sledges and snow shoes.—Each person takes*
*a load on his back; my part of the luggage.—Ex-*
*posed to many hardships.—Several days without*
*victuals —Indians kill three musk oxen, but for*
*want of fire are obliged to eat the meat raw.—Fine*
*weather returns, make a fire, effects of long fasting,*
*stay a day or two to dry some meat in the sun.—Pro-*
*ceed to the Northward, and arrive at Cathawhac-*
*haga, there find some tents of Indians.—A Northern*
*leader called Keelshies meets us, send a letter by*
*him to the Governor.—Transactions at Cathaw-*
*hachaga; leave it, and proceed to the Northward.*
*—Meet several Indians.—My guide not willing to*
*proceed, his reasons for it.—Many more Indians*
*join us —Arrive at Doobaunt Whole River. —Man-*
*ner of ferrying over rivers in the Northern Indian*
*canoes. No rivers in those parts in a useful direct-*
*ion for the natives —Had nearly lost the quadrant and*
*all the powder.—Some reflections on our situation,*
*and the conduct of the Indians.—Find the quadrant*
*and part of the powder.—Observe for the latitude.*
*—Quadrant broke.—Resolve to return again to the*
*Factory.*

D URING my abfence from Prince of
Wales's Fort on my former journey, feveral
Northern Indians arrived in great diftrefs at the
Factory, and were employed in fhooting partridges for the ufe of our people at the Fort. One of
thofe Indians called Conne-e-qu se faid, he had
been very near to the famous river I was engaged

to

to go in queft of.   Accordingly Mr. Norton engaged him and two other Northern Indians to
accompany me on this fecond attempt; but to
avoid all incumbrances as much as poffible, it was
thought advifable not to take any women*, that
the Indians might have fewer to provide for.   I
would not permit any European to go with me,
but two of the home guard (Southern) Indian men
were to accompany me as before.   Indeed the Indians, both Northern and Southern, paid fo little attention to Ifbefter and Merriman on my former journey, particularly in times of fcarcity,
that I was determined not to take them with me
in future; though the former was very defirous
to accompany me again, and was well calculated
to encounter the hardfhips of fuch an undertaking   Merriman was quite fick of fuch excurfions,
and fo far from offering his fervice a fecond time,
feemed to be very thankful that he was once more
arrived in fafety among his friends; for before he
got to the Factory he had contracted a moft violent cold.

Having come to the above refolutions, and finally determined on the number of Indians that were
to accompany us, we were again fitted out with
a large fupply of ammunition, and as many other
ufeful articles as we could conveniently take with
us

---

*This was a propofal of the Governor's, though he well knew we could
not do without their affiftance, both for hauling our baggage, as well as
dreffing fkins for clothing, pitching out tent, getting firing, &c

us, together with a small sample of light trading goods, for presents to the Indians, as before.

My instructions on this occasion amounted to no more than an order to proceed as fast as possible; and for my conduct during the journey, I was referred to my former instructions of November 6th, 1769.

Every thing being in readiness for our departure, on the twenty-third of February I began my second journey, accompanied by three Northern Indians and two of the home-guard (Southern) Indians. I took particular care, however, that Mackachy, though an excellent hunter, should not be of our party, as he had proved himself, during my former journey, to be a sly artful villain.

The snow at this time was so deep on the top of the ramparts, that few of the cannon were to be seen, otherwise the Governor would have saluted me at my departure, as before, but as those honours could not possibly be of any service to my expedition, I readily relinquished every thing of the kind, and in lieu of it, the Governor, officers, and people, insisted on giving me three cheers.

After leaving the Factory, we continued our course in much the same direction as in my former journey, till we arrived at Seal River; when, instead of crossing it, and walking on the barren grounds as before, we followed the course of the river, except in two particular places, where the bends tended so much to the South, that by crossing

ing two necks of land not more than five or fix 1770.
miles wide, we faved the walking of near twenty
miles each time, and ftill çame to the main river March.
again 8th.

The weather had been fo remarkably boifterous
and changeable, that we were frequently obliged
to continue two or three nights in the fame place.
To make up for this inconveniency, deer were fo
plentiful for the firft eight or ten days, that the
Indians killed as many as was neceffaiy , but we
were all fo heavy laden that we could not poffibly
take much of the meat with us. This I foon perceived to be a great evil, which expofed us to fuch
frequent inconveniences, that in cafe of not killing any thing for three or four days together, we
were in great want of provifions, we feldom,
however, went to bed entirely fupperlefs till the
eighth of March, when though we had only walked about eight miles that morning, and expended
all the remainder of the day in hunting, we could
not produce a fingle thing at night, not even a
partridge ¹ nor had we difcerned the track of any
thing that day, which was likely to afford us
hopes of better fuccefs in the morning This being the cafe, we prepared fome hooks and lines
ready to angle for fifh, as our tent was then by the
fide of a lake belonging to Seal River, which
feemed by its fituation to afford fome profpect of
fuccefs

Early in the morning we took down our tent, 9ᵗʰ
and moved about five miles to the Weft by South,

to

to a part of the lake that feemed more commodious for fifhing than that where we had been the
night before.   As foon as we arrived at this place,
fome were immediately employed cutting holes in
the ice, while others pitched the tent, got fire-
wood, &c., after which, for it was early in the
morning, thofe who pitched the tent went a hunting, and at night one of them returned with a
porcupine, while thofe who were angling caught
feveral fine trout, which afforded us a plentiful
fupper, and we had fome trifle left for breakfaft.

Angling for fifh under the ice in winter requires no other procefs, than cutting round holes
in the ice from one to two feet diameter, and let-
ting down a baited hook, which is always kept in
motion, not only to prevent the water from freezing fo foon as it would do if fuffered to remain
quite ftill, but becaufe it is found at the fame time
to be a great means of alluring the fifh to the
hole; for it is always obferved that the fifh in
thofe parts will take a bait which is in motion,
much fooner than one that is at reft.

Early in the morning we again purfued our
angling, and all the forenoon being expended
without any fuccefs, we took down our tent and
pitched it again about eight miles farther to the
Weftward, on the fame lake, where we cut more
holes in the ice for angling, and that night caught
feveral fine pike.   The next day we moved about
five miles to the South Weft, down a fmall river,
where we pitched our tent; and having fet four

19th.

20.h.

fifhing

fiſhing nets, in the courſe of the day we caught many fine fiſh, particularly pike, trout, tittymeg, and a coarſe kind of fiſh known in Hudſon's Bay by the name of Methy*.

To ſet a net under the ice, it is firſt neceſſary to aſcertain its exact length, by ſtretching it out upon the ice near the part propoſed for ſetting it. This being done, a number of round holes are cut in the ice, at ten or twelve feet diſtance from each other, and as many in number as will be ſufficient to ſtretch the net at its full length. A line is then paſſed under the ice, by means of a long light pole, which is firſt introduced at one of the end holes, and, by mean of two forked ſticks, this pole is eaſily conducted or paſſed from one hole to another, under the ice, till it arrives at the laſt. The pole is then taken out, and both ends of the line being properly ſecured, is always ready for uſe  The net is made faſt to one end of the line by one perſon, and hauled under the ice by a ſecond, a large ſtone is tied to each of the lower corners, which ſerves to keep the net expanded, and prevents it riſing from the bottom with every waft of the current. The Europeans ſettled in Hudſon's Bay proceed much in the ſame manner, though they in general take much more pains; but the above method is found quite ſufficient by the Indians.

In order to ſearch a net thus ſet, the two end

C                              holes

---

\* The Methy are generally caught with a hook; and the beſt time for that ſport is in the night, and if the night be dark, the better.

holes only are opened, the line is veered away by one perfon, and the net hauled from under the ice by another; after all the fifh are taken out, the net is eafily hauled back to its former ftation and there fecured as before

As this place feemed likely to afford us a conftant fupply of fifh, my guide propofed to ftay here till the geefe began to fly, which in thofe Northern parts is feldom before the middle of May. His reafons for fo doing feemed well founded. "The weather, he faid, is at this time "too cold to walk on the barren grounds, and "the woods from this part lead fo much to the "Weftward, that were we to continue travelling "in any tolerable fhelter, our courfe would not "be better than Weft South Weft, which would "only be going out of our way, whereas, if we "fhould remain here till the weather permit us "to walk due North, over the barren grounds, "we fhall then in one month get farther ad- "vanced on our journey, than if we were to "continue travelling all the remainder of the "winter in the fweep of the woods"

Thefe reafons appeared to me very judicious, and as the plan feemed likely to be attended with little trouble, it met with my entire approbation. That being the cafe, we took additional pains in building our tent, and made it as commodious as the materials and fituation would admit.

To pitch an Indian's tent in winter, it is firft neceffary to fearch for a level piece of dry ground, which

which cannot be afcertained but by thrufting a
ftick through the fnow down to the ground, all
over the propofed part. When a convenient fpot
is found, the fnow is then cleared away in a circular form to the very mofs, and when it is propofed to remain more than a night or two in one
place, the mofs is alfo cut up and removed, as it
is very liable when dry to take fire, and occafion
much trouble to the inhabitants.    A quantity of
poles are then procured, which are generally proportioned both in number and length to the fize
of the tent cloth, and the number of perfons it is
intended to contain    If one of the poles fhould
not happen to be forked, two of them are tied
together near the top, then raifed erect, and their
buts or lower ends extended as wide as the propofed diameter of the tent, the other poles are
then fet round at equal diftances from each other,
and in fuch order, that their lower ends form a
complete circle, which gives boundaries to the
tent on all fides.  the tent cloth is then faftened
to a light pole, which is always raifed up and put
round the poles from the weather fide, fo that the
two edges that lap over and form the door are
always to the leeward   It muft be underftood
that this method is only in ufe when the Indians
are moving from place to place every day, for
when they intend to continue any time in one
place, they always make the door of their tent to
face the South.

The tent cloth is ufually of thin Moofe leather,

C 2                         dreffed

dreffed and made by the Indians, and in fhape it
nearly refembles a fan-mount inverted; fo that
when the largeft curve inclofes the bottom of the
poles, the fmaller one is always fufficient to cover
the top; except a hole, which is defignedly left
open to ferve the double purpofe of chimney and
window.

The fire is always made on the ground in the
center, and the remainder of the floor, or bottom
of the tent, is covered all over with fmall branches of the pine tree, which ferve both for feats
and beds. A quantity of pine tops and branches
are laid round the bottom of the poles on the outfide, over which the eves of the tent is ftaked
down: a quantity of fnow is then packed over
all, which excludes great part of the external air,
and contributes greatly to the warmth within.
The tent here defcribed is fuch as is made ufe of
by the Southern Indians, and the fame with
which I was furnifhed at the Factory; for that
made ufe of by the Northern Indians is made of
different materials, and is of a quite different
fhape, as fhall be defcribed hereafter.

The fituation of our tent at this time was truly pleafant, particularly for a fpring refidence,
being on a fmall elevated point, which commanded an extenfive profpect over a large lake, the
fhores of which abounded with wood of different
kinds, fuch as pine, larch, birch, and poplar, and
in many places was beautifully contrafted with a
variety of high hills, that fhewed their fnowy
fummits

summits above the talleft woods. About two hundred yards from the tent was a fall, or rapid, which the fwiftnefs of the current prevents from freezing in the coldeft winters. At the bottom of this fall, which empties itfelf into the above lake, was a fine fheet of open water near a mile in length, and at leaft half a mile in breadth; by the margin of which we had our fifhing nets fet, all in open view from the tent.

The remaining part of this month paffed on without any interruption, or material occurrence, to difturb our repofe, worth relating : our fifh-ing nets provided us with daily food, and the In-dians had too much philofophy about them to give themfelves much additional trouble; for during the whole time not one of them offered to look for a partridge, or any thing elfe which could yield a change of diet.

As the time may now be fuppofed to have lain heavy on my hands, it may not be improper to inform the reader how I employed it. In the firft place, I embraced every favourable opportunity of obferving the latitude of the place, the mean of which was 58° 46′ 30′ North; and the longitude by account was 5° 57′ Weft, from Prince of Wales's Fort. I then corrected my reckoning from my laft obfervation; brought up my jour-nal, and filled up my chart, to the place of our refidence I built alfo fome traps, and caught a few martins , and by way of faving my ammuni-tion, fet fome fnares for partridges. The former

is

1772

is performed by means of a few logs, so arranged that when the martin attempts to take away the bait laid for him, he with very little struggle pulls down a small post that supports the whole weight of the trap, when, if the animal be not killed by the weight of the logs, he is confined till he be frozen to death, or killed by the hunter going his rounds

To snare partridges requires no other process than making a few little hedges across a creek, or a few short hedges projecting at right angles from the side of an island of willows, which those birds are found to frequent. Several openings must be left in each hedge, to admit the birds to pass through, and in each of them a snare must be set; so that when the partridges are hopping along the edge of the willows to feed, which is their usual custom, some of them soon get into the snares, where they are confined till they are taken out I have caught from three to ten partridges in a day by this simple contrivance, which requires no further attendance than going round them night and morning

1st

I have already observed that nothing material happened to disturb our repose till the first of April, when to our great surprise the fishing nets did not afford us a single fish. Though some of the preceding days had been pretty successful, yet my companions, like true Indians seldom went to sleep till they had cleared the tent of every article of provision. As nothing was to be caught

caught in the nets, we all went out to angle, but in this we were equally unsuccessful, as we could not procure one fish the whole day. This sudden change of circumstances alarmed one of my companions so much, that he began to think of resuming the use of his gun, after having laid it by for near a month.

Early in the morning we arose, when my guide Connec-cquese went a hunting, and the rest attended the nets and hooks near home; but all with such bad success, that we could not procure enough in one day to serve two men for a supper. This, instead of awakening the rest of my companions, sent them to sleep; and scarcely any of them had the prudence to look at the fishing nets, though they were not more than two or three hundred yards from the tent door.

My guide, who was a steady man, and an excellent hunter, having for many years been accustomed to provide for a large family, seemed by far the most industrious of all my crew; he closely pursued his hunting for several days, and seldom returned to the tent till after dark, while those at the tent passed most of their time in smoking and sleeping

Several days passed without any signs of relief, till the 10th, when my guide continued out longer than ordinary, which made us conjecture that he had met with strangers, or seen some deer, or other game, which occasioned his delay  We all therefore lay down to sleep, having had but little

refresh-

refreſhment for the three preceding days, except a pipe cf tobacco and a draught of water; even partridges had become ſo ſcarce that not one was to be got; the heavy thaws had driven them all out towards the barren grounds. About mid-night, to our great joy, our hunter arrived, and brought with him the blood and fragments of two deer that he had killed. This unexpected ſucceſs ſoon rouſed the ſleepers, who, in an in-ſtant were buſily employed in cooking a large kettle of broth, made with the blood, and ſome fat and ſcraps of meat ſhred ſmall, boiled in it. This might be reckoned a dainty diſh at any time, but was more particularly ſo in our preſent almoſt famiſhed condition.

After partaking of this refreſhment, we reſum-ed our reſt, and early in the morning ſet out in a body for the place where the deer were lying. As we intended to make our ſtay but ſhort, we left our tent ſtanding, containing all our bag-gage.   On our arrival at the place of deſtination, ſome were immediately employed in making a hut or barrocado, with young pine trees, while one man ſkinned the deer, the remainder went a hunting, and in the afternoon returned to the hut, after having killed two deer.

Several days were now ſpent in feaſting and gluttony; during which the Indians killed five more deer and three fine beavers; finding at laſt, however, that there was little proſpect of procuring either more deer or beavers, we deter-mined

mined to return to our tent, with the remains of

what we had already obtained.

The flesh of these deer, though none of the largest, might with frugality have served our small number, (being only six) for some time; but my companions, like other Indians, feasted day and night while it lasted; and were so indolent and unthinking, as not to attend properly to the fishing-nets, so that many fine fish, which had been entangled in the nets, were entirely spoiled, and in about twelve or fourteen days we were nearly in as great distress for provisions as ever.

During the course of our long inactivity, Sawfop-o-kishac, commonly called Soflop, my principal Southern Indian, as he was cutting some birch for spoons, dishes, and other necessary household furniture, had the misfortune to cut his leg in such a manner as to be incapable of walking; and the other Southern Indian, though a much younger man, was so indolent as not to be of any service to me, except hauling part of our luggage, and eating up part of the provisions which had been provided by the more industrious, part of my companions.

On the twenty fourth, early in the day, a great body of Indians was seen to the South West, on the large lake by the side of which our tent stood. On their arrival at our tent we discovered them to be the wives and families of the Northern Indian goose hunters, who were gone to Prince of

Wales's

1770.
April
27th

Wales's Fort to attend the feafon. They were bound toward the barren ground, there to wait the return of their hufbands and relations from the Fort, after the termination of the goofe-feafon.

My guide having for fome days paft determin-ed to move toward the barren ground, this morning we took down our tent, packed up our luggage, and proceeded to the Eaftward in the fame track we came; but Soffop being fo lame as to be obliged to be hauled on a fledge, I eafily prevailed on two of the Indians who had joined us on the 24th, and who were purfuing the fame road, to perform this fervice for him.

27th

After two days good walking in our old track, we arrived at a part of Seal River called She-than-nee, where we pitched our tent and fet both our fifhing-nets, intending to 'ftay there till the geefe began to fly. Though we had feen feveral fwans and fome geefe flying to the Northward, it was the thirteenth of May before we could pro-cure any. On that day the Indians killed two fwans and three geefe. This in fome meafure alleviated our diftrefs, which at that time was very great; having had no other fubfiftence for five or fix days, than a few cranberries, that we gathered from the dry ridges where the fnow was thawed away in fpots, for though we fet our fifhing-nets in the beft judged places, and angled at every part that was likely to afford fuccefs, we only caught three fmall fifh during the whole time.

May
13th

time. Many of the Northern Indians, who had joined us on the 24th of April, remained in our company for some time, and though I well knew they had had a plentiful winter, and had then good ftocks of dried meat by them, and were alfo acquainted with our diftrefs, they never gave me or my Southern companions the leaft fupply, although they had in fecret amply provided for our Northern guides.

By the nineteenth, the geefe, fwans, ducks, gulls, and other birds of paffage, were fo plentiful that we killed every day as many as were fufficient for our fupport, and having ftopped a few days to recruit our fpirits after fo long a faft, on the twenty-third we began once more to proceed toward the barren ground. Soffop having now perfectly recovered from his late misfortune, every thing feemed to have a favourable appearance; efpecially as my crew had been augmented to twelve perfons, by the addition of one of my guide's wives, and five others, whom I had engaged to affift in carrying our luggage, and I well knew, from the feafon of the year, that hauling wou'd foon be at an end for the fummer.

The thaws having been by this time fo great as to render travelling in the woods almoft impracticable, we continue our courfe to the Faß on Seal River, about fixteen miles farther, when we came to a fmall river, and a ftring of lakes connected with it, that tended to the North.

The

1770.    The weather for fome time was remarkably

June    fine and pleafant.  Game of all kinds was exceedingly plentiful, and we continued our courfe
to the Northward on the above river and lakes

1ft.    till the firft of June, when we arrived at a place
called Beralzone.  In our way thither, befide killing more geefe than was neceffary, we fhot two
deer.  One of my companions had now the mif-
fortune to fhatter his hand very much by the
burfting of a gun, but as no bones were broken,
I bound up the wound, and with the affiftance of
fome of Turlington's drops, yellow bafilicon, &c.
which I had with me, foon reftored the ufe of his
hand, fo that in a very fhort time he feemed to
be out of all danger.

4th    After ftopping a few days at Beralzone, to dry
a little venifon and a few geefe, we again proceeded to the Northward on the barren ground;
for on our leaving this place we foon got clear of
all the woods.

5th.    The fnow was by this time fo foft as to render
walking in fnow-fhoes very laborious; and
though the ground was bare in many places, yet
at times, and in particular places, the fnow-drifts
were fo deep, that we could not poffibly do with-

6th    out them.  By the fixth, however, the thaws
were fo general, and the fnows fo much melted,
that as our fnow-fhoes were attended with more
trouble than fervice, we all confented to throw

10th.    them away.  Till the tenth, our fledges proved
ferviceable, particularly in croffing lakes and
ponds

ponds on the ice; but that mode of travelling now growing dangerous on account of the great thaws, we determined to throw away our fledges, and every one to take a load on his back.

This I found to be much harder work than the winter carriage, as my part of the luggage confifted of the following articles, viz the quadrant and its ftand, a trunk containing books, papers, &c. a land-compafs, and a large bag containing all my wearing apparel; alfo a hatchet, knives, files, &c. befide feveral fmall articles, intended for prefents to the natives. The aukwardnefs of my load, added to its great weight, which was upward of fixty pounds, and the exceffive heat of the weather, rendered walking the moft laborious tafk I had ever encountered; and what confiderably increafed the hardfhip, was the badnefs of the road, and the coarfenefs of our lodging, being, on account of the want of proper tents, expofed to the utmoft feverity of the weather. The tent we had with us was not only too large, and unfit for barren ground fervice, where no poles were to be got, but we had been obliged to cut it up for fhoes, and each perfon carried his own fhare. Indeed my guide behaved both negligently and ungeneroufly on this occafion; as he never made me, or my Southern Indians, acquainted with the nature of pitching tents on the barren ground; which had he done, we could eafily have procured a fet of poles before we left the woods. He took care, however, to

procure

procure a fet for himfelf and his wife, and when the tent was divided, though he made fhift to get a piece large enough to ferve him for a complete little tent, he never afked me or my Southern Indians to put our heads into it

Befide the inconvenience of being expofed to the open air, night and day, in all weathers, we experienced real diftrefs from the want of victuals When provifions were procured, it often happened that we could not make a fire, fo that we were obliged to eat the meat quite raw, which at fifft, in the article of fifh particularly, was as little relifhed by my Southern companion, as myfelf

Notwithftanding thefe accumulated and complicated hardfhips, we continued in perfect health and good fpirits, and my guide, though a perfect niggard of his provifions, efpecially in times of fcarcity, gave us the ftrongeft affurance of foon arriving at a plentiful country, which would not only afford us a certain fupply of provifions, but where we fhould meet with other Indians, who probably would be willing to carry part of our luggage. This news naturally gave us great confolation; for at that time the weight of our conftant loads was fo great, that when Providence threw any thing in our way, we could not carry above two days provifions with us, which indeed was the chief reafon of our being fo frequently in want.

From the twentieth to the twenty third we walked

walked every day near twenty miles, without
any other fubfiftence than a pipe of tobacco, and
a drink of water when we pleafed . even partridges and gulls, which fome time before were
in great plenty, and eafily procured, were now fo
fcarce and fhy, that we could rarely get one ; and
as to geefe, ducks, &c. they had all flown to the
Northward to breed and molt.

Early in the morning of the twenty-third, we
fet out as ufual, but had not walked above feven
or eight miles before we faw three mufk-oxen
grazing by the fide of a fmall lake   The Indians immediately went in purfuit of them ; and
as fome of them were expert hunters, they foon
killed the whole of them.   This was no doubt
very fortunate ; but, to our great mortification,
before we could get one of them fkinned, fuch a
fall of rain came on, as to put it quite out of our
power to make a fire, which, even in the fineft
weather, could only be made of mofs, as we were
near an hundred miles from any woods.   This
was poor comfort for people who had not broke
their faft for four or five days.   Neceffity, however, has no law, and having been before initi-
ated into the method of eating raw meat, we
were the better prepared for this repaft : but this
was by no means fo well relifhed, either by me
or the Southern Indians, as either raw venifon or
raw fifh had been   for the flefh of the mufk-ox
is not only coarfe and tough, but fmells and
taftes fo ftrong of mufk as to make it very difa-
agreeable

greeable when raw, though it is tolerable eating when properly cooked. The weather continued so remarkably bad, accompanied with conftant heavy rain, fnow and fleet, and our neceffities were so great by the time the weather permitted us to make a fire, that we had nearly eat to the amount of one buffalo quite raw,

Notwithftanding I muftered up all my philofophy on this occafion, yet I muft confefs that my fpirits began to fail me. Indeed our other misfortunes were greatly aggravated by the inclemency of the weather, which was not only cold, but fo very wet that for near three days and nights, I had not one dry thread about me. When the fine weather returned, we made a fire, though it was only of mofs, as I have already obferved; and having got my cloaths dry, all things feemed likely to go on in the old channel, though that was indifferent enough; but I endeavoured, like a failor after a ftorm, to forget paft misfortunes.

None of our natural wants, if we except thirft, are fo diftreffing, or hard to endure, as hunger; and in wandering fituations, like that which I now experienced, the hardfhip is greatly aggravated by the uncertainty with refpect to its duration, and the means moft proper to be ufed to remove it, as well as by the labour and fatigue we muft necefiarily undergo for that purpofe, and the difappointments which too frequently fruftrate our beft concerted plans and moft ftrenuous

nuous exertions it not only enfeebles the body, but 'epreffes the fpirits, in fpite of every effort to prevent it. Befides, for want of action, the ftomach fo far lofes its digeftive powers, that after long fafting it refumes its office with pain and reluctance. During this journey I have too frequently experienced the dreadful effects of this calamity, and more than once been reduced to fo low a ftate by hunger and fatigue, that when Providence threw any thing in my way, my ftomach has fcarcely been able to retain more than two or three ounces, without producing the moft oppreffive pain. Another difagreeable circumftance of long fafting is, the extreme difficulty and pain attending the natural evacuations for the firft time, and which is fo dreadful, that of it none but thofe who have experienced can have an adequate idea.

To record in detail each day's fare fince the commencement of this journey, would be little more than a dull repetition of the fame occurrences. A fufficient idea of it may be given in a few words, by obferving that it may juftly be faid to have been either all feafting, or all famine: fometimes we had too much, feldom juft enough, frequently too little, and often none at all. It will be only neceffary to fay that we have tafted many times two whole days and nights; twice upwards of three days, and once, while at Shethan-nee, near feven days, during which we tafted not a mouthful of any thing, except a few

D                    cran-

cranberries, water, fcraps of old leather, and burnt bones. On thofe prefling occafions I have frequently feen the Indians examine their ward-robe, which confifted chiefly of fkin-clothing, and confider what part could beft be fpared; fometimes a piece of an old, half-rotten deer fkin, and at others a pair of old fhoes, were facrificed to alleviate extreme hunger. The relation of fuch uncommon hardfhips may perhaps gain lit-tle credit in Europe; while thofe who are con-verfant with the hiftory of Hudfon's Bay, and who are thoroughly acquainted with the diftrefs which the natives of the country about it fie-quently endure, may confider them as no more than the common occurrences of an Indian life, in which they are frequently driven to the ne-ceffity of eating one another.*

Knowing

* It is the general opinion of the Southern Indians, that when any of their tribe have been driven to the neceffity of eating human flefh, they become fo fond of it, that no perfon is fafe in their company  And though it is well known they are never guilty of making this horrid repaft but when driven to it by neceffity, yet thofe who have made it are not only fhunned, but fo univerfally detefted by all who know them, that no Indians will tent with them, and they are frequently murdered flily  I have feen feveral of thofe poor wretches who, unfortunately for them, have come under the above defcription, and though they were perfons much efteemed before hunger had driven them to this act, were after-wards fo univerfally defpifed and neglected, that a fmile never graced their countenances  deep melancholy has been feated on their brows, while the eye moft expreffively fpoke the dictates of the heart, and feemed to fay, ' Why do you defpife me for my misfortunes? the peri-" od is probably not far diftant, when you may be driven to the like ne-" ceffity ''

In the Spring of the year 1775, when I was building Cumberland
House,

Knowing that our conftant loads would not permit us to carry much provifions with us, we agreed to continue a day or two to refrefh ourfelves, and to dry a little meat in the fun, as it thereby not only becomes more portable, but is always ready for ufe. On the twenty-fixth, all that remained of the mufk-ox flefh being properly dried and fit for carriage, we began to proceed on our journey Northward, and on the thirtieth of June arrived at a fmall river, called Cathawhachaga, which empties itfelf into a large lake called Yath-kyed-whoie, or White Snow Lake. Here we found feveral tents of Northern Indians, who had been fome time employed fpearing deer in their canoes, as they croffed the above mentioned little river. Here alfo we met

1770.
June.
26th.
30th.

D 2

a Nor-

---

Hotf, an Indian, whofe name was Wapoos, came to the fettlement, at a time when fifteen tents of Indians were on the plantations they examined him very minutely, and found he had come a confiderable way by himfelf, without a gun, or ammunition This made many of them conjecture he had met with, and killed, fome perfon by the way, and this was the more eafily credited, from the care he took to conceal a bag of provifions, which he had brought with him, in a lofty pine tree near the houfe.

Being a ftranger, I invited him in, though I faw he had nothing for trade, and during that interview, fome of the Indian women examined his legs, and gave it as their opinion that the meat contained was human flefh in confequence, it was not without the interference of fome principal Indians, whofe liberality of fentiment was more extenfive than that in the others, the poor creature faved his life. Many of the men cleaned and loaded their guns, others had their bows and arrows ready, and even the women took poffeffion of the hatchets, to kill this poor inoffenfive wretch, for no crime but that of travelling about two hundred miles by himfelf, unaffifted by fire-arms for fupport in his journey.

a Northern Indian Leader, or Captain, called Keelſhies, and a ſmall party of his crew, who were bound to Prince of Wales's Fort, with furs and other commodities for trade  When Keel ſhies was made acquainted with the intent of my journey, he readily offered his ſervice to bring me any thing from the Factory that we were likely to ſtand in need of, and though we were then in latitude 63° 4' North, and longitude 7° 12' Weſt from Churchill, yet he promiſed to join us again, at a place appointed by my guide, by the ſetting in of the Winter.  In conſequence of this offer, I looked over our ammunition and other articles; and finding that a little powder, ſhot, tobacco, and a few knives, were likely to be of ſervice before the journey could be completed, I determined to ſend a letter to the governor of Prince of Wales's Fort, to adviſe him of my ſitu-ation, and to deſire him to ſend by the bearer a certain quantity of the above articles; on which Keelſhies and his crew proceeded on their jour-ney for the Factory the ſame day.

Cathawhachaga was the only river we had ſeen ſince the breaking up of the ice that we could not ford; and as we had not any canoes with us, we were obliged to get ferried acroſs by the ſtrange Indians.  When we arrived on the North ſide of this river, where the Indians reſided, my guide propoſed to ſtop ſome time, to dry and pound ſome meat to take with us; to which I readily conſented.  We alſo ſet our fiſhing-nets,
                                                    and

and caught a confiderable quantity of very fine fifh; fuch as tittemeg, barble, &c.

The number of deer which croffed Cathawha-chaga, during our ftay there, was by no means equal to our expectations, and no more than juft fufficient to fupply our prefent wants, fo that after waiting feveral days in fruitlefs expectati-on, we began to prepare for moving; and ac-cordingly, on the fixth of July, we fet out, though we had not at that time as much victu-als belonging to our company as would furnifh us a fupper. During our ftay here, we had each day got as much fifh or flefh as was fufficient for prefent expenditure, but, being in hopes of bet-ter times, faved none

Before we left Cathawhachaga, I made feveral obfervations for the latitude, and found it to be 63° 4 North I alfo brought up my journal, and filled up my chart to that time Every thing being now ready for our departure, my guide informed me that in a few days a canoe would be abfolutely neceffary, to enable us to crofs fome unfordable rivers which we fhould meet, and could not avoid. This induced me to purchafe one at the eafy rate of a fingle knife, the full value of which did not exceed one penny. It muft be obferved, that the man who fold the canoe had no farther occafion for it, and was glad to take what he could get; but had he been tho-roughly acquainted with our neceffities he moft affuredly would have had the confcience to

have

have afked goods to the amount of ten beaver fkins at leaft

This additional piece of luggage obliged me to engage another Indian; and we were lucky enough at that time to meet with a poor forlorn fellow, who was fond of the office, having never been in a much better ftate than that of a beaft of burthen  Thus, provided with a canoe, and a man to carry it, we left Cathawhachaga, as has been obferved, on the fixth of July, and conti- nued our courfe to the North by Weft, and Noith North Weft; and that night put up by the fide of a fmall bay of White Snow Lake, where we angled, and caught feveral fine trout, fome of which weighed not lefs than fourteen or fixteen pounds  In the night heavy rain came on, which

9th  continued three days; but the ninth proving fine weather, and the fun difplaying his beams very powerfuily, we dried our clothes, and proceeded to the Northward  Toward the evening, how- ever, it began again to rain fo exceffively, that it was with much difficulty we kept our powder and books dry

17th  On the feventeenth, we faw many mufk-oxen, feveral of which the Indians killed, when we agreed to ftay here a day or two, to dry and pound * fome of the carcafes to take with us

The

* To prepare meat in this manner  it requires no farther opeiation than cuting the lean parts of the animal nto thin flices, and drying it in the fun, or by a flow fire, till, after beating it between two ftones, it is reduced to a ccarfe powder

The flefh of any animal, when it is thus prepared,
is not only hearty food, but is always ready for
ufe, and at the fame time very portable    In moft
parts of Hudfon's Bay it is known by the name
of Thew hagon, but amongft the Northern Indians it is called Achees.

Having prepared as much dried flefh as we
could tranfport, we proceeded to the Northward;
and at our departure left a great quantity of meat
behind us, which we could neither eat nor carry
away. This was not the firft time we had fo done;
and however wafteful it may appear, it is a practice fo common among all the Indian tribes, as
to be thought nothing of.   On the twenty-fecond, we met feveral ftrangers, whom we joined
in purfuit of the deer, &c. which were at this
time fo plentiful, that we got every day a fufficient number for our fupport, and indeed too
frequently killed feveral merely for the tongues,
narrow, and fat.

After we had been fome time in company with
thofe Indians, I found that my guide feemed to
hefitate about proceeding any farther, and that
he kept pitching his tent backward and forward,
from place to place, after the deer, and the reft
of the Indians.   On my afking him his reafon for
fo doing, he anfwered, that as the year was too
far advanced to admit of our arrival at the Coppermine River that Summer, he thought it more
advifable to pafs the Winter with fome of the
Indians then in company, and alleged that there
                                                could

1770. could be no fear of our arriving at that river
early in the Summer of one thousand seven hundred and seventy-one.  As I could not pretend
to contradict him. I was entirely reconciled to his
proposal, and accordingly we kept moving to the
Westward with the other Indians.  In a few
days, many others joined us from different quarters, so that by the thirtieth of July we had in
all above seventy tents, which did not contain
less than six hundred persons.  Indeed our encampment at night had the appearance of a small
town; and in the morning, when we began to
move, the whole ground (at least for a large
space all round) seemed to be alive, with men,
women, children, and dogs.  Though the land
was entirely barren, and destitute of every kind
of herbage. except wish-a capucca * and moss, yet
the deer were so numerous that the Indians not
only killed as many as were sufficient for our large
number, but often several merely for the skins,
marrow, &c. and left the carcases to rot, or to be
devoured by the wolves, foxes, and other beasts
of prey.

In our way to the Westward we came to several
rivers, which, though small and of no note, were
so deep as not to be fordable, particularly Doo-
baunt River†.  On those occasions only, we
had

_July_

30th

* Wish-a capucca is the name given by the natives to a plant which is
found all over the country bordering on Hudson's Bay, and an infusion
of it is used as tea by all the Europeans settled in that country

† This river, as well as all others deserving that appellation which I
crossed

had recourfe to our canoe, which, though of the
common fize, was too fmall to carry more than
two perfons; one of whom always lies down at
full length for fear of making the canoe top-hea-
vy, and the other fits on his heels and paddles.
This method of ferrying over rivers, though
tedious, is the moft expeditious way thefe poor
people can contrive; for they are fometimes obliged to carry their canoes one hundred and fifty,
or two hundred miles, without having occafion
to make ufe of them; yet at times they cannot
do without them; and were they not very fmall
and portable, it would be impoffible for one man
to carry them, which they are often obliged to
do, not only the diftance above mentioned, but
even the whole Summer

The perfon I engaged at Cathawhachaga to car- 6th
ry my canoe proving too weak for the tafk, another of my crew was obliged to exchange loads
with him, which feemed perfectly agreeable to all
parties; and as we walked but fhort days journies, and deer were very plentiful, all things went
on every fmoothly. Nothing material happened
till the eighth, when we were near lofing the 8th
quadrant and all our powder from the following
circumftance: the fellow who had been releafed
from carrying the canoe proving too weak, as hath
been

croffed during this part of my journey ran to the Eaft and North Eaft,
and both them and the lakes were perfectly frefh, and inhabited by fifh
that are well known never to frequent falt water

been already obferved, had, after the exchange, nothing to carry but my powder and his own trifles, the latter were indeed very inconfiderable, not equal in fize and weight to a foldier's knapfack. As I intended to have a little fport with the deer, and knowing his load to be much lighter than mine, I gave him the quadrant and ftand to carry, which he took without the leaft hefitation, or feeming ill will. Having thus eafed myfelf for the prefent of a heavy and cumberfome part of my load, I fet out early in the morning with fome of the Indian men; and after walking about eight or nine miles, faw, from the top of a high hill, a great number of deer feeding in a neighbouring valley, on which we laid down our loads and erected a flag, as a fignal for the others to pitch their tents there for the night. We then purfued our hunting, which proved very fuccefsful. At night, however, when we came to the hill where we had left our baggage, I found that only part of the Indians had arrived, and that the man who had been entrufted with my powder and quadrant, had fet off another way, with a fmall party of Indians that had been in our company that morning. The evening being far advanced, we were obliged to defer going in fearch of him till the morning, and as his track could not be eafily difcovered in the Summer, the Southern Indians, as well as myfelf, were very uneafy, fearing we had loft the powder, which was to provide us with food and raiment the remainder of

our

our journey   The very uncourteous behaviour
of the Northern Indians then in company, gave
me little hopes of receiving aſſiſtance from them,
any longer than I had wherewithal to reward them
for their trouble and expence; for during the
whole time I had been with them, not one of them
had offered to give me the leaſt morſel of victuals,
without aſking ſomething in exchange, which, in
general, was three times the value of what they
could have got for the ſame articles, had they carried them to the Factory, though ſeveral hundred
miles diſtant.

So inconſiderate were thoſe people, that wherever they met me, they always expected that I
had a great aſſortment of goods to relieve their
neceſſities; as if I had brought the Company's
warehouſe with me   Some of them wanted
guns, all wanted ammunition, iron-work, and
tobacco; many were ſolicitous for medicine; and
others preſſed me for different articles of clothing:
but when they found I had nothing to ſpare, except a few nick-nacks and gewgaws, they made
no ſcruple of pronouncing me a "poor ſervant,
"noways like the Governor at the Factory, who,
"they ſaid, they never ſaw, but he gave them
"ſomething uſeful." It is ſcarcely poſſible to
conceive any people ſo void of common underſtanding, as to think that the ſole intent of my
undertaking this fatiguing journey, was to carry a large aſſortment of uſeful and heavy implements, to give to all that ſtood in need of them;
but

but many of them would aſk me for what they
wanted with the ſame freedom, and apparently
with the ſame hopes of ſucceſs, as if they had
been at one of the Company's Factories.    Others,
with an air of more generoſity, offered me furs
to trade with at the ſame ſtandard as at the Factory; without conſidering how unlikely it was that
I ſhould increaſe the enormous weight of my load
with articles which could be of no more uſe to me
in my preſent ſituation than they were to themſelves

This unaccountable behaviour of the Indians
occaſioned much ſerious reflection on my part;
as it ſhowed plainly how little I had to expect if
I ſhould, by any accident, be reduced to the neceſſity of depending upon them for ſupport, ſo
that, though I laid me down to reſt, ſleep was a
ſtranger to me that night.    The following beautiful lines of Dr. Young I repeated above an hundred times

" Tired Nature's ſweet reſtorer, balmy Sleep
" He, like the world, his ready viſit pays
" Where fortune ſmiles; the wretched he forſakes
" Swift on his downy pinion flies from woe,
" And lights on lids unſullied with a tear'    NIGHT THOUGHT-

After paſſing the night in this melancholy
manner, I got up at day-break, and, with the two
Southern Indians, ſet out in queſt of our deſer-
ter.    Many hours elapſed in fruitleſs ſearch after
him, as we could not diſcover a ſingle track in
the direction which we were informed he had
taken.

taken. The day being almost spent without the least appearance of succels, I propofed repaiiing to the place where I had delivered the quadrint to him, in hopes of feeing fome track in the mofs that might lead to the way the Indians were gone whom oui defeiter had accompanied On our aiiival at that place, we found they had ftruck down toward a little river which they had croff-ed the morning before, and there, to our great joy, we found the quadrant and the bag of pow-dei lying on the top of a high ftone, but not a human being was to be feen. On examining the powder, we found that the bag had been opened, and pait of it taken out, but, notwithftanding our lofs was very confiderable, we retuined with light hearts to the place at which we had been the night before, where we found our baggage fafe, but all the Indians gone they had, howe-ver, been fo confiderate as to fet up marks to direct v what couife to fteer. By the time we had adjufted our bundles, the day was quite fpent; feeing, however, a fmoke, or rather a fire, in the direction we were ordered to fteer, we bent our way towards it, and a little after ten o'clock at night came up with the main body of the Indi-ans; when, after refrefhing ourfelves with a plentiful fupper, the firft morfel we had tafted that day, we retired to ieft, which I at leaft en-joyed with better fuccefs than the preceding night.

In the morning of the eleventh we proceeded on to the Weft, and Weft by South; but on the twelfth

twelfth did not move. This gave us an opportunity of endeavouring to afcertain the latitude
by a meredian altitude, when we found the place
to be in 63° 10 North nearly.  It proving rather
cloudy about noon, though exceeding fine weather, I let the quadrant ftand, in order to obtain
the latitude more exactly by two altitudes; but,
to my great mortification, while I was eating my
dinner, a fudden guft of wind blew it down;
and as the ground where it ftood was very ftoney,
the bubble, the fight-vane, and vernier, were entirely broke to pieces, which rendered the inftrument ufelefs.  In confequence of this misfortune
I refolved to return again to the Fort, though we
were then in the latitude of 63" 10' North, and
about 10° 40' Weft longitude from Churchill
River.

CHAP.

## C H A P. III

Tranfactions from the Time the Quadrant was broken, till I arrived at the Factory.

*Several strange Indians join us from the Northward.— They plundered me of all I had ; but did not plunder the Southern Indians.—My guide plundered.—We begin our return to the Factory.—Meet with other Indians, who join our company.—Collect deer-skins for clothing, but could not get them dreffed —Suffer much hardfhip from the want of tents and warm clothing.—Moft of the Indians leave us.—Meet with Matonabbee.—Some account of him, and his behaviour to me and the Southern Indians —We remain in his company fome time —His obfervations on my two unfuccefsful attempts —We leave him, and proceed to a place to which he directed us, in order to make fnow fhoes and fledges.—Join Matonabbee again, and proceed towards the Factory in his company.— Ammunition runs fhort.—Myfelf and four Indians fet off poft for the Factory —Much bewildered in a fnow ftorm , my dog is frozen to death , we lie in a bufh of willows.—Proceed on our journey.—Great difficulty in croffing a jumble of rocks.—Arrive at the Fort.*

THE day after I had the misfortune to break the quadrant, feveral Indians joined me from the Northward, fome of whom plundered me

1770.
Auguft 13th.

me and my companions of almoſt every uſeful article we had, among which was my gun, and
notwithſtanding we were then on the point of
returning to the Factory, yet, as one of my companions' guns was a little out of order, the loſs
was likely to be ſeverely felt; but it not being
in my power to recover it again, we were obliged to reſt contented.

Nothing can exceed the cool deliberation of
thoſe villains; a committee of them entered my
tent*. The ringleader ſeated himſelf on my left-
hand. They firſt begged me to lend them my
ſkipertogan † to fill a pipe of tobacco  After
ſmoking two or three pipes, they aſked me for
ſeveral articles which I had not, and among others
for a pack of cards, but on my anſwering that I
had not any of the articles they mentioned,  one
of them put his hand on my baggage, and aſked
if it was mine.  Before I could anſwer in the affirmative, he and the reſt of his companions (ſix
in number) had all my treaſure ſpread on the
ground.  One took one thing, and another another, till at laſt nothing was left but the empty
bag, which they permitted me to keep.  At
length

---

* This only conſiſted of three walking ſticks ſtuck into the gro nd,
and a blanket thrown over them

† Skipertogan is a ſmal bag that conta ns a flint and ſteel, alſo a pipe
and tobacco as well as touchwood, &c for making a fire  Some of theſe
bags may be called truly elegan , b ng richly ornamented with beads,
porcup ne qu ll , moose-ha r &c a work always performed by the women, and d ev are, w th much propr ety, greatly eſteemed by moſt Europeans for the neatneſs o the r workmanſ p

length, confidering that, though I was going to
the Factory, I fhould want a knife to cut my victuals, an awl to mend my fhoes, and a needle to
mend my other clothing, they readily gave me
thefe articles, though not without making me
underftand that I ought to look upon it as a great
favour  Finding them poffeffed of fo much generofity, I ventured to folicit them for my ra-
zors; but thinking that one would be fufficient
to fhave me during my paffage home, they made
no fcruple to keep the other; luckily they chofe
the worft  To complete their generofity, they
permitted me to take as much foap as I thought
would be fufficient to wafh and fhave me during
the remainder of my journey to the Factory.

They were more cautious in plundering the
Southern Indians, as the relation of fuch outrages
being committed on them might occafion a war
between the two nations; but they had nothing
of that kind to dread from the Englifh.  However, the Northern Indians had addrefs enough to
talk my home-guard Indians out of all they had:
fo that before we left them, they were as clean
fwept as myfelf, excepting their guns, fome ammunition, an old hatchet, an ice-chiffel, and a file
to fharpen them.

It may probably be thought ftrange that my
guide, who was a Northern Indian, fhould permit his countrymen to commit fuch outrages on
thofe under his charge; but being a man of little note, he was fo far from being able to protect

E                    us,

me and my companions of almoſt every uſeful article we had, among which was my gun; and
notwithſtanding we were then on the point of
returning to the Factory, yet, as one of my companions' guns was a little out of order, the loſs
was likely to be ſeverely felt, but it not being
in my power to recover it again, we were obliged to reſt contented.

Nothing can exceed the cool deliberation of
thoſe villains; a committee of them entered my
tent\*. The ringleader ſeated himſelf on my left-
hand. They firſt begged me to lend them my
ſkipertogan † to fill a pipe of tobacco After
ſmoking two or three pipes, they aſked me for
ſeveral articles which I had not, and among otheis
for a pack of cards; but on my anſwering that I
had not any of the articles they mentioned, one
of them put his hand on my baggage, and aſked
if it was mine. Before I could anſwer in the affirmative, he and the reſt of his companions (ſix
in number) had all my treaſure ſpread on the
ground. One took one thing, and another another, till at laſt nothing was left but the empty
bag, which they permitted me to keep. At
length

* Th s only confiſted of three walk rg ſticks ſtuck into the gro nd,
and a blarket thrown cre them

† Sk pertcg i s a ſmall naz th contairs a flint and ſteel, alſo a p pe
and tobacco as well as t uchwood &c for mak ng a fire Some of theſe
bags may be called truly elegan , being richly ornamented with beads,
porcup ne qu l s, morſe-h r &c a work alway s performed by the women, and they are with much pcp e , greatly eſteemed by moſt Europeans for the neatneſs c their workman ſ p

length, confidering that, though I was going to
the Factory, I fhould want a knife to cut my victuals, an awl to mend my fhoes, and a needle to
mend my other clothing, they readily gave me
thefe articles, though not without making me
underftand that I ought to look upon it as a great
favour. Finding them poffeffed of fo much generofity, I ventured to folicit them for my ra-
zors; but thinking that one would be fufficient
to fhave me during my paffage home, they made
no fcruple to keep the other, luckily they chofe
the worft. To complete their generofity, they
permitted me to take as much foap as I thought
would be fufficient to wafh and fhave me during
the remainder of my journey to the Factory.

They were more cautious in plundering the
Southern Indians, as the relation of fuch outrages
being committed on them might occafion a war
between the two nations; but they had nothing
of that kind to dread from the Englifh. However, the Northern Indians had addrefs enough to
talk my home-guard Indians out of all they had:
fo that before we left them, they were as clean
fwept as myfelf, excepting their guns, fome ammunition, an old hatchet, an ice-chiffel, and a file
to fharpen them.

It may probably be thought ftrange that my
guide, who was a Northern Indian, fhould permit his countrymen to commit fuch outrages on
thofe under his charge; but being a man of little note, he was fo far from being able to protect
E                               us,

us, that he was obliged to submit to nearly the same outrage himself.   On this occasion he assumed a great air of generosity, but the fact was, he gave freely what it was not in his power to protect

19th

Early in the morning of the nineteenth, I set out on my return, in company with several Northern Indians, who were bound to the Factory with furrs and other commodities in trade  This morning the Indian who took my gun, returned it to me, it being of no use to him, having no ammunition  The weather for some time proved fine, and deer were very plentiful, but as the above ravagers had materially lightened my load, by taking every thing from me, except the quadrant, books, &c this part of my journey was the easiest and most pleasant of any I had experienced since my leaving the Fort.   In our way we frequently met with other Indians, so that scarcely a day passed without our seeing several smokes made by other strangers.   Many of those we met joined our party, having furrs and other commodities for trade.

31st

The deer's hair being now of a proper length for clothing, it was necessary, according to the custom, to procure as many of their skins, while in season, as would make a suit of warm clothing for the Winter: and as each grown person requires the prime parts of from eight to eleven (those skins in proportion to their size) to make a complete suit, it must naturally be supposed that

this

this addition to my burthen was very considerable. My load, however cumberfome and heavy, was yet very bearable; but, after I had carried it feveral weeks, it proved of no fervice; for we had not any women properly belonging to our company, confequently had not any perfon to drefs them; and fo uncivil were the other Indians, that they would neither exchange them for others of an inferior quality already dreffed, nor permit their women to drefs them for us, under pretence that they were always employed in the like duty for themfelves and families, which was by no means the cafe; for many of them had fufficient time to have done every little fervice of that kind that we could have required of them. The truth was, they were too well informed of my poverty to do any acts of generofity, as they well knew I had it not then in my power to reward them for their trouble I never faw a fet of people that poffeffed fo little humanity, or that could view the diftreffes of their fellow-creatures with fo little feeling and unconcern, for though they feem to have a great affection for their wives and children, yet they will laugh at and ridicule the diftrefs of every other perfon who is not immediately related to them.

This behaviour of the Indians made our fituation very difagreeable, for as the fall advanced, we began to feel the cold very feverely for want of proper clothing. We fuffered alfo greatly from the inclemency of the weather, as we had no

tent

1776.   tent to shelter us.   My guide was entirely exempt-
September   ed from all those inconveniences, having procured a good warm suit of clothing; and, as one of
his wives had long before joined our party, he
was provided with a tent, and every other necef-
15th.   fary confistent with their manner of living · but
the old fellow was so far from interesting himself
in our behalf, that he had, for some time before,
entirely withdrawn from our company, and
though he then continued to carry the greatest
part of our little remains of ammunition, yet he
did not contribute in the smallest degree towards
our support.   As deer, however, were in great
plenty, I felt little or no inconvenience from his
neglect in this respect.

17th          Provisions still continued very plentiful; which
was a singular piece of good fortune, and the only circumstance which at this time could contribute to our happiness or safety, for notwithstanding the early season of the year, the weather was
remarkably bad and severely cold, at least it appeared so to us, probably from having no kind of
skin-clothing.   In this forlorn state we continued
our course to the South East; and, to add to the
gloominess of our situation, most of the Northern
Indians who had been in our company all the first
part of the fall, were by this time gone a-head, as
we could not keep up with them for want of
snow-shoes.

20.          In the evening of the twentieth, we were joined from the Westward by a famous Leader, call-
ed

ed Matonabbee, mentioned in my inftructions;
who, with his followers, or gang, was alfo going to Prince of Wales's Fort, with furrs, and other articles for trade   This leader, when a youth, refided feveral years at the above Fort, and was not only a perfect mafter of the Southern Indian language, but by being frequently with the Company's fervants, had acquired feveral words of Englifh, and was one of the men who brought the lateft accounts of the Coppermine River; and it was on his information, added to that of one I-dot-le-ezey, (who is fince dead,) that this expedition was fet on foot.

The courteous behaviour of this ftranger ftruck me very fenfibly.   As foon as he was acquainted with our diftrefs, he got fuch fkins as we had with us dreffed for the Southern Indians, and furnifhed me with a good warm fuit of otter and other fkins · but, as it was not in his power to provide us with fnow-fhoes, (being then on the barren ground,) he directed us to a little river which he knew, and where there was a fmall range of woods, which, though none of the beft, would, he faid, furnifh us with temporary fnow-fhoes and fledges, that might materially affift us during the remaining part of our journey.   We fpent feve- ral nights in company with this Leader, though we advanced towards the Fort at the rate of ten or twelve miles a day, and as provifions abounded, he made a grand feaft for me in the Southern Indian ftile, where there was plenty of good eat-

ing,

ing, and the whole concluded with singing and dancing, after the Southern Indian style and manner. In this amusement my home-guard Indians bore no inconsiderable part, as they were both men of some consequence when at home, and well known to Matonabbee. but among the other Northern Indians, to whom they were not known, they were held in no estimation; which indeed is not to be wondered at, when we consider that the value of a man among those people, is always proportioned to his abilities in hunting, and as my two Indians had not exhibited any great talents that way, the Northern Indians shewed them as much respect as they do in common to those of very moderate talents among themselves

During my conversation with this Leader, he asked me very seriously, If I would attempt another journey for the discovery of the Coppermines? And on my answering in the affirmative, provided I could get better guides than I had hitherto been furnished with, he said he would readily engage in that service, provided the governor at the Fort would employ him. In answer to this, I assured him his offer would be gladly accepted, and as I had already experienced every hardship that was likely to accompany any future trial, I was determined to complete the discovery, even at the risque of life itself Matonabbee assured me, that by the accounts received from his own countrymen, the Southern Indians, and myself, it was very probable I might not experience
                                                                so

so much hardship during the whole journey, as I 1770.
had already felt, though scarcely advanced one ~~~~ October
third part of the journey

He attributed all our misfortunes to the miscon-
duct of my guides, and the very plan we pursued,
by the desire of the Governor, in not taking any
women with us on this journey, was. he said, the
principal thing that occasioned all our wants:
" for, said he, when all the men are heavy laden,
" they can neither hunt nor travel to any consider-
" able distance, and in case they meet with suc-
" cefs in hunting, who is to carry the produce of
" their labour? Women, added he, were made
' for labour, one of them can carry, or haul, as
' much as two men can do  They also pitch our
" tents, make and mend our clothing, keep us
' warm at night, and, in fact, there is no such
" thing as travelling any confiderable distance or
" for any length of time, in this country, without
" their affistance  " Women, said he again,
" though they do every thing, are maintained at
' a trifling expence, for as they always stand
' cook, the very licking of their fingers in scarce
" times. is sufficient for their subsistence " This,
however odd it may appear, is but too true a description of the situation of women in this country, it is at least so in appearance, for the women
always carry the provisions, and it is more than
probable they help themselves when the men are
not present

Early in the morning of the twenty-third, I 23d.
                                    struck

ftruck out of the road to the Faftward, with my
two companions and two or three Northern Indians, while Matonabbee and his crew continued
their courfe to the Factory, promifing to walk fo
flow that we might come up with them again;
and in two days we arrived at the place to which
we were directed   We went to work immediately in making fnow-fhoe frames and fledges;
but notwithftanding our utmoft endeavours, we
could not complete them in lefs than four days.
On the firft of November we again proceeded on
our journey toward the Factory; and on the
fixth, came up with Matonabbee and his gang:
after which we proceeded on together feveral
days; when I found my new acquaintance, on all
occafions, the moft fociable, kind, and fenfible Indian I had ever met with.   He was a man well
known, and, as an Indian, of univerfal knowledge,
and generally refpected.

Deer proved pretty plentiful for fome time, but
to my great furprife, when I wanted to give Matonabbee a little ammunition for his own ufe, I
found that my guide, Conreaquefè, who had it
all under his care, had fo embezzled or otherways
expended it, that only ten balls and about three
pounds of powder remained; fo that long before
we arrived at the Fort we were obliged to cut up
an ice-chiffel into fquare lumps, as a fubftitute for
ball.   It is, however, rather dangerous firing
lumps of iron out of fuch flight barrels as are
brought to this part of the world for trade.
Thefe

These, though light and handy, and of course well adapted for the use of both English and Indians in long journies, and of sufficient strength for leaden shot or ball, are not strong enough for this kind of shot, and strong fowling-pieces would not only be too heavy for the laborious ways of hunting in this country, but their bores being so much larger, would require more than double the quantity of ammunition that small ones do; which, to Indians at least, must be an object of no inconsiderable importance.

I kept company with Matonabbee till the twentieth, at which time the deer began to be so scarce that hardly a fresh track could be seen, and as we were then but a few days walk from the Fort, he advised me to proceed on with all speed, while he and his companions followed at leisure Accordingly, on the twenty-first, I set out post-haste, accompanied by one of the home guard (Southern) Tribe, and three Northern Indians. That night we lay on the South side of Egg River, but, long before day-break the next morning, the weather being so bad, with a violent gale of wind from the North West, and such a drift of snow, that we could not have a bit of fire: and as no good woods were near to afford us shelter, we agreed to proceed on our way: especially as the wind was on our backs, and though the weather was bad near the surface we could frequently see the moon, and sometimes the stars, to direct us in our course. In this situation we continued walk-

ing

ing the whole day, and it was not till after ten at
night that we could find the smallest tuft of woods
to put up in, for though we well knew we must
have paffed by feveral hummocks of fhrubby woods
that might have afforded us fome fhelter, yet the
wind blew fo hard, and the fnow drifted fo exceffively thick, that we could not fee ten yards
before us the whole day.  Between feven and
eight in the evening my dog, a valuable brute,
was frozen to death, fo that his fledge, which
was a very heavy cne, I was obliged to haul
Between nine and ten at night we arrived at a
fmall creek, on which we walked about three
quarters of a mile, when we came to a large tuft
of tall willows, and two or three fets of old
tent-poles.   Being much jaded, we determined
not to proceed any farther that night, fo we
went to work, and made the beft defence againft
the weather that the fituation of the place and
our materials would admit   Our labour confifted only in digging a hole in the fnow, and fixing
a few deer fkins up to windward of us, but the
moft difficult tafk was that of making a fire.
When this was once accomplifhed, the old tent
poles amply fupplied us with fewel.  By the time
we had finifhed this bufinefs, the weather began
to moderate, and the drift greatly to abate, fo
that the moon and the *Aurora Borealis* fhone out
with great fplendor, and there appeared every
fymptom of the return of fine weather.  After
eating a plentiful fupper of venifon, therefore,
of which we had a fufficent ftock to laft us to
the

the Fort, we laid down and got a little sleep The next day proving fine and clear, though excessively sharp, we proceeded on our journey early in the morning, and at night lay on the South East side of Seal River. We should have made a much longer day's journey, had we not been greatly embarrassed at setting out, by a jumble of rocks, which we could not avoid without going greatly out of our way. Here I must observe, that we were more than fortunate in not attempting to leave the little creek where we had fixed our habitation the preceding night, as the spot where we lay was not more than two or three miles distant from this dangerous place ; in which, had we fallen in with it in the night, we must unavoidably have been bewildered, if we had not all perished, as notwithstanding the advantage of a clear day, and having used every possible precaution, it was with the utmost difficulty that we crossed it without broken limbs. Indeed it would have been next to an impossibility to have done it in the night

1770.

November 23d

The twenty-fourth and twenty-fifth proved fine clear weather, though excessively cold, and in the afternoon of the latter, we arrived at Prince of Wales's Fort, after having been absent eight months and twenty-two days, on a fruitless, or at least an unsuccessful journey.

24th
25th.

CHAP.

## C H A P. IV.

Tranfactions during our Stay at Prince of Wales's Fort, and the former part of our third Expedition, till our Arrival at Clowey, where we built Canoes, in May 1771.

*Preparations for our departure.—Refufe to take any of the home-guard Indians with me —By fo doing, I offend the Governor.—Leave the Fort a third time. —My inftructions on this expedition —Provifions of all kinds very fcarce —Arrive at the woods, where we kill fome deer.—Arrive at Ifland Lake.—Matonabbee taken ill —Some remarks thereon —Join the remainder of the Indians' families —Leave Ifland Lake.—Defcription thereof.—Deer plentiful — Meet a ftrange Indian.—Alter out courfe from Weft North Weft to Weft by South.—Crofs Cathawhach-aga River, Coffed Lake, Snow Bird Lake, and Pike Lake —Arrive at a tent of ftrangers, who are employed in fnaring deer in a pound —Defcription of the pound —Method of proceeding.—Remarks thereon.—Proceed on our journey.—Meet with feveral parties of Indians, by one of whom I fent a letter to the governor at Prince of Wales's Fort.—Arrive at Thleweyazayeth.—Employment there —Proceed to the North North Weft and North.—Arrive at Clowey, —One of the Indian's wives taken in labour. —Remarks thereon —Cuftoms obferved by the Northern Indians on thofe occafions.*

ON

ON my arrival at the Fort, I informed the Go- 1770.
vernor, of Matonabbee's being fo near. On
the twenty-eighth of November he arrived. Not- <sub></sub>November 28th
withftanding the many difficulties and hardfhips
which I had undergone during my two unfuccefsful attempts, I was fo far from being folicited
on this occafion to undertake a third excurfion,
that I willingly offered my fervice, which was
readily accepted, as my abilities and approved
courage, in perfevering under difficulties, were
thought noways inferior to the tafk.

I then determined to engage Matonabbee to be
my guide, to which he readily confented, and
with a freedom of fpeech and correctnefs of language not commonly met with among Indians,
not only pointed out the reafons which had occafioned all our misfortunes in my two former
attempts, but defcribed the plan he intended to
purfue, which at the fame time that it was highly fatisfactory to me, did honour to his penetration and judgment; as it proved him to be a man
of extenfive obfervation with refpect to times, feafons, and places; and well qualified to explain
every thing that could contribute either to facili-
tate or retard the eafe or progrefs of travelling in
thofe dreary parts of the world.

Having engaged Matonabbee, therefore, as my
guide, I began to make preparations for our departure; but Mr. Norton, the Governor, having
been very fully occupied in treding with a large
body of Indians, it was the feventh of December December.
before 7th

before I could obtain from him my dispatches. It may not be improper to observe, that he again wanted to force some of the home guard Indians (who were his own relations*) into our company, merely

---

* ‡ ... an Indian, he was born at Prince of Wales's Fort, but had been in England nine years, and considering the small sum which was expended on his education had made some progress in literature. At his return to Hudson's Bay he entered into all the abominable vices of his countrymen. He kept for his own use five or six of the finest Indian girls which he could select, and ... notwithstanding his own uncommon propensity to the sex, took every means in his power to prevent any European from having intercourse with the women of the country, for which purpose he proceeded to them ... ridiculous length. To his own friends and country he was so partial, that he set more value on, and showed more respect to one of their favourite dogs, than he ever did to his first officer. Among his miserable and ignorant countrymen he passed for a proficient in physic, and always kept a box of poison, to administer to those who refused him their wives or daughters.

With all these bad qualities, no man took more pains to inculcate virtue, morality, and continence on others, always painting, in the most odious colours, the jealous and revengeful disposition of his Indians, when any attempt was made on the chastity of their wives or daughters. Lectures of this kind, from a man of established virtue might have had some effect, but when it came from one who was grown to live in open defiance of common decency, and had many women himself, they were always heard with indignation, and considered as the hypocritical cant of a selfish debauchee, who wished to engross every woman in the country to himself.

His apartments were not only convenient but elegant, and always crowded with his favourite Indians; at night he locked the doors, and put the keys under his pillow, so that in the morning his dining-room was generally, for the want of necessary convenience, worse than a hog stye. As he advanced in years his jealousy increased, and he actually poisoned two of his women because he thought them partial to other objects more suitable to their ages. He was a most notorious smuggler, but though he put many thousands into the pockets of the Captains, he seldom put a shilling into his own.

An inflammation in his bowels occasioned his death on the 29th of December 1779, and though he died in the most excruciating pain, he retained his jealousy to the last, for a few minutes before he expired, happening to see an officer laying hold of the hand of one of his women who was standing

merely with a view that they might engrofs all
the credit of taking care of me during the journey:
but I had found them of fo little ufe in my two
former attempts, that I abfolutely refufed them;
and by fo doing, offended Mr. Norton to fuch a
degree, that neither time nor abfence could ever
afterwards eradicate his diflike of me, fo that at
my return he ufed every means in his power to
treat me ill, and to render my life unhappy.
However, to deal with candour on this occafion,
it muft be acknowledged to his honour, that whatever our private animofities might have been, he
did not fuffer them to interfere with public bufinefs; and I was fitted out with ammunition, and
every other article which Matonabbee thought
could be wanted   I was alfo furnifhed, as before,
with a fmall affortment of light trading goods, as
prefents to the far diftant Indians.

At laft I fucceeded in obtaining my inftructions,
which were as follows:

> " ORDERS *and* INSTRUCTIONS *for Mr.* SAMUEL
> " HEARNE, *going on his third Expedition to the*
> " *North of Churchill River, in queft of a North*
> " *Weft Paffage, Copper Mines, or any other thing*
> " *that may be ferviceable to the Britifh Nation in*
> "                                 *general,*

1770.

December.

---

fitting by the fire, he bellowed out, in as loud a voice as his fituation
could admit, " God " d—n you for a b——h, if I live I'll knock out your
brains   A few minutes after making this elegant apoftrophe, he expired
in the greateft agonies that can poffibly be conceived.

This I declare to be the real character and manner of life of the late Mr
Mofes Norton

" *general, cr the Hudson's Bay Company in par-*
" *ticular ; in the year* 1770.

" Mr. Samuel Hearne,

" SIR,

" As you have offered your fervice a third time
" to go in fearch of the Copper Mine River, &c.
" and as Matonabbee, a leading Indian, who has
" been at thofe parts, is willing to be your guide,
" we have accordingly engaged him for that fer-
" vice ; but having no other inftrument on the
" fame conftruction with the quadrant you had
" the misfortune to break, we have furnifhed you
" with an Elton's quadrant, being the moft pro-
" per inftrument we can now procure for mak-
" ing obfervations on the land

" The above Leader, Matonabbee, and a few of
" his beft men, which he has felected for that pur-
" pofe, are to provide for you, affift you in all
" things, and conduct you to the Copper Mine
" River; where you muft be careful to obferve
" the latitude and longitude, alfo the courfe of
" the river, the depth of the water, the fituation
" of the Copper Mines, &c. but your firft in-
" ftructions, of November fixth, one thoufand fe-
" ven hundred and fixty-nine, being fufficiently
" full, we refer you to every part thereof for
" the better regulation of your conduct during
" this journey.

                                        " As

" As you and your Indian companions are fit-
" ted out with every thing that we think is necef-  ᘏᘓ
" fary, (or at leaft as many ufeful articles as the
" nature of travelling in thofe parts will admit
" of,) you are hereby defired to proceed on your
" journey as foon as poffible; and your prefent
" guide has promifed to take great care of you,
" and conduct you out and home with all conve-
" nient fpeed.

    " I conclude with my beft wifhes for your
" health and happinefs, together with a fuc-
" cefsful journey and a quick return in fafety.
" Amen.

    * (Signed) MOSES NORTON, Governor.
" Dated at Prince of Wales's Fort,
    " 7th December, 1770."


On the feventh of December I fet out on my
third journey; and the weather, confidering
the feafon of the year, was for fome days pretty
mild.   One of Matonabbee's wives being ill, occafioned us to walk fo flow, that it was the thirteenth before we arrived at Seal River; at which
time two men and their wives left us, whofe loads,
when added to thofe of the remainder of my crew,
made a very material difference, efpecially as
Matonabbee's wife was fo ill as to be obliged to be
hauled on a fledge.
    Finding deer and all other game very fcarce,
and not knowing how long it might be before
                    F                    we

we could reach any place where they were in greater plenty, the Indians walked as far each day as their loads and other circumftances would conveniently permit.   On the fixteenth, we arrived at Egg River, where Matonabbee and the reft of my crew had laid up fome provifions and other neceffaries, when on their journey to the Fort   On going to the place where they thought the provifions had been carefully fecured from all kinds of wild beafts, they had the mortification to find that fome of their countrymen, with whom the Governor had firft traded and difpatched from the Fort, had robbed the ftore of every article, as well as of fome of their moft ufeful implements.   This lofs was more feverely felt, as there was a total want of every kind of game; and the Indians, not expecting to meet with fo great a difappointment, had not ufed that œconomy in the expenditure of the oatmeal and other provifions which they had received at the Fort, as they probably would have done, had they not relied firmly on finding a fupply at this place.   This difappointment and lofs was borne by the Indians with the greateft fortitude; and I did not hear one of them breathe the leaft hint of revenge in cafe they fhould ever difcover the offenders   the only effect it had on them was, that of making them put the beft foot foremoft. This was thought fo neceffary, that for fome time we walked every day from morning till night.
The

The days, however, being short, our sledges
heavy, and some of the road very bad, our progress seldom exceeded sixteen or eighteen miles
a day, and some days we did not travel so
much.

On the eighteenth, as we were continuing our
course to the North West, up a small creek that
empties itself into Egg River, we saw the tracks
of many deer which had crossed that part a few
days before; at that time there was not a fresh
track to be seen: some of the Indians, however,
who had lately passed that way, had killed more
than they had occasion for, so that several joints
of good meat were found in their old tent-
places; which, though only sufficient for one
good meal, were very acceptable, as we had been
in exceeding straitened circumstances for many
days.

On the nineteenth, we pursued our course in
the North West quarter; and, after leaving the
above-mentioned creek, traversed nothing but entire barren ground, with empty bellies, till the
twenty-seventh; for though we arrived at some
woods on the twenty sixth, and saw a few deer,
four of which the Indians killed, they were at
so great a distance from the place on which we
lay, that it was the twenty-seventh before the
meat was brought to the tents. Here the Indians
proposed to continue one day, under pretence of
repairing their sledges and snow shoes; but from

the

the little attention they paid to thoferepairs, I was led to think that the want of food was the chief thing that detained them, as they never ceafed eating the whole day. Indeed for many days before we had been in great want, and for the laft three days had not tafted a morfel of any thing, except a pipe of tobacco and a drink of fnow water, and as we walked daily from mor- ning till night, and were all heavy laden, our ftrength began to fail. I muft confefs that I ne- ver fpent fo dull a Chriftmas, and when I recol- lected the merry feafon which was then paffing, and reflected on the immenfe quantities, and great variety of delicacies which were then ex- pending in every part of Chriftendom, and that with a profufion bordering on wafte, I could not refrain from wifhing myfelf again in Europe, if it had been only to have had an opportunity of alleviating the extreme hunger which I fuffered with the refufe of the table of any one of my ac- quaintance. My Indians, however, ftill kept in good fpirits; and as we were then acrofs all the barren ground, and faw a few frefh tracks of deer, they began to think that the worft of the road was over for that winter, and flattered me with the expectation of foon meeting with deer and other game in greater plenty than we had done fince our departure from the Fort

28. Early in the morning of the twenty-eighth, we again fet out, and directed our courfe to the Weftward,

Weftward, through thick fhrubby woods, confifting chiefly of ill-fhaped ftunted pines, with fmall
dwarf junipers, intermixed here and there, particularly round the margins of ponds and fwamps,
with dwarf willow bufhes, and among the
rocks and fides of the hills were alfo fome fmall
poplars.

On the thirtieth, we arrived at the Eaft fide of
Ifland Lake, where the Indians killed two large
buck deer; but the rutting feafon was fo lately
over, that their flefh was only eatable by thofe
who could not procure better food  In the evening, Matonabbee was taken very ill; and from
the nature of his complaint, I judged his illnefs
to have proceeded from the enormous quantity
of meat that he had eat on the twenty-feventh,
as he had been indifpofed ever fince that time.
Nothing is more common with thofe Indians,
after they have eat as much at a fitting as would
ferve fix moderate men, than to find themfelves
out of order, but not one of them can bear to hear
that it is the effect of eating too much · in defence of which they fay, that the meaneft of the
animal creation knows when hunger it fatisfied,
and will leave off accordingly.  This, however,
is a falfe affertion, advanced knowingly in fupport of an abfurd argument; for it is well known
by them, as well as all the Southern Indians, that
the black bear, who, for fize and the delicacy of
its flefh, may juftly be called a refpectable animal, is fo far from knowing when its hunger is
fatisfied,

satisfied, that, in the Summer, when the berries
are ripe, it will gorge to such a degree, that it frequently, and even daily, vomits up great quantities of new-swallowed fruit, before it has undergone any change in the stomach, and immediately renews its repast with as much eager-
ness as before

Notwithstanding the Northern Indians are at
times so voracious, yet they bear hunger with a
degree of fortitude which, as Mr. Ellis justly ob-
serves of the Southern Indians, " is much easier
" to admire, than to imitate " I have more than
once seen the Northern Indians, at the end of
three or four days fasting, as merry and jocose on
the subject, as if they had voluntarily imposed it
on themselves; and would ask each other in the
plainest terms, and in the merriest mood, If they
had any inclination for an intrigue with a strange
woman? I must acknowledge that examples of
this kind were of infinite service to me, as they
tended to keep up my spirits on those occasions
with a degree of fortitude that would have been
impossible for me to have done had the Indians
behaved in a contrary manner, and expressed
any apprehension of starving.

31      Early in the morning of the thirty-first, we continued our journey, and walked about fourteen
miles to the Westward on Island Lake, where we
fixed our residence, but Matonabbee was at this
time so ill as to be obliged to be hauled on a
sledge the whole day    The next morning, however,

ever, he fo far recovered as to be capable of walking; when we proceeded on to the Weft and
Weft by North, about fixteen miles farther on the
fame Lake, till we arrived at two tents, which
contained the remainder of the wives and families
of my guides, who had been waiting there for
the return of their hufbands from the Fort. Here
we found only two men, though there were upward of twenty women and children; and as
thofe two men had no gun or ammunition, they
had no other method of fupporting themfelves
and the women, but by catching fifh, and fnaring
a few rabbits: the latter were fcarce, but the former were eafily caught in confiderable numbers
either with nets or hooks. The fpecies of fifh
generally caught in the nets are tittemeg, pike,
and barble; and the only forts caught with
hooks are trout, pike, burbut, and a fmall fifh,
erroneoufly called by the Englifh tench: the Southern Indians called it the toothed tittemeg, and
the Northern Indians call it *faint eah* They are
delicate eating, being nearly as firm as a perch,
and generally very fat. They feldom exceed a
foot in length, and in fhape much refemble a
gurnard, except that of having a very long broad
fin on the back, like a perch, but this fin is not
armed with fimilar fpikes. The fcales are large,
and of a footy brown. They are generally moft
efteemed when broiled or roafted with the fcales
on, of courfe the fkin is not eaten.

As the Captain [Matonabbee] and one man
were

were indifpofed, we did not move on the fecond of January; but early in the morning of the third fet out, and walked about feven miles to the North Weftward, five of which were on the above mentioned Lake; when the Indians having killed two deer, we put up for the night.

Ifland Lake (near the center) is in latitude 60° 45' North, and 102° 25' Weft longitude, from London; and is, at the part we croffed, about thirty-five miles wide. but from the North Eaft to the South Weft it is much larger, and entirely full of iflands, fo near to each other as to make the whole Lake refemble a jumble of ferpentine rivers and creeks; and it is celebrated by by the natives as abounding with great plenty of fine fifh during the beginning of the Winter. At different parts of this Lake moft part of the wives and families of thofe Northern Indians who vifit Prince of Wales's Fort in October and November generally refide, and wait for their return; as there is little fear of their being in want of provifions, even without the affiftance of a gun and ammunition, which is a point of real confequence to them. The Lake is plentifully fupplied with water from feveral fmall rivulets and creeks which run into it at the South Weft end; and it empties itfelf by means of other fmall rivers which run to the North Eaft, the principal of which is Nemace-a-feepee-a-fifh, or Little Fifh River. Many of the iflands, as well as the main land round this Lake, abound with

dwarf

dwarf woods, chiefly pines; but in fome parts
intermixed with larch and fmall birch trees.
The land, like all the reft which lies to the North
of Seal River, is hilly, and full of rocks; and
though none of the hills are high, yet as few of
the woods grow on their fummits, they in general
fhew their fnowy heads far above the woods
which grow in the vallies, or thofe which are
fcattered about their fides.

After leaving Ifland Lake, we continued our
old courfe between the Weft and North Weft,
and travelled at the eafy rate of eight or nine miles
a day. Provifions of all kinds were fcarce till
the fixteenth, when the Indians killed twelve
deer. This induced us to put up, though early
in the day; and finding great plenty of deer in
the neighbourhood of our little encampment, it
was agreed by all parties to remain a few days,
in order to dry and pound fome meat to make it
lighter for carriage.

Having, by the twenty-fecond, provided a fufficient ftock of provifion, properly prepared, to
carry with us, and repaired our fledges and fnow-
fhoes, we again purfued our courfe in the North
Weft quarter; and in the afternoon fpoke with a
ftranger, an Indian, who had one of Matonabbee's
wives under his care. He did not remain in our
company above an hour, as he only fmoked part
of a few pipes with his friends, and returned
to his tent, which could not be far diftant from
the place where we lay that night, as the woman
and

and her two children joined us next morning, before we had taken down our tent and made ready for moving. Thofe people were the firft ftrangers whom we had met fince we left the Fort, though we had travelled feveral hundred miles; which is a proof that this part of the country is but thinly inhabited. It is a truth well known to the natives, and doubtlefs founded on experience, that there are many very extenfive tracts of land in thofe parts, which are incapable of affording fupport to any number of the human race even during the fhort time they are paffing through them, in the capacity of emigrants, from one place to the other, much lefs are they capable of affording a conftant fupport to thofe who might wifh to make them their fixed refidence at any feafon of the year    It is true, that few rivers or lakes in thofe parts are entirely deftitute of fifh; but the uncertainty of meeting with a fufficient fupply for any confiderable time together, makes the natives very cautious how they put their whole dependance on that article, as it has too frequently been the means of many hundreds, being ftarved to death.

234    By the twenty-third, deer were fo plentiful that the Indians feemed to think that, unlefs the feafon, contrary to expectation and general experience, fhould prove unfavourable, there would be no fear of our being in want of provifions during the reft of the Winter, as deer had always

ways been known to be in great plenty in the direction which they intended to walk.

On the third of February, we continued our
courfe to the Weft by North and Weft North
Weft, and were fo near the edge of the woods,
that the barren ground was in fight to the Northward  As the woods trended away to the Weft,
we were obliged to alter our courfe to Weft by
South, for the fake of keeping among them, as
well as the deer  In the courfe of this day's
walk we faw feveral ftrangers, fome of whom
remained in our company, while others went on
their refpective ways.

On the fixth, we croffed the main branch of
Cathawhachaga River, which, at that part, is
about three quarters of a mile broad, and after
walking three miles farther, came to the fide of
Coffed Whore, or Partridge, Lake; but the day
being far fpent, and the weather exceffively cold,
we put up for the night.

Early in the morning of the feventh, the weather being ferene and clear, we fet out, and
croffed the above mentioned Lake, which at
that part is about fourteen miles wide, but from
the South South Weft to North North Eaft is
much larger.  It is impoffible to defcribe the in-
tenfenefs of the cold which we experienced this
day; and the difpatch we made in croffing
the lake is almoft incredible, as it was performed
by the greateft part of my crew in lefs than two
hours, though fome of the women, who were

heavy

heavy laden, took a much longer time.  Several
of the Indians were much frozen, but none of
them more difagreeably fo than one of Matonabbee's wives, whofe thighs and buttocks were in
a manner incrufted with froft; and when thawed, feveral blifters arofe, nearly as large as fheeps'
bladders.  The pain the poor woman fuffered on
this occafion was greatly aggravated by the laughter and jeering of her companions, who faid
that fhe was rightly ferved for belting her clothes
fo high.  I muft acknowledge that I was not in
the number of thofe who pitied her, as I thought
fhe took too much pains to fhew a clean heel and
good leg; her garters being always in fight,
which, though by no means confidered here as
bordering on indecency, is by far too airy to
withftand the rigorous cold of a fevere winter in
a high Northern latitude.  I doubt not that the
laughter of her companions was excited by fimilar
ideas.

When we got on the Weft fide of Partridge
Lake we continued our courfe for many days toward the Weft by South and Weft South Weft,
when deer were fo plentiful, and the Indians
killed fuch vaft numbers, that notwithftanding
we frequently remained three, four, or five days
in a place, to eat up the fpoils of our hunting,
yet at our departure we frequently left great
quantities of good meat behind us, which we
could neither eat nor carry with us.  This conduct is the more excufable among people whofe
wandering

wandering manner of life and contracted ideas make every thing appear to them as the effect of mere chance. The great uncertainty of their ever visiting this or that part a second time, induces them to think there is nothing either wrong or improvident in living on the best the country will afford, as they are passing through it from place to place; and they seem willing that those who come after them should take their chance, as they have done.

On the twenty-first, we crossed The-whole-kyed Whoie, or Snowbird Lake, which at that part was about twelve or thirteen miles wide, though from North to South it is much larger. As deer were as plentiful as before, we expended much time in killing and eating them. This Matonabbee assured me was the best way we could employ ourselves, as the season would by no means permit us to proceed in a direct line for the Copper-mine River; but when the Spring advanced, and the deer began to draw out to the barren ground, he would then, he said, proceed in such a manner as to leave no room to doubt of our arrival at the Copper-mine River in proper time

On the second of March, we lay by the side of Whooldyah'd Whoie or Pike Lake, and not far from Doo-baunt Whoie River. On the next day we again began to cross the above mentioned Lake, but after walking seven miles on it to the West South West, we arrived at a large tent of Northern

Northern Indians, who had been living there from the beginning of the Winter, and had found a plentiful subsistence by catching deer in a pound. This kind of employment is performed in the following manner:

When the Indians design to impound deer, they look out for one of the paths in which a number of them have trod, and which is observed to be still frequented by them. When these paths cross a lake, a wide river, or a barren plain, they are found to be much the best for the purpose; and if the path run through a cluster of woods, capable of affording materials for building the pound, it adds considerably to the commodiousness of the situation. The pound is built by making a strong fence with brushy trees, without observing any degree of regularity, and the work is continued to any extent, according to the pleasure of the builders. I have seen some that were not less than a mile round, and am informed that there are others still more extensive. The door, or entrance of the pound, is not larger than a common gate, and the inside is so crowded with small counter-hedges as very much to resemble a maze; in every opening of which they set a snare, made with thongs of parchment deer-skins well twisted together, which are amazingly strong. One end of the snare is usually made fast to a growing pole; but if no one of a sufficient size can be found near the place where the snare is set, a loose pole is substituted in its room, which is always of such size

and

and length that a deer cannot drag it far before it gets entangled among the other woods, which are all left ftanding except what is found neceſſary for making the fence, hedges, &c.

The pound being thus prepared, a row of fmall brufhwood is ftuck up in the fnow on each fide the door or entrance; and thefe hedge-rows are continued along the open part of the lake, river, or plain, where neither ftick nor ftump befides is to be feen, which makes them the more diftinctly obferved. Thefe poles, or brufh-wood, are generally placed at the diftance of fifteen or twenty yards from each other, and ranged in fuch a manner as to form two fides of a long acute angle, growing gradually wider in proportion to the diftance they extend from the entrance of the pound, which fometimes is not lefs than two or three miles; while the deer's path is exactly along the middle, between the two rows of brufh-wood.

Indians employed on this fervice always pitch their tent on or near to an eminence that affords a commanding profpect of the path leading to the pound; and when they fee any deer going that way, men, women, and children walk along the lake or river-fide under cover of the woods, till they get behind them, then ftep forth to open view, and proceed towards the pound in the form of a crefcent. The poor timorous deer finding themfelves purfued, and at the fame time taking the two rows of brufhy poles to be two ranks of people ftationed to prevent their paffing on either fide,

fide, run ftraight forward in the path till they get
into the pound.   The Indians then clofe in,  and
block up  the  entrance with fome brufhy trees,
that have been cut down and lie at hand for that
purpofe.   The deer being thus enclofed,  the women and children walk round the pound,  to prevent  them  from  breaking  or jumping over the
fence, while the men are employed fpearing fuch
as are entangled in the fnares,  and fhooting with
bows and arrows thofe which remain loofe in the
pound.

This  method  of  hunting,  if it deferves  the
name, is fometimes fo  fuccefsful, that many families fubfift  by  it  without having occafion  to
move their tents above once  or  twice during the
courfe of a whole winter ,  and when the Spring
advances, both the deer and Indians draw out to
the  Eaftward,  on  the  ground  which is entirely
barren, or at leaft what is fo called in thofe parts,
as it neither produces trees or fhrubs of any kind,
fo that mofs and fome little grafs is all the herbage which is to be found on it.   Such an eafy
way  of  procuring  a  comfortable  maintenance in
the Winter  months,  (which is by far the worft
time of the year,) is wonderfully well adapted to
the fupport of the aged and infirm, but is too apt
to occafion an habitual indolence in the young and
active,  who frequently fpend a whole Winter in
this indolent manner : and as thofe parts of the
country  are almoft  deftitute of  every animal of
the furr kind, it cannot be fuppofed that thofe
who

who indulge themfelves in this indolent method of procuring food can be mafters of any thing for trade; whereas thofe who do not get their livelihood at fo eafy a rate, generally procure furrs enough during the Winter to purchafe a fufficient fupply of ammunition, and other European goods, to laft them another year. This is nearly the language of the more induftrious among them, who, of courfe, are of moft importance and value to the Hudfon's Bay Company, as it is from them the furrs are procured which compofe the greateft part of Churchill trade. But in my opinion, there cannot exift a ftronger proof that mankind was not created to enjoy happinefs in this world, than the conduct of the miferable beings who inhabit this wretched part of it, as none but the aged and infirm, the women and children, a few of the more indolent and unambitious part of them, will fubmit to remain in the parts where food and clothing are procured in this eafy manner, becaufe no animals are produced there whofe furrs are valuable. And what do the more induftrious gain by giving themfelves all this additional trouble? The real wants of thefe people are few, and eafily fupplied, a hatchet, an icechiffel, a file, and a knife, are all that is required to enable them, with a little induftry, to procure a comfortable livelihood; and thofe who endeavour to poffefs more, are always the moft unhappy, and may, in fact, be faid to be only flaves and carriers to the reft, whofe ambition never leads

G                    them

them to any thing beyond the means of procuring food and clothing. It is true, the carriers pride themselves much on the respect which is shewn to them at the Factory; to obtain which they frequently run great risques of being starved to death in their way thither and back; and all that they can possibly get there for the furrs they procure after a year's toil, seldom amounts to more than is sufficient to yield a bare subsistence, and a few furrs for the ensuing year's market; while those whom they call indolent and mean-spirited live generally in a state of plenty, without trouble or risque, and consequently must be the most happy, and, in truth, the most independent also. It must be allowed that they are by far the greatest philosophers, as they never give themselves the trouble to acquire what they can do well enough without. The deer they kill, furnishes them with food, and a variety of warm and comfortable clothing, either with or without the hair, according as the seasons require, and it must be very hard indeed, if they cannot get furrs enough in the course of two or three years, to purchase a hatchet, and such other edge-tools as are necessary for their purpose. Indeed those who take no concern at all about procuring furrs, have generally an opportunity of providing themselves with all their real wants from their more industrious countrymen, in exchange for provisions, and ready-dressed skins for clothing

It is undoubtedly the duty of every one of the Com-

Company's fervants to encourage a fpirit of induftry among the natives, and to ufe every means in
their power to induce them to procure furrs and
other commodities for trade, by afluring them of
a ready purchafe and good payment for every
thing they bring to the factory : and I can truly
fay, that this has ever been the grand object of my
attention. But I muft at the fame time confefs,
that fuch conduct is by no means for the real benefit of the poor Indians, it being well known
that thofe who have the leaft intercourfe with the
Factories, are by far the happieft. As their whole
aim is to procure a comfortable fubfiftence, they
take the moft prudent methods to accomplifh it;
and by always following the lead of the deer, are
feldom expofed to the griping hand of famine,
fo frequently felt by thofe who are called the annual traders. It is true, that there are few of the
Indians, whofe manner of life I have juft defcribed, but have once in their lives at leaft vifited
Prince of Wales's Fort ; and the hardfhips and
dangers which moft of them experienced on thofe
occafions, have left fuch a lafting impreffion on
their minds, that nothing can induce them to repeat their vifits · nor is it, in fact, the intereft of
the company that people of this eafy turn, and
who require only as much iron-work at a time as
can be purchafed with three or four beaver fkins,
and that only once in two or three years, fhould
be invited to the Factories; becaufe what they beg
and fteal while there, is worth, in the way of

G 2                                        trade

trade, three times the quantity of furrs which
they bring.   For this reason, it is much more for
the interest of the Company that the annual traders should buy up all those small quantities of
furrs, and bring them in their own name, than
that a parcel of beggars should be encouraged to
come to the Factory with scarcely as many furrs
as will pay for the victuals they eat while they are
on the plantation

I have often heard it observed, that the Indians
who attend the deer-pounds might, in the course
of a winter, collect a vast number of pelts, which
would well deserve the attention of those who are
called carriers or traders, but it is a truth,
though unknown to those speculators, that the
deer skins at that season are not only as thin as a
bladder, but are also full of warbles, which render them of little or no value    Indeed, were they
a more marketable commodity than they really
are, the remote situation of those pounds from the
Company's Factories, must for ever be an unsur-
mountable barrier to the Indians bringing any of
those skins to trade.   The same observation may
be made of all the other Northern Indians, whose
chief support, the whole year round, is venison ;
but the want of heavy draught in Winter, and
water-carriage in summer, will not permit them
to bring many deer skins to market, not even
those that are in season, and for which there has
always been great encouragement given

We stopped only one night in company with the
Indians

Indians whom we met on Pike Lake, and in the 1771. morning of the fourth, proceeded to crofs the re- March mainder of that Lake, but, though the weather 4'th was fine, and though the Lake was not more than twenty-feven miles broad at the place where we croffed it, yet the Indians loft fo much time at play, that it was the feventh before we arrived on 7th the Weft fide of it    During the whole time we were croffing it, each night we found either points of land, or iflands, to put up in.  On the eighth, 8th. we lay a little to the Faft North Eaft of Black Bear Hill, where the Indians killed two deer, which were the firft we had feen for ten days, but hav- ing plenty of dried meat and fat with us, we were by no means in want during any part of that time    On the ninth, we proceeded on our courfe 9th to the Weftward, and foon met with as great plenty of deer as we had feen during any part of our journey, which, no doubt, made things go on fmooth and eafy : and as the Spring advanced, the rigour of the winter naturally abated, fo that at times we had fine pleafant weather over-head, though it was never fo warm as to occafion any thaw, unlefs in fuch places as lay expofed to the mid-day fun, and were fheltered from all the cold winds.

On the nineteenth, as we were continuing our 19th. courfe to the Weft and Weft by South, we faw the tracks of feveral ftrangers, and on following the main path, we arrived that night at five tents of Northern Indians, who had refided there great

part

1771.  part of the Winter, fnaring deei in the fame man-
Ma ch   ner as thofe before mentioned.    Indeed, it fhould
        feem that this, as well as fome other places, had
        been frequented more than once on this occafion;
        for the wood that had been cut down for fewel,
20th    and other ufes, was almoft incredible.    Before
        morning, the weather became fo bad, and the
        ftorm continued to rage with fuch violence, that
        we did not move for feveral days; and as fome
        of the Indians we met with at this place were go-
        ing to Prince of Wales's Fort in the Summer, I
        embraced the opportunity of fending by them a
        Letter to the Chief at that Fort, agreeably to the
        tenor of my inftructions.    By fumming up my
        courfes and diftances from my laft obfervation,
        for the weather at that time would not permit
        me to obferve, I judged myfelf to be in latitude
        61° 30 North, and about 19° 60' of longitude to
        tne Weft of Churchill River.    This, and fome
        accounts of the ufage I received from the natives,
        with my opinion of the future fuccefs of the
        journey, formed the contents of my Letter.

2 d         On the twenty-third, the weather became fine
        and moderate, fo we once more purfued our way,
26.h    and the next day, as well as on the twenty-fixth,
        faw feveral more tents of Northern Indians, who
        were employed in the fame manner as thofe we
        had formerly met, but fome of them having had
        bad fuccefs, and being relations or acquaintances
        of part of my crew, joined our company, and
        proceeded with us to the Weftward.    Though
                                                    the

the deer did not then keep regular paths, so as to enable the Indians to catch them in pounds, yet they were to be met with in great abundance in scattered herds, so that my companions killed as many as they pleased with their guns.

We still continued our course to the West and West by South, and on the eighth of April, arrived at a small Lake, called Thelewey-aza-yeth; but with what propriety it is so called I cannot discover, for the meaning of Thelewey-aza-yeth is Little Fish Hill. probably so called from a high hill which stands on a long point near the West end of the lake. On an island in this Lake we pitched our tents, and the Indians finding deer very numerous, determined to stay here some time, in order to dry and pound meat to take with us; for they well knew, by the season of the year, that the deer were then drawing out to the barren ground, and as the Indians proposed to walk due North on our leaving the Lake, it was uncertain when we should again meet with any more As several Indians had during the Winter joined our party, our number had now increased to seven tents, which in the whole contained not less than seventy persons.

Agreeably to the Indians' proposals we remained at Thelewey-aza-yeth ten days, during which time my companions were busily employed (at their intervals from hunting) in preparing small staves of birch-wood, about one and a quarter inch square, and seven or eight feet long. These

serve

serve as tent-poles all the summer, while on the barren ground, and as the fall advances, are converted into snow-shoe frames for Winter use. Birchrind, together with timbers and other wood-work for building canoes, were also another object of the Indian's attention while at this place; but as the canoes were not to be set up till our arrival at Clowey, (which was many miles distant,) all the wood-work was reduced to its proper size, for the sake of making it light for carriage.

As to myself, I had little to do, except to make a few observations for determining the latitude, bringing up my journal, and filling up my chart to the present time. I found the latitude of this place 61° 30 North, and its longitude, by my account, 19° West of Prince of Wales's Fort

18th    Having a good stock of dried provisions, and most of the necessary work for canoes all ready, on the eighteenth we moved about nine or ten miles to the North North West, and then came to a tent of Northern Indians who were tenting on the North side of Thelewey aza River. From these Indians Matonabbee purchased another wife; so that he had now no less than seven, most of whom would for size have made good grenadiers. He prided himself much in the height and strength of his wives, and would frequently say, few women would carry or haul heavier loads, and though they had, in general, a very masculine appearance, yet he preferred them to those of a more delicate form and moderate stature.

In

In a country like this, where a partner in exceflive hard labour is the chief motive for the union, and the fofter endearments of a conjugal life are only confidered as a fecondary object, there feems to be great propriety in fuch a choice, but if all the men were of this way of thinking, what would become of the greater part of the women, who in general are but of low ftature, and many of them of a moft delicate make, though not of the ex- acteft proportion, or moft beautiful mould? Take them in a body, the women are as deftitute of real beauty as any nation I ever faw, though there are fome few of them, when young, who are to- lerable; but the care of a family, added to their conftant hard labour, foon make the moft beau- tiful among them look old and wrinkled, even before they are thirty, and feveral of the more ordinary ones at that age are perfect antidotes to love and gallantry. This, however, does not ren- der them lefs dear and valuable to their owners, which is a lucky circumftance for thofe women, and a certain proof that there is no fuch thing as any rule or ftandard for beauty. Afk a Nor- thern Indian, what is beauty? he will anfwer, a broad flat face, fmall eyes, high cheek-bones, three or four broad black lines a-crofs each cheek, a low forehead, a large broad chin, a clumfy hook-nofe, a tawny hide, and breafts hanging down to the belt. Thofe beauties are greatly heightened, or at leaft rendered more valuable, when the poffef- for is capable of dreffing all kinds of fkins, con-

verting

verting them into the different parts of their
clothing, and able to carry eight or ten * stone in
Summer, or haul a much greater weight in Winter. These, and other similar accomplishments,
are all that are sought after, or expected, of a
Northern Indian woman. As to their temper, it
is of little consequence; for the men have a wonderful facility in making the most stubborn comply with as much alacrity as could possibly be expected from those of the mildest and most obliging turn of mind, so that the only real difference
is, the one obeys through fear, and the other com-
plies cheerfully from a willing mind; both knowing that what is commanded must be done. They
are, in fact, all kept at a great distance, and the
rank they hold in the opinion of the men cannot
be better expressed or explained, than by observing the method of treating or serving them at
meals, which would appear very humiliating, to
an European woman, though custom makes it sit
light on those whose lot it is to bear it. It is necessary to observe, that when the men kill any
large beast, the women are always sent to bring it
to the tent: when it is brought there, every operation it undergoes, such as splitting, drying,
pounding, &c. is performed by the women.
When any thing is to be prepared for eating, it is
the women who cook it; and when it is done,
the wives and daughters of the greatest Captains

in

* The stone here meant is fourteen pounds

in the country are never ferved, till all the males,
even thofe who are in the capacity of fervants,
have eaten what they think proper, and in times
of fcarcity it is frequently their lot to be left without a fingle morfel. It is, however, natural to
think they take the liberty of helping themfelves
in fecret; but this muft be done with great prudence, as capital embezzlements of provifions in
fuch times are looked on as affairs of real confequence, and frequently fubject them to a very
fevere beating  If they are practifed by a woman
whofe youth and inattention to domeftic concerns
cannot plead in her favour, they will for ever be
a blot in her character, and few men will chufe to
have her for a wife.

Finding plenty of good birch growing by the
fide of Theley-aza River, we remained there for a
few days, in order to complete all the wood-work
for the canoes, as well as for every other ufe for
which we could poffibly want it on the barren
ground, during our Summer's cruife.  On the
twentieth, Matonabbee fent one of his brothers,
and fome others, a-head, with birch-rind and
wood work for a canoe, and gave them orders to
proceed to a fmall Lake near the barren ground
called Clowey, where they were defired to make
all poffible hafte in building the canoe, that it
might be ready on our arrival.

Having finifhed fuch wood-work as the Indians
thought would be neceffary, and having augmented our ftock of dried meat and fat, the
twenty-

twenty-firft was appointed for moving, but one of the women having been taken in labour, and it being rather an extraordinary cale, we were detained more than two days. The inftant, however, the poor woman was delivered, which was not until fhe had fuffered all the pains ufually felt on thofe occafions for near fifty-two hours, the fignal was made for moving when the poor crea-ture took her infant on her back and fet out with the reft of the company; and though another perfon had the humanity to haul her fledge for her, (for one day only,) fhe was obliged to car-ry a confiderable load befide her little charge, and was frequently obliged to wade knee deep in water and wet fnow. Her very looks, exclufive of her moans, were a fufficient proof of the great pain fhe endured, infomuch that although fhe was a perfon I greatly difliked, her diftrefs at this time fo overcame my prejudice, that I never felt more for any of her fex in my life; indeed her fighs pierced me to the foul, and rendered me very mi-ferable, as it was not in my power to relieve her.

When a Northern Indian woman is taken in la-bour, a fmall tent is erected for her, at fuch a dif-tance from the other tents that her cries cannot eafily be heard, and the other women and young girls are her conftant vifitants. no male, except children in arms, ever offers to approach her. It is a circumftance perhaps to be lamented, that thefe people never attempt to affift each other on thofe occafions, even in the moft critical cafes.
This

This is in fome meafure owing to delicacy, but more probably to an opinion they entertain that nature is abundantly fufficient to perform every thing required, without any external help whatever  When I informed them of the affiftance which European women derive from the fkill and attention of our midwives, they treated it with the utmoft contempt, ironically obferving, "that " the many hump-backs, bandy-legs, and other " deformities, fo frequent among the Englifh, " were undoubtedly owing to the great fkill of " the perfons who affifted in bringing them into " the world, and to the extraordinary care of " their nurfes afterward "

A Northern Indian woman after child-birth is reckoned unclean for a month or five weeks; during which time fhe always remains in a fmall tent placed at a little diftance from the others, with only a female acquaintance or two, and during the whole time the father never fees the child. Their reafon for this practice is, that children when firft born are fometimes not very fightly, having in general large heads, and but little hair, and are, moreover, often difcoloured by the force of the labour, fo that were the father to fee them to fuch great difadvantage, he might probably take a diflike to them, which never afterward could be removed.

The names of the children are always given to them by the parents, or fome perfon near of kin. Thofe of the boys are various, and generally de-
rived

rived from some place, season, or animal; the names of the girls are chiefly taken from some part or property of a Martin, such as, the White Martin, the Black Martin, the Summer Martin, the Martin's Head, the Martin's Foot, the Martin's Heart, the Martin's Tail, &c.*

23d       On the twenty-third, as I hinted above, we began to move forward, and to shape our course nearly North; but the weather was in general so hot, and so much snow had, in consequence, been melted, as made it bad walking in snow-shoes, and such exceeding heavy hauling, that it
May
3d.       was the third of May before we could arrive at Clowey, though the distance was not above eighty-five miles from Thelewey-aza-yeth. In our way we crossed part of two small Lakes, called Tittameg Lake and Scartack Lake; neither of which are of any note, though both abound with fine fish.

* Matonabbee had eight wives, and they were all called Martins

CHAP.

# C H A P. V

Tranfactions at Clowey, and on our Journey, till our Arrival at the Copper mine River.

*Several ftrange Indians join us —Indians employed building canoes, defcription and ufe of them.—— More Indians join us, to the amount of fome hundreds. —Leave Clowey.—Receive intelligence that Keel-fhies was near us.—Two young men difpatched for my letters and goods —Arrive at Pefhew Lake; crofs part of it, and make a large fmoke.—One of Matonabbee's wives elopes.—Some remarks on the ratives.—Keelfhies joins us, aid delivers my letters, but the goods were all expended.—A Northern Indian wifhes to take one of Matonabbee's wives from him, matters compromifed, but had like to have proved fatal to my progrefs.—Crofs Pefhew Lake, when I make proper arrangements for the remainder of my journey.—Many Indians join our party, in order to make war on the Efquimaux at the Copper River —Preparations made for that purpofe while at Clowey.—Proceed on our journey to the North.— Some remarks on the way.—Crofs Cogead Lake on the ice —The fun did not fet —Arrive at Conge-cathawhachaga.—Find feveral Copper Indians there. —Remarks and tranfactions during our ftay at Con-gecathawhachaga.—Proceed on our journey.—Wea-ther very bad.—Arrive at the Stoney Mountains.— Some account of them.—Crofs part of Buffalo Lake*

*on*

*on the ice —Saw many muſk-oxen —Deſcription of*
*them.—Went with ſome Indians to view Grizzle-*
*bear Hill.—Ju a ſtrange Northern Indian Leader,*
*called O'iſe, in company with ſome Copper Indians.*
*—Their behaviour to me.—Arrive at the Copper-*
*mine River.*

1771.    THE Lake Clowey is not much more than
~~~~~~       twelve miles broad in the wideſt part.  A
May      ſmall river which runs into it on the Weſt ſide, is
said by the Indians to join the Athapuſcow Lake.

3d.      On our arrival at Clowey on the third of May,
we found that the Captain's brother, and thoſe
who were ſent a-head with him from Theley-aza
River, had only got there two days before us,
and, on account of the weather, had not made the
leaſt progreſs in building the canoe, the plan of
which they had taken with them.  The ſame day
we got to Clowey ſeveral other Indians joined us
from different quarters, with intent to build their
canoes at the ſame place  Some of thoſe indians
had reſided within four or five miles, to the South
Eaſt of Clowey all the Winter, and had procured a plentiful livelihood by ſnaring deer, in
the manner which has been already deſcribed

Immediately after our arrival at Clowey, the Indians began to build their canoes, and embraced
every convenient opportunity for that purpoſe:
but as warm and dry weather only is fit for this
buſineſs, which was by no means the caſe at preſent, it was the eighteenth of May before the ca-
                                                      noes

noes belonging to my party could be completed On the nineteenth we began to proceed on our journey, but Matonabbee's canoe meeting with some damage, which took near a whole day to repair, we were detained till the twentieth.

Thofe veffels, though made of the fame mate-rials with the canoes of the Southern Indians, dif-fer from them both in fhape and conftruction; they are alfo much finaller and lighter, and though very flight and fimple in their conftruction, are neverthelefs the beft that could poffibly be con-trived for the ufe of thofe poor people, who are frequently obliged to carry them a hundred, and fometimes a hundred and fifty miles at a time, without having occafion to put them into the wa-ter. Indeed, the chief ufe of thefe canoes is to ferry over unfordable rivers, though fometimes, and at a few places, it muft be acknowledged, that they are of great fervice in killing deer, as they enable the Indians to crofs rivers and the narrow parts of lakes, they are alfo ufeful in kill-ing fwans, geefe, ducks, &c in the moulting feafon.

All the tools ufed by an Indian in building his canoe, as well as in making his fnow-fhoes, and every other kind of wood-work, confift of a hatchet, a knife, a file, and an awl, in the ufe of which they are fo dextrous, that every thing they make is executed with a neatnefs not to be ex-celled by the moft expert mechanic, affifted with every tool he could wifh.

In fhape the Northern Indian canoe bears fome

H                                              refemresemblance to a weaver's shuttle; being flat-bottomed, with straight upright sides, and sharp at each end, but the stern is by far the widest part, as there the baggage is generally laid, and occasionally a second person, who always lies down at full length in the bottom of the canoe. In this manner they carry one another across rivers and the narrow parts of lakes in those little vessels, which seldom exceed twelve or thirteen feet in length, and are from twenty inches to two feet broad in the widest part. The head, or fore part, is unnecessarily long, and narrow, and is all covered over with birch-bark, which adds considerably to the weight, without contributing to the burthen of the vessel. In general, these Indians make use of the single paddle, though a few have double ones, like the Esquimaux: the latter, however, are seldom used, but by those who lie in wait to kill deer as they cross rivers and narrow lakes*.

During

* See Plate IV where Fig A represents the bottom of the canoe, Fig B being the fore part. Fig C is the complete frame of one before it is covered with the bark of the birch-tree: it is represented on an artificial bank, which the natives raise to build it on. Fig D is an end view of a set of timbers bent and lashed in their proper shape, and left to dry. Fig E is the representation of a complete canoe. Fig F represents one of their paddles. Fig G a spear with which they kill deer, and Fig H, their mode of carrying the canoe.

The following references are to the several parts of the canoe. Fig C.
1 The stem 2 The stern post 3 Two forked sticks supporting the stem and stern-post. 4. The gunwales 5 Small rods placed between the timber and birch-back that covers them. 6 The timbers 7 The keelson 8 Large stones placed there to keep the bottom steady till the sides are sewed on

**Reference**

A  *The Bottom of the Canoe*

B  *The Fore part*

C  *The Frame, compleat*

D  *A set of Timbers bent and lashed in their proper shape for drying*

E  *A Canoe compleat*

F  *A Paddle*

G  *A spear to kill Deer with in the Water*

H  *The method of carrying the Canoe in Summer*

**Reference to the Skeleton**

1  *The Stem*

2  *Stern post*

3 3  *Two forked sticks, supporting the Stem & Stern*

4  *The Gunwalls*

5  *Small Rods placed between the Timbers & the Birch rind*

6  *The Timbers*

7  *The Kelson*

8  *Large Stones to keep the Bottom steady all the sides are sewed to*

During our ftay at Clowey we were joined by upward of two hundred Indians from different quarters, moft of whom built canoes at this place, but as I was under the protection of a principal man, no one offered to moleft me, nor can I fay they were very clamorous for any thing I had. This was undoubtedly owing to Matonabbee's informing them of my true fituation, which was, that I had not, by any means, fufficient neceffaries for myfelf, much lefs to give away. The few goods which I had with me were intended to be referved for the Copper and Dogribbed Indians, who never vifit the Company's Factories. Tobacco was, however, always given away; for every one of any note, who joined us, expected to be treated with a few pipes, and on fome occafions it was fcarcely poffible to get off without prefenting a few inches * to them; which, with the conftant fupplies which I was obliged to furnifh my own crew, decreafed that article of my ftock fo faft, that notwithftanding I had yet advanced fo fmall a part of my journey, more than one half of my ftore was expended. Gun powder and fhot alfo were articles commonly afked for by moft of the Indians we met; and in general thefe were dealt round to them with a liberal hand by my guide Matonabbee. I muft, however, do him the juftice to acknowledge, that what

H 2                                              he

---

* The tobacco ufed in Hudfon's Bay is the Brafil tobacco, which is twifted into the form of a rope, of near an inch diameter, and then wound into a large roll, from which it is taken by meafures of length, for the natives.

1771.

he diftributed was all his own, which he had purchafed at the Factory, to my certain knowledge
he bartered one hundred and fifty martins' fkins
for powder only, befides a great number of beaver, and other furrs, for fhot, ball, iron-work,
and tobacco. purpofely to give away among his
countrymen, as he had certainly as many of thefe
articles given to him as were, in his opinion, fufficient for our fupport during our journey out and
home.

May
20 a

Matonabbee's canoe having been repaired, on
the twentieth we left Clowey, and proceeded
Northward  That morning a fmall gang of ftrangers joined us, who informed my guide, that Captain Keelfhies was within a day's walk to the
Southward  Keelfhies was the man by whom I
had fent a letter to Prince of Wales's Fort, from
Cathawhachaga, in the beginning of July one
thoufand feven hundred and feventy, but not
long after that, having the misfortune to break
my quadrant, I was obliged to return to the Fort
a fecond time, and though we faw many fmokes,
and fpoke with feveral Indians on my return that
year, yet he and I miffed each other on the barren
ground, and I had not feen or heard of him fince
that time.

As Matonabbee was defirous that I fhould receive my letters, and alfo the goods I had written
for, he difpatched two of his young men to bring
them  We continued our journey to the Northward; and the next day faw feveral large fmokes

at

at a great diftance to the Eaftward on the barren
ground, which were fuppofed to be made by fome
parties of Indians bound to Prince of Wales's Fort
with furrs and other commodities for trade

On the twenty fecond and twenty third, we
proceeded to the North, at the rate of fourteen or
fifteen miles a day, and in the evening of the latter, got clear of all the woods, and lay on the barren ground. The fame evening the two young
men who were fent for my letters, &c returned,
and told me that Keelfhies had promifed to join
us in a few days, and deliver the things to me
with his own hand.

The twenty-fourth proved bad and rainy weather, fo that we only walked about feven miles,
when finding a few blafted ftumps of trees, we
pitched our tents It was well we did fo, for towards night we had exceffively bad weather, with
loud thunder, ftrong lightning, and heavy rain,
attended with a very hard gale of wind from the
South Weft, toward the next morning, however, the wind veered round to the North Weft,
and the weather became intenfely cold and frofty.
We walked that day about eight miles to the
Northward, when we were obliged to put up,
being almoft benumbed with cold. There we
found a few dry ftumps, as we had done the day
before, which ferved us for fewel*.

The

* I have obferved, during my feveral journies in thofe parts, that all the
way to the North of Seal River the edge of the wood is faced with old wi
the ed

1771.

Mar
26 h
27th

The weather on the twenty-fixth was fo bad, with fnow and thick drifting fleet, that we did not move; but the next morning proving fine and pleafant, we dried our things, and walked about twelve miles to the Northward, moft of the way on the ice of a fmall river which runs into Pefhew Lake*. We then faw a fmoke to the Southward, which we judged to be made by Keelfhies, fo we put up for the night by the fide of the above-mentioned Lake, where I expected we fhould

28 h

have waited for his arrival, but, to my great furprize, on the morrow we again fet forward, and walked twenty-two miles to the Northward on Pefhew Lake, and in the afternoon pitched our tents on an ifland, where, by my defire, the Indians made a large fmoke, and propofed to ftay a day or two for Captain Keelfhies

In

three ftumps and trees which have been blown down by the wind They are moftly of the fort which is called here Juniper but were feldom of any confiderable fize Thofe blafted trees are found in fome parts to extend to the diftance of twenty miles from the living woods, and detached patches of them are much farther off, which is a proof that the cold has been encreafing in thofe parts for fome ages Indeed, fome of the older Northern Indians have affured me, that they have heard their fathers and grandfathers fay they remembered the greateft part of thofe places where the trees are now blafted and dead, in a flourifhing ftate, and that they were remarkable for abounding with deer It is a well-known fact, that many deer are fond of frequenting thofe plains where the juniper trees abound near barren grounds, particularly in fine weather during the Winter but in heavy gales of wind they either take fhelter in the thick woods, or go to the open plains The Indians, who never want a reafon for any thing, fay, that the deer quit the thin ftraggling woods during the high winds, becaufe the noding of the trees, when at a confiderable diftance from each other, frightens them, but in the midft of a thick foreft, the conftant rufling of the branches lulls them into fecurity, and renders them an eafy prey to a fkilful hunter

* Probably the fame with Partridge Lake in the Map

In the night, one of Matonabbee's wives and
another woman eloped: it was suppofed they
went off to the Eaftward, in order to meet their
former hufbands, from whom they had been
fometime before taken by force    This affair made
more noife and buftle than I could have suppofed, and Matonabbee feemed entirely disconcert-
ed, and quite inconfolable for the lofs of his wife.
She was certainly by far the handfomeft of all his
flock, of a moderate fize, and had a fair complexion, fhe apparently poffeffed a mild temper, and
very engaging manners    In fact, fhe feemed to
have every good quality that could be expected in
a Northern Indian woman, and that could render
her an agreeable companion to an inhabitant of
this part of the world.    She had not, however,
appeared happy in her late fituation, and chofe
rather to be the fole wife of a fprightly young
fellow of no note, (though very capable of maintaining her,) than to have the feventh or eighth
fhare of the affection of the greateft man in the
country. I am forry to mention an incident which
happened while we were building the canoes at
Clowey, and which by no means does honour to
Matonabbee: it is no lefs a crime than that of
having actually ftabbed the hufband of the above-
mentioned girl in three places, and had it not
been for timely affiftance, would certainly have
murdered him, for no other reafon than becaufe
the poor man had fpoken difrefpectfully of him
for having taken his wife away by force. The cool
deliberation

1771.
Ma

deliberation with which Matonabbee committed this bloody action, convinced me it had been a long premeditated defign; for he no fooner heard of the man's arrival, than he opened one of his wives' bundles, and with the greateſt compofure, took out a new long box-handled knife, went into the man's tent, and, without any preface whatever, took him by the collar, and began to execute his horrid defign   I he poor man anticipating his danger, fell on his face, and called for affiftance; but before any could be had he received three wounds in the back   Fortunately for him, they all happened on the fhoulder-blade, fo that his life was fpared   When Matonabbee returned to his tent, after committing this horrid deed, he fat down as compofedly as if nothing had happened, called for water to wafh his bloody hands and knife, fmoked his pipe as ufual, feemed to be perfectly at eafe, and afked if I did not think he had done right ?

It has ever been the cuftom among thofe people for the men to wreftle for any woman to whom they are attached; and, of courfe, the ftrongeit party always carries off the prize.   A weak man, unleſs he be a good hunter and well-beloved, is feldom permitted to keep a wife that a ftronger man thinks worth his notice · for at any time when the wives of thofe ftrong wreftlers are heavy-laden either with furrs or provifions, they make no fcruple of tearing any other man's wife from his bofom, and making her bear a part of

his

his luggage  This cuſtom prevails throughout all
their tribes, and cauſes a great ſpirit of emulation among their youth, who are upon all occaſions, from their childhood, trying their ſtrength
and ſkill in wreſtling  This enables them to protect their property, and particularly their wives,
from the hands of thoſe powerful raviſhers ; ſome
of whom make almoſt a livelihood by taking what
they pleaſe from the weaker parties, without making them any return.  Indeed, it is repreſented
as an act of great generoſity, if they condeſcend
to make an unequal exchange, as, in general,
abuſe and inſult are the only return for the loſs
which is ſuſtained.

The way in which they tear the women and
other property from one another, though it has
the appearance of the greateſt brutality, can
ſcarcely be called fighting.  I never knew any of
them receive the leaſt hurt in theſe rencontres ;
the whole buſineſs conſiſts in hauling each other
about by the hair of the head ; they are ſeldom
known either to ſtrike or kick one another.  It
is not uncommon for one of them to cut off his
hair and to greaſe his ears, immediately before the
conteſt begins.  This, however, is done private-
ly ; and it is ſometimes truly laughable, to ſee one
of the parties ſtrutting about with an air of great
importance, and calling out, " Where is he?
" Why does he not come out ?" when the other
will bolt out with a clean ſhorned head and greaſ-
ed ears, ruſh on his antagoniſt, ſeize, him by
the

the hair, and though perhaps a much weaker man, foon drag him to the ground, while the ſtronger is not able to lay hold on him. It is veiy frequent on thoſe occaſions for each party to have ſpies, to watch the other's motions, which puts them more on a footing of equality. For want of hair to pull, they ſeize each other about the waiſt, with legs wide extended, and try their ſtrength, by endeavouring to vie who can firſt throwthe other down.

On theſe wreſtling occaſions the ſtanders-by never attempt to interfere in the conteſt ; even one brother offers not to aſſiſt another, unleſs it be with advice, which, as it is always delivered openly on the field during the conteſt, may, in fact, be ſaid to be equally favourable to both parties. It ſometimes happens that one of the wreſt-lers is ſuperior in ſtrength to the other; and if a woman be the cauſe of the conteſt, the weaker is frequently unwilling to yield, notwithſtanding he is greatly overpowered. When this happens to be the caſe, the relations and friends, or other bye-ſtanders, will ſometimes join to perſuade the weaker combatant to give up the conteſt, leſt, by continuing it, he ſhould get bruiſed and hurt, without the leaſt probability of being able to protect what he is contending for. I obſerved that very few of thoſe people were diſſatisfied with the wives which had fallen to their lot, for whenever any conſiderable number of them were in company, ſcarcely a day paſſed without ſome overtures being made for conteſts of this kind ; and

it

it was often very unpleafant to me, to fee the object of the conteft fitting in penfive filence watching her fate, while her hufband and his rival were
contending for the prize   I have indeed not only
felt pity for thofe poor wretched victims, but the
utmoft indignation, when I have feen them won,
perhaps, by a man  whom they mortally hated.
On thofe occafions their  grief  and reluctance to
follow their new lord has been fo  great, that the
bufinefs has often ended in the greateft brutality ;
for, in the ftruggle, I  have  feen  the poor girls
ftripped quite naked, and carried by main force to
their new lodgings.   At other times it was pleafant enough to fee a fine girl led off the field from
a hufband fhe difliked, with a tear in one eye and
a finger on the other ·  for cuftom,  or delicacy if
you pleafe, has taught them to think it neceffary
to whimper a little, let the  change be ever fo
much to their inclination.  I have throughout this
account given the women the appellation of girls,
which is pretty applicable,  as the objects of conteft are generally young, and without any family:
few of the men chufe to be at the trouble of maintaining other people's children, except on particular occafions, which will be taken  notice of hereafter.

   Some of the old men,  who are famous on account of their fuppofed fkill in conjuration, have
great influence in perfuading the  rabble from
committing thofe outrages; but the humanity of
thefe fages is feldom known to extend beyond
                                              their

their own families.  In defence of them they will exert their utmoft influence , but when their own relations are guilty of the fame crime, they feldom interfere  This partial conduct creates fome fecret,  and feveral open enemies ; but the generality of their neighbours are deterred, through fear or fuperftition, from executing their revenge, and even from talking difrefpectfully of them, unlefs it be behind their backs , which is a vice of which almoft every Indian in this country, without exception, is guilty.

Notwithftanding the Northern Indians are fo covetous, and pay fo little regard to private property as to take every advantage of bodily ftrength to rob their neighbours,  not only of their goods, but of their wives, yet they are, in other refpects, the mildeft tribe,  or nation, that is to be found on the borders of Hudfon's Bay.  for let their affronts or loffes be ever fo great, they never will feek any other revenge than that of wreftling. As for murder, which is fo common among all the tribes of Southern Indians, it is feldom heard of among them  A murderer is fhunned and deterted by all the tribe,  and is obliged to wander up and down,  forlorn and forfaken even by his own relations and former friends.  In that refpect a murderer may truly be compared to Cain, after he had killed his brother Abel.  The cool reception he meets with by all who know him, occafions him to grow melancholy, and he never leaves any place but the whole company fay
" There

" There goes the murderer !" The women, it is true, sometimes receive an unlucky blow from their husbands for misbehaviour, which occasions their death, but this is thought nothing of: and for one man or woman to kill another out of revenge, or through jealousy, or on any other account, is so extraordinary, that very few are now existing who have been guilty of it. At the present moment I know not one, beside Matonabbee, who ever made an attempt of that nature; and he is, in every other respect, a man of such universal good sense, and, as an Indian, of such great humanity, that I am at a loss how to account for his having been guilty of such a crime, unless it be by his having lived among the Southern Indians so long, as to become tainted with their bloodthirsty, revengeful, and vindictive disposition.

Early in the morning of the twenty-ninth, captain Keelshies joined us. He delivered to me a packet of letters, and a two-quart keg of French brandy, but assured me, that the powder, shot, tobacco, knives, &c which he received at the Fort for me, were all expended. He endeavoured to make some apology for this, by saying, that some of his relations died in the Winter, and that he had, according to their custom, throw all his own things away, after which he was obliged to have recourse to my ammunition and other goods, to support himself and a numerous family. The very affecting manner in which he related this story, often crying like a child, was a great proof of his extreme

extreme forrow, which he wifhed to perfuade me
arofe from the recollection of his having embezzled fo much of my property, but I was of a different opinion, and attributed his grief to arife
from the remembrance of his deceafed relations.
However, as a fmall recompence for my lofs, he
prefented we with four ready-dreffed moofe-fkins,
which was, he faid, the only retribution he could
then make.   The moofe-fkins, though not the
twentieth part of the value of the goods which
he had embezzled, were in reality more acceptable to me, than the ammunition and the other
articles would have been, on account of their
great ufe as fhoe-leather, which at that time was
a very fcarce article with us, whereas we had plenty of powder and fhot.

On the fame day that Keelfhies joined us, an Indian man, who had been fome time in our company, infifted on taking one of Matonabbee's
wives from him by force, unlefs he complied with
his demands, which were, that Matonabbee
fhould give him a certain quantity of ammunition, fome pieces of iron-work, a kettle, and feveral
other articles; every one of which, Matonabbee
was obliged to deliver, or lofe the woman; for
the other man far excelled him in ftrength.   Matonabbee was more exafperated on this occafion,
as the fame man had fold him the woman no longer ago than the nineteenth of the preceding
April.   Having expended all the goods he then
poffeffed, however, he was determined to make
                                             another

another bargain for her; and as she was what may be called a valuable woman in their estimation, that is, one who was not only tolerably personable, but reckoned very skilful in manufacturing the different kinds of leather, skins, and furrs, and at the same time very clever in the performance of every other domestic duty required of the sex in this part of the world, Matonabbee was more unwilling to part with her, especially as he had so lately suffered a loss of the same kind.

This dispute, which was after some hours decided by words and presents, had like to have proved fatal to my expedition; for Matonabbee, who at that time thought himself as great a man as then lived, took this affront so much to heart, especially as it was offered in my presence, that he almost determined not to proceed any farther toward the Copper-mine River, and was on the point of striking off to the Westward, with an intent to join the Athapuscow Indians, and continue with them, he being perfectly well acquainted with all their leaders, and most of the principal Indians of that country, from whom, during a former residence among them of several years, he said he had met with more civility than he ever did from his own countrymen. As Matonabbee seemed resolutely bent on his design, I had every reason to think that my third expedition would prove equally unsuccessful with the two former. I was not, however, under the least apprehension for my own safety, as he promised

to

to take me with him, and procure me a paffage to Prince of Wales's Fort, with fome of the Athapufcow Indians, who at that time annually vifited the Factory in the way of trade   After waiting till I thought Matonabbee's paffion had a little abated, I ufed every argument of which I was mafter in favour of his proceeding on the journey; affuring him not only of the future efteem of the prefent Governor of Prince of Wales's Fort, but alfo of that of all his fucceffors as long as he lived, and that even the Hudfon's Bay Company themfelves would be ready to acknowledge his affiduity and perfeverance, in conducting a bufinefs which had fo much the appearance, of proving advantageous to them.   After fome converfation of this kind, and a good deal of intreaty, he at length confented to proceed, and promifed to make all poffible hafte.   Though it was then

29th.  late in the afternoon, he gave orders for moving, and accordingly we walked about feven miles that night, and put up on another ifland in Pefhew Lake.   The preceding afternoon the Indians had killed a few deer, but our number was then fo great, that eight or ten deer would fcarcely afford us all a tafte.   Thefe deer were the firft we had feen fince our leaving the neighbourhood of Thelewey-aza-yeth; fo that we had lived all the time on the dried meat which had been prepared before we left that place in April.

30th.     The thirtieth proved bad, rainy weather; we walked, however, about ten miles to the Northward,

ward, when we arrived on the North fide of Pefhew Lake, and put up. Here Matonabbee immediately began to make every neceffary arrangement for facilitating the executing of our defign;
and as he had promifed to make all poffible hafte,
he thought it expedient to leave moft of his wives
and all his children in the care of fome Indians,
then in our company, who had his orders to proceed to the Northward at their leifure; and who,
at a particular place appointed by him, were to
wait our return from the Copper-mine River.
Having formed this refolution, Matonabbee felected two of his young wives who had no children, to accompany us; and in order to make
their loads as light as poffible, it was agreed that
we fhould not take more ammunition with us
than was really neceffary for our fupport, till we
might expect again to join thofe Indians and the
women and children. The fame meafures were
alfo adopted by all the other Indians of my party;
particularly thofe who had a plurality of wives,
and a number of children

As thefe matters took fome time to adjuft, it
was near nine o'clock in the evening of the thirty-firft before we could fet out; and then it was
with much difficulty that Matonabbee could perfuade his other wives from following him, with
their children and all their lumber, for fuch was
their unwillingnefs to be left behind, that he was
obliged to ufe his authority before they would
confent, confequently they parted in anger, and

I we.

we no fooner began our march, than they fet up a moft woeful cry, and continued to yell moft piteoufly as long as we were within hearing. This mournful fcene had fo little effect on my party, that they walked away laughing, and as merry as ever. The few who expreffed any regret at their departure from thofe whom they were to leave behind, confined their regard wholly to their children, particularly to the youngeft, fcarcely ever mentioning their mother.

Though it was fo late when we left the women, we walked about ten miles that night before we ftopped. In our way we faw many deer, feveral of which the Indians killed. To talk of travelling and killing deer in the middle of the night, may at firft view have the appearance of romance, but our wonder will fpeedily abate, when it is confidered that we were then to the Northward of 64° of North latitude, and that, in confequence of it, though the Sun did not remain the whole night above the horizon, yet the time it remained below it was fo fhort, and its depreffion even at midnight fo fmall at this feafon of the year, that the light, in clear weather, was quite fufficient for the purpofe both of walking, and hunting any kind of game.

It fhould have been obferved, that during our ftay at Clowey a great number of Indians entered into a combination with thofe of my party to accompany us to the Copper-mine River; and with no other intent than to murder the Efquimaux, who

who are underftood by the Copper Indians to frequent that river in confiderable numbers This
fcheme, notwithftanding the trouble and fatigue,
as well as danger, with which it muft be obviou-
fly attended, was neverthelefs fo univerfally approved by thofe people, that for fome time almoft
every man who joined us propofed to be of the
party. Accordingly, each volunteer, as well as
thofe who were properly of my party, prepared
a target, or fhield, before we left the woods of
Clowey. Thofe targets were compofed of thin
boards, about three quarters of an inch thick, two
feet broad, and three feet long, and were intended to ward off the arrows of the Efquimaux.
Notwithftanding thefe preparations, when we
came to leave the women and children, as has
been already mentioned, only fixty volunteers
would go with us, the reft, who were nearly as
many more, though they had all prepared targets,
reflecting that they had a great diftance to walk,
and that no advantage could be expected from
the expedition, very prudently begged to be ex-
cufed, faying, that they could not be fpared for fo
long a time from the maintenance of their wives
and families; and particularly, as they did not
fee any then in our company, who feemed willing
to encumber themfelves with fuch a charge. This
feemed to be a mere evafion, for I am clearly of
opinion that poverty on one fide, and avarice on
the other, were the only impediments to their
joining our party; had they poffeffed as many

I 2          European

1771.   European goods to fquander away among their
May     countrymen as Matonabbee and thofe of my party
        did, in all probability many might have been found
        who would have been glad to have accompanied us.

When I was acquainted with the intentions of
my companions, and faw the warlike preparations
that were carrying on, I endeavoured as much as
poffible to perfuade them from putting their inhuman defign into execution, but fo far were my
intreaties from having the wifhed-for effect, that
it was concluded I was actuated by cowardice;
and they told me, with great marks of derifion,
that I was afraid of the Efquimaux   As I knew
my perfonal fafety depended in a great meafure
on the favourable opinion they entertained of me
in this refpect, I was obliged to change my tone,
and replied, that I did not care if they rendered
the name and race of the Efquimaux extinct;
adding at the fame time, that though I was no
enemy to the Efquimaux, and did not fee the
neceffity of attacking them without caufe, yet if
I fhould find it neceffary to do it, for the protection of any one of my company, my own fafety
out of the queftion, fo far from being afraid of a
poor defencelefs Efquimaux, whom I defpifed
more than feared, nothing fhould be wanting on
my part to protect all who were with me.   This
declaration was received with great fatisfaction,
and I never afterwards ventured to interfere with
any of their war-plans.  Indeed, when I came to
confider ferioufly, I faw evidently that it was the
                                          highest

higheft folly for an individual like me, and in my
fituation, to attempt to turn the current of a national prejudice which had fubfifted between
thofe two nations from the earlieft periods, or at
leaft as long as they had been acquainted with the
exiftence of each other

Having got rid of all the women, children, dogs,
heavy baggage, and other incumbrances, on the
firft of June we purfued our journey to the Northward with great fpeed; but the weather was in
general fo precarious, and the fnow, fleet, and
rain fo frequent, that notwithftanding we embraced every opportunity which offered, it was
the fixteenth of June before we arrived in the latitude of 67° 30', where Matonabbee had propofed that the women and children fhould wait our
return from the Copper-mine River.

In our way hither we croffed feveral lakes on
the ice, of which Thoy noy-kyed Lake and Thoy-
coy-lyned Lake were the principal   We alfo
croffed a few inconfiderable creeks and rivers,
which were only ufeful as they furnifhed a fmall
fupply of fifh to the natives   The weather, as I
have before obferved, was in general difagreeable,
with a great deal of rain and fnow.   To make up
for that inconvenience, however, the deer were
fo plentiful, that the Indians killed not only a fufficient quantity for our daily fupport, but frequently great numbers merely for the fat, marrow and tongues   To induce them to defift from
this practice, I often interefted myfelf, and endeavoured,

voured, as much as poffible, to convince them in the cleareft terms of which I was mafter, of the great impropriety of fuch wafte; particularly at a time of the year when their fkins could not be of any ufe for clothing, and when the anxiety to proceed on our journey would not permit us to ftay long enough in one place to eat up half the fpoils of their hunting. As national cuftoms, however, are not eafily overcome, my remonftrances proved ineffectual, and I was always anfwered, that it was certainly right to kill plenty, and live on the beft, when and where it was to be got, for that it would be impoffible to do it where every thing was fcarce. and they infifted on it, that killing plenty of deer and other game in one part of the country, could never make them fcarcer in another. Indeed, they were fo accuftomed to kill every thing that came within their reach, that few of them could pafs by a fmall bird's neft, without flaying the young ones, or deftroying the eggs.

From the feventeenth to the twentieth, we walked between feventy and eighty miles to the North Weft and North North Weft, the greater part of the way by Cogead Lake, but the Lake being then frozen, we croffed all the creeks and bays of it on the ice.

On the twenty-firft we had bad rainy weather, with fo thick a fog that we could not fee our way: about ten o'clock at night, however, it became fine and clear, and the Sun fhone very bright;
indeed

indeed it did not fet all that night, which was a
convincing proof, without any obfervation, that
we were then confiderably to the North of the
Arctic Polar Circle

As foon as the fine weather began, we fet out
and walked about feven or eight miles to the
Noithward, when we came to a branch of Conge-
ca-tha-wha-chaga River, on the North fide of
which we found feveral Copper Indians, who
were affembled, according to annual cuftom, to kill
deer as they crofs the river in their little canoes.

The ice being now broken up, we were, for the
firft time this Summer, obliged to make ufe of our
canoes to ferry acrofs the river. which would
have proved very tedious, had it not been for the
kindnefs of the Copper Indians, who fent all their
canoes to our affiftance. Though our number
was not much lefs than one hundred and fifty,
we had only three canoes, and thofe being of the
common fize, could only carry two perfons each,
without baggage. It is true, when water is
fmooth, and a raft of three or four of thofe canoes
is well fecured by poles lafhed acrofs them, they
will carry a much greater weight in proportion,
and be much fafer, as there is fcarcely a poffibility
of their overfetting, and this is the general mode
adopted by the people of this country in croffing
rivers when they have more than one canoe with
them.

Having arrived on the North fide of this river,
we found that Matonabbee, and feveral others in

our

our company, were perfonally acquainted with moft of the Copper Indians whom we found there. The latter feemed highly pleafed at the interview with our party, and endeavoured, by every means in their power, to convince our company of their readinefs to ferve us to the utmoft; fo that by the time we had got our tents pitched, the ftrangers had provided a large quantity of dried meat and fat, by way of a feaft, to which they invited moft of the principal Indians who accompanied me, as well as Matonabbee and myfelf, who were prefented with fome of the very beft.

It it natural to fuppofe, that immediately after our arrival the Copper Indians would be made acquainted with the nature and intention of our journey This was no fooner done than they expreffed their entire approbation, and many of them feemed willing and defirous of giving every affiftance, particularly by lending us feveral canoes, which they affured us would be very ufeful in the remaining part of our journey, and contribute both to our eafe and difpatch. It muft be obferved, that thefe canoes were not entirely entrufted to my crew, but carried by the owners themfelves who accompanied us, as it would have been very uncertain where to have found them at our return from the Copper River.

Agreeably to my inftructions, I fmoked my calumet of peace with the principal of the Copper Indians, who feemed highly pleafed on the occafion; and, from a converfation held on the fubject

ject of my journey, I found they were delighted
with the hopes of having an Europein settlement
in their neighbourhood, and feemed to have no
idea that any impediment could prevent fuch a
fcheme from being carried into execution.  Climates and feafons had no weight with them, nor
could they fee where the difficulty lay in getting
to them; for though they acknowledged that
they had never feen the fea at the mouth of the
Copper River clear of ice, yet they could fee
nothing that fhould hinder a fhip from approaching it; and they innocently enough obferved,
that the water was always fo fmooth between
the ice and fhore that even fmall boats might
get there with great eafe and fafety.  How a fhip
was to get between the ice and the fhore, never
once occurred to them.

Whether it was from real motives of hofpitali-
ty, or from the great advantages which they expected to reap by my difcoveries, I know not;
but I muft confefs that their civility far exceeded
what I could expect from fo uncivilized a tribe,
and I was exceedingly forry that I had nothing of
value to offer them.  However, fuch articles as I
had, I diftributed among them, and they were
thankfully received by them.  Though they have
fome European commodities among them, which
they purchafe from the Northern Indians, the
fame articles from the hands of an Englifhman
were more prized.  As I was the firft whom they
had ever feen, and in all probability might be the
                                          laft,

1771.
June

laſt, it was curious to ſee how they flocked about me, and expreſſed as much deſire to examine me from top to toe, as an European Naturaliſt would a non-deſcript animal. They, however, found and pronounced me to be a perfect human being, except in the colour of my hair and eyes: the former, they ſaid, was like the ſtained hair of a buffaloe's tail, and the latter, being light, were like thoſe of a gull. The whiteneſs of my ſkin alſo was, in their opinion, no ornament, as they ſaid it reſembled meat which had been ſodden in water till all the blood was extracted On the whole, I was viewed as ſo great a curioſity in this part of the world, that during my ſtay there, whenever I combed my head, ſome or other of them never failed to aſk for the hairs that came off, which they carefully wrapped up, ſaying, " When I ſee you again, you ſhall again ſee your " hair.

23d

The day after our arrival at Congecathawha-chaga, Matonabbee diſpatched his brother, and ſeveral Copper Indians, to Copper-mine River, with orders to acquaint any Indians they might meet, with the reaſon of my viſiting thoſe parts, and alſo when they might probably expect us at that river. By the bearers of this meſſage I ſent a preſent of tobacco and ſome other things, to induce any ſtrangers they met to be ready to give us aſſiſtance, either by advice, or in any other way which might be required.

As Matonabbee and the other Indians thought
it

it advifable to leave all the women at this place,
and proceed to the Copper-mine River without
them, it was thought neceffary to continue here
a few days, to kill as many deer as would be fufficient for their fupport during our abfence. And
notwithftanding deer were fo plentiful, yet our
numbers were fo large, and our daily confumption
was fo great, that feveral days elapfed before the
men could provide the women with a fufficient
quantity, and then they had no other way of
preferving it, than by cutting it in thin flices and
drying it in the Sun. Meat, when thus prepared,
is not only very portable, but palatable; as all
the blood and juices are ftill remaining in the
meat, it is very nourifhing and wholefome food;
and may, with care, be kept a whole year without the leaft danger of fpoiling. It is neceffary,
however, to air it frequently during the warm
weather, otherwife it is liable to grow mouldy:
but as foon as the chill air of the fall begins, it
requires no farther trouble till next Summer.

We had not been many days at Congecathawhachaga before I had reafon to be greatly concerned at the behaviour of feveral of my crew to
the Copper Indians. They not only took many
of their young women, furrs, and ready-dreffed
fkins for clothing, but alfo feveral of their bows
and arrows, which were the only implements
they had to procure food and raiment, for the
future fupport of themfelves, their wives, and families. It may probably be thought, that as thefe
weapons are of fo fimple a form, and foe afily con-
structed,

ftructed, they might foon be replaced, without any other trouble or expence than a little labour, but this fuppofition can only hold good in places where proper materials are eafily procured, which was not the cafe here  if it had, they would not have been an object of plunder.  In the midft of a foreft of trees, the wood that would make a Northern Indian a bow and a few arrows, or indeed a bow and arrows ready made, are not of much value, no more than the man's trouble that makes them · but carry that bow and arrows feveral hundred miles from any woods and place where thofe are the only weapons in ufe, their intrinfic value will be found to increafe, in the fame proportion as the materials which are made are lefs attainable\*.

To do Matonabbee juftice on this occafion, I muft fay that he endeavoured as much as poffible to perfuade his countrymen from taking either furrs, clothing, or bows, from the Copper Indians, without making them fome fatisfactory return; but if he did not encourage, neither did he endeavour to hinder them from taking as many women as they pleafed.  Indeed, the Copper Indian women feem to be much efteemed by our Northern traders; for what reafon I know not, as they are in reality the fame people in every refpect; and their language differs not fo much as the dialects of fome of the neareft counties in England do from each other.

It

---

\* See Poftlethwayt on the article of Labour,

It is not furprifing that a plurality of wives is cuftomary among thefe people, as it is fo well adapted to their fituation and manner of life    In my opinion no race of people under the Sun have a greater occafion for fuch an indulgence.   Their annual haunts, in queft of furrs, is fo remote from any European fettlement, as to render them the greateft travellers in the known world,  and as they have neither horfe nor water carriage, every good hunter is under the neceffity of having feveral perfons to affift in carrying his furrs to the Company's Fort, as well as carrying back the European goods which he receives in exchange for them.   No perfons in this country are fo proper for this work as the women, becaufe they are inured to carry and haul heavy loads from their childhood, and to do all manner of drudgery; fo that thofe men who are capable of providing for three, four, five, fix, or more women, generally find them humble and faithful fervants, affectionate wives, and fond and indulgent mothers to their children.   Though cuftom makes this way of life fit apparently eafy on the generality of the women, and though, in general, the whole of their wants feem to be comprized in food and clothing only,  yet nature at times gets the better of cuftom, and the fpirit of jealoufy makes its appearance among them : however, as the hufband is always arbitrator, he foon fettles the bufinefs, though perhaps not always to the entire fatisfaction of the parties.

Much

Much does it redound to the honour of the Northern Indian women when I affirm, that they are the mildeft and moft virtuous females I have feen in any part of North America, though fome think this is more owing to habit, cuftom, and the fear of their hufbands, then from real inclination  It is undoubtedly well known that none can manage a Northern Indian woman fo well as a Northern Indian man, and when any of them have been permitted to remain at the Fort, they have, for the fake of gain, been eafily prevailed on to deviate from that character, and a few have, by degrees, become as abandoned as the Southern Indians, who are remarkable throughout all their tribes for being the moft debauched wretches under the Sun. So far from laying any reftraint on their ferfual appetites, as long as youth and inclination laft, they give themfelves up to all manner of even inceftuous debauchery, and that in fo beaftly a manner when they are intoxicated, a ftate to which they are peculiarly addicted, that the brute creation are not lefs regardlefs of decency. I know that fome few Europeans, who have had little opportunity of feeing them, and of enquiring into their manners, have been very lavifh in their praife  but every one who has had much intercourfe with them, and penetration and induftry enough to ftudy their difpofitions, will agree, that no accomplifhments whatever in a man, is fufficient to conciliate the affections,

or

or preferve the chaftity of a Southern Indian woman*.

The

* Notwithftanding this is the general character of the Southern Indian
women, as they are called on the coafts of Hudfon's Bay, and who are the
fame tribe with the Canadian Indian, I am happy to have it in my power
to infert a few lines to the memory of one of them, whom I knew from
her infancy, and who, I can truly affirm, was directly the reverfe of the
picture I have drawn

MARY, the daughter of MOSES NORTON, many years Chief at Prince
of Wales's Fort, in Hudson's Bay, though born and brought up in a country of all others the leaft favourable to virtue and virtuous principles, poffeffed them, and every other good and amiable quality, in the moft eminent degree

Without the affiftance of religion, and with no education but what fhe
received among the diffolute natives of her country, fhe would have fhone
with fuperior luftre in any other country for, if an engaging perfon, gen-
tle manners, an eafy freedom, arifing from confcioufnefs of innocence, an
amiable modefty, and an unrivalled delicacy of fentiment, are graces and
virtues which render a woman lovely, none ever had greater pretenfions
to general efteem and regard while her benevolence, humanity, and fcrupulous adherence to truth and honefty would have done honour to the
moft enlightened and devout Chriftian

Dutiful, obedient, and affectionate to her parents, fteady and faithful to
her friends, grateful and humble to her benefactors, eafily forgiving and
forgetting an injury, careful not to offend any, and courteous and kind to
all, fhe was, neverthelefs, fuffered to perifh by the rigours of cold and hunger, amidft her own relations, at a time when the griping hand of famine
was by no means feverely felt by any other member of their company,
and it may truly be faid that fhe fell a martyr to the principles of virtue
This happened in the Winter of the year 1782, after the French had deftroyed Prince of Wales's Fort, at which time fhe was in the twenty-fecond year of her age

Human nature fhudders at the bare recital of fuch brutality, and reafon
fhrinks from the tafk of accounting for the decrees of Providence on fuch
occafions as this but they are the ftrongeft affurances of a future ftate, fo
infinitely fuperior to the prefent, that the enjoyment of every pleafure in
this world by the moft worthlefs and abandoned wretch, or the moft innocent and virtuous won an perifhing by the moft excruciating of all deaths,
are matters equally indifferent But,

> Peace to the afhes, and the virtuous mind
> Of her who lived in peace with all mankind,

Learn'd

1771.
The Northern Indian women are in general fo far from being like thofe I have above defcribed, that it is very uncommon to hear of their ever been guilty of incontinency, not even thofe who are confined to the fixth or even eighth part of a man.

It is true, that were I to form my opinion of thofe women from the behaviour of fuch as I have been more particularly acquainted with, I fhould have little reafon to fay much in their favour, but impartiality will not permit me to make a few of the worft characters a ftandard for the general conduct of all of them. Indeed it is but reafonable to think that travellers and interlopers will be always ferved with the moft commodious, though perhaps they pay the beft price for what they have.

It

I earn'd from the heart, unknowing of difguife,
Truth in her thoughts, and candour in her eyes,
Stranger alike to envy and to pride,
Good fenfe her light and Nature all her guide,
But now removed from all the ills of life,
Here refts the pleafing friend and faithful wife          WALLER

Her father was, undoubtedly, very blameable for bringing her up in the tender manner which he did, rendering her by that means not only incapable of bearing the fatigues and hardfhips which the reft of her country-women think little of, but of providing for herfelf. This is, indeed, too frequent a practice among Europeans in that country, who bring up their children in fo indulgent a manner, that when they retire, and leave their offspring behind they find themfelves fo helplefs, as to be unable to provide for the few wants to which they are fubject. The late Mr Ferdinand Jacobs, many years Chief at York Fort, was the only perfon whom I ever knew that acted in a different manner, though no man could poffibly be fonder of his children in other refpects, yet as there were fome that he could not bring to England, he had them brought up entirely among the natives, fo that when he left the country, they fcarcely ever felt the lofs, though they regretted the abfence of a fond and indulgent parent.

It may appear ftrange, that while I am extoll- ing the chaftity of the Northern Indian women, I fhould acknowledge that it is a very common cuftom among the men of this country to ex- change a night's lodging with each other's wives. But this is fo far from being confidered as an act which is criminal, that it is efteemed by them as one of the ftrongeft ties of friendfhip between two families, and in cafe of the death of either man, the other confiders himfelf bound to fupport the children of the deceafed. Thofe people are fo far from viewing this engagement as a mere ceremo- ny, like moft of our Chriftian god-fathers and god-mothers, who, notwithftanding their vows are made in the moft folemn manner, and in the prefence of both God and man, fcarcely ever af- terward remember what they have promifed, that there is not an inftance of a Northern In- dian having once neglected the duty which he is fuppofed to have taken upon himfelf to perform. The Southern Indians, with all their bad qualities, are remarkably humane and charitable to the wi- dows and children of departed friends, and as their fituation and manner of life enable them to do more acts of charity with lefs trouble than falls to the lot of a Northern Indian, few widows or orphans are ever unprovided for among them.

Though the Northern Indian men make no fcru- ple of having two or three fifters for wives at one time, yet they are very particular in obferving a proper diftance in the confanguinity of thofe they

K                                    admit

1771.
June

admit to the above-mentioned intercourfe with their wives  The Southern Indians are lefs fcrupulous on thofe occafions, among them it is not at all uncommon for one brother to make free with another brother's wife or daughter*, but this is held in abhorrence by the Northern Indians.

July
1ft.

By the time the Indians had killed as many deer as they thought would be fufficient for the fupport of the women during our abfence, it was the firft of July, and during this time I had two good obfervations, both by meridional and double altitudes; the mean of which determined the latitude of Congecathawhachaga to be 68° 46' North; and its longitude, by account, was 24° 2' Weft from Prince of Wales's Fort, or 118° 15' Weft of the meridian of London.

2d

On the fecond, the weather proved very bad, with much fnow and fleet; about nine o'clock
at

---

* Moft of the Southern Indians as well the Athapufcow and Neheaway tribes, are ent rely without fcruple in this refpect  It is notoriously known, that many of them cohabit occafionally with their own mothers, and frequently efpoufe their fifters and daughters.  I have known feveral of them who, after having lived in that ftate for fome time with their daughters, have given them to their fons, and all parties been perfectly reconciled to it

In fact, notwithftanding the feverity of the climate, the licentioufnefs of the inhabitants cannot be exceeded by any of the Eaftern nations, whofe luxurious manner of life, and genial clime  feem more adapted to excite extraordinary paffions, than the fevere cold of the frigid Zone

It is true, that few of thofe who live under the immediate protection of the Englifh ever take either their fifters or daughters for wives, which is probably owing to the fear of incurring their difpleafure, but it is well known that acts of inc_t too often take place among them, though perhaps not fo frequently as among the foreign Indians

at night, however, it grew more moderate, and
fomewhat clearer, fo that we fet out, and walked
about ten miles to the North by Weft, when we
lay down to take a little fleep  At our departure from Congecathawhachaga, feveral Indians
who had entered the war lift, rather chofe to ftay
behind with the women, but their lofs was amply fupplied by Copper Indians, who accompanied
us in the double capacity of guides and warriors.

On the third the weather was equally bad with
that of the preceding day; we made fhift, however, to walk ten or eleven miles in the fame direction we had done the day before, and at laft
were obliged to put up, not being able to fee our
way for fnow and thick drift.  By putting up,
no more is to be underftood than that we got to
leeward of a great ftone, or into the crevices of
the rocks, where we regaled ourfelves with fuch
provifions as we had brought with us, fmoked
our pipes, or went to fleep, till the weather permitted us to proceed on our journey.

On the fourth, we had rather better weather,
though conftant light fnow, which made it very
difagreeable under foot.  We neverthelefs walked twenty-feven miles to the North Weft, fourteen of which were on what the Indians call the
Stony Mountains; and furely no part of the
world better deferves that name.  On our firft
approaching thefe mountains, they appeared to
be a confufed heap of ftones, utterly inacceffible
to the foot of man. but having fome Copper In-

dians

dians with us who knew the beſt road, we made a tolerable ſhift to get on, though not without being obliged frequently to crawl on our hands and knees. Notwithſtanding the intricacy of the road, there is a very viſible path the whole way acroſs theſe mountains, even in the moſt difficult parts. and alſo on the ſmooth rocks, and thoſe parts which are capable of receiving an impreſſi-on, the path is as plain and well-beaten, as any bye foot-path in England By the ſide of this path there are, in different parts, ſeveral large, flat, or table ſtones, which are covered with ma-ny thouſands of ſmall pebbles. Theſe the Cop-per Indians ſay have been gradually increaſed by paſſengers going to and from the mines; and on its being obſerved to us that it was the univerſal cuſtom for every one to add a ſtone to the heap, each of us took up a ſmall ſtone in order to in-creaſe the number, for good luck.

Juſt as we arrived at the foot of the Stony Mountains, three of the Indians turned back, ſay-ing, that from every appearance, the remainder of the journey ſeemed likely to be attended with more trouble than would counterbalance the pleaſure they could promiſe themſelves by going to war with the Eſquimaux

On the fifth, as the weather was ſo bad, with conſtant ſnow, fleet, and rain, that we could not ſee our way, we did not offer to move. but the

ſixth proving moderate, and quite fair till toward noon, we ſet out in the morning, and walked about

about eleven miles to the North Weft; when perceiving bad weather at hand, we began to look out for fhelter among the rocks, as we had done the four preceding nights, having neither tents nor tentpoles with us The next morning fifteen more of the Indians deferted us, being quite fick of the road, and the uncommon badnefs of the weather. Indeed, though thefe people are all inured to hardfhips, yet their complaint on the prefent occafion was not without reafon; for, from our leaving Congecathawhachaga we had fcarcely a dry garment of any kind, or any thing to fkreen us from the inclemency of the weather, except rocks and caves; the beft of which were but damp and unwholefome lodging. In fome the water was conftantly dropping from the rock that formed the roof, which made our place of retreat little better than the open air; and we had not been able to make one fpark of fire (except what was fufficient to light a pipe) from the time of our leaving the women on the fecond inftant, it is true, in fome places there was a little mofs, but the conftant fleet and rain made it fo wet, as to render it as impoffible to fet fire to it as it would be to a wet fpunge.

We had no fooner entered our places of retreat than we regaled ourfelves with fome raw venifon which the Indians had killed that morning; the fmall ftock of dried provifions we took with us when we left the women being now all expended.

Agreeably

Agreeably to our expectations, a very sudden and heavy gale of wind came on from the North West, attended with so great a fall of snow, that the oldest Indian in company said, he never saw it exceeded at any time of the year, much less in the middle of Summer. The gale was soon over, and by degrees it became a perfect calm: but the flakes of snow were so large as to surpass all credibility, and fell in such vast quantities, that though the shower only lasted nine hours we were in danger of being smothered in our caves.

On the seventh, we had a fresh breeze at North West, with some flying showers of small rain, and at the same time a constant warm sunshine, which soon dissolved the greatest part of the new-fallen snow. Early in the morning we crawled out of our holes, which were on the North side of the Stony Mountains, and walked about eighteen or twenty miles to the North West by West. In our way we crossed part of a large lake on the ice, which was then far from being broken up. This lake I distinguished by the name of Buffalo, or Musk Ox Lake, from the number of those animals that we found grazing on the margin of it; many of which the Indians killed, but finding them lean, only took some of the bulls' hides for shoe-soals. At night the bad weather returned, with a strong gale of wind at North East, and very cold rain and sleet.

This

This was the firſt time we had ſeen any of the
muſk oxen ſince we left the Factory. It has been
obſerved that we ſaw a great number of them in
my firſt unſucceſsful attempt, before I had got an
hundred miles from the Factory; and indeed I
once perceived the tracks of two of thoſe animals
within nine miles of Prince of Wales's Fort.
Great numbers of them alſo were met with in my
ſecond journey to the North: ſeveral of which
my companions killed, particularly on the ſeven-
teenth of July one thouſand ſeven hundred and
ſeventy. They are alſo found at times in conſiderable numbers near the ſea-coaſt of Hudſon's
Bay, all the way from Knapp's Bay to Wager
Water, but are moſt plentiful within the Arctic
Circle. In thoſe high latitudes I have frequently
ſeen many herds of them in the courſe of a day's
walk, and ſome of thoſe herds did not contain
leſs than eighty or an hundred head. The number of bulls is very few in proportion to the
cows; for it is rare to ſee more than two or three
full-grown bulls with the largeſt herd and from
the number of the males that are found dead, the
Indians are of opinion that they kill each other
in contending for the females. In the rutting
ſeaſon they are ſo jealous of the cows, that they
run at either man or beaſt who offers to approach
them; and have been obſerved to run and bellow
even at ravens, and other large birds, which
chanced to light near them. They delight in the
moſt ſtony and mountainous parts of the barren
ground,

1771.
Jul.

ground, and are feldom found at any great diftance from the woods. Though they are a beaft of great magnitude, and apparently of a very unwieldy inactive ftructure, yet they climb the rocks with great eafe and agility, and are nearly as furefooted as a goat · like it too, they will feed on any thing, though they feem fondeft of grafs, yet in Winter, when that article cannot be had in fufficient quantity, they will eat mofs, or any other herbage they can find, as alfo the tops of willows and the tender branches of the pine tree. They take the bull in Auguft, and bring forth their young the latter end of May, or beginning of June, and they never have more than one at a time.

The mufk-ox, when full grown, is as large as the generality, or at leaft as the middling fize, of Englifh black cattle*, but their legs, though large, are not fo long, nor is their tail longer than that of

* Mr Dragge fays, in his voyage, vol. p. 260, that the mufk ox is lower than a deer, but larger as to bell, and quarters whi h is very far from the truth  hey are of the fize I h ve here defcribed them, and the Indian always eft mate the flefh of a full-grown cow to be equal in quantity to three deer. I am forry alfo to be obliged to contradict my friend Mr Graham, who fays that the flefh of this animal is carried on fledges to Prince Wales's Fort, to the amount of three or four thoufand pounds annually. To the amount of near one thoufand pounds may have been purchafed from the natives in fome particular years, but t more frequently happens that not an ounce is bought one year out of five. In fact, it is by no means efteemed by the company s fervants, and of courfe no great encouragement is given to introduce it, but if it had been otherwife, the general direction is fo remote from the fettlement, that it would not be worth the Indians while to haul it to the Fort. So that in fact, all that has ever been carried to Prince of Wales's Fort, has moft afluredly been killed out of a herd that has been accidentally found within a moderate diftance of the fettlement, perhaps an hundred miles, which is only thought a ftep by an Indian.

of a bear, and, like the tail of that animal, it always bends downward and inward, fo that it is
entirely hid by the long hair of the rump and
hind quarters. the hunch on their fhoulders is
not large, being little more in proportion than
that of a deer: their hair is in fome parts very
long, particularly on the belly, fides, and hind
quarters; but the longeft hair about them, particularly the bulls, is under the throat, extending
from the chin to the lower part of the cheft, between the fore-legs; it there hangs down like a
horfe's mane inverted, and is full as long, which
makes the animal have a moft formidable appearance. It is of the hair from this part that the
Efquimaux make their mufketto wigs, and not
from the tail, as is afferted by Mr. Ellis*; their
tails, and the hair which is on them, being too
fhort for that purpofe. In Winter they are provided with a thick fine wool, or furr, that grows
at the root of the long hair, and fhields them from
the intenfe cold to which they are expofed during
that feafon; but as the Summer advances, this
furr loofens from the fkin, and, by frequently
rolling themfelves on the ground, it works out
to the end of the hair, and in time drops off, leaving little for their Summer clothing except the
long hair. This feafon is fo fhort in thofe high
latitudes, that the new fleece begins to appear,
almoft as foon as the old one drops off; fo that
by the time the cold becomes fevere, they are
again provided with a Winter drefs

The

* Voyage to Hudf's Bay, p 232

The flefh of the mufk-ox noways refembles that of the Weftern buffalo, but is more like that of the moofe or elk, and the fat is of a clear white, flightly tinged with a light azure  The calves and young heifers are good eating, but the flefh of the bulls both fmells and taftes fo ftrong of mufk, as to render it very difagreeable. even the knife that cuts the flefh of an old bull will fmell fo ftrong of mufk, that nothing but fcowring the blade quite bright can remove it, and the handle will retain the fcent for a long time  Though no part of a bull is free from this fmell, yet the parts of generation, in particular the *urethra*, are by far the moft ftrongly impregnated.  The urine itfelf muft  contain this fcent in a very great degree ; for the fheaths of the bull's *penis* are corroded with a brown gummy fubftance, which is nearly as high-fcented with mufk as that faid to be produced by the civet cat ; and after having been kept for feveral years, feems not to lofe any of its quality.

On the eighth, the weather was fine and moderate, though not without fome fhowers of rain. Early in the morning we fet out, and walked eighteen miles to the Northward.  The Indians killed fome deer, fo we put up by the fide of a fmall creek, that afforded a few willows, with which we made a fire for the firft time fince our leaving Congecathawhachaga ; confequently it was here that we cooked our firft meal for a whole week. This, as may naturally be fuppofed, was well relifhed

lifhed by all parties, the Indians as well as myfelf. And as the Sun had, in the courfe of the day, dried our clothing, in fpite of the fmall fhowers of rain, we felt ourfelves more comfortable than we had done fince we left the women. The place where we lay that night, is not far from Griz-zled Bear Hill; which takes its name from the numbers of thofe animals that are frequently known to refort thither for the purpofe of bring-ing forth their young in a cave that is found there. The wonderful defcription which the Copper Indi-ans gave of this place exciting the curiofity of fe-veral of my companions as well as myfelf, we went to view it, but on our arrival at it found little worth remarking about it, being no more than a high lump of earth, of a loamy quality, of which kind there are feveral others in the fame neighbourhood, all ftanding in the middle of a large marfh, which makes them refemble fo many iflands in a lake. The fides of thefe hills are quite perpendicular; and the height of Grizzled Bear Hill, which is the largeft, is about twenty feet above the level ground that furrounds it. Their fummits are covered with a thick fod of mofs and long grafs, which in fome places pro-jects over the edge; and as the fides are conftantly mouldering away, and wafhing down with every fhower of rain during the fhort Summer, they muft in time be levelled with the marfh in which they are fituated. At prefent thofe iflands, as I call them, are excellent places of retreat for the

birds

birds which migrate there to breed; as they can bring forth their young in perfect safety from every beaft except the Quequehatch, which, from the fharpnefs of its claws and the amazing ftrength of its legs, is capable of afcending the moft diffi-cult precipices.

On the fide of the hill that I went to furvey, there is a large cave which penetrates a confidera-ble way into the rock, and may probably have been the work of the bears, as we could difco-ver vifible marks that fome of thofe beafts had been there that Spring. This, though deemed very curious by fome of my companions, did not appear fo to me, as it neither engaged my atten-tion, nor raifed my furprife, half fo much as the fight of the many hills and dry ridges on the Eaft fide of the marfh, which are turned over like ploughed land by thofe animals, in fearching for ground-fquirrels, and perhaps mice, which con-ftitute a favourite part of their food. It is fur-prifing to fee the extent of their refearches in queft of thofe animals, and ftill more to view the enormous ftones rolled out of their beds by the bears on thofe occafions. At firft I thought thefe long and deep furrows had been effected by light-ning; but the natives affured me they never knew any thing of the kind happen in thofe parts, and that it was entirely the work of the bears feeking for their prey.

On the ninth, the weather was moderate and cloudy, with fome flying fhowers of rain. We

fet

set out early in the morning, and walked about forty miles to the North and North by East. In our way we saw plenty of deer and musk-oxen. several of the former the Indians killed, but a smart shower of rain coming on just as we were going to put up, made the moss so wet as to render it impracticable to light a fire. The next day proving fine and clear, we set out in the morning, and walked twenty miles to the North by West and North North West; but about noon the weather became so hot and sultry as to render walking very disagreeable; we therefore put up on the top of a high hill, and as the moss was then dry, lighted a fire, and should have made a comfortable meal, and been otherwise tolerably happy, had it not been for the muskettoes, which were uncommonly numerous, and their stings almost insufferable. The same day Matonabbee sent several Indians a-head, with orders to proceed to the Copper-mine River as fast as possible, and acquaint any Indians they might meet, of our approach. By those Indians I also sent some small presents, as the surest means to induce any strangers they found, to come to our assistance.

The eleventh was hot and sultry, like the preceding day. In the morning we walked ten or eleven miles to the North West, and then met a Northern Indian Leader, called Oule eye, and his family, who were, in company with several Copper Indians, killing deer with bows and arrows and spears, as they crossed a little river, by the side

1771.
July

10th

11th

1771.   fide of which we put up, as did alfo the above-
        mentioned Indians*.   That afternoon I fmoked
Ja'y    my calumet of peace with thefe ftrangers, and
        found them a quite different fet of people, at leaft
        in principle, from thofe I had feen at Congeca-
        thawhachaga · for though they had great plenty
        of provifions, they neither offered me nor my
        companions a mouthful, and would, if they had
        been permitted, have taken the laft garment from
        off my back, and robbed me of every article I
        poffeffed.   Even my Northern companions could
        not help taking notice of fuch unaccountable be-
        haviour.   Nothing but their poverty protected
        them from being plundered by thofe of my crew;
        and had any of their women been worth no-
        tice, they would moft affuredly have been preff-
        ed into our fervice.

12th        The twelfth was fo exceedingly hot and fultry,
13th    that we did not move; but early in the morning
        of the thirteenth, after my companions had taken
        what dry provifions they chofe from our unfoci-
        able ftrangers, we fet out, and walked about fif-
        teen or fixteen miles to the North and North by
        Eaft, in expectation of arriving at the Copper-
        mine River that day; but when we had reached
        the top of a long chain of hills, between which
        we were told the river ran, we found it to be no
        more than a branch of it which empties itfelf in-
        to the main river about forty miles from its in-
                                                    flux

---

* This river runs nearly North Eaft, and in all probability empties itfelf into the Northern Ocean, not far from the Copper River

flux into the fea. At that time all the Copper Indians were difpatched different ways, fo that there was not one in company, who knew the fhorteft cut to the main river. Seeing fome woods to the Weftward, and judging that the current of the rivulet ran that way, we concluded that the main river lay in that direction, and was not very remote from our prefent fituation. We therefore directed our courfe by the fide of it, when the Indians met with feveral very fine buck deer, which they deftroyed; and as that part we now traverfed afforded plenty of good fire-wood, we put up, and cooked the moft comfortable meal to which we had fat down for fome months. As fuch favourable opportunities of indulging the appetite happen but feldom, it is a general rule with the Indians which we did not neglect, to exert every art in dreffing our food which the moft refined fkill in Indian cookery has been able to invent, and which confifts chiefly in boiling, broiling, and roafting : but of all the difhes cooked by thofe people, a *beeatee*, as it is called in their language, is certainly the moft delicious, at leaft for a chance, that can be prepared from a deer only, without any other ingredient. It is a kind of haggis, made with the blood, a good quantity of fat fhred fmall, fome of the tendereft of the flefh, together with the heart and lungs cut, or more commonly torn into fmall fhivers, all which is put into the ftomach, and roafted, by being fufpended before the fire by a ftring. Care muft be

taken

taken that it does not get too much heat at firft, as the bag would thereby be liable to be burnt, and the contents be let out. When it is fufficiently done, it will emit fteam, in the fame manner as a fowl or a joint of meat; which is as much as to fay, Come, eat me now: and if it be taken in time, before the blood and other contents are too much done, it is certainly a moft delicious morfel, even without pepper, falt, or any other feafoning.

After regaling ourfelves in the moft plentiful manner, and taking a few hours reft, (for it was almoft impoffible to fleep for the mufkettoes,) we once more fet forward, directing our courfe to the North Weft by Weft; and after walking about nine or ten miles, arrived at that long wifh-ed-for fpot, the Copper-mine River.

CHAP.

## C H A P. VI

Tranſactions at the Copper-mine River, and till we
joined all the women to the South of Cogead
Lake.

*Some Copper Indians join us —Indians ſend three ſpies
down the river.—Begin my ſurvey.—Spies return,
and give an account of five tents of Eſquimaux.—Indians conſult the beſt method to ſteal on them in the
night, and kill them while aſleep.—Croſs the river.
—Proceedings of the Indians as they advance towards the Eſquimaux tents.—The Indians begin the
maſſacre while the poor Eſquimaux are aſleep, and
ſlay them all.—Much affected at the ſight of one
young woman killed cloſe to my feet.—The behaviour
of the Indians on this occaſion.—Their brutiſh treatment of the dead bodies.—Seven more tents ſeen on
the oppoſite ſide of the river.—The Indians haraſs
them, till they fly to a ſhoal in the river for ſafety.
—Behaviour of the Indians after killing thoſe Eſquimaux.—Croſs the river, and proceed to the tents
on that ſide —Plunder their tents, and deſtroy their
utenſils.—Continue my ſurvey to the river's mouth.
—Remarks there —Set out on my return.—Arrive
at one of the Copper mines —Remarks on it —Many
attempts made to induce the Copper Indians to carry
their own goods to market —Obſtacles to it.—Villany and cruelty of Keelſhies to ſome of thoſe poor Indians.—Leave the Copper-mine, and walk at an*

L                                      *amazing*

*amazing rate till we join the women, by the side of*
*CogeadWhoie ‥ Much foot-foundered.——The appear-*
*ance very alarming, but soon changes for the better.*
*—Proceed to the southward, and join the remainder*
*of the women and children.——Many other Indians*
*arrive with them.*

1771.

July
14th.

WE had scarcely arrived at the Copper-mine River when four Copper Indians joined us, and brought with them two canoes. They had seen all the Indians who were sent from us at various times, except Matonabbee's brother and three others that were first dispatched from Congecathawhachaga.

On my arrival here I was not a little surprised to find the river differ so much from the description which the Indians had given of it at the Factory; for, instead of being so large as to be navigable for shipping, as it had been represented by them, it was at that part scarcely navigable for an Indian canoe, being no more than one hundred and eighty yards wide, every where full of shoals, and no less than three falls were in sight at first view.

Near the water's edge there is some wood, but not one tree grows on or near the top of the hills between which the river runs. There appears to have been formerly a much greater quantity than there is at present; but the trees seem to have been set on fire some years ago, and, in consequence, there is at present ten sticks lying on the ground, for one green one which is growing befide

fide them. The whole timber appears to have been, even in its greateſt proſperity, of ſo crook-ed and dwarfiſh a growth as to render it of little uſe for any purpoſe but fire-wood

Soon after our arrival at the river-fide, three Indians were ſent off as ſpies, in order to ſee if any Eſquimaux were inhabiting the river-fide between us and the fea. After walking about three quar-ters of a mile by the fide of the river, we put up, when moſt of the Indians went a hunting, and killed ſeveral muſk-oxen and ſome deer. They were employed all the remainder of the day and night in ſplitting and drying the meat by the fire. As we were not then in want of proviſions, and as deer and other animals were ſo plentiful, that each day's journey might have provided for it-ſelf, I was at a loſs to account for this unuſal œco-nomy of my companions; but was ſoon inform-ed, that thoſe preparations were made with a view to have victuals enough ready-cooked to ſerve us to the river's mouth, without being obliged to kill any in our way, as the report of the guns, and the ſmoke of the fires, would be liable to alarm the natives, if any ſhould be near at hand, and give them an opportunity of eſcaping.

Early in the morning of the fifteenth, we ſet out, when I immediately began my ſurvey, which I continued about ten miles down the river, till heavy rain coming on we were obliged to put up; and the place where we lay that night was the end, or edge of the woods, the whole ſpace be-

tween

1771.
Jun

tween it and the fea being entirely barren hills and wide open marfhes. In the courfe of this day's furvey, I found the river as full of fhoals as the part which I had feen before; and in many places it was fo greatly diminifhed in its width, that in our way we paffed by two more capital falls.

16 h

Early in the morning of the fixteenth, the weather being fine and pleafant, I again proceeded with my furvey, and continued it for ten miles farther down the river, but ftill found it the fame as before, being every where full of falls and fhoals. At this time (it being about noon) the three men who had been fent as fpies met us on their return, and informed my companions that five tents of Efquimaux were on the weft fide of the river. The fituation, they faid, was very convenient for furprizing them; and, according to their account, I judged it to be about twelve miles from the place we met the fpies. When the Indians received this intelligence, no farther attendance or attention was paid to my furvey, but their whole thoughts were immediately engaged in planning the beft method of attack, and how they might fteal on the poor Efquimaux the enfuing night, and kill them all while afleep. To accomplifh this bloody defign more effectually, the Indians thought it neceffary to crofs the river as foon as poffible; and, by the account of the fpies, it appeared that no part was more convenient for the purpofe than that where we had met them, it being there very fmooth,

and

and at a confiderable diftance from any fall.  Accordingly, after the Indians had put all their guns,
fpears, targets, &c. in good order, we croffed the
river, which took up fome time.

When we arrived on the Weft fide of the river,
each painted the front of his target or fhield ;
fome with the figure of the Sun, others with that
of the Moon, feveral with different kinds of birds
and beafts of prey, and many with the images of
imaginary beings, which, according to their filly
notions, are the inhabitants of the different elements, Farth, Sea, Air, &c.

On enquiring the reafon of their doing fo, I
learned that each man painted his fhield with the
image of that being on which he relied moft for
fuccefs in the intended engagement.   Some were
contented with a fingle reprefentation, while
others, doubtful, as I fuppofe, of the quality and
power of any fingle being, had their fhields covered to the very margin with a group of hieroglyphics quite unintelligible to every one except the
painter.   Indeed, from the hurry in which this
bufinefs was neceffarily done, the want of every
colour but red and black, and the deficiency of
fkill in the artift. moft of thofe paintings had more
the appearance of a number of accidental blotches, than " of any thing that is on the earth, or in
" the water under the earth ;" and though fome
few of them conveyed a tolerable idea of the
thing intended, yet even thefe were many degrees
worfe than our country fignpaintings in England.

When

When this piece of fuperftition was completed, we began to advance towards the Efquimaux tents; but were very careful to avoid croffing any hills, or talking loud, for fear of being feen or overheard by the inhabitants; by which means the diſtance was not only much greater than it otherwife would have been, but, for the fake of keeping in the loweft grounds, we were obliged to walk through entire fwamps of ftiff marly clay, fometimes up to the knees. Our courfe, however, on this occafion, though very ferpentine, was not altogether fo remote from the river as entirely to exclude me from a view of it the whole way: on the contrary, feveral times (according to the fituation of the ground) we advanced fo near it, as to give me an opportunity of convincing myfelf that it was as unnavigable as it was in thofe parts which I had furveyed before, and which entirely correfponded with the accounts given of it by the fpies.

It is perhaps worth remarking, that my crew, though an undifciplined rabble, and by no means accuftomed to war or command, feemingly acted on this horrid occafion with the utmoft uniformity of fentiment. There was not among them the leaſt altercation or feparate opinion; all were united in the general caufe, and as ready to follow where Matonabbee led, as he appeared to be ready to lead, according to the advice of an old Copper Indian, who had joined us on our firft arrival at the river where this bloody bufinefs was firft propofed

Never

Never was reciprocity of intereſt more generally regarded among a number of people, than it
was on the preſent occaſion by my crew, for not
one was a moment in want of any thing that
another could ſpare; and if ever the ſpirit of
diſintereſted friendſhip expanded the heart of a
Northern Indian, it was here exhibited in the
moſt extenſive meaning of the word. Property
of every kind that could be of general uſe now
ceaſed to be private, and every one who had any
thing which came under that deſcription, ſeemed
proud of an opportunity of giving it, or lending
it to thoſe who had none, or were moſt in want
of it.

The number of my crew was ſo much greater
than that which five tents could contain, and the
warlike manner in which they were equipped ſo
greatly ſuperior to what could be expected of the
poor Eſquimaux, that no leſs than a total maſſacre of every one of them was likely to be the caſe,
unleſs Providence ſhould work a miracle for their
deliverance.

The land was ſo ſituated that we walked under
cover of the rocks and hills till we were within
two hundred yards of the tents. There we lay
in ambuſh for ſome time, watching the motions
of the Eſquimaux; and here the Indians would
have adviſed me to ſtay till the fight was over,
but to this I could by no means conſent; for I
conſidered that when the Eſquimaux came to be
ſurpriſed, they would try every way to eſcape,
and

and if they found me alone, not knowing me from an enemy, they would probably proceed to violence againſt me when no perſon was near to aſſiſt. For this reaſon I determined to accompany them, telling them at the ſame time, that I would not have any hand in the murder they were about to commit, unleſs I found it neceſſary for my own ſafety. The Indians were not diſpleaſed at this propoſal; one of them immediately fixed me a ſpear, and another lent me a broad bayonet for my protection, but at that time I could not be provided with a target; nor did I want to be encumbered with ſuch an unneceſſary piece of lumber

While we lay in ambuſh, the Indians performed the laſt ceremonies which were thought neceſſary before the engagement. Theſe chiefly conſiſted in painting their faces; ſome all black, ſome all red, and others with a mixture of the two; and to prevent their hair from blowing into their eyes, it was either tied before and behind, and on both ſides, orelſe cut ſhort all round. The next thing they conſidered was to make themſelves as light as poſſible for running; which they did, by pulling off their ſtockings, and either cutting off the ſleeves of their jackets, or rolling them up cloſe to their arm-pits; and though the muſkettoes at that time were ſo numerous as to ſurpaſs all credibility, yet ſome of the Indians actually pulled off their jackets and entered.

entered the lifts quite naked, except their breech-
cloths and fhoes.   Fearing I might have occafion
to run with the reft, I thought it alfo advifeable to
pull off my ftockings and cap, and to tie my hair
as clofe up as poffible.

By the time the Indians had made themfelves
thus completely frightful, it was near one o'clock
in the morning of the feventeenth; when finding all the Efquimaux quiet in their tents, they
rufhed forth from their ambufcade, and fell on
the poor unfufpecting creatures, unperceived till
clofe to the very eves of the tents, when they
foon began the bloody maffacre, while I ftood
neuter in the rear.

In a few feconds the horrible fcene commenced;
it was fhocking beyond defcription; the poor unhappy victims were furprifed in the midft of their
fleep, and had neither time nor power to make
any refiftance, men, women, and children, in all
upwards of twenty, ran out of their tents ftark
naked, and endeavoured to make their efcape;
but the Indians having poffeffion of all the land-
fide, to no place could they fly for fhelter.   One
alternative only remained, that of jumping into
the river, but, as none of them attempted it,
they all fell a facrifice to Indian barbarity!

The fhrieks and groans of the poor expiring
wretches were truly dreadful; and my horror
was much increafed at feeing a young girl, feemingly about eighteen years of age, killed fo near
me, that when the firft fpear was ftuck into her

fide

fide she fell down at my feet, and twisted round my legs, so that it was with difficulty that I could disengage myself from her dying grasps    As two Indian men pursued this unfortunate victim, I solicited very hard for her life, but the murderers made no reply till they had stuck both their spears through her body, and transfixed her to the ground. They then looked me sternly in the face, and began to ridicule me, by asking if I wanted an Esquimaux wife, and paid not the smallest regard to the shrieks and agony of the poor wretch, who was twining round their spears like an eel! Indeed, after receiving much abusive language from them on the occasion, I was at length obliged to desire that they would be more expeditious in dispatching their victim out of her misery, otherwise I should be obliged, out of pity, to assist in the friendly office of putting an end to the existence of a fellow-creature who was so cruelly wounded.    On this request being made, one of the Indians hastily drew his spear from the place where it was first lodged, and pierced it through her breast near the heart.   The love of life, however, even in this most miserable state, was so predominant, that though this might justly be called the most merciful act that could be done for the poor creature, it seemed to be unwelcome, for though much exhausted by pain and loss of blood, she made several efforts to ward off the friendly blow.   My situation and the terror of my mind at beholding this butchery, cannot

easily

eafily be conceived, much lefs defcribed ; though I fummed up all the fortitude I was mafter of on the occafion, it was with difficulty that I could refrain from tears ; and I am confident that my features muft have feelingly exprefled how fincerely I was affected at the barbarous fcene I then witneffed ; even at this hour I cannot reflect on the tranfactions of that horrid day without fhedding tears.

The brutifh manner in which thefe favages ufed the bodies they had fo cruelly bereaved of life was fo fhocking, that it would be indecent to defcribe it ; particularly their curiofity in examining, and the remarks they made, on the formation of the women ; which, they pretended to fay, differed materially from that of their own. For my own part I muft acknowledge, that however favourable the oppoitunity for determining that point might have been, yet my thoughts at the time were too much agitated to admit of any fuch remarks, and I firmly believe, that had there actually been as much difference between them as there is faid to be between the Hottentots and thofe of Europe, it would not have been in my power to have marked the diftinction. I have reafon to think, however, that there is no ground for the affertion ; and really believe that the declaration of the Indians on this occafion, was utterly void of truth, and proceeded only from the implacable hatred they bore to the whole tribe of people of whom I am fpeaking.

When

When the Indians had Completed the murder
of the poor Efquimaux, feven other tents on the
Eaft fide the river immediately engaged their attention : very luckily, however, our canoes and
baggage had been left at a little diftance up the
river, fo that they had no way of croffing to get
at them. The river at this part being little more
than eighty yards wide, they began firing at them
from the Weft fide. The poor Efquimaux on the
oppofite fhore, though all up in arms, did not attempt to abandon their tents; and they were fo
unacquainted with the nature of fire-arms, that
when the bullets ftruck the ground, they ran in
crowds to fee what was fent them, and feemed
anxious to examine all the pieces of lead which
they found flattened againft the rocks. At length
one of the Efquimaux men was fhot in the calf of
his leg, which put them in great confufion. They
all immediately embarked in their little canoes,
and paddled to a fhoal in the middle of the river,
which being fomewhat more than a gun-fhot
from any part of the fhore, put them out of the
reach of our barbarians.

When the favages difcovered that the furviving Efquimaux had gained the fhore above mentioned, the Northern Indians began to plunder
the tents of the deceafed of all the copper utenfils they could find, fuch as hatchets, bayonets,
knives, &c. after which they affembled on the top
of an adjacent high hill, and ftanding all in a
clufter, fo as to form a folid circle, with their

fpears

spears erect in the air, gave many shouts of victory, constantly clashing their spears against each other, and frequently calling out *tima! tima*! by way of derision to the poor surviving Esquimaux, who were standing on the shoal almost knee-deep in water. After parading the hill for some time, it was agreed to return up the river to the place where we had left our canoes and baggage, which was about half a mile distant, and then to cross the river again and plunder the seven tents on the East side. This resolution was immediately put in force; and as ferrying across with only three or four canoes ‡ took a considerable time, and as we were, from the crookedness of the river and the form of the land, entirely under cover, several of the poor surviving Esquimaux, thinking probably that we were gone about our business, and meant to trouble them no more, had returned from the shoal to their habitations. When we approached their tents, which we did under cover of the rocks, we found them busily employed tying up bundles. These the Indians seized with their usual ferocity; on which, the Esquimaux having their canoes lying ready in the water, immediately embarked, and all of them got safe to the former shoal, except an old man, who was so intent on collecting his things, that

* *Tima* in the Esquimaux language is a friendly word similar to *what cheer?*

‡ When the fifteen Indians turned back to the Stony Mountains they took two or three canoes with them, some of our crew that were sent ahead as messengers had not yet returned, which occasioned the number of our canoes to be so small.

that the Indians coming upon him before he could reach his canoe, he fell a sacrifice to their fury: I verily believe not lefs than twenty had a hand in his death, as his whole body was like a cullender. It is here neceffary to obferve that the fpies when on the look-out, could not fee thefe feven tents, though clofe under them, as the bank, on which they ftood, ftretched over them.

It ought to have been mentioned in its proper place, that in making our retreat up the river, after killing the Efquimaux on the Weft fide, we faw an old woman fitting by the fide of the water, killing falmon, which lay at the foot of the fall as thick as a fhoal of herrings Whether from the noife of the fall, or a natural defect in the old woman's hearing, it is hard to determine, but certain it is, fhe had no knowledge of the tragical fcene which had been fo lately tranfacted at the tents, though fhe was not more than two hundred yards from the place. When we firft perceived her, fhe feemed perfectly at eafe, and was entirely furrounded with the produce of her labour. From her manner of behaviour, and the appearance of her eyes, which were as red as blood, it is more than probable that her fight was not very good; for fhe fcarcely difcerned that the Indians were enemies, till they were within twice the length of their fpears of her. It was in vain that fhe attempted to fly, for the wretches of my crew transfixed her to the ground in a few feconds, and butchered her in the moft favage manner.

manner There was fcarcely a man among them
who had not a thruft at her with his fpear, and
many in doing this, aimed at torture, rather
than immediate death, as they not only poked out
her eyes, but ftabbed her in many parts very remote from thofe which are vital.

It may appear ftrange, that a perfon fuppofed to
be almoft blind fhould be employed in the bufinefs of fifhing, and particularly with any degree
of fuccefs; but when the multitude of fifh is taken
into the account, the wonder will ceafe. Indeed
they were fo numerous at the foot of the fall,
that when a light pole, armed with a few fpikes,
which was the inftrument the old woman ufed,
was put under water, and hauled up with a jerk,
it was fcarcely poffible to mifs them. Some of
my Indians tried the method, for curiofity, with
the old woman's ftaff, and feldom got lefs than
two at a jerk, fometimes three or four. Thofe
fifh, though very fine, and beautifully red, are but
fmall, feldom weighing more (as near as I could
judge) than fix or feven pounds, and in general
much lefs Their numbers at this place were almoft incredible, perhaps equal to any thing that
is related of the falmon in Kamfchatka, or any
other part of the world. It does not appear that
the Efquimaux have any other method of catching the fifh, unlefs it be by fpears and darts; for
no appearance of nets were difcovered either at
their tents, or on any part of the fhore. This is
the cafe with all the Efquimaux on the Weft fide

of

1771.   of Hudfon's Bay; fpearing in Summer, and ang-
Juſy    ling in Winter, are the only methods they have
        yet devifed to catch fiſh, though at times their
        whole dependance for fupport is on that article*.
                                                    When

---

* When the Efquimaux wro refide near Churchill River travel in Winter, it is always from lake to lake, or from river to river, where they have
formed magazines of provifions, and heaps of mofs for firing   As fome
of thofe places are at a confiderable diſtance from each other, and fome of
the lakes of confiderable width, they frequently pitch their tents on the
ice, and inſtead of having a fire, which the feverity of the climate fo much
requires, they cut holes in the ice within their tents, and there ſt and
angle for fiſh, if they meet with any fuccefs, the fiſh are eaten alive out of
the water, and when they are thirſty, water, their ufual beverage, is at
hand
    When I firſt entered into the employment of the Hudfon's Bay Compa-
ny, it was as Mate of one of their ſloops which was employed in trading
with the Efquimaux, I had therefore frequent opportunities of obferving
the miferable manner in which thofe people live   In the courfe of our
trade with them we frequently purchafed feveral feal-ſkin bags, which we
fuppofed were full of oil, but on opening them have fometimes found
great quantities of venifon, feals, and fea-horfe paws, as well as falmon,
and as thefe were of no ufe to us, we always returned them to the Indians,
who eagerly devoured them, though fome of the articles had been perhaps
a whole year in that ſtate, and they feemed to exult greatly in having fo
over-reached us in the way of trade, as to have fometimes one third of
their bargain returned                                    .
    This method of preferving their food, though it effectually guards it from
the external air, and from the flies, does not prevent putrefaction entirely, though it renders its progrefs very flow   Pure train oil is of fuch a
quality that it never freezes folid in the coldeſt Winters, a happy circum-
ſtance for thofe people, who are condemned to live in the moſt rigorou-
ci mate without the affiſtance of fire   While thefe magazines laſt, they
have nothing more to do when hunger affails them, but to open one of the
bags, take out a fide of venifon, a few feals, fea-horfe paws, or fome half
rotten falmon, and without any preparation, ſt down and make a meal
and the lake or river by which they pitch their tent, affords them water
which is their conſtant drink   Befides the extraordinary food already men
tioned, they have feveral other diſhes equally difguſting to an Europear
palate, I will only mention one, as it was more frequently part of their
repaſt when I vifited their tents, than any other, except fiſh   The diſh I
                                                              allude

When the Indians had plundered the feven
tents of all the copper utenfils, which feemed the
only things worth their notice, they threw all the
tents and tent-poles into the river, deftroyed a
vaft quantity of dried falmon, mufk-oxen flefh,
and other provifions; broke all the ftone kettles;

M                             and

allude to, is made of the raw liver of a deer, cut in fmall pieces of about an
inch fquare, and mixed up with the contents of the ftomach of the fame
animal, and the farther digeftion has taken place, the better it is fuited to
their tafte    It is impoffible to defcribe or conceive the pleafure they feem
to enjoy when eating fuch unaccountable food    nay, 1 have even feen
them eat whofe handfuls of maggots that were produced in meat by fly-
blows, and it is their conftant cuftom, when their nofes bleed by any accident, to lick their blood into their mouths, and fwallow it    Indeed, if we
confider the inhofpitable part of the globe they are deftined to inhabit,
and the great diftreffes to which they are frequently driven by hunger in
confequence of it, we fhall no longer be furprized at finding they can relifh
any thing in common with the meaneft of the animal creation, but rather
admire the wifdom and kindnefs of Providence in forming the palates and
powers of all creatures in fuch a manner as is beft adapted to the food, climate, and every other circumftance which may be incident to their refpective fituations

It is no lefs true, that thefe people, when I firft knew them, would not
eat any of our provifions, fugar, raifins, figs, or even bread, for though
fome of them would put a bit of it into their mouths, they foon fpit it out
again with evident marks of diflike, fo that they had no greater relifh for
our food than we had for theirs    At prefent, however, they will eat any
part of our provifions, either frefh or falted, and fome of them will drink
a draft of porter, or a little brandy and water, and they are now fo far
civilized, and attached to the Fnglifh, that 1 am perfuaded any of the
company's fervants who could habituate themfelves to their diet and manner of life, might now live as fecure under their protection, as under that
of any of the tribes of Indians who border on Hudfon s Bay

They live in a ftate of perfect freedom, no one apparently claiming the
fuperiority over, or acknowledging the leaft fubordination to another, except what is due from children to their parents, or fuch of their kin as take
care of them when they are young and incapable of providing for then-
felves    There is, however, reafon to think that, when grown up to man-
hood, they pay fome attention to the advice of the old men, on account of
their experience

and, in fact, did all the mifchief they poffibly
could to diftrefs the poor creatures they could not
murder, and who were ftanding on the fhoal before mentioned, obliged to be woeful fpectators of
their great, or perhaps irreparable lofs

After the Indians had completed this piece of
wantonnefs we fat down, and made a good meal
of frefh falmon which were as numerous at the
place where we now refted, as they were on the
Weft fide of the river. When we had finifhed
our meal, which was the firft we had enjoyed for
many hours, the Indians told me that they were
again ready to affift me in making an end of my
furvey. It was then about five o'clock in the
morning of the feventeenth, the fea being in fight
from the North Weft by Weft to the North Eaft,
about eight miles diftant. I therefore fet inftant-
ly about commencing my furvey, and purfued it
to the mouth of the river, which I found all the
way fo full of fhoals and falls that it was not navigable even for a boat, and that it emptied itfelf
into the fea over a ridge or bar. The tide was
then out, but I judged from the marks which I
faw on the edge of the ice, that it flowed about
twelve or fourteen feet, which will only reach a
little way within the river's mouth. The tide
being out, the water in the river was perfectly
frefh, bu I am certain of its being the fea, or
fome branch of it, by the quantity of whalebone
and feal-fkins which the Efquimaux had at their
tents, and alfo by the number of feals which I
faw

fiw on the ice   At the mouth of the river, the
fea is full of iflands and fhoals, as far as I could
fee with the affiftance of a good pocket telefcope.
The ice was not then broke up, but was melted
away for about three quarters of a mile from the
main fhore, and to a little diftance round the
iflands and fhoals.

By the time I had completed this furvey, it was
about one in the morning of the eighteenth; but
in thofe high latitudes, and at this feafon of the
year, the Sun is always at a good height above
the horizon, fo that we had not only day light,
but fun fhine the whole night: a thick fog and
drizzling rain then came on, and finding that
neither the river nor fea were likely to be of any
ufe, I did not think it worth while to wait for fair
weather to determine the latitude exactly by an
obfervation; but by the extraordinary care I
took in obferving the courfes and diftances when
I walked from Congecathawhachaga where I had
two good obfervations, the latitude may be depended upon within twenty miles at the utmoft.
For the fake of form however, after having had
fome confultation with the Indians, I erected a
mark, and took poffeffion of the coaft, on behalf
of the Hudfon's Bay Company

Having finifhed this bufinefs, we fet out on our
return, and walked about twelve miles to the
South by Eaft, when we ftopped and took a little
fleep, which was the firft time that any of us had
clofed our eyes from the fifteenth inftant, and it

was

was now fix o'clock in the morning of the eigh-teenth. Here the Indians killed a mufk ox, but the mofs being very wet, we could not make a fire, fo that we were obliged to eat the meat raw, which was intolerable, as it happened to be an old beaft.

Before I proceed farther on my return, it may not be improper to give fome account of the river, and the country adjacent; its productions, and the animals which conftantly inhabit thofe drea-ry regions, as well as thofe that only migrate thi-ther in Summer, in order to breed and rear their young, unmolefted by man. That I may do this to better purpofe, it will be neceffary to go back to the place where I firft came to the river, which was about forty miles from its mouth.

Befide the ftunted pines already mentioned, there are fome tufts of dwarf willows; plenty of Wifhacumpuckey, (as the Englifh call it, and which they ufe as tea); fome jackafheypuck, which the natives ufe as tobacco; and a few cran-berry and heathberry bufhes; but not the leaft appearance of any fruit

The woods grow gradually thinner and fmaller as you approach the fea; and the laft little tuft of pines that I faw is about thirty miles from the mouth of the river, fo that we meet with no-thing between that fpot and the fea-fide but bar-ren hills and marfhes.

The general courfe of the river is about North by Eaft; but in fome places it is very crooked,

and

Here I fell in with the River

feet

A Fall of 7 feet

Bends

A Fall of 10 feet

Pond

End of

0    1    2    3    4    5    6    7    8

A Scale of English 2 2 Miles not to a Degree

A Plan
of the
COPPER MINE RIVER
Surveyed by
SAMUEL HEARNE
July. 1771

Here we crossed the River
to the Esquimaux

A fine level Country
River steep from West

the Banks of the
to feet high

fine Man

Longitude 112° 30' West of Greenwich

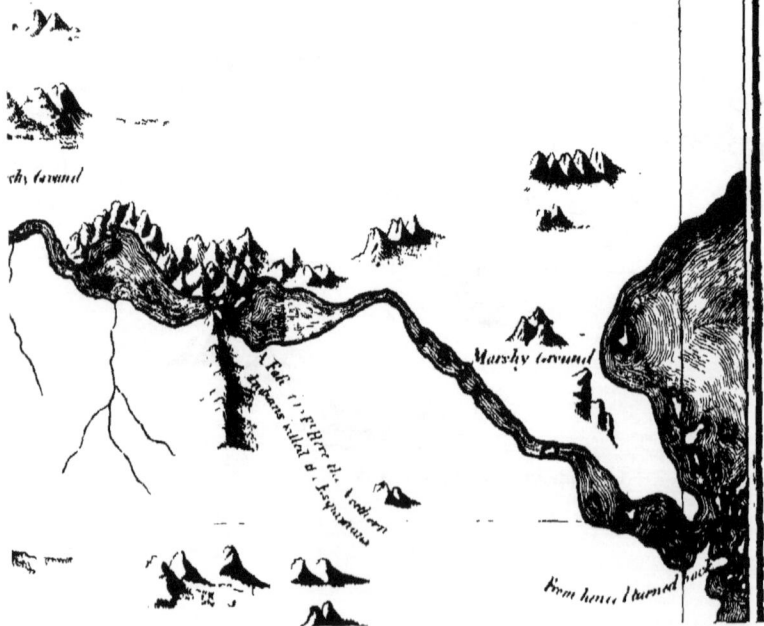

Marshy Ground

Marshy Ground

From hence I turned back

and its breadth varies from twenty yards to four
or five hundred.  The banks are in general a folid
rock, both fides of which correfpond fo exactly
with each other, as to leave no doubt that the
channel of the river has been caufed by fome ter-
rible convulfion of nature; and the ftream is fupplied by a variety of little rivulets, that rufh down
the fides of the hills, occafioned chiefly by the
melting of the fnow.  Some of the Indians fay,
that this river takes its rife from the North Weft
fide of Large White Stone Lake, which is at the
diftance of near three hundred miles on a ftraight
line; but I can fcarcely think that is the cafe,
unlefs there be many intervening lakes, which
are fupplied by the vaft quantity of water that is
collected in fo great an extent of hilly and mountainous country : for were it otherwife, I fhould
imagine that the multitude of fmall rivers, which
muft empty themfelves into the main ftream in
the courfe of fo great a diftance, would have formed a much deeper and ftronger current than I difcovered, and occafioned an annual deluge at the
breaking up of the ice in the Spring, of which
there was not the leaft appearance, except at Bloody Fall, where the river was contracted to the
breadth of about twenty yards.  It was at the
foot of this fall that my Indians killed the Efquimaux ; which was the reafon why I diftinguifhed
it by that appellation.  From this fall, which is
about eight miles from the fea-fide, there are very
few hills, and thofe not high.  The land between

them

1771.<br>July

them is a stiff loam and clay, which, in some parts, produces patches of pretty good grafs, and in others tallish dwarf willows · at the foot of the hills alfo there is plenty of fine scurvy grafs.

The Esquimaux at this river are but low in stature, none exceeding the middle size, and though broad set, are neither well-made nor strong bodied Their complexion is of a dirty copper colour ; some of the women, however, are more fair and ruddy. Their dress much refembles that of the Greenlanders in Davis's Straits, except the women's boots, which are not stiffened out with whalebone, and the tails of their jackets are not more than a foot long

Their arms and fishing-tackle are bows and arrows, spears, lances, darts, &c. which exactly refemble thofe made ufe of by the Efquimaux in Hudfon's Straits, and wnich have been well defcribed by Crantz*, but, for want of good edge-tools, are far inferior to them in workmanship. Their arrows are either shod with a trianglar piece of black stone, like slate, or a piece of copper ; but most commonly the former.

The body of their canoes is on the fame construction as that of the other Esquimaux, and there is no unneceffary prow-projection beyond the body of the veffel, thefe, like their arms and other utenfils, are, for the want of better tools, by no means fo neat as thofe I have feen in Hudfon's Bay and Straits. The double-bladed paddle

dle

---

* See hift of Greenland, vol . p 132—136

dle is in univerfal ufe among all the tribes of this people.

Their tents are made of parchment deer-fkins in the hair, and are pitched in a circular form, the fame as thofe of the Efquimaux in Hudfon's Bay  Thefe tents are undoubtedly no more than their Summer habitations, for I faw the remains of two miferable hovels, which, from the fituation, the ftructure, and the vaft quantity of bones, old fhoes, fcraps of fkins, and other rubbifh lying near them,  had certainly been fome of their Winter retreats.  Thefe houfes were fituated on the South fide of a hill, one half of them were under-ground, and the upper parts clofely fet round with poles, meeting at the top in a conical form, like their fummer-houfes or tents  Thefe tents when inhabited, had undoubtedly been covered with fkins, and in Winter entirely over-fpread with the fnow drift, which muft have greatly contributed to their warmth.  They were fo fmall, that they did not contain more than fix or eight perfons each, and even that number of any other people would have found them but miferable habitations.

Their houfehold furniture chiefly confifts of ftone kettles, and wooden troughs of various fizes, alfo difhes, fcoops, and fpoons, made of the buffalo or mufk-ox horns  Their kettles are formed of a pepper and falt coloured ftone; and though the texture appears to be very coarfe, and as porous as a drip-ftone, yet they are perfectly
tight,

tight, and will found as clear as a china bowl. Some of thofe kettles are fo large as to be capable of containing five or fix gallons; and though it is impoffible thefe poor people can perform this arduous work with any other tools than harder ftones, yet they are by far fuperior to any that I had ever feen in Hudfon's Bay; every one of them being ornamented with neat mouldings round the rim, and fome of the large ones with a kind of flute-work at each corner. In fhape they were a long fquare, fomething wider at the top than bottom, like a knife-tray, and ftrong handles of the fohd ftone were left at each end to lift them up.

Their hatchets are made of a thick lump of copper, about five or fix inches long, and from one and a half to two inches fquare; they are bevilled away at one end like a mortice-chiffel. This is lafhed into the end of a piece of wood about twelve or fourteen inches long, in fuch a manner as to act like an adze. in general they are applied to the wood like a chiffel, and driven in with a heavy club, inftead of a mallet. Neither the weight of the tool nor the fharpnefs of the metal will admit of their being handled either as adze or axe, with any degree of fuccefs

The men's bayonets and women's knives are alfo made of copper. the former are in fhape like the ace of fpades, with the handle of deers horn a foot long, and the latter exactly refemble thofe defcribed by Crantz. Samples of both thefe implements
plements

plements I formerly fent home to James Fitzge-
rald, Efq then one of the Hudfon's Bay Committee.

Among all the fpoils of the twelve tents which
my companions plundered, only two fmall pieces
of iron were found; one of which was about an
inch and a half long, and three eighths of an inch
broad, made into a woman's knife, the other was
barely an inch long, and a quarter of an inch wide,
This laft was rivetted into a piece of ivory, fo as
to form a man's knife, known in Hudfon's Bay
by the name of *Mokeatoggan*, and is the only inftrument ufed by them in fhaping all their wood-
work

Thofe people had a fine and numerous breed of
dogs, with fharp erect ears, fharp nofes, bufhy
tails, &c. exactly like thofe feen among the Efquimaux in Hudfon's Bay and Straits. They were
all tethered to ftones, to prevent them, as I fuppofe, from eating the fifh that were fpread all over
the rocks to dry. I do not recollect that my
companions killed or hurt one of thofe animals;
but after we had left the tents, they often wifhed they had taken fome of thofe fine dogs with
them.

Though the drefs, canoes, utenfils, and many
other articles belonging to thefe people, are very
fimilar to thofe of Hudfon's Bay, yet there is one
cuftom that prevails among them—namely, that
of the men having all the hair of their heads pulled out by the roots—which pronounces them to
be

be of a different tribe from any hitherto feen either on the coaft of Labradore, Hudfon's Bay, or Davis's Straits. The women wore their hair at full length, and exactly in the fame ftile as all the other Efquimaux women do whom I have feen.

When at the fea-fide, (at the mouth of the Copper River,) befides feeing many feals on the ice, I alfo obferved feveral flocks of fea-fowl flying about the fhores, fuch as, gulls black-heads, loons. old wives, ha ha-wie's, dunter geefe, arctic gulls, and willicks In the adjacent ponds alfo were fome fwans and geefe in a moulting ftate, and in the marfhes fome curlews and plover; plenty of hawks-eyes, (*i. e.* the green plover,) and fome yellow-legs; alfo feveral other fmall birds, that vifit thofe Northern parts in the Spring to breed and moult, and which doubtlefs return Southward as the fall advances My reafon for this conjecture is founded on a certain knowledge that all thofe birds migrate in Hudfon's Bay, and it is but reafonable to think that they are lefs capable of withftanding the rigour of fuch a long and cold Winter as they muft neceffarily experience in a country which is fo many degrees within the Arctic Circle, as that is where I now faw them.

That the mufk-oxen, deer, bears, wolves, wolvarines, foxes, Alpine hares, white owls, ravens, partridges, ground-fquirrels, common fquirrels, ermins, mice, &c. are the conftant inhabitants of thofe parts, is not to be doubted. In many places, by the fides of the hills, where the fnow lay to a

great

great depth, the dung of the mufk-oxen and
deer was lying in fuch long and continued heaps,
as clearly to point out that thofe places had been
their much-frequented paths during the preceding Winter. There were alfo many other fimilar
appearances on the hills, and other parts, where
the fnow was entirely thawed away, without any
print of a foot being vifible in the mofs, which
is a certain proof that thefe long ridges of dung
muft have been dropped in the fnow as the beafts
were paffing and repaffing over it in the Winter.
There are likewife fimilar proofs that the Alpine
hare and the partridge do not migrate, but remain
there the whole year the latter we found in
confiderable flocks among the tufts of willows
which grow near the fea.

It is perhaps not generally known, even to the
curious, therefore may not be unworthy of obfervation, that the dung of the mufk-ox, though fo
large an animal, is not larger, and at the fame time
fo near the fhape and colour of that of the Alpine
hare, that the difference is not eafily diftinguifhed but by the natives, though in general the quantity may lead to a difcovery of the animal to
which it belongs.

I did not fee any birds peculiar to thofe parts,
except what the Copper Indians call the " Alarm
" Bird," or Bird of Warning " In fize and colour it refembles a Cobadekoock, and is of the
owl genus The name is faid to be well adapted
to its qualities, for when it perceives any people,

or

or beaft, it directs its way towards them immediately, and after hovering over them fome
time, flies round them in circles, or goes a-head
in the fame direction in which they walk    They
repeat their vifits frequently ; and if they fee any
other moving objects, fly alternately from one
party to the other, hover over them for fome time,
and make a loud fcreaming noife, like the crying
of a child.    In this manner they are faid fometimes to follow paffengers a whole day.    The Copper Indians put great confidence in thofe birds,
and fay they are frequently apprized by them of
the approach of ftrangers, and conducted by
them to herds of deer and mufk-oxen ; which,
without their affiftance, in all probability, they never could have found.

The Efquimaux feem not to have imbibed the
fame opinion of thofe birds ; for if they had, they
muft have been apprized of our approach toward
their tents, becaufe all the time the Indians lay in
ambufh, (before they began the maffacre,) a
large flock of thofe birds were continually flying
about, and hovering alternately over them and
the tents, making a noife fufficient to awaken any
man out of the foundeft fleep

After a fleep of five or fix hours we once more
fet out, and walked eighteen or nineteen miles to
the South South Eaft, when we arrived at one of
the copper mines, which lies, from the river's
mouth about South South Eaft, diftant about
twenty-nine or thirty miles

Thi<

This mine, if it deferve that appellation, is no more than an entire jumble of rocks and gravel, which has been rent many ways by an earthquake. Through thefe ruins there runs a fmall river; but no part of it, at the time I was there, was more than knee-deep.

The Indians who were the occafion of my undertaking this journey, reprefented this mine to be fo rich and valuable, that if a factory were built at the river, a fhip might be ballafted with the oar, inftead of ftone; and that with the fame eafe and difpatch as is done with ftones at Churchill River. By their account the hills were entirely compofed of that metal, all in handy lumps, like a heap of pebbles. But their account differed fo much from the truth, that I and almoft all my companions expended near four hours in fearch of fome of this metal, with fuch poor fuccefs, that among us all, only one piece of any fize could be found. This, however, was remarkably good, and weighed above four pounds*. I believe the copper has formerly been in much greater plenty; for in many places, both on the furface and in the cavities and crevices of the rocks, the ftones are much tinged with verdigrife.

It may not be unworthy the notice of the curious, or undeferving a place in my Journal, to remark,

* This piece of Copper is now in the pof effon of the Hudfon . Bay Company.

1771. remark, that the Indians imagine that every bit
of copper they find refembles fome object in nature, but by what I faw of the large piece, and
fome fmaller ones which were found by my companions, it requires a great fhare of invention to
make this out. I found that different people had
different ideas on the fubject, for the large piece
of copper above mentioned had not been found
long before it had twenty different names. One
faying that it refembled this animal, and another
that it reprefented a particular part of another;
at laft it was generally allowed to refemble an
Alpine hare couchant: for my part, I muft confefs that I could not fee it had the leaft refemblance to any thing to which they compared it.
It would be endlefs to enumerate the different
parts of a deer, and other animals, which the
Indians fay the beft pieces of copper refemble · it
may therefore be fufficient to fay, that the largeft
pieces, with the feweft branches and the leaft drofs,
are the beft for their ufe, as by the help of fire,
and two ftones, they can beat it out to any fhape
they wifh

Before Churchill River was fettled by the Hudfon's Bay Company, which was not more than
fifty years previous to this journey being undertaken, the Northern Indians had no other metal but copper among them, except a fmall quantity of iron-work, which a party of them who
vifited York Fort about the year one thoufand
feven hundred and thirteen, or one thoufand feven

ven hundred and fourteen, purchafed, and a few pieces of old iron found at Churchill River, which had undoubtedly been left there by Captain Monk. This being the cafe, numbers of them from all quarters uſed every Summer to refort to thefe hills in fearch of copper; of which they made hatchets, ice chiffels, bayonets, knives, awls, arrow-heads, &c.*  The many paths that had been beaten by the Indians on thefe occaſions, and which are yet, in many places, very perfect, efpecially on the dry ridges and hills, is furprifing; in the vallies and marfhy grounds, however, they are moftly grown over with herbage, fo as not to be difcerned

The Copper Indians fet a great value on their native metal even to this day; and prefer it to iron, for almoſt every uſe except that of a hatchet,

---

* There is a ftrange tradition among thofe people, that the firft perfon who difcovered thofe mines was a woman, and that fhe conducted them to the place for feveral years, but as fhe was the only woman in company, fome of the men took fuch liberties with her as made her vow revenge on them, and fhe is faid to have been a great conjurer  Accordingly when the men had loaded themfelves with copper, and were going to return fhe refufed to accompany them, and faid fhe would fit on the mine till fhe funk into the ground, and that the copper fhould fink with her  The next year, when the men went for more copper, they found her funk up to the waift, though ftill alive and the quantity of copper much decreafed, and on their repeat ng their vifit the year following, fhe had quite difappeared, and all the principal part of the mine with her, fo that after that period nothing remained on the furface but a few fmall pieces, and thofe were fcattered at a confiderable diftance from each other  Before that period they fay the copper lay on the furface in fuch large heaps, that the Indians had nothing to do but turn it over, and pick fuch pieces as would beft fuit the different uſes for which they intended it.

et, a knife, and an awl. for thefe three neceffary implements, copper makes but a very poor fubftitute   When they exchange copper for iron-work with our trading Northern Indians, which is but feldom, the ftandard is an ice-chiffel of copper for an ice-chiffel of iron, or an ice chiffel and a few arrow-heads of copper, for a half-worn hatchet; but when they barter furrs with our Indians, the eftablifhed rule is to give ten times the price for every thing they purchafe that is given for them at the Company's Factory.   Thus, a hatchet that is bought at the Factory for one beaver-fkin, or one cat-fkin, or three ordinary martins' fkins, is fold to thofe people at the advanced price of one thoufand *per cent.;* they alfo pay in proportion, for knives, and every other fmaller piece of iron-work.   For a fmall brafs kettle of two pounds, or two pounds and a half weight, they pay fixty martins, or twenty beaver in other kinds of furrs*.   If the kettles are not bruifed, or ill-ufed in any other refpect, the Northern

* What is meant by Beaver in other kind of furrs, muft be underftood as follows   For the eafier trading with the Indians, as well as for the more correctly keeping their accounts, the Hudfon's Bay Company have made a full-grown beaver-fkin the ftandard by which they rate all other furs, according to their refpective values   Thus in feveral fpecies of furrs, one fkin is valued at the rate of four beaver fkins, fome at three, and others at two, whereas thofe of an inferior quality are rather at one, and thofe of ftill lefs value confidered fo inferior to that of a beaver, that from fix to twenty of their fkins are only valued as equal to one beaver fkin in the way of trade, and do not fetch one-fourth of the price at the London market   In this manner the term "Made Beaver" is to be underftood

thein traders have the confcience at times to exact fomething more. It is at this extravagant
price that all the Copper and Dog-ribbed Indians,
who traffic with our yearly traders, fupply themfelves with iron-work, &c.

From thofe two tribes our Northern Indians
ufed formerly to purchafe moft of the furrs they
brought to the Company's Factory; for their own
country produced very few of thofe articles,
and being, at that time, at war with the Southern
Indians, they were prevented from penetrating
far enough backwards to meet with many animals of the furr kind; fo that deer-fkins, and
fuch furrs as they could extort from the Copper
and Dog-ribbed Indians, compofed the whole of
their trade; which, on an average of many years,
and indeed till very lately, feldom or ever exceeded fix thoufand *Made Beaver per annum.*

At prefent happy it is for them, and greatly to
the advantage of the Company, that they are in
perfect peace, and live in friendfhip with their
Southern neighbours. The good effect of this
harmony is already fo vifible, that within a few
years the trade from that quarter has increafed
many thoufands of Made Beaver annually, fome
years even to the amount of eleven thoufand
fkins*. Befides the advantage arifing to the

N                    Company

* Since this Journal was written, the Northern Indians, by annually vifiting their Southern friends, the Athapufcow Indians, have contracted the
fmall-

Company from this increafe, the poor Northern Indians reap innumerable benefits from a fine and plentiful country, with the produce of which they annually load themfelves for trade, without giving the leaft offence to the proper inhabitants.

Several attempts have been made to induce the Copper and Dog-ribbed Indians to vifit the Company's Fort at Churchill River, and for that purpofe many prefents have been fent, but they never were attended with any fuccefs. And though

---

fmall pox, which has carried off nine-tenths of them, and par icularly thofe people who compofed the trade at Churchill Factory The few furvivors follow the example of their Southern ne ghbours, and all trade with the Canadians, who are fettled in the heart of the Athapufcow country fo that a verv few years has proved my fhort fightednefs, and that it would have been much more to the advantage of the Company, as well as have prevented the depopulation of the Northern Indian country, if they had ftill remained at war with the Southern tribes, and never attempted to better the r fituation At the fame time, t is impoffible to fay what increafe of trade might not, in time, have arifen from a conftant and regular traffic with the different tribes of Copper and Dog ribbed Indians But having been to ally neglected for feveral years, they have now funk into the r original barbarifm and extreme indigence, and a war has erfued between the two tribes, for the fake of a few remnants of iron-work which was left among them, and the Dog-ribbed Indians were fo numerous, and fo fuccefsful as to deftroy almoft the whole race of the Copper Indians

While I was writing this Note, I was informed by fome Northern Indians, that the few which remain of the Copper tribe have found their way to one of the Canadian houfes in the Athapufcow Indians country, where they get fupplied with every thing at lefs, or about half the price they were formerly obliged to give, fo that the few furviving Northern Indians, as well as the Hudfon's Bay Company, have now loft every fhadow of any future trade from that quarter, unlefs the Company will eftablifh a fettlement with the Athapufcow country, and underfell the Canadians

though several of the Copper Indians have visited
Churchill, in the capacity of servants to the Northern Indians, and were generally sent back loaded with presents for their countrymen, yet the
Northern Indians always plundered them of the
whole soon after they left the Fort.   This kind of
treatment, added to the many inconveniencies
that attend so long a journey, are great obstacles
in their way, otherwise it would be as possible
for them to bring their own goods to market, as
for the Northern Indians to go so far to purchase
them on their own account, and have the same
distance to bring them as the first proprietors
would have had   But it is a political scheme of our
Northern traders to prevent such an intercourse,
as it would greatly lessen their consequence and
emolument. Superstition, indeed, will, in all probability, be a lasting barrier against those people
ever having a settled communication with our
Factory, as few of them chuse to travel in countries so remote from their own, under a pretence
that the change of air and provisions (though exactly the same to which they are accustomed) are
highly prejudicial to their health, and that not
one out of three of those who have undertaken
the journey, have ever lived to return   The
first of these reasons is evidently no more than
gross superstition, and though the latter is but
too true, it has always been owing to the treachery and cruelty of the Northern Indians, who took
them under their protection.

N 2                                       It

It is but a few years fince, that Captain Keelfhies, who is frequently mentioned in this Journal, took twelve of thefe people under his charge,
all heavy laden with the moft voluable furrs;
and long before they arrived at the Fort, he and
the reft of his crew had got all the furrs from
them, in payment for provifions for their fupport, and obliged them to carry the furrs on their
account

On their arrival at Prince of Wales's Fort,
Keelfhies laid claim to great merit for having
brought thofe ftrangers, fo richly laden, to the
Factory, and affured the Governor that he might,
in future, expect a great increafe in trade from
that quarter, through his intereft and affiduity.
One of the ftrangers was dubbed with the name
of Captain, and treated accordingly, while at the
Fort, that is, he was dreffed out in the beft manner, and at his departure, both himfelf and all
his countrymen were loaded with prefents, in
hopes that they would not only repeat the vifit
themfelves, but by difplaying fo much generofity,
many of their countrymen would be induced to
accompany them

There feems to be great propriety in the conduct of the Governor* on this occafion; but however well-intended, it had quite the contrary effect, for Keelfhies and the reft of his execrable
gang, not content with fharing all the furrs thofe
poor people had carried to the Fort, determined
to

* Mr Mofes Norton

to get alfo all the European goods that had been
given to them by the Governor   As neither
Keelfhies nor any of his gang had the courage to
kill the Copper Indians, they concerted a deep-
laid fcheme for their deftruction; which was to
leave them on an ifland.   With this view, when
they got to the propofed fpot, the Northern Indians took care to have all the  baggage belonging
to the Copper Indians ferried acrofs to the main,
and having ftripped them of fuch parts of their
clothing as they thought worthy their notice,
went off with all the canoes, leaving them all
behind on the ifland, where they perifhed for
want.   When I was on my journey to the Fort
in June one thoufand feven hundred and feventy-
two, I faw the bones of thofe poor people, and
had the foregoing account from my guide Matonabbee; but it was not made known to the Governor for fome years afterward, for fear of pre-
judicing him againft Keelfhies.

A fimilar circumftance had nearly happened to
a Copper Indian who accompanied me to the Fort
in one thoufand feven hundred and feventy-two:
after we were all  ferried acrofs Seal River, and
the poor man's bundle of furrs on the South-fide,
he was left alone on the oppofite fhore; and no
one except Matonabbee would go over for him.
The wind at that time blew fo hard, that Matonabbee ftripped himfelf quite naked, to be ready
for fwimming in cafe the canoe fhould overfet;
but he foon brought the Copper Indian fafe over,

to

to the no fmall mortification of the wretch who had the charge of him, and who would gladly have poffeffed the bundle of furrs at the expence of the poor man's life

When the Northern Indians returned for the Factory that year, the above Copper Indian put himfelf under the protection of Matonabbee, who accompanied him as far North as the latitude 64°, where they faw fome Copper Indians, among whom was the young man's father, into whofe hands Matonabbee delivered him in good health, with all his goods fafe, and in good order

Soon after we had left the Copper-mine, there came on a thick fog with rain, and at intervals heavy fhowers of fnow. This kind of weather continued for fome days, and at times it was fo thick, that we were obliged to ftop for feveral hours together, as we were unable to fee our way, and the road was remarkably rocky and intricate

22d

At three o'clock in the morning of the twenty-fecond, Matonabbee's brother and one of the Copper Indians, who had been firft difpatched a-head from Congecathawhachaga, overtook us. During their abfence they had not difcovered any Indians who could have been ferviceable to my expedition. They had, however, been at the Copper River, and feeing fome marks fet up there to direct them to return, they had made the beft of their way, and had not flept from the
time

time they left the river till they joined us, though the diftance was not lefs than a hundred miles When they arrived we were afleep, but we foon awakened, and began to proceed on our jour-ney. That day we walked forty two miles; and in our way paffed Buffalo Lake: at night, we put up about the middle of the Stony Moun-tains. The weather was exceffively hot and fultry.

On the twenty-third, the weather continued much the fame as on the preceding day. Early in the morning we fet out, and walked forty-five miles the fift day, during which the Indians kill-ed feveral fine fat buck deer.

About one o'clock in the morning of the twen-ty-fourth, we flopped and took a little refrefh-ment, as we had alfo done about noon the pre-ceding day; but the Indians had been fo long from their wives and families, that they promif-ed not to fleep till they faw them, efpecially as we were then in fight of the hills of Congecatha-whachaga, where we had left the laft of them. After refting about an hour, we proceeded on our way, and at fix in the morning arrived at Congecathawhachaga; when, to our great difap-pointment, we found that all our women had got fet acrofs the river before the Copper Indians left that part; fo that when we arrived, not an In-dian was to be found, except an old man and his family, who had arrived in our abfence, and

was

was waiting at the croffing-place with fome furrs for Matonabbee, who was fo nearly related to the old man as to be his fon-in-law, having one of his daughters for a wife. The old man had another with him, who was alfo offered to the great man, but not accepted

Our ftay at this place may be faid to have been of very fhort duration; for on feeing a large fmoke to the Southward, we immediately croffed the river, and walked towards it, when we found that the women had indeed been there fome days before, but were gone; and at their departure had fet the mofs on fire, which was then burning, and occafioned the fmoke we had feen. By this time the afternoon was far advanced, we purfued, however, our courfe in the direction which the women took, for their track we could eafily dif-cover in the mofs. We had not gone far, before we faw another fmoke at a great diftance, for which we fhaped our courfe; and, notwithftand-ing we redoubled our pace, it was eleven o'clock at night before we reached it, when, to our great mortification, we found it to be the place where the women had flept the night before; having in the morning, at their departure, fet fire to the mofs which was then burning.

The Indians, finding that their wives were fo near as to be within one of their ordinary day's walk, which feldom exceeded ten or twelve miles, determined not to reft till they had joined them.

Accordingly

Accordingly we purfued our courfe, and about two o'clock in the morning of the twenty-fifth, come up with fome of the women, who had then pitched their tents by the fide of Coge-ad Lake.

From our leaving the Copper-mine River to this time we had travelled fo hard, and taken fo little reft by the way, that my feet and legs had fwelled confiderably, and I had become quite ftiff at the ankles. In this fituation I had fo little power to direct my feet when walking, that I frequently knocked them againft the ftones with fuch force, as not only to jar and diforder them, but my legs alfo, and the nails of my toes were bruifed to fuch a degree, that feveral of them feftered and dropped off. To add to this mifhap, the fkin was entirely chafed off from the tops of both my feet, and between every toe, fo that the fand and gravel, which I could by no means exclude, irritated the raw parts fo much, that for a whole day before we arrived at the women's tents, I left the print of my feet in blood almoft at every ftep I took. Several of the Indians began to complain that their feet alfo were fore; but, on examination, not one of them was the twentieth part in fo bad a ftate as mine.

This being the firft time I had been in fuch a fituation, or feen any body foot-foundered, I was much alarmed, and under great apprehenfions for the confequences. Though I was but little
fatigued

fatigued in body, yet the excruciating pain I fuffered when walking, had fuch an effect on my
fpirits, that if the Indians had continued to travel
two or three days longer at that unmerciful rate,
I muft unavoidably have been left behind; for
my feet were in many places quite honey-comb-
ed, by the dirt and gravel eating into the raw
flefh.

As foon as we arrived at the women's tents, the
firft thing I did, was to wafh and clean my feet
in warm water, then I bathed the fwelled parts
with fpirits of wine, and dreffed thofe that were
raw with Turner's cerate, foon after which I be-
took myfelf to reft.   As we did not move on the
following day, I perceived that the fwelling
abated, and the raw parts of my feet were not
quite fo much inflamed.  This change for the
better gave me the ftrongeft affurance that reft
was the principal thing wanted to effect a fpeedy
and complete cure of my painful though in reality very fimple diforder, (foot-foundering,) which
I had before confidered to be an affair of the
greateft confequence

Reft, however, though effential to my fpeedy
recovery, could not at this time be procured; for
as the Indians were defirous of joining the remainder of their wives and families as foon as poffible,
they would not ftop even a fingle day; fo that
on the twenty-feventh we again began to move;
and though they moved at the rate of eight or
nine

nine miles a day, it was with the utmoft difficulty that I could follow them  Indeed the weather
proved remarkably fine and pleafant, and the
ground was in general pretty dry, and free from
ftones; which contributed greatly to my eafe
in walking, and enabled me to keep up with the
natives.

On the thirty-firft of July, we arrived at the
place where the wives and families of my companions had been ordered to wait our return from
the Copper-mine River.  Here we found feveral
tents of Indians, but thofe belonging to Matonabbee, and fome others of my crew, had not arrived.  We faw, however, a large fmoke to the
Eaftward, which was fuppofed had been made by
them, as no other Indians were expected from
that quarter.  Accordingly, the next morning,
Matonabbee fent fome of his young men in queft
of them, and on the fifth, they all joined us;
when, contrary to expectation, a great number
of other Indians were with them; in all, to the
amount of more than forty tents.  Among thofe
Indians, was the man who Matonabbee ftabbed
when we were at Clowey.  With the greateft fub-
miffion he led his wife to Matonabbee's tent, fet
her down by his fide, and retired, without faying
a word.  Matonabbee took no notice of her,
though fhe was bathed in tears, and by degrees,
after reclining herfelf on her elbow for fome time,
fhe lay down, and, fobbing, faid, *fee'd dinne, fee'd
dinne !*

1771.

July

31ft

Auguft
1ft

5th

1771. *dinne!* which is, My hufband, my hufband! On
which Matonabbee told her, that if fhe had re-
Auguft. fpected him as fuch, fhe would not have run away
from him; and that fhe was at liberty to go
where fhe pleafed. On which fhe got up, with
feeming reluctance, though moft affuredly with a
light heart, and returned to her former hufband's
tent.

CHAP.

## C H A P.  VII.

Remarks from the Time the Women joined us till our Arrival at the Athapuſcow Lake.

*Several of the Indians ſick.—Method uſed by the conju-*
*rors to relieve one man, who recovers.—Matonabbee*
*and his crew proceed to the South Weſt.—Moſt of the*
*other Indians ſeparate, and go their reſpective ways.*
*—Paſs by White Stone Lake.—Many deer killed*
*merely for their ſkins.—Remarks thereon, and on the*
*deer, reſpecting ſeaſons and places.—Arrive at Point*
*Lake.—One of the Indian's wives being ſick, is left*
*behind to periſh above-ground.—Weather very bad,*
*but deer plenty.—Stay ſome time at Point Lake to*
*dry meat, &c.—Winter ſet in —Superſtitious cuſtoms*
*obſerved by my companions, after they had killed the*
*Eſquimaux at Copper River.—A violent gale of wind*
*overſets my tent and breaks my quadrant.—Some*
*Copper and Dog-ribbed Indians join us.—Indians*
*propoſe to go to the Athapuſcow Country to kill*
*mooſe.—Leave Point Lake, and arrive at the wood's*
*edge.—Arrive at Anawd Lake.—Tranſactions*
*there—Remarkable inſtance of a man being cured*
*of the palſey by the conjurors.—Leave Anawd Lake*
*—Arrive at the great Athapuſcow Lake.*

SEVERAL of the Indians being very ill, the conjurers, who are always the doctors, and pretend to perform great cures, began to try their ſkill

skill to effect their recovery.   Here it is neceffary to remark, that they ufe no medicine either for internal or external complaints, but perform all their cures by charms.   In ordinary cafes, fucking the part affected,  blowing, and finging to it; haughing, fpitting, and at the fame time uttering a heap of unintelligible jargon, compofe the whole procefs of cure.   For fome inward complaints; fuch as, griping in the inteftines, difficulty of making water, &c. it is very common to fee thofe jugglers blowing into the *anus*, or into the parts adjacent, till their eyes are almoft ftarting out of their heads · and this operation is performed indifferently on all, without regard either to age or fex   The accumulation of fo large a quantity of wind is at times apt to occafion fome extraordinary emotions, which are not eafily fuppreffed by a fick perfon ; and as there is no vent for it out by the channel through which it was conveyed thither, it fometimes occafions an odd fcene between the doctor and his patient; which I once wantonly called an engagement, but for which I was afterward exceedingly forry, as it highly offended feveral of the Indians ; particularly the juggler and the fick perfon, both of whom were men I much efteemed, and, except in that moment of levity, it had ever been no lefs my inclination than my intereft to fhew them every refpect that my fituation would admit.

I have often admired the great pains thefe jugglers take to receive their credulous countrymen,
while

while at the fame time they are indefatigably induftrious and perfevering in their efforts to relieve
them. Being naturally not very delicate, they
frequently continue their windy procefs fo long,
that I have more than once feen the doctor quit
his patient with his face and breaft in a very difagreeable condition. However laughable this
may appear to an European, cuftom makes it very indecent, in their opinion, to turn any thing
of the kind to ridicule.

When a friend for whom they have a particular
regard is, as they fuppofe, dangeroufly ill, befide
the above methods, they have recourfe to another
very extraordinary piece of fuperftition, which
is no lefs than that of pretending to fwallow
hatchets, ice-chiffels, broad bayonets, knives, and
the like; out of a fuperftitious notion that undertaking fuch defperate feats will have fome influence in appeafing death, and procure a refpite
for their patient

On fuch extraordinary occafions a conjuring-
houfe is erected, by driving the ends of four long
fmall fticks, or poles, into the ground at right
angles, fo as to form a fquare of four, five, fix,
or feven feet, as may be required The tops of
the poles are tied together, and all is clofe covered with a tent-cloth or other fkin, exactly in the
fhape of a fmall fquare tent, except that there is
no vacancy left at the top to admit the light. In
the middle of this houfe, or tent, the patient is
laid, and is foon followed by the conjurer, or
conjurers.

conjurers. Sometimes five or fix of them give
their joint-affiftance, but before they enter, they
ftrip themfelves quite naked, and as foon as they
get into the houfe, the door being well clofed,
they kneel round the fick perfon or perfons, and
begin to fuck and blow at the parts effected, and
then in a very fhort fpace of time fing and talk
as if converfing with familiar fpirits, which they
fay appear to them in the fhape of different beafts
and birds of prey. When they have had fufficient
conference with thofe neceffary agents, or fhadows,
as they term them, they afk for the hatchet, bayonet, or the like, which is always prepared by
another perfon, with a long ftring faftened to it
by the haft, for the convenience of hauling it up
again after they have fwallowed it; for they
very wifely admit this to be a very neceffary precaution, as hard and compact bodies, fuch as iron
and fteel, would be very difficult to digeft, even
by the men who are enabled to fwallow them.
Befides, as thofe tools are in themfelves very ufeful, and not always to be procured, it would be
very ungenerous in the conjurers to digeft them,
when it is known that barely fwallowing them
and hauling them up again is fully fufficient to
anfwer every purpofe that is expected from them.

At the time when the forty and odd tents of
Indians joined us, one man was fo dangeroufly ill,
that it was thought neceffary the conjurers fhould
ufe fome of thofe wonderful experiments for his
recovery; one of them therefore immediately, confented

fented to fwallow a broad bayonet. Accordingly,
a conjuring-houfe was erected in the manner
above defcribed, into which the patient was conveyed, and he was foon followed by the conjurer,
who, after a long preparatory difcourfe, and the
neceſſary conference with his familiar fpirits, or
ſhadows, as they call them, advanced to the door
and aſked for the bayonet, which was then ready
prepared, by having a ſtring faſtened to it, and a
ſhort piece of wood tied to the other end of the
ſtring, to prevent him from fwallowing it. I
could not help obferving that the length of the
bit of wood was not more than the breadth of
the bayonet . however, as it anfwered the intended purpofe, it did equally well as if it had been as
long as a handfpike.

Though I am not fo credulous as to believe that
the conjurer abfolutely fwallowed the bayonet,
yet I muſt acknowledge that in the twinkling of
an eye he conveyed it to—God knows where;
and the fmall piece of wood, or one exactly like
it, was confined clofe to his teeth. He then pa-
raded backward and forward before the conjuring-houfe for a ſhort time, when he feigned to be
greatly diſordered in his ſtomach and bowels;
and, after making many wry faces, and groaning
moſt hideoufly, he put his body into feveral di-
ſtorted attitudes, very fuitable to the occafion. He
then returned to the door of the conjuring-houfe,
and after making many ſtrong efforts to vomit,
by the help of the ſtring he at length, and after
tugging at it fome time, produced the bayonet,

O                              which

which apparently he hauled out of his mouth, to the no small surprize of all present. He then looked round with an air of exultation, and strutting into the conjuring-houfe, where he renewed his incantations, and continued them without intermiffion twenty-four hours. Though I was not clofe to his elbow when he performed the above feat, yet I thought myfelf near enough (and I can affure my readers I was all attention) to have detected him. Indeed I muft confefs that it appeared to me to be a very nice piece of deception, efpecially as it was performed by a man quite naked.

Not long after this flight of-hand work was over, fome of the Indians afked me what I thought of it; to which I anfwered, that I was too far off to fee it fo plain as I could wifh; which indeed was no more than the ftricteft truth, becaufe I was not near enough to detect the deception. The fick man, however, foon recovered; and in a few days afterwards we left that place and proceeded to the South Weft.

9th

On the ninth of Auguft, we once more purfued our journey, and continued our courfe in the South Weft quarter, generally walking about feven or eight miles a day, All the Indians, however, who had been in our company, except twelve tents, ftruck off different ways. As to myfelf, having had feveral days reft, my feet were completely healed, though the fkin remained very tender for fome time.

From

From the nineteenth to the twenty fifth, we
walked by the fide of Thaye-chuck-gyed Whoie, 
or Large Whiteftone Lake, which is about forty
miles long from the North Eaft to the South
Weft, but of very unequal breadth   A river from
the North Weft fide of this lake is faid to run in
a ferpentine manner a long way to the Weftward;
and then tending to the Northward, compofes
the main branch of the Copper-mine River, as
has been already mentioned; which may or may
not be true.   It is certain, however, that there
are many rivulets, which empty themfelves into
this lake from the South Eaft; but as they are all
fmall ftreams, they may probably be no more
than what is fufficient to fupply the conftant de-
creafe occafioned by the exhalations, which, during the fhort Summer, fo high a Northern latitude always affords.

Deer were very plentiful the whole way; the
Indians killed great numbers of them daily, merely for the fake of their fkins, and at this time of
the year their pelts are in good feafon, and the
hair of a proper length for clothing.

The great deftruction which is made of the
deer in thofe parts at this feafon of the year only, is almoft incredible, and as they are never
known to have more than one young one at a
time, it is wonderful they do not become fcarce:
but fo far is this from being the cafe, that the old-
eft Northern Indian in all their tribe will affirm
that the deer are as plentiful now as they ever have

O 2                                  been;

been; and though they are remarkably scarce some years near Churchill river, yet it is said, and with great probability of truth, that they are more plentiful in other parts of the country than they were formerly. The scarcity or abundance of these animals in different places at the same season is caused, in a great measure, by the winds which prevail for some time before; for the deer are supposed by the natives to walk always in the direction from which the wind blows, except when they migrate from East to West, or from West to East, in search of the opposite sex, for the purpose of propagating their species.

It requires the prime part of the skins of from eight to ten deer to make a complete suit of warm clothing for a grown person during the Winter; all of which should, if possible, be killed in the month of August, or early in September; for after that time the hair is too long, and at the same time so loose in the pelt, that it will drop off with the slightest injury.

Beside these skins, which must be in the hair, each person requires several others to be dressed into leather, for stockings and shoes, and light Summer clothing; several more are also wanted in a parchment state, to make *clewla* as they call it, or thongs to make netting for their snow-shoes, snares for deer, sewing for their sledges, and, in fact, for every other use where strings or lines of any kind are required: so that each person, on an average, expends, in the course of a year, upwards

of

of twenty deer fkins in clothing and other domeftic ufes, exclufive of tent cloths, bags, and many
other things which it is impoffible to remember,
and unneceffary to enumerate.

All fkins for the above-mentioned purpofes
are, if poffible, procured between the beginning
of Auguft and the middle of October ; for when
the rutting feafon is over, and the Winter fets in,
the deer-fkins are not only very thin, but in general full of worms and warbles ; which render
them of little ufe, unlefs it be to cut into fine
thongs, of which they make fifhing-nets, and nets
for the heels and toes of their fnow-fhoes. Indeed the chief ufe that is made of them in Winter is for the purpofe of food; and really when
the hair is properly taken off, and all the warbles
are fqueezed out, if they are well-boiled, they are
far from being difagreeable  The Indians, however, never could perfuade me to eat the warbles,
of which fome of them are remarkably fond, particularly the children. They are always eaten
raw and alive, out of the fkin; and are faid, by
thofe who like them, to be as fine as goofeberries.
But the very idea of eating fuch things, exclufive
of their appearance, (many of them being as
large as the firft joint of the little finger,) was
quite fufficient to give me an unalterable difguft
to fuch a repaft ; and when I acknowledge that
the warbles out of the deers backs, and the domeftic lice, were the only two things I ever faw
my companions eat, of which I could not, or did
not,

not partake, I truft I fhall not be reckoned over-delicate in my appetite

The month of October is the rutting feafon with the deer in thofe parts, and after the time of their courtfhip is over, the bucks feparate from the does, the former proceed to the Weftward, to take fhelter in the woods during the Winter, and the latter keep out in the barren ground the whole year. This, though a general rule, is not without fome exceptions, for I have frequently feen many does in the woods, though they bore no proportion to the number of bucks. This rule, therefore, only ftands good refpecting the deer to the North of Churchill River; for the deer to the Southward live promifcuoufly among the woods, as well as in the plains, and along the banks of rivers, lakes, &c. the whole year.

The old buck's horns are very large, with many branches, and always drop off in the month of November, which is about the time they begin to approach the woods This is undoubtedly wifely ordered by Providence, the better to enable them to efcape from their enemies through the woods; otherwife they would become an eafy prey to wolves and other beafts, and be liable to get entangled among the trees, even in ranging about in fearch of food. The fame opinion may probably be admitted of the Southern deer, which always refide among the woods, but the Northern deer, though by far the fmalleft in this country, have much the largeft horns, and the branches are fo long, and at the fame time fpread

fo

fo wide, as to make them more liable to be entangled among the under-woods, than any other
fpecies of deer that I have noticed. The young
bucks in thofe parts do not fhed their horns fo
foon as the old ones : I have frequently feen them
killed at or near Chriftmas, and could difcover
no appearance of their horns being loofe. The
does do not fhed their horns till the Summer; fo
that when the buck's horns are ready to drop off,
the horns of the does are all hairy, and fcarcely
come to their full growth.

The deer in thofe parts are generally in motion
from Eaft to Weft, or from Weft to Eaft, according to the feafon, or the prevailing winds, and
that is the principal reafon why the Northern Indians are always fhifting their ftation. From
November till May, the bucks continue to the
Weftward, among the woods, when their horns
begin to fprout; after which they proceed on
to the Laftward, to the barren grounds, and the
does that have been on the barren ground all the
Winter, are taught by inftinct to advance to the
Weftward to meet them, in order to propagate
their fpecies. Immediately after the rutting feafon is over, they feparate, as hath been mentioned above. The old vulgar faying, fo generally
received among the lower clafs of people in England, concerning the bucks fhedding their yards,
or more properly the glands of the *penis*, yearly,
whether it be true in England or not, is certainly
not true in any of the countries bordering on

Hudfon's

Hudfon's Bay. A long refidence among the Indians has enabled me to confirm this affertion
with great confidence, as I have feen deer killed
every day throughout the year; and when I
have mentioned this circumftance to the Indians,
either Northern or Southern, they always affured
me that they never obferved any fuch fymptoms.
With equal truth I can affert, and that from
ocular demonftration, that the animal which is
called the Alpine Hare in Hudfon's Bay, actually
undergoes fomething fimilar to that which is vulgarly afcribed to the Englifh deer. I have feen
and handled feveral of them, who had been killed juft after they had coupled in the Spring,
with the *penifes* hanging out, dried up, and fhri-
velled, like the navel-ftring of young animals;
and on examination I always found a paffage
through them for the urine to pafs. I have
thought proper to give this remark a place in my
Journal, becaufe, in all probability, it is not generally known, even to thofe gentlemen who have
made natural hiftory their chief ftudy, and if
their refearches are of any real utility to mankind,
it is furely to be regretted that Providence
fhould have placed the greateft part of them too
remote from want to be obliged to travel for
ocular proofs of what they affert in their publications; they are therefore wifely content to ftay
at home, and enjoy the bleffings with which they
are endowed, refting fatisfied to collect fuch information for their own amufement, and the
grati-

gratification of the public, as thofe who are ne-
ceffitated to be travellers are able or willing to
give them  It is true, and I am forry it is fo,
that I come under the latter defcription; but
hope I have not, or fhall not, in the courfe of this
Journal, advance any thing that will not ftand
the teft of experiment, and the fkill of the moft
competent judges.

After leaving White Stone Lake, we continued
our courfe in the South Weft quarter, feldom
walking more than twelve miles a day, and frequently not half that diftance.

On the third of September, we arrived at a
fmall river belonging to Point Lake, but the weather at this time proved fo boifterous, and there
was fo much rain, fnow, and froft, alternately,
that we were obliged to wait feveral days before
we could crofs it in our canoes; and the water
was too deep, and the current too rapid, to attempt fording it.  During this interruption,
however, our time was not entirely loft, as deer
were fo plentiful that the Indians killed numbers
of them, as well for the fake of their fkins, as
for their flefh, which was at prefent in excellent
order, and the fkins in proper feafon for the fun-
dry ufes for which they are deftined.

In the afternoon of the feventh, the weather
became fine and moderate, when we all were
ferried acrofs the river; and the next morning
fhaped our courfe to the South Weft, by the fide
of point Lake.  After three days journey, which
only

only confifted of about eighteen miles, we came to a few fmall fcrubby woods, which were the firft that we had feen from the twenty-fifth of May, except thofe we had perceived at the Coppei-mine River

One of the Indian's wives, who for fome time had been in a confumption, had for a few days paft become fo weak as to be incapable of travelling, which. among thofe people, is the moft deplorable ftate to which a human being can poffibly be brought. Whether fhe had been given over by the doctors, or that it was for want of friends among them, I cannot tell, but certain it is, that no expedients were taken for her recovery; fo that, without much ceremony, fhe was left unaffifted, to perifh above-ground.

Though this was the fiift inftance of the kind I had feen, it is the common, and indeed the conftant practice of thofe Indians, for when a grown perfon is fo ill, efpecially in the Summer, as not to be able to walk, and too heavy to be carried, tney fay it is better to leave one who is paft recovery, than for the whole family to fit down by them and ftarve to death; well knowing that they cannot be of any fervice to the afflicted. On thofe occafions, therefore, the friends or relations of the fick generally leave them fome victuals and water, and, if the fituation of the place will afford it, a little firing. When thofe articles are provided, the perfon to be left is acquainted with the road which the others intend to go,

and

and then, after covering them well up with deer
fkins, &c. they take their leave, and walk away
crying

Sometimes perfons thus left, recover, and
come up with their friends, or wander about till
they meet with other Indians, whom they accompany till they again join their relations. Inftances of this kind are feldom known. The poor
woman above mentioned, however, came up with
us three feveral times, after having been left in
the manner defcribed. At length, poor creature! fhe dropt behind, and no one attempted to
go back in fearch of her

A cuftom apparently fo unnatural is perhaps
not to be found among any other of the human
race. if properly confidered, however, it may
with juftice be afcribed to neceffity and felf-prefervation, rather than to the want of humanity
and focial feeling, which ought to be the charac-
teriftic of men, as the nobleft part of the creation Neceffity, added to national cuftom, contributes principally to make fcenes of this kind lefs
fhocking to thofe people, than they muft appear
to the more civilized part of mankind.

During the early part of September, the weather was in general cold, with much fleet and
fnow, which feemed to promife that the Winter
would fet in early. Deer at this time being very
plentiful, and the few woods we met with affording tent-poles and firing, the Indians propofed to
remain where we were fome time, in order to
dr efs

drefs fkins, and provide our Winter clothing; alfo to make fnow-fhoes and temporary fledges, as well as to prepare a large quantity of dried meat and fat to carry with us; for by the accounts of the Indians, they have always experienced a great fcarcity of deer, and every other kind of game, in the direction they propofed we fhould go when we left Point Lake.

Toward the middle of the month, the weather became quite mild and open, and continued fo till the end of it, but there was fo much conftant and inceffant rain, that it rotted moft of our tents. On the twenty-eighth, however, the wind fettled in the North Weft quarter, when the weather grew fo cold, that by the thirtieth all the ponds, lakes, and other ftanding waters, were frozen over fo hard that we were enabled to crofs them on the ice without danger.

28th.

30th.

Among the various fuperftitious cuftoms of thofe people, it is worth remarking, and ought to have been mentioned it its proper place, that immediately after my companions had killed the Ffquimaux at the Copper River, they confidered themfelves in a ftate of uncleannefs, which induced them to practife fome very curious and unufual ceremonies. In the firft place, all who were abfolutely concerned in the murder were prohibited from cooking any kind of victuals, either for themfelves or others. As luckily there were two in company who had not fhed blood, they were employed always as cooks till we joined

ed

ed the women.    This circumftance was exceedingly favourable on my fide ; for had there been
no perfons of the above defcription in company,
that talk, I was told, would have fallen on me ;
which would have been no lefs fatiguing and troublefome, than humiliating and vexatious

When the victuals were cooked, all the murderers took a kind of red earth, or oker, and painted all the fpace between the nofe and chin, as well
as the greater part of their cheeks, almoft to the
ears, before they would tafte a bit, and would not
drink out of any other difh, or fmoke out of any
other pipe, but their own; and none of the
others feemed willing to drink or fmoke out of
theirs.

We had no fooner joined the women, at our
return fiom the expedition, than there feemed to
be an univerfal fpirit of emulation among them,
vying who fhould firft make a fuit of ornaments
for their hufbands, which confifted of bracelets for
the wrifts, and a band for the forehead, compofed of porcupine quills and moofe-hair, curioufly
wrought on leather.

The cuftom of painting the mouth and part of
the cheeks before each meal, and drinking and
fmoking out of their own utenfils, was ftrictly
and invariable obferved, till the Winter began to
fet in ; and during the whole of that time they
would never kifs any of their wives or children.
They refrained alfo from eating many parts of
the deer and other animals, particularly the head,
entrails,

entrails, and blood, and during their uncleanness, their victuals were never fodden in water, but dried in the fun, eaten quite raw, or broiled, when a fire fit for the purpofe could be procured.

When the time arrived that was to put an end to thefe ceremonies, the men, without a female being prefent, made a fire at fome diftance from the tents, into which they threw all their ornaments, pipe-ftems, and difhes, which were foon confumed to afhes, after which a feaft was prepared, confifting of fuch articles as they had long been prohibited from eating, and when all was over, each man was at liberty to eat, drink, and fmoke as he pleafed; and alfo to kifs his wives and children at difcretion, which they feemed to do with more raptures than I had ever known them do it either before or fince.

October came in very roughly, attended with heavy falls of fnow, and much drift On the fixth at night, a heavy gale of wind from the North Weft put us in great diforder, for though the few woods we paffed had furnifhed us with tent-poles and fewel, yet they did not afford us the leaft fhelter whatever. The wind blew with fuch violence, that in fpite of all our endeavours, it overfet feveral of the tents, and mine, among the reft, fhared the difafter, which I cannot fufficiently lament, as the but-ends of the weather tent-poles fell on the quadrant, and though it was in a ftrong wainfcot cafe, two of the bubbles, the
index,

index, and feveral other parts were broken,
which rendeied it entuely ufelefs. This being the
cafe, I did not think it worth carriage, but broke
it to pieces, and gave the brafs-work to the Indians, who cut it into fmall lumps, and made ufe of
it inftead of ball.

On the twenty-third of October, feveral Copper and a few Dog-ribbed Indians came to our
tents laden with furrs which they fold to fome
of my crew for fuch iron-work as they had to
give in exchange. This vifit, I afterwards found,
was by appointment of the Copper Indians whom
we had feen at Congecathawhachaga, and who,
in their way to us, had met the Dog ribbed Indians, who were alfo glad of fo favourable an opportunity of purchafing fome of thofe valuable
articles, though at a very extravagant price: for
one of the Indians in my company, though not
properly of my party, got no lefs than forty
beaver fkins, and fixty maitins, for one piece of
iron which he had ftole when he was laft at the
Fort*.

One of thofe ftrangers had about forty beaver
fkins, with which he intended to pay Matonabbee an old debt, but one of the other Indians
feized

---

* The p ece of iron above mentioned was the coulter of a new-fafhioned
plough, invented by Captain John Foxler, Late Governor at Chorchll
River, with which he had a large piece of ground ploughed, and afterwards fowed with oats  but the part being nothing but a hot burning
fand, like the Spanifh lines at Gibraltar, the fuccefs may eafily be guefl-
ed, which was, that it did not produce a fingle grain.

feized the whole, notwithftanding he knew it to be in fact Matonabbee's property. This treatment, together with many other infults, which he had received during my abode with him, made him renew his old refolution of leaving his own country, and going to refide with the Athapuf-cow Indians.

As the moft interefting part of my journey was now over, I did not think it neceffary to interfere in his private affairs; and therefore did not endeavour to influence him either one way or the other: out of complaifance, therefore rather than any thing elfe, I told him, that I thought fuch behaviour very uncourteous, efpecially in a man of his rank and dignity. As to the reafon of his determination, I did not think it worth while to enquire into it; but, by his difcourfe with the other Indians, I foon underftood that they all intended to make an excurfion into the country of the Athapufcow Indians, in order to kill moofe and beaver. The former of thofe animals are never found in the Northern Indian territories; and the latter are fo fcarce in thofe Northern parts, that during the whole Winter of one thoufand feven hundred and feventy, I did not fee more than two beaver houfes. Martins are alfo fcarce in thofe parts, for during the above period, I do not think that more than fix or eight were killed by all the Indians in my company. This exceedingly fmall number, among fo many

people,

people, may with great truth be attributed to the indolence of the Indians, and the wandering life which they lead, rather than to the great fcarcity of the martins. It is true, that our moving fo frequently from place to place, did at times make it not an object worth while to build traps; but had they taken the advantage of all favourable opportunities, and been poffeffed of half the induftry of the Company's fervants in the Bay, they might with great eafe have caught as many hundreds, if not fome thoufands; and when we confider the extent of ground which we walked over in that time, fuch a number would not have been any proof of the martins being very plentiful.

Except a few martins; wolves, quiquehatches, foxes, and otters, are the chief furrs to be met with in thofe parts, and few of the Northern Indians chufe to kill either the wolf or the quiquehatch, under a notion that they are fomething more than common animals. Indeed, I have known fome of them fo bigotted to this opinion, that having by chance killed a quiquehatch by a gun which had been fet for a fox, they had left it where it was killed, and would not take off its fkin. Notwithftanding this filly notion, which is too frequently to be obferved among thofe people, it generally happens that there are fome in every gang who are lefs fcrupulous, fo that none of thofe furrs are ever left to rot; and even thofe who make a point of not killing the ani-

P

mals

mals themfelves, are ready to receive their fkins from other Indians, and carry them to the Fort for trade.

By the thirtieth of October, all our clothing, fnowfhoes, and temporary fledges, being completed, we once more began to prepare for moving; and on the following day fet out, and walked five or fix miles to the Southward.

From the firft to the fifth of November we walked on the ice of a large lake, which, though very confiderable both in length and breadth, is not diftinguifhed by any general name; on which account I gave it the name of No Name Lake. On the South fide of this lake we found fome wood, which was very acceptable, being the firft that we had feen fince we left Point Lake.

No Name Lake is about fifty miles long from North to South, and, according to the account of the Indians, is thirty-five miles wide from Eaft to Weft  It is faid to abound with fine fifh; but the weather at the time we crofled it was fo cold, as to render it impoffible to fit on the ice any length of time to angle. A few exceedingly fine trout, and fome very large pike, however, were caught by my companions.

When we arrived on the South fide of the above lake, we fhaped our courfe to the South Weft; and though the weather was in general very cold, yet as we every night found tufts of wood,

wood, in which we could pitch our tents, we 1771.
were enabled to make a better defence againſt the November
weather, than we had had it in our power to do
for ſome time paſt.

On the tenth of November, we arrived at the 10th.
edge of the main woods; at which time the
Indians began to make proper ſledges, ſome ſnow-
ſhoes, &c after which we proceeded again to
the South Weſt. But deer and all other kinds
of game were ſo ſcarce the whole way, that, except a few partridges, nothing was killed by any
in company: we had, neverthelefs, plenty of
the proviſion which had been prepared at Point
Lake.

On the twentieth of the ſame month, we ar- 20th
rived at Anaw'd Whoie, or the Indian Lake.
In our way we croſſed part of Methy Lake, and
walked near eighty miles on a ſmall river belonging to it, which empties itſelf into the Great
Athapuſcow Lake*. While we were walking
on the above little river, the Indians ſet fiſhing-
nets under the ice every night; but their labour
was attended with ſo little ſucceſs, that all they
caught ſerved only as a delicacy, or to make a
little change in our diet; for the quantity was too
trifling to occaſion any conſiderable ſaving of our
other proviſions.

Anaw'd Lake, though ſo ſmall as not to exceed
twenty miles wide in the broadeſt part, is cele-
P 2 brated

* The courſe of this river is near'y South Weſt

brated by the natives for abounding with plenty
of fish during the Winter; accordingly the Indians set all their nets, which were not a few, and
met with such success, that in about ten days the
roes only were as much as all the women could
haul after them.

Tittimeg and barble, with a few small pike,
were the only fish caught at this part; the roes of
which, particularly those of the tittimeg, are more
esteemed by the Northern Indians, to take with
them on a journey, than the fish itself; for about
two pounds weight of these roes, when well bruis-
ed, will make near four gallons of broth, as thick
as common burgoe; and if properly managed,
will be as white as rice, which makes it very
pleasing to the eye, and no less agreeable to the
palate.

The land round this lake is very hilly, though
not mountainous, and chiefly consists of rocks
and loose stones; there must, however, be a small
portion of soil on the surface, as it is in most parts
well clothed with tall poplars, pines, fir, and
birch; particularly in the vallies, where the poplars, pine, and birch seem to thrive best; but
the firs were as large, and in as flourishing a state,
on the very summit of the hills, as in any other
part.

Rabbits were here so plentiful, particularly on
the South and South East side of the lake, that
several of the Indians caught twenty or thirty in
a night with snares; and the wood-partridges
were

were fo numerous in the fir trees, and fo tame,
that I have known an Indian kill near twenty of
them in a day with his bow and arrows. The
Northern Indians call this fpecies of the partridge
Day; and though their flefh is generally very
black and bitter, occafioned by their feeding on
the brufh of the fir tree, yet they make a variety,
or change of diet, and are thought exceedingly
good, particularly by the natives, who, though
capable of living fo hard, and at times eating very ungrateful food, are neverthelefs as fond of
variety as any people whom I ever faw; and will
go as great lengths, according to their circumftances, to gratify their palates, as the greateft epicure in England. As a proof of this affertion, I
have frequently known Matonabbee, and others
who could afford it, for the fake of variety only,
fend fome of their young men to kill a few partridges at the expence of more ammunition than
would have killed deer fufficient to have maintained their families many days; whereas the partridges were always eaten up at one meal: and to
heighten the luxury on thefe occafions, the partridges are boiled in a kettle of fheer fat, which it
muft be allowed renders them beyond all defcription finer flavoured than when boiled in water or
common broth. I have alfo eat deer-fkins boiled in fat, which were exceedingly good.

As during our ftay at Anaw'd Lake feveral of
the Indians, were fickly, the doctors undertook
to adminifter relief; particularly to one man, who
had

had been hauled on a fledge by his brother for two months. His diforder was the dead palfey, which affected one fide, from the crown of his head to the fole of his foot. Befides this dreadful diforder, he had fome inward complaints, with a total lofs of appetite; fo that he was reduced to a mere fkeleton, and fo weak as to be fcarcely capable of fpeaking. In this deplorable condition, he was laid in the center of a large conjuring-houfe, made much after the manner as that which has been already defcribed. And that nothing might be wanting toward his recovery, the fame man who deceived me in fwallowing a bayonet in the Summer, now offered to fwallow a large piece of board, about the fize of a barrel-ftave, in order to effect his recovery. The piece of board was prepared by another man, and painted according to the direction of the juggler, with a rude reprefentation of fome beaft of prey on one fide, and on the reverfe was painted, according to their rude method, a refemblance of the fky.

Without entering into a long detail of the preparations for this feat, I fhall at once proceed to obferve, that after the conjurer had held the neceffary conference with his invifible fpirits, or fhadows, he afked if I was prefent; for he had heard of my faying that I did not fee him fwallow the bayonet fair: and on being anfwered in the affirmative, he defired me to come nearer; on which the mob made a lane for me to pafs,
and

and I advanced clofe to him, and found him

ftanding at the conjuring-houfe door as naked as
he was born.

When the piece of board was delivered to him,
he propofed at firft only to fhove one-third of it
down his throat, and then walk round the company afterward to fhove down another third;
and fo proceed till he had fwallowed the whole,
except a fmall piece of the end, which was left behind to haul it up again. When he put it to his
mouth it apparently flipped down his throat like
lightning, and only left about three inches fticking without his lips, after walking backwards
and forwards three times, he hauled it up again,
and ran into the conjuring-houfe with great precipitation. This he did to all appearance with
great eafe and compofure, and notwithftanding
I was all attention on the occafion, I could not
detect the deceit; and as to the reality of its being a piece of wood that he pretended to fwallow, there is not the leaft reafon to doubt of it,
for I had it in my hand, both before and immediately after the ceremony.

To prevent a variety of opinions on this occafion, and to leffen the apparent magnitude of the
miracle, as well as to give fome colour to my
fcepticifm, which might otherwife perhaps appear
ridiculous, it is neceffary to obferve, that this feat
was performed in a dark and exceffively cold
night, and although there was a large fire at
fome diftance, which reflected a good light, yet
there

there was great room for collufion : for though the conjurer himfelf was quite naked, there were feveral of his fraternity well-clothed, who attended him very clofe during the time of his attempting to fwallow the board, as well as at the time of his hauling it up again.

For thefe reafons it is neceffary alfo to obferve, that on the day preceding the performance of this piece of deception, in one of my hunting excurfions, I accidentally came acrofs the conjurer as he was fitting under a bufh, feveral miles from the tents, where he was bufily employed fhaping a piece of wood exactly like that part which ftuck out of his mouth after he had pretended to fwallow the remainder of the piece. The fhape of the piece which I faw him making was this, ; which exactly refembled the forked end of the main piece, the fhape of which was this, . So that when his attendants had concealed the main piece, it was eafy for him to ftick the fmall point into his mouth, as it was reduced at the fmall end to a proper fize for the purpofe.

Similar proofs may eafily be urged againft his fwallowing the bayonet in the Summer, as no perfon lefs ignorant than themfelves can poffibly place any belief in the reality of thofe feats; yet on the whole, they muft be allowed a confiderable fhare of dexterity in the performance of thofe tricks, and a wonderful deal of perfeverance in what they do for the relief of thofe whom they undertake to cure.

Not

Not long after the above performance had taken place, fome of the Indians began to afk me what I thought of it. As I could not have any plea for faying that I was far off, and at the fame time not caring to affront them by hinting my fufpicions of the deceit, I was fome time at a lofs for an anfwer: I urged, however, the impoffibility of a man's fwallowing a piece of wood, that was not only much longer than his whole back, but nearly twice as broad as he could extend his mouth. On which fome of them laughed at my ignorance, as they were pleafed to call it ; and faid, that the fpirits in waiting fwallowed, or otherwife concealed, the ftick, and only left the forked end apparently fticking out of the conjurer's mouth. My guide, Matonabbee, with all his other good fenfe, was fo bigotted to the reality of thofe performances, that he affured me in the ftrongeft terms, he had feen a man, who was them in company, fwallow a child's cradle, with as much eafe as he could fold up a piece of paper, and put it into his mouth ; and that when he hauled it up again, not the mark of a tooth, or of any violence, was to be difcovered about it.

This ftory fo far exceeded the feats which I had feen with the bayonet and board, that, for the fake of keeping up the farce, I began to be very inquifitive about the fpirits which appear to them on thofe occafions, and their form ; when I was told that they appeared in various fhapes, for almoft every conjurer had his peculiar attendant ;

but

1771.

November

but that the fpirit which attended the man who pretended to fwallow the piece of wood, they faid, generally appeared to him in the fhape of a cloud. This I thought very a-propos to the prefent occafion; and I muft confefs that I never had fo thick a cloud thrown before my eyes before or fince; and had it not been by accident, that I faw him make a counterpart to the piece of wood faid to be fwallowed, I fhould have been ftill at a lofs how to account for fo extraordinary a piece of deception, performed by a man who was entirely naked

As foon as our conjurer had executed the above feat, and entered the conjuring-houfe as already mentioned, five other men and an old woman, all of whom were great profeffors of that art, ftripped themfelves quite naked and followed him, when they foon began to fuck, blow, fing, and dance, round the poor paralytic; and continued fo to do for three days and four nights, without taking the leaft reft or refrefhment, not even fo much as a drop of water. When thefe poor deluding and deluded people came out of the conjuring-houfe, their mouths were fo parched with thirft as to be quite black, and their throats fo fore, that they were fcarcely able to articulate a fingle word, except thofe that ftand for *yes* and *no* in their language.

After fo long an abftinence they were very careful not to eat or drink too much at one time, particularly for the firft day; and indeed fome of
them,

them, to appearance, were almoſt as bad as the 1771.
poor man they had been endeavouring to relieve. November
But great part of this was feigned, for they lay
on their backs with their eyes fixed, as if in the
agonies of death, and were treated like young
children; one perſon ſat conſtantly by them, moi-
ſtening their mouths with fat, and now and then
giving them a drop of water. At other times a
ſmall bit of meat was put into their mouths, or
a pipe held for them to ſmoke. This farce only
laſted for the firſt day; after which they ſeemed
to be perfectly well, except the hoarſeneſs, which
continued for a conſiderable time afterwards.
And it is truly wonderful, though the ſtricteſt
truth, that when the poor ſick man was taken
from the conjuring-houſe, he had not only recovered his appetite to an amazing degree, but was
able to move all the fingers and toes of the ſide
that had been ſo long dead. In three weeks he
recovered ſo far as to be capable of walking, and
at the end of ſix weeks went a hunting for his
family. He was one of the perſons * particularly engaged to provide for me during my journey;
and after his recovery from this dreadful-diſor-
der, accompanied me back to Prince of Wales's
Fort in June one thouſand ſeven hundred and
ſeventy-two, and ſince that time he has frequently viſited the Factory, though he never had a
healthy

* His name was Cuſ-abyagh, the Northern Indian name for the Rock
Partridge

healthy look afterwards, and at times feemed troubled with a nervous complaint. It may be added, that he had been formerly of a remarkable lively difpofition; but after his laft illnefs he always appeared thoughtful, fometimes gloomy, and, in fact, the diforder feemed to have changed his whole nature; for before that dreadful paralytic ftroke, he was diftinguifhed for his good-nature and benevolent difpofition; was entirely free from every appearance of avarice, and the whole of his wifhes feemed confined within the narrow limits of poffeffing as many goods as were abfolutely neceffary, with his own induftry, to enable him to fupport his family from feafon to feafon; but after this event, he was the moft fractious, quarrelfome, difcontented, and covetous wretch alive.

Though the ordinary trick of thefe conjurers may be eafily detected, and juftly exploded, being no more than the tricks of common jugglers, yet the apparent good effect of their labours on the fick and difeafed is not fo eafily accounted for. Perhaps the implicit confidence placed in them by the fick may, at times, leave the mind fo perfectly at reft, as to caufe the diforder to take a favourable turn; and a few fuccefsful cafes are quite fufficient to eftablifh the doctor's character and reputation: But how this confideration could operate in the cafe I have juft mentioned I am at a lofs to fay; fuch, however, was the fact, and I leave it to be accounted for by others.

When

When thefe jugglers take a diflike to, and
threaten a fecret revenge on any perfon, it often
proves fatal to that perfon ; as, from a firm belief that the conjurer has power over his life, he
permits the very thoughts of it to prey on his
fpirits, till by degrees is brings on a diforder
which puts an end to his exiftence*: and fometimes

* As a proof of this, Matonabbee, (who always thought me poffeffed of
this art,) on his arrival at Prince of Wales's Fort in the Winter of 1778,
informed me, that a man whom I had never feen but once, had treated him
in fuch a manner that he was afraid of his life, in confequence of which
he preffed me very much to kill him, though I was then feveral hundreds
of miles diftant  On which, to pleafe this great man to whom I owed fo
much, and not expecting that any harm could poffibly arife from it, I
drew a rough fketch of two human figures on a piece of paper, in the atti-
tude of wreftling  in the hand of one of them, I drew the figure of a bayonet pointing to the breaft of the other  This is me, faid I to Matonabbee, pointing to the figure which was holding the bayonet, and the other,
is your enemy  Oppofite to thofe figures I drew a pine tree, over which
I placed a large human eye, and out of the tree projected a human hand
This paper I gave to Matonabbee, with inftructions to make it as public-
ly known as p ble.  Sure enough, the following year, when he came in
to trade, he informed me that the man was dead, though at that time he
was not lefs than three hundred miles from Prince of Wales's Fort  He
affured me that the man was in perfect health when he heard of my defign
againft him, but almoft immediately afterwards became quite gloomy,
and refufing all kind of fuftenance, in a very few days died  After this I
was frequently applied to on the fame account, both by Matonabbee and
other leading Indians, but never thought proper to comply with their
requefts, by which means I not only preferved the credit I gained on the
firft attempt, but always kept them in awe, and in fome degree of refpect
and obedience to me  In fact, ftrange as it may appear, it is almoft abfolutely neceffary that the chiefs at this place fhould profefs fomething a
little fupernatural, to be able to deal with thofe people  The circumftance here recorded is a fact well known to Mr William Jefferfon,
who fucceeded me at Churchill Factory, as well as to all the officers and
many of the common men who were at Prince of Wales's Fort at the
time.

times a threat of this kind caufes the death of a whole family; and that without any blood being fhed, or the leaft apparent moleftation being offered to any of the parties.

Having dried as many fifh and fifh-roes as we could conveniently take with us, we once more packed up our ftores, and, on the firft day of December, fet out, and continued our courfe to the South Weft, leaving Anaw'd Lake on the South Weft. Several of the Indians being out of order, we made but fhort days journies.

From the firft to the thirteenth, we walked along a courfe of fmall lakes, joined to each other by fmall rivers, or creeks, that have communication with Anaw'd Lake.

In our way we caught daily a few fifh by angling, and faw many beaver houfes, but thefe were generally in fo difficult a fituation, and had fo many ftones in the compofition of them, that the Indians killed but few, and that at a great expence of labour and tools.

On the thirteenth, one of the Indians killed two deer, which were the firft that we had feen fince the twentieth of October. So that during a period of near two months, we had lived on the dried meat that we had prepared at Point Lake, and a few fifh; of which the latter was not very confiderable in quantity, except what was caught at Anaw'd Lake. It is true, we alfo caught a few rabbits, and at times the wood-partridges were

fo plentiful, that the Indians killed confiderable
numbers of them with their bows and arrows,
but the number of mouths was fo great, that all
which was caught from our leaving Point Lake,
though if enumerated, they might appear very
confiderable, would not have afforded us all a
bare fubfiftence; for though I and fome others
experienced no real want, yet there were many
in our company who could fcarcely be faid to
live, and would not have exifted at all, had it not
been for the dry meat we had with us.

When we left the above-mentioned lakes we
fhaped a courfe more to the Southward, and on
the twenty-fourth, arrived at the North fide of
the great Athapufcow Lake. In our way we faw
many Indian deer, and beaver were very plentiful, many of which the Indians killed, but the
days were fo fhort, that the Sun only took a cir-
cuit of a few points of the compafs above the horizon, and did not, at its greateft altitude, rife,
half-way up the trees. The brilliancy of the
*Aurora Borealis*, however, and of the Stars, even
without the affiftance of the Moon, made fome
amends for that deficiency; for it was frequently fo light all night, that I could fee to read a very fmall print. The Indians make to difference
between night and day when they are hunting of
beaver; but thofe *noΩurnal* lights are always
found infufficient for the purpofe of hunting deer
or moofe.

1771.
December

24th

I do

I do not remember to have met with any travellers into high Northern latitudes, who remarked their having heard the Northern Lights make
any noise in the air as they vary their colours or
position; which may probably be owing to the
want of perfect silence at the time they made their
observations on those meteors. I can positively
affirm, that in still nights I have frequently heard
them make a rustling and crackling noise, like
the waving of a large flag in a fresh gale of wind.
This is not peculiar to the place of which I am
now writing, as I have heard the same noise very
plain at Churchill River; and in all probability
it is only for want of attention that it has not
been heard in every part of the Northern hemis-
phere where they have been known to shine
with any considerable degree of lustre. It is, however, very probable that these lights are sometimes much nearer the earth than they are at
others, according to the state of the atmosphere,
and this may have a great effect on the sound:
but the truth or falsehood of this conjecture I
leave to the determinations of those who are better skilled in natural philosophy than I can pretend
to be.

Indian deer (the only species found in those
parts, except the moose) are so much larger than
those which frequent the barren grounds to the
North of Churchill River, that a small doe is
equal in size to a Northern buck. The hair of
the

the former is of a fandy red during the Winter,
and their horns, though much ftronger, are not
fo long and branchy as are thofe of the latter
kind. Neither is the flefh of thofe deer fo much
efteemed by the Northern Indians, as that of the
fmaller kind, which inhabit the more Eaftern and
Northern parts of the country. Indeed, it muft
be allowed to be much coarfer, and of a different
flavour; inafmuch as the large Lincolnfhire mutton differs from grafs lamb. I muft acknowledge,
however, that I always thought it very good.
This is that fpecies of deer which are found fo
plentiful near York Fort and Severn River. They
are alfo at times found in confiderable numbers
near Churchill River; and I have feen them killed as far North, near the fea-fide, as Seal River:
But the fmall Northern Indian deer are feldom
known to crofs Churchill River, except in fome
very extraordinary cold feafons, and when the
Northern winds have prevailed much in the preceding fall; for thofe vifits are always made in
the Winter. But though I own that the flefh
of the large Southern deer is very good, I muft at
the fame time confefs that the flefh of the fmall
Northern deer, whether buck or doe, in their proper feafon, is by far more delicious and the fineft
I have ever eaten, either in this country or any
other; and is of that peculiar quality, that it never cloys. I can affirm this from my own experience; for, after living on it entirely, as it may
be faid, for twelve or eighteen months fucceffive-

Q                               ly,

ly, I fcarcely ever wifhed for a change of food; though when fifh or fowl came in my way, it was very agreeable.

The beaver being fo plentiful, the attention of my companions was chiefly engaged on them, as they not only furnifhed delicious food, but their fkins proved a valuable acquifition, being a principal article of trade, as well as a ferviceable one for clothing, &c.

The fituation of the beaver-houfes is various. Where the beavers are numerous they are found to inhabit lakes, ponds, and rivers, as well as thofe narrow creeks which connect the numerous lakes with which this country abounds; but the two latter are generally chofen by them when the depth of water and other circumftances are fuitable, as they have then the advantage of a current to convey wood and other neceffaries to their habitations, and becaufe, in general, they are more difficult to be taken, than thofe that are built in ftanding water.

There is no one particular part of a lake, pond, river, or creek, of which the beavers make choice for building their houfes on, in preference to another; for they fometimes build on points, fometimes in the hollow of a bay, and often on fmall iflands; they always chufe, however, thofe parts that have fuch a depth of water as will refift the froft in Winter, and prevent it from freezing to the bottom

The beaver that build their houfes in fmall rivers

vers or creeks, in which the water is liable to be drained off when the back supplies are dried up by the froft, are wonderfully taught by inftinct to provide againft that evil, by making a dam quite acrofs the river, at a convenient diftance from their houfes  This I look upon as the moft curious piece of workmanfhip that is performed by the beaver; not fo much for the neatnefs of the work, as for its ftrength and real fervice; and at the fame time it difcovers fuch a degree of fagacity and forefight in the animal, of approaching evils, as is little inferior to that of the human fpecies, and is certainly peculiar to thofe animals.

The beaver-dams differ in fhape according to the nature of the place in which they are built. If the water in the river or creek have but little motion, the dam is a'moft ftraight, but when the current is more rapid, it is always made with a confiderable curve, convex toward the ftream. The materials made ufe of in thofe dams are drift-wood, green willows, birch, and poplars, if they can be got; alfo mud and ftones, intermixed in fuch a manner as muft evidently contribute to the ftrength of the dam; but in thefe dams there is no other order or method obferved, except that of the work being carried on with a regular fweep, and all the parts being made of equal ftrength

In places which have been long frequented by beaver undifturbed, their dams, by frequent re-

pairing,

pairing, become a folid bank, capable of refifting a great force both of water and ice; and as the willow, poplar, and birch generally take root and fhoot up, they by degrees form a kind of regular planted hedge, which I have feen in fome places fo tall, that birds have built their nefts among the branches.

Though the beaver which build their houfes in lakes and other ftanding waters, may enjoy a fufficient quantity of their favourite element without the affiftance of a dam, the trouble of getting wood and other neceffaries to their habitations without the help of a current, muft in fome meafure counterbalance the other advantages which are reaped from fuch a fituation, for it muft be obferved, that the beaver which build in rivers and creeks, always cut their wood above their houfes, fo that the current, with little trouble, conveys it to the place required.

The beaver-houfes are built of the fame materials as their dams, and are always proportioned in fize to the number of inhabitants, which feldom exceed four old, and fix or eight young ones, though, by chance, I have feen above double that number.

Thefe houfes, though not altogether unworthy of admiration, fall very fhort of the general defcription given of them, for inftead of order or regulation being obferved in rearing them, they are of a much ruder ftructure than their dams.

Thofe

Those who have undertaken to describe the inside of beaver-houses, as having several apartments appropriated to various uses, such as eating, sleeping, store-houses for provisions, and one for their natural occasions, &c. must have been very little acquainted with the subject, or, which is still worse, guilty of attempting to impose on the credulous, by representing the greatest falsehoods as real facts. Many years constant residence among the Indians, during which I had an opportunity of seeing several hundreds of those houses, has enabled me to affirm that every thing of the kind is entirely void of truth; for, notwithstanding the sagacity of those animals, it has never been observed that they aim at any other conveniencies in their houses, than to have a dry place to lie on; and there they usually eat their victuals, which they occasionally take out of the water.

It frequently happens, that some of the large houses are found to have one or more partitions, if they deserve that appellation; but that is no more than a part of the main building, left by the sagacity of the beaver to support the roof. On such occasions it is common for those different apartments, as some are pleased to call them, to have no communication with each other but by water, so that in fact they may be called double or treble houses, rather than different apartments of the same house. I have seen a large beaver-house built in a small island, that had near a dozen apart-

apartments under one roof: and, two or three
of thefe only excepted, none of them had any
communication with each other but by water  As
there were beaver enough to inhabit each apart-
ment, it is more than probable that each family
knew its own, and always entered at their own
door, without having any farther connection
with their neighbours than a friendly intercourfe;
and to join their united labours in erecting their
feparate habitations, and building their dams
where required  It is difficult to fay whether
their intereft on other occafions was anyways reciprocal.  The Indians of my party killed twelve
old beaver, and twenty-five young and half grown
ones out of the houfe above mentioned, and on
examination found that feveral had efcaped their
vigilance, and could not be taken but at the expence of more trouble than would be fufficient
to take double the number in a lefs difficult
fituation*.

Travellers who affert that the beaver have two
doors to their houfes, one on the land fide, and
the other next the water, feem to be lefs acquainted with thofe animals than others who affign them
an elegant fuite of apartments.  Such a proceeding would be quite contrary to their manner of
life, and at the fame time would render their
houfes of no ufe, either to protect them from their
enemies,

---

* The difficulty here alluded to  was the numberlefs vaults the beaver
had in the fides of the pond, and the immenfe thicknefs of the houfe in
fome part

enemies, or guard them againſt the extreme cold
in Winter.

The quiquehatches, or wolvereens, are great
enemies to the beaver, and if there were a
paſſage into their houſes on the land-ſide, would
not leave one of them alive wherever they
came.

I cannot refrain from ſmiling, when I read the
accounts of different Authors who have written
on the œconomy of thoſe animals, as there ſeems
to be a conteſt between them, who ſhall moſt exceed in fiction. But the Compiler of the Won-
ders of Nature and Art ſeems, in my opinion, to
have ſucceeded beſt in this reſpect; as he has not
only collected all the fictions into which other
writers on the ſubject have run, but has ſo greatly improved on them, that little remains to be
added to his account of the beaver, beſide a vocabulary of their language, a code of their laws, and
a ſketch of their religion, to make it the moſt
complete natural hiſtory of that animal which can
poſſibly be offered to the public.

There cannot be a greater impoſition, or indeed
a groſſer inſult, on common underſtanding, than
the wiſh to make us believe the ſtories of ſome of
the works aſcribed to the beaver, and though it
is not to be ſuppoſed that the compiler of a general work can be intimately acquainted with every
ſubject of which it may be neceſſary to treat, yet a
very moderate ſhare of underſtanding is ſurely
ſufficient to guard him againſt giving credit to
ſuch

such marvellous tales, however smoothly they may be told, or however boldly they may be asserted, by the romancing traveller.

To deny that the beaver is possessed of a very considerable degree of sagacity, would be as absurd in me, as it is in those Authors who think they cannot allow them too much  I shall willingly grant them their full share, but it is impossible for any one to conceive how, or by what means, a beaver, whose full height when standing erect does not exceed two feet and a half, or three feet at most, and whose fore-paws are not much larger than a half-crown piece, can "drive " stakes as thick as a man's leg into the ground " three or four feet deep "  Their " wattling " those stakes with twigs," is equally absurd ; " and their "plaistering the inside of their houses " with a composition of mud and straw, and " swimming with mud and stones on their tails," are still more incredible.  The form and size of the animal, notwithstanding all its sagacity,  will not admit of its performing such feats ; and it would be as impossible for a beaver to use its tail as a trowel, except on the surface of the ground on which it walks, as it would have been for Sir James Thornhill to have painted the dome of St. Paul's cathedral without the assistance of scaffolding  The joints of their tail will not admit of their turning it over their backs on any occasion whatever, as it has a natural inclination to bend downwards, and it is not without some considerable

rable exertion that they can keep it from trailing
on the ground.    This being the cafe, they cannot
fit erect like a fquirrel, which is their common
pofture: particularly when eating, or when they
are cleaning themfelves, as a cat or fquirrel does,
without having their tails bent forward between
their legs, and which may not improperly be called their trencher.

So far are the beaver from driving ftakes into
the ground when building their houfes, that they
lay moft of the wood crofswife, and nearly hori-
zontal, and without any other order than that of
leaving a hollow or cavity in the middle, when
any unneceffary branches project inward, they
cut them off with their teeth, and throw them in
among the reft, to prevent the mud from falling
through the roof.    It is a miftaken notion, that
the wood-work is firft completed and then plai-
ftered, for the whole of their houfes, as well as
their dams, are from the foundation one mafs of
wood and mud, mixed with ftones, if they can
be procured.    The mud is always taken from
the edge of the bank, or the bottom of the creek
or pond, near the door of the houfe, and though
their fore-paws are fo fmall, yet it is held clofe
up between them, under their throat, that they
carry both mud and ftones, while they always
drag the wood with their teeth

All their work is executed in the night, and
they are fo expeditious in completing it, that in
the courfe of one night I have known them to
have

have collected as much mud at their houfes as to have amounted to fome thoufands of their little handfuls; and when any mixture of grafs or ftraw has appeared in it, it has been, moft affuredly, mere chance, owing to the nature of the ground from which they had taken it. As to their defignedly making a compofition for that purpofe, it is entirely void of truth.

It is a great piece of policy in thofe animals, to cover, or plaifter, as it is ufually called, the outfide of their houfes every fall with frefh mud, and as late as poffible in the Autumn, even when the froft becomes pretty fevere; as by this means it foon freezes as hard as a ftone, and prevents their common enemy, the quiquehatch, from difturbing them during the Winter. And as they are frequently feen to walk over their work, and fometimes to give a flap with their tail, particularly when plunging into the water, this has, without doubt, given rife to the vulgar opinion that they ufe their tails as a trowel, with which they plaifter their houfes, whereas that flapping of the tail is no more than a cuftom, which they always preferve, even when they become tame and domeftic, and more particularly fo when they are ftartled

Their food chiefly confifts of a large root, fomething refembling a cabbage-ftalk, which grows at the bottom of the lakes and rivers. They eat alfo the bark of trees, particularly that of the poplar, birch, and willow; but the ice

pre-

preventing them from getting to the land in Winter, they have not any barks to feed upon during that feafon, except that of fuch fticks as they cut down in Summer, and throw into the water oppofite the doors of their houfes, and as they generally eat a great deal, the roots above mentioned conftitute a chief part of their food during the Winter  In fummer they vary their diet, by eating various kinds of herbage, and fuch berries as grow near their haunts during that feafon.

When the ice breaks up in the fpring, the beaver always leave their houfes, and rove about the whole Summer, probably in fearch of a more commodious fituation; but in cafe of not fucceeding in their endeavours, they return again to their old habitations a little before the fall of the leaf, and lay in their Winter ftock of woods. They feldom begin to repair the houfes till the froft commences, and never finifh the outer-coat till the cold is pretty fevere, as hath been already mentioned.

When they fhift their habitations, or when the increafe of their number renders it neceffary to make fome addition to their houfes, or to erect new ones, they begin felling the wood for thefe purpofes early in the Summer, but feldom begin to build till the middle or latter end of Auguft, and never complete their houfes till the cold weather be fet in.

Not-

Notwithstanding what has been so repeatedly reported of those animals assembling in great bodies, and jointly erecting large towns, cities, and commonwealths, as they have sometimes been called, I am confident, from many circumstances, that even where the greatest numbers of beaver are situated in the neighbourhood of each other, their labours are not carried on jointly in the erection of their different habitations, nor have they any reciprocal interest, except it be such as live immediately under the same roof, and then it extends no farther than to build or keep a dam which is common to several houses. In such cases it is natural to think that every one who receives benefit from such dams, should assist in erecting it, being sensible of its utility to all.

Persons who attempt to take beaver in Winter should be thoroughly acquainted with their manner of life, otherwise they will have endless trouble to effect their purpose, and probably without success in the end; because they have always a number of holes in the banks, which serve them as places of retreat when any injury is offered to their houses, and in general it is in those holes that they are taken.

When the beaver which are situated in a small river or creek are to be taken, the Indians sometimes find it necessary to stake the river across, to prevent them from passing, after which, they endeavour to find out all their holes or places of retreat in the banks. This requires much practice

tice

tice and experience to accomplifh, and is performed in the following manner· Every man being furnifhed with an ice-chifel, lafhes it to the end of a fmall ftaff about four or five feet long; he then walks along the edge of the binks, and keeps knocking his chifels againft the ice   Thofe who are well acquainted with that kind of work well know by the found of the ice when they are oppofite to any of the beaver' holes or vaults. As foon as they fufpect any, they cut a hole through the ice big enough to admit an old beaver, and in this manner proceed till they have found out all their places of retreat, or at leaft as many of them as poffible.   While the principal men are thus employed, fome of the underftrappers, and the women, are bufy in breaking open the houfe, which at times is no eafy talk; for I have frequently known thefe houfes to be five and fix feet thick, and one in particular, was more than eight feet thick on the crown.   When the beaver find that their habitations are invaded, they fly to their holes in the banks for fhelter; and on being perceived by the Indians, which is eafily done, by attending to the motion of the water, they block up the entrance with ftakes of wood, and then haul the beaver out of its hole, either by hand, if they can reach it, or with a large hook made for that purpofe, which is faftened to the end of a long ftick.

In this kind of hunting, every man has the fole right to all the beaver caught by him in the holes

or

or vaults; and as this is a conftant rule, each perfon takes care to mark fuch as he difcovers, by
fticking up the branch of a tree, or fome other
diftinguifhing poft, by which he may know them.
All that are caught in the houfe alfo are the property of the perfon who finds it.

The fame regulations are obferved, and the
fame procefs ufed in taking beaver that are found
in lakes and other ftanding waters, except it be
that of ftaking the lake acrofs, which would be
both unneceffary and impoffible. Taking beaver-
houfes in thefe fituations is generally attended
with lefs trouble and more fuccefs than in the
former.

The beaver is an animal which cannot keep
under water long at a time; fo that when their
houfes are broke open, and all their places of retreat difcovered, they have but one choice left, as
it may be called, either to be taken in their houfes or their vaults: in general they prefer the latter; for where there is one beaver caught in the
houfe, many thoufands are taken in their vaults
in the banks. Sometimes they are caught in nets,
and in the Summer very frequently in traps. In
Winter they are very fat and delicious; but the
trouble of rearing their young, the thinnefs of
their hair, and their conftantly roving from place
to place, with the trouble they have in providing
againft the approach of Winter, generally keep
them very poor during the fummer feafon, at
which time their flefh is but indifferent eating,
and

and their fkins of fo little value, that the Indians generally finge them, even to the amount of many thoufands in one Summer. They have from two to five young, at a time. Mr. Dobbs, in his Account of Hudfon's Bay, enumerates no lefs than eight different kinds of beaver, but it muft be underftood that they are all of one kind and fpecies; his diftinctions arife wholly from the different feafons of the year in which they are killed, and the different ufes to which their fkins are applied which is the fole reafon that they vary fo much in value.

Jofeph Lefranc, or Mr Dobbs for him, fays, that a good hunter can kill fix hundred beaver in one feafon, and can only carry one hundred to market. If that was really the cafe in Lefranc's time, the canoes muft have been much fmaller than they are at prefent, for it is well known that the generality of the canoes which have vifited the Company's Factories for the laft forty or fifty years, are capable of carrying three hundred beaver-fkins with great eafe, exclufive of the Indians luggage, provifions, &c.

If ever a particular Indian killed fix hundred beaver in one Winter, (which is rather to be doubted, it is more than probable that many in his company did not kill twenty, and perhaps fome none at all, fo that by diftributing them among thof who had bad fuccefs, and others who had no abilities for that kind of hunting, there would

would be no neceffity of leaving them to rot, or for finging them in the fire, as related by the Author. During my refidence among the Indians I have known fome individuals kill more beaver, and other heavy furrs, in the courfe of a Winter, than their wives could manage ; but the ove plus was never wantonly deftroyed, but always given to their relations, or to thofe who had been lefs fuccefsful, fo that the whole of the great hunters labours were always brought to the Factory. It is indeed too frequently a cuftom among the Southern Indians to finge many otters, as well as beaver; but this is feldom done, except in Summer, when their fkins are of fo little value as to be fcarcely worth the duty; on which account it has been always thought impolitic to encourage the natives to kill fuch valuable animals at a time when their fkins are not in feafon.

The white beaver, mentioned by Lefranc, are fo rare, that inftead of being " blown upon by the Company's Factors," as he afferts, I rather doubt whether one-tenth of them ever faw one during the time of their refidence in this country. In the courfe of twenty years experience in the countries about Hudfon's Bay, though I travelled fix hundred miles to the Weft of the fea-coaft, I never faw but one white beaver-fkin, and it had many reddifh and brown hairs along the ridge of the back, and the fides and belly were of a gloffy
filvery

filvery white. It was deemed by the Indians a
great curiofity; and I offered three times the
ufual price for a few of them, if they could be got,
but in the courfe of ten years that I remained
there afterwards, I could not procure another;
which is a convincing proof there is no fuch thing
as a breed of that kind, and that a variation from
the ufual colour is very rare

Black beaver, and that of a beautiful glofs, are
not uncommon: perhaps they are more plentiful
at Churchill than at any other Factory in the
Bay, but it is rare to get more than twelve
or fifteen of their fkins in the courfe of one year's
trade.

Lefranc, as an Indian, muft have known better
than to have informed Mr. Dobbs that the beaver have from ten to fifteen young at a time, or
if he did, he muft have deceived him wilfully;
for the Indians, by killing them in all ftages of
geftation, have abundant opportunities of afcertaining the ufual number of their offspring. I
have feen fome hundreds of them killed at the
feafons favourable for thofe obfervations, and
never could difcover more than fix young in one
female, and that only in two inftances; for the
ufual number, as I have before obferved, is from
two to five.

Befides this unerring method of afcertaining
the real number of young which any animal has
at a time, there is another rule to go by, with

R                          refpect

respect to the beaver, which experience has proved to the Indians never to vary or deceive them,
that is by diffection; for on examining the womb
of a beaver, even at a time when not with young,
there is always found a hardish round knob for
every young she had at the laft litter. This is a
circumftance I have been particularly careful to
examine, and can affirm it to be true, from real
experience.

Moft of the accounts, nay I may fay all the
accounts now extant, refpecting the beaver, are
taken from the authority of the French who have
refided in Canada; but thofe accounts differ fo
much from the real ftate and œconomy of all the
beaver to the North of that place, as to leave
great room to fufpect the truth of them altogether. In the firft place, the affertion that they
have two doors to their houfes, one on the land-
fide, and the other next the water, is, as I have
before obferved, quite contrary to fact and common fenfe, as it would render their houfes of no
ufe to them, either as places of fhelter from the
inclemency of the extreme cold in Winter, or as
a retreat from their common enemy the quiquehatch. The only thing that could have made
M Du Pratz, and other French writers, conjecture that fuch a thing did exift, muft have been
from having feen fome old beaver houfes which
had been taken by the Indians, for they are always obliged to make a hole in one fide of the
houfe

houfe before they can drive them out; and it is
more than probable that in fo mild a climate as
Canada, the Indians do generally make thofe holes
on the land fide\*, which without doubt gave rife
to the fuggeftion.

In refpect to the beaver dunging in their houfes,
as fome perfons affert, it is quite wrong as they
always plunge into the water to do it.  I am the
better enabled to make this affertion, from having kept feveral of them till they became fo domefticated as to anfwer to their name, and follow
thofe to whom they were accuftomed, in the fame
manner as a dog would do, and they were as
much pleafed at being fondled, as any animal I
ever faw.  I had a houfe built for them, and a
fmall piece of water before the door, into which
they always plunged when they wanted to eafe
nature; and their dung being of light a fubftance,
immediately rifes and floats on the furface; then
feparates and fubfides to the bottom.  When
the Winter fets in fo as to freeze the water folid,
they ftill continue their cuftom of coming out
of their houfe, and dunging and making water
on the ice, and when the weather was fo cold
that I was obliged to take them into my houfe,

R 2                    they

---

\* The Northern Indians think that the fagacity of the beaver directs
them to make that part of their houfe which fronts the North fuch
thicker than any other part, with a view of defending themfelves from
the cold winds which generally blow from that quarter during the Winter, and for this reafon the Northern Indians generally break open that
fide of the beaver houfes which exactl front the South

they always went into a large tub of water which
I set for that purpofe : so that they made not the
leaft dirt, though they were kept in my own fit-
ting-room, where they were the conftant companions of the Indian women and children, and
were fo fond of their company, that when the
Indians were abfent for any confiderable time,
the beaver difcovered great figns of uneafinefs,
and on their return fhewed equal marks of pleafure, by fondling on them, crawling into their
laps, laying on their backs, fitting erect like a
fquirrel, and behaving to them like children who
fee their parents but feldom.   In general, during
the Winter they lived on the fame food as the
women did, and were remarkably fond of rice
and plum-pudding : they would eat partridges
and frefh venifon very freely, but I never tried
them with fifh, though I have heard they will at
times prey on them.   In fact, there are few of
the granivorous animals that may not be brought
to be carnivorous.   It is well known that our domeftic poultry will eat animal food : thoufands
of geefe that come to London market are fattened
on tallow-craps ; and our horfes in Hudfon's Bay
would not only eat all kinds of animal food, but
alfo drink freely of the wafh, or pot-liquor, intended for the hogs.   And we are affured by the
moft authentic Authors, that in Iceland, not only
black cattle, but alfo the fheep, are almoft entirely fed on fifh and fifh bones during the Winter
                                                feafon.

feafon. Even in the Ifles of Orkney, and that in
Summer, the fheep attend the ebbing of the tide
as regular as the Efquimaux curlew, and go down
to the fhore which the tide has left, to feed on
the fea-weed. This, however, is through neceffity, for even the famous Ifland of Pomona* will
not afford them an exiftence above high-water-
mark.

With refpect to the inferior, or flave-beaver, of
which fome Authors fpeak, it is, in my opinion,
very difficult for thofe who are beft acquainted
with the œconomy of this animal to determine
whether there are any that deferve that appellation or not. It fometimes happens, that a beaver
is caught, which has but a very indifferent coat,
and which has broad patches on the back, and
fhoulders almoft wholly without hair. This is
the only foundation for afferting that there is an
inferior, or flave-beaver, among them. And
when one of the above defcription is taken, it is
perhaps too haftily inferred that the hair is worn
off from thofe parts by carrying heavy loads:
whereas it is moft probable that it is caufed by a
diforder that attacks them fomewhat fimilar to
the mange, for were that falling off of the hair
occafioned by performing extra labour, it is natural to think that inftances of it would be more
frequent than they are, as it is rare to fee one of
them

* This being the largeft of the Orkney Iflands, is called by the Inhab-
tants the Main Land.

them in the courfe of feven or ten years.  I have feen a whole houfe of thofe animals that had no-thing on the furface of their bodies but the fine foft down ; all the long hairs having molted off. This and every other deviation from the general run is undoubtedly owing to fome particular dif-order.

CHAP.

## C H A P. VIII.

Tranfactions and Remarks from our Arrival on the South Side of the Athapufcow Lake, till our Arrival at Prince of Wales's Fort on Churchill River.

*Crofs the Athapufcow Lake.—Defcription of it and its productions, as far as could be difcovered in Winter, when the fnow was on the ground. Fifh found in the lake.—Defcription of the buffalo;— of the moofe or elk, and the method of dreffing their fkins.—Find a woman alone that had not feen a human face for more than feven months.—Her account how fhe came to be in that fituation, and her curious method of procuring a livelihood.—Many of my Indians wreftled for her.—Arrive at the Great Athapufcow River.—Walk along the fide of the River for feveral days, and then ftrike off to the Eaftward.—Difficulty in getting through the woods in many places.—Meet with fome ftrange Northern Indians on their return from the Fort.—Meet more ftrangers, whom my companions plundered, and from whom they took one of their young women.—Curious manner of life which thofe ftrangers lead, and the reafon they gave for roving fo far from their ufual refidence.—Leave the fine level country of the Athapufcows, and arrive at the Stony Hills of the Northern Indian Country.—Meet fome ftrange Northern Indians, one of whom carried a letter for me to Prince*

*Prince of Wales's Fort, in March one thousand seven
hundred and seventy-one, and now gave me an answer to it, dated twentieth of June following.—
Indians begin preparing wood-work and birch rind
for canoes.—The equinoctial gale very severe.—
Indian method of running the moose deer down by
speed of foot.—Arrival at Theeleyaza River.—
See some strangers—The brutality of my companions—A tremendous gale and snow-drift.—Meet
with more strangers;—remarks on it.—Leave all
the elderly people and children, and proceed directly
to the Fort.—Stop to build canoes, and then advance—Several of the Indians die through hunger,
and many others are obliged to decline the journey for
want of ammunition.—A violent storm and inunda-
tion, that forced us to the top of a high hill, where
we suffered great distress for more than two days.
—Kill several deer.—The Indians method of pre-
serving the flesh without the assistance of salt.—See
several Indians that were going to Knapp's Bay—
Game of all kinds remarkably plentiful.—Arrive at
the Factory.*

1772.
January
9th.

AFTER expending some days in hunting beaver, we proceeded to cross the Athapuscow Lake; but as we had lost much time in
hunting deer and beaver, which were very plentiful on some of the islands, it was the ninth of
January before we arrived on the South side.

This lake from the best information which I
could get from the natives, is about one hundred
and

A WINTER VIEW in the ATHAPUSCOW LAKE, by Saml HEARNE 1771

and twenty leagues long from East to West, and twenty wide from North to South. The point where we croffed it is faid to be the narroweft. It is full of iflands; moft of which are clothed with fine tall poplars, birch, and pines, and are well flocked with Indian deer. On fome of the large iflands we alfo found feveral beaver, but this muft be underftood only of fuch iflands as had large ponds in them; for not one beaver-houfe was to be feen on the margin of any of them.

The lake is ftored with great quantities of very fine fifh; particularly between the iflands, which in fome parts are fo clofe to each other as to form very narrow channels, like little rivers, in which I found (when angling for fifh) a confiderable current fetting to the Eaftward.

The fifh that are common in this lake, as well as in moft of the other lakes in this country, are pike, trout, perch, barble, tittameg, and methy; the two laft are names given by the natives to two fpecies of fifh which are found only in this country. Befides thefe, we alfo caught another kind of fifh, which is faid by the Northern Indians to be peculiar to this lake; at leaft none of the fame kind have been met with in any other. The body of this fifh much refembles a pike in fhape; but the fcales, which are very large and ftiff, are of a beautifully bright filver colour: the mouth is large, and fituated like that of a pike; but when open, much refembles that of a fturgeon;

and

and though not provided with any teeth, takes a bait as ravenously as a pike or a trout. The fizes we caught were from two feet long to four feet. Their flesh, though delicately white, is very soft, and has so rank a taste, that many of the Indians, except they are in absolute want, will not eat it. The northern Indians call this fish Shees The trout in this lake are of the largest size I ever saw: some that were caught by my companions could not, I think, be less than thirty-five or forty pounds weight. Pike are also of an incredible size in this extensive water; here they are seldom molested, and have multitudes of smaller fish to prey upon. If I say that I have seen some of these fish that were upwards of forty pounds weight, I am sure I do not exceed the truth.

Immediately on our arrival on the South side of the Athapuscow Lake, the scene was agreeably altered, from an entire jumble of rocks and hills, for such is all the land on the North side, to a fine level country, in which there was not a hill to be seen, or a stone to be found: so that such of my companions as had not brass kettles, loaded their sledges with stones from some of the last islands, to boil their victuals with in their birch-rind kettles, which will not admit of being exposed to the fire. They therefore heat stones and drop them into the water in the kettle to make it boil.

Buffalo, moose, and beaver were very plentiful; and we could discover, in many parts through which

which we paffed, the tracks of martins, foxes, quiquehatches, and other animals of the furr kind; fo that they were by no means fcarce: but my companions never gave themfelves the leaft trouble to catch any of the three laft mentioned animals; for the buffalo, moofe, and beaver engaged all their attention, perhaps principally fo on account of the excellency of their flefh; whereas the flefh of the fox and quiquehatch are never eaten by thofe people, except when they are in the greateft diftrefs, and then meiely to fave life. their reafons for this fhall be given in a fubfequent part of my Journal.

The buffalo in thofe parts, I think, are in general much larger than the Englifh black cattle; particularly the bulls, which, though they may not in reality be taller than the largeft fize of the Englifh oxen, yet to me always appeared to be much larger. In fact, they are fo heavy, that when fix or eight Indians are in company at the fkinning of a large bull, they never attempt to turn it over while entire, but when the upper fide is fkinned, they cut off the leg and fhoulder, rip up the belly, take out all the inteftines, cut off the head, and make it as light as poffible, before they turn it to fkin the under fide. The fkin is in fome places of an incredible thicknefs, particularly about the neck, where it often exceeds an inch The horns are fhort, black, and almoft ftraight, but very thick at the roots or bafe.

The

1772.
January

The head of an old bull is of a great size and weight indeed : some which I have seen were so large, that I could not without difficulty lift them from the ground\*; but the heads of the cows are much smaller. Their tails are, in general, about a foot long, though some appear to be exclusive of the long brush of hair at the end, longer. The hair on the tails of the bulls is generally of a fine glossy black, but the brush at the end of the cows' tails is always of a rusty brown, probably owing to being stained with their urine.

The hair of the body is soft and curled, somewhat approaching to wool; it is generally of a sandy brown, and of an equal length and thickness all over the body: but on the head and neck it is much longer than it is on any other part.

The Indians, after reducing all the parts of the skin to an equal thickness by scraping, dress them in the hair for clothing, when they are light, soft, warm, and durable. They also dress some of those skins into leather without the hair, of which they make tents and shoes; but the grain

is

* It is remarked by Mr Catesby, in his description of this animal, that no man can lift one of their heads  Those I saw in the Athapuscow country are such as I have described , and I am assured by the Company's servants, as well as the Indians who live near Hudson's House, that the buffalos there are much smaller, so that the species Mr Catesby saw, or wrote of, must have been much larger, or have had very large heads, for it is well known that a man of any tolerable strength can lift two and a half, or three hundred pounds weight  I think that the heads of his buffalos are too heavy for the bodies, as the bodies of those I saw in the Athapuscow country appear to have been of equal weight with his

is remarkably open and fpungy, by no means
equal in goodnefs to that of the fkin of the moofe .
nor am I certain that the curriers or tanners in
Europe could manufacture thefe fkins in fuch a
manner as to render them of any confiderable
value; for, to appearance, they are of the fame
quality which the fkins of the mufk-ox, which
are held in fo little eftimation in England, that
when a number of them was fent home from
Churchill Factory, the Company iffued out orders
the year following, that unlefs they could be purchafed from the Indians at the rate of four fkins
for one beaver, they would not anfwer the expence
of fending home; a great proof of their being of
very little value.

The buffalos chiefly delight in wide open
plains, which in thofe parts produce very long
coarfe grafs, or rather a kind of fmall flags and
rufhes, upon which they feed; but when purfued
they always take to the woods  They are of
fuch an amazing ftrength, that when they fly
through the woods from a purfuer, they frequently brufh down trees as thick as a man's arm;
and be the fnow ever fo deep, fuch is their ftrength
and agility that they are enabled to plunge
through it fafter than the fwifteft Indian can run
in fnow-fhoes. To this I have been an eye-wit-
nefs many times, and once had the vanity to think
that I could have kept pace with them; but
though I w , at that time celebrated for being
particularly fleet of foot in fnow fhoes, I foon
found

found that I was no match for the buffalos, notwithftanding they were then plunging through
fuch deep fnow, that their bellies made a trench
in it as large as if many heavy facks had been
hauled through it. Of all the large beafts in thofe
parts the buffalo is eafieft to kill, and the moofe
are the moft difficult; neither are the deer very
eafy to come at, except in windy weather: indeed
it requires much practice, and a great deal of patience, to flay any of them, as they will by no
means fuffer, a direct approach, unlefs the hunter
be entirely fheltered by woods or willows. The
flefh of the buffalo is exceedingly good eating;
and fo entirely free from any difagreeable fmell or
tafte, that it refembles beef as nearly as poffible:
the flefh of the cows, when fome time gone with
calf, is efteemed the fineft, and the young calves,
cut out of their bellies, are reckoned a great delicacy indeed. The hunch on their backs, or more
properly on their fhoulders, is not a large flefhy
lump, as fome fuppofe, but is occafioned by the
bones that form the withers being continued to
a greater length than in moft other animals.
The flefh which furrounds this part being fo equally intermixed with fat and lean, is reckoned
among the niceft bits The weight, however, is
by no means equal to what has been commonly
reported. The tongue is alfo very delicate, and
what is moft extraordinary, when the beafts are
in the pooreft ftate, which happens regularly at
certain feafons, their tongues are then very fat
and

and fine; fome fay, fatter than when they are in
the beft order, the truth of which, I will not
confirm. They are fo efteemed here, however,
that many of them are brought down to the
Company's Factory at York as prefents, and are
efteemed a great luxury, probably for no other
reafon but that they are far-fetched; for they
are by no means fo large, and I think them not
fo fine, as a neat's tongue in England.

The moofe deer is alfo a large beaft, often exceeding the largeft horfe both in height and bulk;
but the length of the legs, the bulk of the body,
the fhortnefs of the neck, and the uncommon
length of the head and ears, without any appearance of a tail, make them have a very aukward
appearance. The males far exceed the females
in fize, and differ from them in colour. The
hair of the male, which is long, hollow, and foft,
like that of a deer, is at the points nearly black,
but a little way under the furface it is of an afh-
colour, and at the roots perfectly white The
hair of the female is of a fandy brown, and in
fome parts, particularly under the throat, the
belly, and the flank, is nearly white at the furface, and moft delicately fo at the root.

Their legs are fo long, and their necks fo fhort,
that they cannot graze on level ground like other
animals, but are obliged to brouze on the tops of
large plants and the leaves of trees during the
Summer, and in Winter they always feed on the
tops of willows, and the fmall branches of the
biich-

birch-tree; on which account they are never found during that feafon but in fuch places as can afford them a plentiful fupply of their favourite food: and though they have no fore-teeth in the upper-jaw, yet I have often feen willows and fmall birch-trees cropped by them, in the fame manner as if they had been cut by a gardener's fheers, though fome of them were not fmaller than common pipe-ftems; they feem particularly partial to the red willow.

In Summer they are generally found to frequent the banks of rivers and lakes, probably with no other view than to have the benefit of getting into the water, to avoid the innumerable multitudes of mufkettos and other flies that pefter them exceedingly during that feafon. There is alfo a variety of water-plants, of which the moofe are very fond, and which are adapted to their neceffities in a peculiar manner during the Summer feafon, as they can eafily brouze on them when nearly emerged in water, to avoid the torment of the flies.

The head of the moofe is, as I have obferved, remarkably long and large, not very unlike that of a horfe; but the nofe and noftrils are at leaft twice as large. The ears are about a foot long, and large; and they always ftand erect. Their faculty of hearing is fuppofed to be more acute than either their fight or fcent; which makes it very difficult to kill them, efpecially as the Indians in thofe parts have no other method

of

of doing it but by creeping after them, among the trees and bushes, till they get within gun-shot, taking care always to keep to leeward of the moose, for fear of being overheard. In Summer, when they frequent the margins of rivers and lakes, they are often killed by the Indians in the water, while they are crossing rivers, or swim- ming from the main to islands, &c. When pursu- ed in this manner, they are the most inoffensive of all animals, never making any resistance, and the young ones are so simple, that I remember to have seen an Indian paddle his canoe up to one of them, and take it by the poll without the least opposition : the poor harmless animal seeming at the same time as contented along side the canoe, as if swimming by the side of its dam, and look- ing up in our faces with the same fearless inno- cence that a house-lamb would, making use of its fore-foot almost every instant to clear its eyes of muskettoes, which at that time were remarkably numerous.

I have also seen women and boys kill the old moose in this situation, by knocking them on the head with a hatchet ; and in the Summer of one thousand seven hundred and seventy-five, when I was on my passage from Cumberland House to York Fort, two boys killed a fine buck moose in the water, by forcing a stick up its fundament; for they had neither gun, bow, nor arrows with them. The common deer are far more dangerous to approach in canoes, as they kick up their hind

S                                  legs

legs with such violence as to endanger any birch-
rind canoe that comes within their reach, for
which reason all the Indians who kill deer upon
the water are provided with a long stick that will
reach far beyond the head of the canoe.

The moose are also the easiest to tame and do-
mesticate of any of the deer kind. I have repeatedly seen them at Churchill as tame as sheep*,
and even more so; for they would follow their
keeper any distance from home, and at his call
return with him, without the least trouble, or
ever offering to deviate from the path†.

The flesh of the moose is very good, though the
grain is but coarse, and it is much tougher than
any other kind of venison. The nose is most excellent, as is also the tongue, though by no means
so fat and delicate as that of the common deer.
It is perhaps worth remarking, that the livers of
the

---

* The moose formerly sent to his Majesty was from that place. A young
male was also put on board the ship, but it died on the passage, otherwise it
is probable they might have propagated in this country.

† Since the above was written, the same Indian that brought all the
above-mentioned young moose to the Factory hall, in the year 1777, two
others, so tame, that when on his passage to Prince of Wales's Fort in a
canoe, the moose always followed him long the bank of the river, and at
night, or on any other occasion when the Indians landed, the young moose
generally came and fondled on them, in the same manner as the most domestic animal would have done, and never offered to stray from the tents.
Unfortunately, in crossing a deep bay in one of the lakes, (on a fine day,)
all the Indians that were not interested in the safe landing of those engaging creatures, paddled from point to point, and the man that owned them,
not caring to go so far about by himself, accompanied the others, in hopes
they would follow him round as usual, but at night the young moose did
not arrive, and as the howling of some wolves was heard in that quarter,
it was supposed they had been devoured by them, as they were never afterward seen.

the moofe are never found, not even at any time of the year; and, like the other deer, they have no gall. The fat of the inteftines is hard, like fuet, but all the external fat is foft, like that of a breaft of mutton, and when put into a bladder, is as fine as marrow  In this they differ from all the other fpecies of deer, of which the external fat is as hard as that of the kidnies.

The moofe in all their actions and attitudes appear very uncouth, and when difturbed, never run, only make a kind of trot, which the length of their legs enables them to do with great fwiftnefs, and apparently with much eafe, but were the country they inhabit free from under-wood, and dry under-foot, fo that horfemen and dogs might follow them, they would become an eafy prey, as they are both tender-footed and fhort-winded · But of this more hereafter*.

The fkins of the moofe, when dreffed by the natives, make excellent tent-covers and fhoe-leather; and in fact every other part of their clothing  Thefe, like the fkins of the buffalo, are of very unequal thicknefs  Some of the Indian women, who are acquainted with the manufacture of them, will, by means of fcraping, render them as even as a piece of thick cloth, and when well dreffed they are very foft; but not being dreff-

S 2                                    ed

*Mr Du Pratz, in his defcription of this animal, fays, it is never found farther North than Cape Breton and Nova Scotia  but I have feen them in great numbers in the Athapufcow Country, which cannot be much fhort of 60° North latitude

ed in oil, they always grow hard after being wet,
unlefs great care be taken to keep rubbing them
all the time they are drying.   The fame may be
faid of all the Indian-dreffed leather, except that
of the wewafkifh, which will wafh as well as
fhammoy-leather, and always preferve its foftnefs.

The female moofe never have any horns, but the
males have them of a prodigious fize and weight,
and very different in fhape from thofe of the
common deer.   The extremity of each horn is
palmated to the fize of a common fhovel, from
which a few fhort branches fhoot out, and the
fhaft of the horn is frequently as large as a common man's wrift.   They fhed them annually like
the common deer.   The horns of the moofe are
frequently found to exceed fixty pounds weight;
and their texture,  though of a large fize and of
fuch rapid growth, is much harder than any other
fpecies of deer-horns in thofe parts.

Though the flefh  of the moofe is efteemed by
moft Indians both  for its flavour and fubftance,
yet the Northern Indians of my crew did not
reckon either it or the flefh of the buffalo fubftantial food.   This I fhould think entirely proceeded from prejudice, efpecially with refpect to
the moofe, but the flefh of the buffalo, though fo
fine to the eye, and pleafing to the tafte, is fo
light and eafy of digeftion, as not to be deemed
fubftantial food by any Indian in this country,
either Northern or Southern.   The moofe have
from one to three young at a time, and generally
bring

bring them forth in the latter end of April, or

beginning of May.

Soon after our arrival no the South-fide of
Athapufcow Lake, Matonabbee propofed continuing our courfe in the South Weft quarter, in
hopes of meeting fome of the Athapufcow Indians; becaufe I wifhed, if poffible, to purchafe a
tent, and other ready-dreffed fkins from them,
as a fupply of thofe articles would at this time
have been of material fervice to us, being in great
want both of tents and fhoe-leather: and though
my companions were daily killing either moofe or
buffalo, the weather was fo exceffively cold, as to
render dreffing their fkins not only very troublefome, but almoft impracticable, efpecially to the
generality of the Northern Indians, who are not
well acquainted with the manufacture of that kind
of leather.

To drefs thofe fkins according to the Indian
method, a lather is made of the brains and fome
of the fofteft fat or marrow of the animal, in
which the fkin is well foaked, when it is taken
out, and not only dried by the heat of a fire, but
hung up in the fmoke for feveral days; it is then
taken down, and well foaked and wafhed in warm
water, till the grain of the fkin is perfectly open,
and has imbibed a fufficient quantity of water,
after which it is taken out and wrung as dry as
poffible, and then dried by the heat of a flow fire;
care being taken to rub and ftretch it as long as
any moifture remains in the fkin. By this fimple
method,

method, and by fcraping them afterwaids, fome
of the moofe fkins are made very delicate both to
the eye and the touch.

11.b    On the eleventh of January, as fome of my
companions were hunting, they faw the track of a
ftrange fnow-fhoe, which tney followed; and at a
confiderable diftance came to a little hut, where
they difcovered a young woman fitting alone  As
they found that fhe underftood their language,
they brought her with them to the tents.   On
examination, fhe proved to be one of the Weftern
Dogribbed Indians, who had been taken prifoner
by the Athapufcow Indians in the Summer of one
thoufand feven hundred and feventy , and in the
following Summer, when the Indians that took
her prifoner were near this part, fhe had eloped
from them, with an intent to return to her own
countr' ; but the diftance being fo great, and having after fhe was taken prifoner, been carried in
a canoe the whole way, the turnings and windings of the rivers and lakes were fo numeious,
that fhe forgot the track , fo fhe built the hut in
which we found her, to protect her from the weather during the Winter, and here fhe had refided
from the firft fetting in of the fall.

From her account of the moons paft fince her
elopement, it appeared that fhe had been near feven months without feeing a human face , during
all which time fhe had fupported herfelf very
well by fnaring partridges, rabbits, and fquirrels, fhe had alfo killed two or three beaver, and
fome porcupines  That fhe did not feem to have
been

been in want is evident, as fhe had a fmall ftock 1772.
of provifions by her when fhe was difcovered; January.
and was in good health and condition, and I
think one of the fineft women, of a real Indian, that I have feen in any part of North
America.

The methods practifed by this poor creature to
procure a livelihood were truly admirable, and
are great proofs that neceffity is the real mother
of invention. When the few deer-finews that
fhe had an opportunity of taking with her were
all expended in making fnares, and fewing her
clothing, fhe had nothing to fupply their place
but the finews of the rabbits legs and feet; thefe
fhe twifted together for that purpofe with great
dexterity and fuccefs. The rabbits, &c. which
fhe caught in thofe fnares, not only furnifhed her
with a comfortable fubfiftence, but of the fkins
fhe made a fuit of neat and warm clothing for
the Winter. It is fcarcely poffible to conceive
that a perfon in her forlorn fituation could be fo
compofed as to be capable of contriving or executing any thing that was not abfolutely neceffary to her exiftence, but there were fufficient
proofs that fhe had extended her care much farther, as all her clothing, befide being calculated
for real fervice, fhewed great tafte, and exhibited no little variety of ornament. The materials,
though rude, were very curioufly wrought, and
fo judicioufly placed, as to make the whole of
her

her garb have a very pleasing, though rather romantic appearance.

Her leisure hours from hunting had been employed in twisting the inner rind or bark of willows into small lines, like net-twine, of which she
had some hundred fathoms by her; with this she
intended to make a fishing-net as soon as the
Spring advanced.    It is of the inner bark of
willows, twisted in this manner, that the Dog-
ribbed Indians make their fishing-nets, and they
are much perferable to those made by the Northern Indians*.

Five or six inches of an iron hoop, made into
a knife, and the shank of an arrow head of iron,
which served her as an awl, were all the metals
this poor woman had with her when she eloped; and with these implements she had made
herself complete snow-shoes, and several other useful articles.

Her method of making a fire was equally singular and curious, having no other materials for
that purpose than two hard sulphurous stones.
These, by long friction and hard knocking, produced a few sparks, which at length communi-
cated to some touchwood, but as this method

was

---

* The Northern Indians make their fishing nets with small thongs cut
from raw deer-skins which when dry appear very good, but after being
soaked in water some time, grow so soft and slippery, that when large fish
strike the net, the hitches are very apt to slip and let them escape   Beside this inconvenience, they are very liable to rot   unless they be frequently taken out of the water and dried

was attended with great trouble, and not always
with fuccefs, fhe did not fuffer her fire to go out
all the Winter.    Hence we may conclude that fhe
had no idea of producing fire by friction, in the
manner practifed by the Efquimaux, and many
other uncivilized nations; becaufe if fhe had, the
above mentioned precaution would have been unneceffary.

The fingularity of the circumftance, the come-
linefs of her perfon, and her approved accomplifhments, occafioned a ftrong conteft between feveral of the Indians of my party, who fhould have
her for a wife; and the poor girl was actually
won and loft at wreftling by near half a fcore different men the fame evening.    My guide, Matonabbee who at that time had no lefs than feven
wives, all women grown, befides a young girl of
eleven or twelve years old, would have put in
for the prize alfo, had not one of his wives made
him afhamed of it, by telling him that he had already more wives than he could properly attend.
This piece of fatire, however true, proved fatal to the poor girl who dared to make fo open a
declaration , for the great man, Matonabbee, who
would willingly have been thought equal to eight
or ten men in every refpect, took it as fuch an
affront, that he fell on her with both hands and
feet, and bruifed her to fuch a degree, that after
lingering fome time fhe died.

When the Athapufcow Indians took the above
Dogribbed Indian woman prifoner, they according

ing to the univerfal cuftom of thofe favages, furprifed her and her party in the night, and killed
every foul in the tent, except herfelf and three
other young women. Among thofe whom they
killed, were her father, mother, and hufband.
Her young child, four or five months old, fhe
concealed in a bundle of clothing, and took with
her undifcovered in the night, but when fhe arrived at the place where the Athapufcow Indians
had left their wives, (which was not far diftant,)
they began to examine her bundle, and finding
the child, one of the women took it from her, and
killed it on the fpot.

This laft piece of barbarity gave her fuch a
difguft to thofe Indians, that notwithftanding the
man who took care of her treated her in every
refpect as his wife, and was, fhe faid, remarkably
kind to, and even fond of her; fo far was fhe
from being able to reconcile herfelf to any of the
tribe, that fhe rather chofe to expofe herfelf to
mifery and want, than live in eafe and affluence
among perfons who had fo cruelly murdered her
infant*. The poor woman's relation of this
                                                        fhocking

---

* It is too common a cafe with moft of the tribes of Southern Indians
for the women to defire their hufbands or friends, when going to war,
to bring them a flave, that they may have the pleafure of killing it, and
fome of the inhuman women will accompany their hufbands, and murder the women and children as faft as their hufbands do the men

When I was at Cumberland Houfe, (an inland fettlement that I eftablifhed for the Hadfon's Bay Company in the year 1774) I was particularly acquainted with a very young lady of this extraordinary turn, who,
when I defired fome indians that were going to war to bring me a young
                                                        flave,

fhocking ftory, which fhe delivered in a very affecting manner, only excited laughter among the
favages of my party.

In a converfation with this woman foon afterward, fhe told us, that her country lies fo far to
the Weftward, that fhe had never feen iron, or
any other kind of metal, till fhe was taken prifoner  All of her tribe, fhe obferved, made their
hatchets and ice-chifels of deer's horns, and their
knives of ftones and bones; that their arrows
were fhod with a kind of flate, bones, and deer's
horns; and the inftruments which they employed to make their wood-work were nothing but
beaver's teeth   Though they had frequently
heard of the ufeful materials which the nations
or tribes to the Eaft of them were fupplied with
from the Englifh, fo far were they from drawing
nearer, to be in the way of trading for iron-
work, &c that they were obliged to retreat farther back, to avoid the Athapufcow Indians, who
made furprifing flaughter among them, both in
Winter and Summer.

On the fixteenth, as we were continuing our
courfe

---

flave, which I intended to have brought up as a domeftic, Mifs was equally
defirous that one might be brought to her, for the cruel purpofe of mur-
dering it   It is fcarcely poffible to exprefs my aftonifhment, on hearing
fuch an extraordinary requeft made by a young creature fcarcely fixteen
years old, however, as foon as I recovered from my furprife, I ordered her
to leave the fettlement, which fhe did, with thofe who were going to war,
and it is therefore probable fhe might not be difappointed in her requeft
The next year I was ordered to the command of Prince of Wales's Fort,
and therefore never faw her afterward

courfe in the South Weft quarter, we arrived at the grand Athapufcow River, which at that part is about two miles wide, and empties itfelf into the great lake of the fame name we had fo lately croffed, and which has been already defcribed

The woods about this river, particularly the pines and poplars, are the talleft and ftouteft I have feen in any part of North America. 1 he birch alfo grows to a confiderable fize, and fome fpecies of the willow are likewife tall : but none of them have any trunk, like thofe in England.

The bank of the river in moft parts is very high, and in fome places not lefs than a hundred feet above the ordinary furface of the water. As the foil is of a loamy quality, it is very fubject to moulder or wafh away by heavy rains, even during the fhort Summer allotted to this part of the globe. The breaking up of the ice in the Spring is annually attended with a great deluge, when, I am told, it is not uncommon to fee whole points of land wafhed away by the inundations; and as the wood grows clofe to the edge of the banks, vaft quantities of it are hurried down the ftream by the irrefiftible force of the water and ice, and conveyed into the great lake already mentioned ; on the fhores and iflands of which, there lies the greateft quantity of drift wood I ever faw. Some of this wood is large enough to make mafts for the largeft fhips that are built. The banks of the river in general are fo fteep as to be inacceffible to

either

either man or beaft, except in fome flacks, or
gulleys, that have been wore down by heavy
rains, backwaters, or deluges; and even thofe
flacks are, for the moft part, very difficult to af-
cend, on account of the number of large trees
which lie in the way.

There are feveral low iflands in this river, which
are much frequented by the moofe, for the fake
of the fine willows they produce, which furnifh
them with a plentiful fupply of their favourite
food during the Winter. Some of thofe iflands
are alfo frequently by a number of rabbits; but
as larger game could be procured in great plenty,
thofe fmall animals were not deemed worthy our
notice at prefent.

Befide the grand river already mentioned, there
are feveral others of lefs note, which empty themfelves into the great Athapufcow Lake · There
are alfo feveral fmall rivers and creeks on the
North Eaft fide of the Lake that carry off the fu-
perfluous waters, fome of which, after a variety
of windings through the barren grounds to the
North of Churchill River, are loft in the marfhes
and low grounds, while others, by means of many fmall channels and rivulets, are difcharged into
other rivers and lakes, and at laft, doubtlefs, find
their way into Hudfon's Bay. Thefe rivers,
though numberlefs, are all fo full of fhoals and
ftones, as not to be navigable for an Indian canoe
to any confiderable diftance; and if they were, it
would be of little or no ufe to the natives, as none
of

of them lead within feveral hundred miles of
Churchill River.

Agreeably to Matonabbee's propofal, we continued our courfe up the Athapufcow River for
many days, and though we paffed feveral parts
which we well knew to have been the former
Winter-haunts of the Athapufcow Indians, yet we
could not fee the leaft trace of any of them having been there that feafon. In the preceding
Summer, when they were in thofe parts, they had
fet fire to the woods; and though many months
had elapfed from that time till our arrival there,
and notwithftanding the fnow was then very
deep, the mofs was ftill burning in many places,
which at firft deceived us very much, as we took
it for the fmoke of ftrange tents, but after going
much out of our way, and fearching very diligent-
ly, we could not difcover the leaft track of a
ftranger.

Thus difappointed in our expectations of meeting the Southern Indians, it was refolved (in
Council, as it may be called) to expend as much
time in hunting buffalo, moofe, and beaver as we
could, fo that we might be able to reach Prince
of Wales's Fort a little before the ufual time of
the fhips arrival from England    Accordingly, after having walked upwards of forty miles by the
27th    fide of Athapufcow River, on the twenty-feventh
of January we ftruck off to the Eaftward, and
left the River at that part where it begins to tend
due South.

In

In confequence of this determination of the In- 1772.
dians, we continued our courfe to the Eaftward; January,
but as game of all kinds was very plentiful, we
made but fhort days journies, and often remained
two or three days in one place, to eat up the
fpoils or produce of the chace. The woods
through which we were to pafs were in many places fo thick, that it was neceffary to cut a path
before the women could pafs with their fledges;
and in other places fo much of the woods had formerly been fet on fire and burnt, that we were
frequently obliged to walk farther than we otherwife fhould have done, before we could find green
brufh enough to floor our tents.

From the fifteenth to the twenty-fourth of Fe- February
bruary, we walked along a fmall river that emp- 15th—24th
ties itfelf into the Lake Clowey, near the part
where we built canoes in May one thoufand feven
hundred and feventy-one. This little river is that
which we mentioned in the former part of this
Journal, as having communication with the Athapufcow Lake: but, from appearances, it is of no
confequence whence it takes its rife, or where it
empties itfelf, as one half of it is nearly dry three-
fourths of the year. The intervening ponds,
however, having fufficient depth of water, are,
we may fuppofe, favourable fituations for beaver,
as many of their houfes are to be found in thofe
parts.

On the twenty-fourth, a ftrange Northern In- 24th.
dian leader, called Thlew-fa-nell-ie, and feveral of
his

his followers, joined us from the Eaſtward. This leader preſented Matonabbee and myſelf with a foot of tobacco each, and a two-quart keg of brandy, which he intended as a preſent for the Southern Indians; but being informed by my companions, that there was not the leaſt probability of meeting any, he did not think it worth any farther carriage. The tobacco was indeed very acceptable, as our ſtock of that article had been expended ſome time. Having been ſo long without taſting ſpirituous liquors, I would not partake of the brandy, but left it entirely to the Indians, to whom, as they were numerous, it was ſcarcely a taſte for each. Few of the Northern Indians are fond of ſpirits, eſpecially thoſe who keep at a diſtance from the Fort : ſome who are near, and who uſually ſhoot geeſe for us in the Spring, will drink it at free coſt as faſt as the Southern Indians, but few of them are ever ſo imprudent as to buy it.

The little river lately mentioned, as well as the adjacent lakes and ponds, being well-ſtocked with beaver, and the land abounding with mooſe and buffalo, we were induced to make but ſlow progreſs in our journey. Many days were ſpent in hunting, feaſting, and drying a large quantity of fleſh to take with us, particularly that of the buffalo; for my companions knew by experience, that a few days walk to the Eaſtward of our preſent ſituation would bring us to a part where we ſhould not ſee any of thoſe animals.

The

The ftrangers who had joined us on the twenty fourth informed us, that all were well at Prince of Wales's Fort when they left it laft, which according to their account of the Moons paft fince, muft have been about the fifth of November one thoufand feven hundred and feventy-one. Thefe ftrangers only remained in our company one night before the Leader and part of his crew left us, and proceeded on their journey to the North Weftward, but a few of them having procured fome furrs in the early part of the Winter, joined our party, with an intent to accompany us to the Factory

Having a good ftock of dried meat, fat, &c. prepared in the beft manner for carriage, on the twenty-eighth we fhaped our courfe in the South Eaft quarter, and proceeded at a much greater rate than we had lately done, as little or no time was now loft in hunting The next day we faw the tracks of fome ftrangers, and though I did not perceive any of them myfelf, fome of my companions were at the trouble of fearching for them, and finding them to be poor inoffenfive people, plundered them not only of the few furrs which they had, but took alfo one of their young women from them.

Every additional act of violence committed by my companions on the poor and diftreffed, ferved to increafe my indignation and diflike; this laft act, however, difpleafed me more than all their former actions, becaufe it was committed

T

on a fet of harmlefs creatures, whofe general manner of life renders them the moft fecluded fiom
fociety of any of the human race

Matonabbee affured me, that for more than a
generation paft one family only, as it may be called, (and to which the young men belonged who
were plundered by my companions,) nave taken
up their Winter abode in thofe woods, which
are fituated fo far on the barren ground as to be
quite out of the track of any other Indians.
From the beft accounts that I could colleft, the
latitude of this place muft be about 63½°, or 63°
at leaft, the longitude is very uncertain   From
my own experience I can affirm, that it is fome
hundreds of miles both from the fea-fide and the
main woods to the Weftward.   Few of the trading Northern Indians have vifited this place, but
thofe who have, give a pleafing defcription of it,
all agreeing that it is fituated on the banks of a
river which has communication with feveral fine
lakes.   As the current fets to the North Eaftward, it emplies itfelf, in all probability, into
fome part of Hudfon's Bay, and, from the latitude, no part feems more likely for this communication, than Baker's Lake, at the head of Chefterfield's inlet.   This, however, is mere conjecture. nor is it of any confequence, as navigation
on any of the rivers in thofe parts is not only impracticable, but would be alfo unprofitable, as
they do not lead into a country that produces any
                                                    thing

thing for trade, or that contains any inhabitants worth vifiting.

The accounts given of this place, and the manner of life of its inhabitants, would, if related at full length, fill a volume: let it fuffice to obferve, that the fituation is faid to be remarkably favourable for every kind of game that the barren ground produces at the different feafons of the year; but the continuance of the game with them is in general uncertain, except that of fifh and partridges. That being the cafe, the few who compofe this little commonwealth, are, by long cuftom and the conftant example of their forefathers, poffeffed of a provident turn of mind, with a degree of frugality unknown to every other tribe of Indians in this country except the Efquimaux.

Deer is faid to vifit this part of the country in aftonifhing numbers, both in Spring and Autumn, of which circumftances the inhabitant avail themfelves, by killing and drying as much of their flefh as poffible, particularly in the fall of the year, fo that they feldom are in want of a good Winter's ftock

Geefe, ducks, and fwans vifit here in great plenty during their migrations both in the Spring and Fall, and by much art, joined to an infurmountable patience, are caught in confiderable numbers in fnares*, and, without doubt, make

T 2                              a very

---

* To fnare fwans geefe or ducks, in the water, it requires no other procefs

1772. a very pleaſing change in the food.   It is alſo reported, (though I confeſs I doubt the truth of it,)
February                                          that

proceſs that to make a number of hedges, or fences, project into the water,
at high angles, from the bank of a river, lake or pond, for it is obſerved that thoſe birds generally ſwim in at the margin, for the benefit of feeding on the graſs, &c   Thoſe fences are continued for ſome diſtance from
the ſhore, and ſeparated two or three yards from each other, ſo that openings are left ſufficiently large to let the birds ſwim through   In each of
thoſe openings a ſnare is hung and faſtened to a ſtake, which the bird,
when intangled cannot drag from the bottom, and to prevent the ſnare
from being waſted out of its proper place by the wind, it is ſecured to the
ſtakes which form the opening, with tender graſs, which is eaſily
broken

This method, though it has the appearance of being very ſimple, is neverthelefs attended with much trouble, particula ly when we conſider the
ſmallneſs of their canoes, and the great inconveniency they labour under
in performing works of this kind in the water   Many of the ſtakes uſed
on thoſe occaſions are of a conſiderable length and ſize, and the ſmall branches which form the principal part of the hedges, are not arranged without much caution, for fear of overſetting the canoe, particularly where the
water is deep, as it is in ſome of the lakes   and in many of the rivers the
current is very ſtiff  which renders this buſineſs equally troubleſome
When the lakes and rivers are ſhallow, the natives are frequently at the
pains to make fences from ſhore to ſhore

To ſnare thoſe birds in their neſts requires a conſiderable degree of art
and, as the natives ſay a great deal of cleanlineſs, for they have obſerved,
that when ſnares have been ſet by thoſe whoſe hands were not clean, the
birds would not go to the neſt

Even the gooſe, though ſo ſimple a bird, is notoriouſly known to forſake
its eggs, if they were breathed on by the Indians

The ſmaller ſpecies of birds which make their neſt on the ground, are by
no means ſo delicate, of courſe leſs care is neceſſary to ſnare them   It has
been obſerved that all birds which build in the ground go into their neſt
at one particular ſide, and out of it on the oppoſite   The Indians, thoroughly convinced of this, always ſet the ſnares on the ſide on which the
bird enters the neſt, and if care be taken in ſetting them, ſeldom fail of
ſeizing their object   For ſmall birds, ſuch as larks, and many others of
equal ſize, the Indians only uſe two or three hairs out of their head, but
for larger birds  particularly ſwans, geeſe and ducks, they make ſnares of
deer-ſinews, twiſted like packthread, and occaſionally of a ſmall thong cut
from a parchment deer-ſkin

that a remarkable fpecies of partridges as large as Fnglifh fowls, are found in that part of the country only. Ihofe, as well as the common partidges, it is faid, are killed in confiderable numbers, with fnares, as well as with bows and arrows.

The river and lakes near the little foreft where the family above mentioned had fixed their abode, abound with fine fifh, particularly trout and barble, which are eafily caught, the former with hooks, and the latter in nets. In fact, I have not feen or heard of any part of this country which feems to poffefs half the advantages requifite for a conftant refidence, that are afcribed to this little fpot. The defcendents, however, of the prefent inhabitants muft in time evacuate it for want of wood, which is of fo flow a growth in thofe regions, that what is ufed in one year, exclufive of what is cut down and carried away by the Efquimaux, muft coft many years to replace.

It may probably be thought ftrange that any part of a community, apparently fo commodioufly fituated, and happy within themfelves, fhould be found at fo great a diftance from the reft of their tribe, and indeed nothing but neceffity could poffibly have urged them to undertake a journey of fo many hundred miles as they have done; but no fituation is without its inconveniences, and as their woods contain no birchtrees of fufficient fize, or perhaps none of any fize,

1772.
February

fize, this party had come fo far to the Weftward
to procure birch-rind for making two canoes, and
fome of the fungus that grows on the outfide of
the birch-tree, which is ufed by all the Indians in
thofe parts for tinder   There are two forts of
thefe fungufes which grow on the birch trees;
one is hard, the ufeful part of which much refembles rhubarb, the other is foft and fmooth
like velvet on the outfide, and when laid on hot
afhes for fome time, and well beaten between two
ftones, is fomething like fpunk.   The former is
called by the Northern Indians Jolt-thee, and is
known all over the country bordering on Hudfon's Bay by the name of Pefogan*, it being fo
called by the Southern Indians.   The latter is
only

* The Indians both Northern and Southern have found by experience,
that by boiling the pefogan in water for a confiderable time, the texture is
fo much improved, that when thoroughly dried, fome parts of it will be
nearly as for as fpunce

Some of thofe fungufes are as large as a man's head, the outfide, which
is very hard and black, and much indented with deep cracks, being of no
ufe, is always chopped off with a hatchet   Befides the two forts of
touchwood already mentioned, there is another kind of it in thofe parts,
that I think is infinitely preferable to either   This is found in old decayed
poplars, and lies in fakes of various fizes and thicknefs, fome is not thicker than fhamoy leather, others are as thick as a fhoe-fole   This, like the
fungus of the birch-tree, is always moift when taken from the tree, but
when dry, it is very foft and flexible, and takes fire readily from the
fpark of a fteel, but it is much improved by being kept dry in a bag that
has contained gunpowder   It is rather furprizing that the Indians, whofe
mode of life I have been defcribing, have never acquired the method of
making fire by friction, like the Efquimaux   It is alfo equally furprizing
they do not make ufe of the fkin-canoe   Probably deer-fkins cannot be
manufactured to withstand the water, for it is well known that the Efquimaux ufe always feal-fkins for that purpofe, though they are in the habit
of killing great number of deer

only ufed by the Northern tribes, and is called by them Clalte-ad-dee

By the firft of March we began to leave the fine level country of the Athapufcows, and again to approach the ftony mountains or hills which bound the Northern Indian country. Moofe and beaver ftill continued to be plentiful, but no buffaloes could be feen after the twenty-ninth of February.

As we were continuing our courfe to the Eaft South Eaft, on the fourteenth we difcovered the tracks of more ftrangers, and the next day came up with them. Among thofe Indians was the man who had carried a letter for me in March one thoufand feven hundred and feventy-one, to the Chief at Prince of Wales's Fort, and to which he had brought an anfwer, dated the twenty-firft of June. When this Indian received the letter from me, it was very uncertain what route we fhould take in our return from the Copper River, and, in all probability, he himfelf had not then determined on what fpot he would pafs the prefent winter ; confequently our meeting each other was merely accidental.

Thefe Indians having obtained a few furrs in the courfe of the Winter, joined our party, which now confifted of twenty tents, containing in the whole about two hundred perfons, and indeed our company had not been much lefs during the whofe winter.

From

From the ſtrangers who laſt joined us we received ſome ready-dreſſed mooſe-ſkins for tenting and ſhoe leather; alſo ſome other ſkins for clothing, for all of which the Chief at the Factory was to pay on our arrival.

I cannot ſufficiently lament the loſs of my quadrant, as the want of it muſt render the courſe of my journey from Point Lake, where it was broken, very uncertain, and my watch ſtopping while I was at the Athapuſcow Lake, has contributed greatly to the misfortune, as I am now deprived of every means of eſtimating the diſtances which we walked with any degree of accuracy, particularly in thick weather, when the Sun could not be ſeen.

16 h The Indians were employed at all convenient times in procuring birch-rind and making wood work ready for building canoes; alſo in preparing ſmall ſtaffs of birch-wood, to take with them on the barren ground, to ſerve as tent-poles all the Summer, and which, as hath been already obſerved, they convert into ſnow-ſhoe frames when the Winter ſets in. Here it may be proper to obſerve, that none of thoſe incidental avocations interfere with, or retard the Indians in their journey; for they always take the advantage of every opportunity which offers, as they paſs along, and when they ſee a tree fit for their purpoſe, cut it down, and either ſtrip off the bark, if that be what they want, or ſplit the trunk in pieces;

and

and after hewing it roughly with their hatchet, carry it to the tent, where in the evenings, or in the morning before they set out, they reduce it with their knives to the shape and size which is required

Provisions being plentiful, and the weather fine, we advanced a little each day , and on the nineteenth took up our lodgings by the side of Wholdyeah-chuck'd Whoie, or Large Pike Lake. In our way we crossed another small lake, where we caught some trout by angling, and killed a few deer and one moose.

On the twentieth we crossed Large Pike Lake, which at that part was not more than seven miles wide, but from North North West to the South South East is much longer. The next day we arrived at Bedodid Lake, which in general is not more than three miles wide, and in several places much less; but it is upward of forty miles long, which gives it the appearance of a river. It is said by the Indians to be shut up on all sides, and entirely surrounded with high land, which produces vast quantity of fir trees, but none of them grow to a great height in those parts: their branches, however, spread wider than those of firs of three times their height and thickness do in Europe; so that they resemble an apple-tree in shape, more than any species of the pine. They seem rich in tar, as the wood of them will burn like a candle, and emit as strong a smell, and as much black smoke, as the staves of an old tar-barrel;

barrel; for which reafon no Indians chufe to burn it in their tents, or even out of doors, for the purpofe of cooking their victuals.

The thaws began now to be very confiderable, and the under-woods were fo thick in thefe parts as to render traveling through them very difficult; we therefore took the advantage of walking on the ice of the above-mentioned Lake, which lay nearly in the direction of our courfe; but after proceeding about twenty-two miles on it, the Lake turned more toward the North, on which account we were obliged to leave it, ftriking off to the Eaftward; and after walking fourteen miles farther, we arrived at Noo-fhetht Whoie, or the Hill Ifland Lake, fo called from a very high ifland which ftands in it.

From the twenty-eighth to the thirty-firft of March, we had fo hard a gale of wind from the South, as to render walking on lakes or open plains quite impoffible, and the violence with which the trees were blown down made walking in the woods fomewhat dangerous; but though feveral had narrow efcapes, no accident happened.

312

From the middle to the latter end of March, and in the beginning of April, though the thaw was not general, yet in the middle of the day it was very confiderable: it commonly froze hard in the nights; and the young men took the advantage of the mornings, when the fnow was hard crufted over. and ran down many moofe;

for

for in thofe fituations a man with a good pair of
fnow-fhoes will fcarcely make any impreffion on
the fnow, while the moofe, and even the deer,
will break through it at every ftep up to the belly.   Notwithftanding this, however, it is very
feldom that the Indians attempt to run deer down.
The moofe are fo tender-footed, and fo fhort-
winded, that a good runner will generally tire
them in lefs than a day, and very frequently in
fix or eight hours; though I have known fome
of the Indians continue the chace for two days,
before they could come up with, and kill the
game.   On thofe occafions the Indians, in general, only take with them a knife or bayonet, and
a little bag containing a fet of fire-tackle, and are
as lightly clothed as poffible, fome of them will
carry a bow and two or three arrows, but I never knew any of them take a gun unlefs fuch as
had been blown or burfted, and the barrels cut
quite fhort, which, when reduced to the leaft
poffible fize to be capable of doing any fervice,
muft be too great a weight for a man to run with
in his hand for fo many hours together.

When the poor moofe are incapable of making
farther fpeed, they ftand and keep their purfuers
at bay with their head and fore-feet; in the ufe
of which they are very dexterous, efpecially the
latter, fo that the Indians who have neither a bow
nor arrows, nor a fhort gun, with them, are generally obliged to lafh their knives or bayonets
to the end of a long ftick, and ftab the moofe at
a diftance.

a diftance. For want of this neceffary precaution, fome of the boys and fool-hardy young men,
who have attempted to rufh in upon them, have
frequently received fuch unlucky blows from
their fore-feet, as to render their recover very
doubtful.

The flefh of the moofe, thus killed, is far from
being well-tafted, and I fhould think muft be very
unwholefome, from being over-heated, as by
running fo many hours together, the animal
muft have been in a violent fever, the flefh being foft and clammy, muft have a very difagreeable tafte, neither refembling fifh, flefh, nor
fowl*.

The Southern Indians ufe dogs for this kind of
hunting, which makes it eafier and more expeditious; but the Northern tribes having no dogs
trained to that exercife, are under the neceffity of
doing it themfelves

On the feventh we croffed a part of Thee-lee-
aza River: at which time the fmall Northern
deer were remarkably plentiful, but the moofe
began to be very fcarce, as none were killed after
the third

On

---

* Though I was a fwift runner in thofe days, I never accompanied
the Indians in one of thofe chaces, but have heard many of them fay,
that after a long one, the moofe, when killed, did not produce more
than a quart of blood, the remainder being all fettled in the flefh, which,
in that ftate, muft be ten times worfe tafted, than the fpleen or milt of a
Buccn hog

On the twelfth, we faw feveral fwans flying
to the Northward; they were the firft birds of
paffage we had feen that Spring, except a few
fnow-birds, which always precede the migrating
birds, and confequently are with much propriety
called the harbingers of Spring  The fwans alfo precede all the other fpecies of water-fowl, and
migrate fo early in the feafon, that they find no
open water but at the falls of rivers, where they
are readily met, and fometimes fhot, in confiderable numbers.

On the fourteenth, we arrived at another part
of Ihee-lee-aza River, and pitched our tents not
far from fome families of ftrange Northern Indians, who had been there fome time fnaring deer,
and who were all fo poor as not to have one gun
among them.

The villains belonging to my crew were fo far
from adminiftering to their relief, that they
robbed them of almoft every ufeful article in their
poffeffion, and to complete their cruelty, the men
joined themfelves in parties of fix, eight, or ten
in a gang, and dragged feveral of their young
women to a little diftance from their tents, where
they not only ravifhed them, but otherwife ill-
tieated them, and that in fo barbarous a manner,
as to endanger the lives of one or two of them.
Humanity on this, as well as on feveral other
fimilar occafions during my refidence among
thofe wretches, prompted me to upbraid them
                                        with

with their barbarity , but fo far were my remonftrances from having the defired effect, that they
afterwards made no fcruple of telling me in the
plaineft terms that if any female relation of mine
had been there, fhe fhould have been ferved in
the fame manner.

Deer being plentiful, we remained at this place
ten days, in order to dry and prepare a quantity
of the flefh and fat to carry with us , as this was
the laft time the Indians expected to fee fuch
plenty until they met them again on the barren
ground. During our ftay here, the Indians completed the wood-work for their canoes, and procured all their Summer tent-poles, &c., and while
we were employed in this neceffary bufinefs, the
thaw was fo great that the bare ground began to
appear in many places, and the ice in the rivers,
where the water was fhallow and the current
rapid, began to break up, fo that we were in
daily expectation of feeing geefe, ducks and other
birds of paffage.

25th   On the twenty-fifth, the weather, being cool
and favourable for travelling, we once more fet
out, and that day walked twenty miles to the
Eaftward; as fome of the women had not
joined us, we did not move on the two following days.

28th   On the twenty-eighth, having once more muftered all our forces, early in the morning we fet
out, and the next day paffed by Thleweyaza Yeth,

the

the place at which we had prepared wood-work
for canoes in the Spring one thoufand feven hundred and feventy-one.

As the morning of the fiift of May was exceedingly fine and pleafant, with a light air from
the South, and a great thaw, we walked eight
or nine miles to the Eaft by North, when a heavy
fall of fnow came on, which was followed, or
indeed more properly accompanied, by a hard
gale of wind from the north Weft. At the time
the bad weather began, we were on the top of
a high barren hill, a confiderable diftance from
any woods, judging it to be no more than a
fquall, we fat down, in expectation of its foon
paffing by. As the night, however, advanced,
the gale increafed to fuch a degree, that it was
impoffible for a man to ftand upright; fo that
we were obliged to lie down, without any other
defence againft the weather, than putting our
fledges and other lumber to windward of us,
which in reality was of no real fervice, as it only
harboured a great drift of fnow, with which in
fome places we were covered to the depth of two
or three feet; and as the night was not very
cold, I found myfelf, and many others who were
with me, long before morning in a puddle of
water, occafioned by the heat of our bodies melting the fnow.

The fecond proved fine pleafant weather, with
warm funfhine. In the morning, having dried

all

1772. all our clothing, we proceeded on our journey.
May In the afternoon we arrived at the part at which
my guide intended we fhould build our canoes,
but having had fome difference with his countrymen, he altered his mind, and determined to proceed to the Eaftward, as long as the feafon would
permit, before he attempted to perform that duty.

3d Accordingly, on the third, we purfued our way,
and as that and the following day were very
cold, which made us walk Lrifkly, we were enabled to make good days' journies; but the fifth
was fo hot and fultry, that we only walked about
thirteen miles in our old courfe to the Eaft by
North, and then halted about three-quarters of a
mile to the South of Black Bear Hill, a place
which I had feen in the Spring of one thoufand
feven hundred and feventy-one.

On the fixth, the weather was equally hot with
the preceding day; in the morning, however, we
moved on eleven miles to the Eaft, and then met
feveral ftrange Indians, who informed us that a
few others, who had a tolerable cargo of furrs,
and were going to the Factory that Summer,
were not far diftant.

On receiving this intelligence, my guide, Matonabbee, fent a meffenger to defire their company. This was foon complied with, as it is an
univerfal practice with the Indian Leaders, both
Northern and Southern, when going to the company's Factory, to ufe their influence and intereft

reft in convaffing for companions, as they find
by experience that a large gang gains them much
refpect. Indeed, the generality of Europeans
who refide in thofe parts, being utterly unacquainted with the manners and cuftoms of the Indians, have conceived fo high an opinion of thofe
Leaders, and their authority, as to imagine that
all who accompany them on thofe occafions are
entirely devoted to their fervice and command
all the year; but this is fo far from being the
cafe, that the authority of thofe great men, when
abfent from the Company's Factory, never extends beyond their own family, and the trifling
refpect which is fhown them by their countrymen
during their refidence at the Factory, proceeds
only from motives of intereft.

The Leaders have a very difagreeable talk to
perform on thofe occafions; for they are not only obliged to be the mouth-piece, but the beggars
for all their friends and relations for whom they
have a regard, as well as for thofe whom at other
times they have reafon to fear. Thofe unwelcome commiffions, which are impofed on them
by their followers, joined to their own defire of
being thought men of great confequence and intereft with the Englifh, make them very troublefome. And if a Governor deny them any
thing which they afk, though it be only to give
away to the moft worthlefs of their gang, they
immediately turn fulky and impertinent to the
higheft degree, and however rational they may

U                                          be

be at other times, are immediately divested of
every degree of reason, and raise their demands
to so exorbitant a pitch, that after they have received to the amount of five times the value of
all the furrs they themselves have brought, they
never cease begging during their stay at the Factory, and, after all, few of them go away thoroughly satisfied*.

After

* As a proof of this assertion I take the liberty, though a little foreign
to the narrative of my journey, to insert one instance, out of many hundreds of the kind that happen at the different Factories in Hudson's Bay,
but perhaps no where so frequently as at Churchill  In October 1776,
my old guide, Matonabbee, came at the head of a large gang of Northern
Indians, to trade at Prince of Wale's Fort, at which time I had the honour to command  When the usual ceremonies had passed, I dressed him
out as a Captain of the first rank and also clothed his six wives from top
to toe  after which, that is to say, during his stay at the Factory, which
was ten days, he begged seven lieutenants' coats, fifteen common coats,
eighteen hats, eighteen shirts, eight guns, one hundred and forty pounds
weight of gunpowder with shot, ball and flints in proportion, together
with many hatchets, ice chissels, files, bayonets, knives, and a great quantity of tobacco, cloth, blankets, combs, looking-glasses, stockings, handker-
chiefs, &c besides numberless small articles, such as awls, needles, paint,
steels, &c  in all to the amount of upwards of seven hundred beaver in the
way of trade, to give away among his followers  This was exclusive of his
own present, which consisted of a variety of goods to the value of four hundred beaver more  But the most extraordinary of his demands was twelve
pounds of powder, twenty eight pounds of shot and ball, four pounds
of tobacco, some articles of clothing, and several pieces of ironwork, &c.
to give to two men who had hauled his tent and other lumber the preceding Winter  This demand was so very unreasonable, that I made some
scruple, or at least hesitated to comply with it, hinting that he was the person who ought to satisfy those men for their services, but I was soon an-
swered, That he did not expect to have been denied such a trifle as that was,
and for the future he would carry his goods where he could get his own
price for them  On my asking him where that was? he replied, in a ve-
nolent tone, "To the Canadian Traders"  I was glad to comply with
his demands, and I here insert the anecdote, as a specimen of an Indian's
conscience.

After stopping four days at this place, Matonabbee, and all the Indians who were to accompany me to the Fort, agreed to leave the elderly
people and young children here, in the care of
some Indians who were capable of providing for
them, and who had orders to proceed to a place
called Cathawhachaga, on the barren grounds,
and there wait the return of their relations from
the Factory.  Matters of this kind being settled,
apparently to the entire satisfaction of all parties,
we resumed our journey on the eleventh of May,
and that at a much brisker pace than we could
probably have done when all the old people and
young children were with us.  In the afternoon
of the same day we met some other Northern
Indians, who were also going to the Fort with
furrs, those joined our party, and at night we
all pitched our tents by the side of a river that
empties itself into Doo-baunt Lake  This day
all of us threw away our snow-shoes, as the
ground was so bare in most places as not to require any such assistance; but sledges were occasionally serviceable for some time, particularly
when we walked on the ice of rivers or lakes.

The weather on the twelfth was so exceedingly hot and sultry, and the water so deep on the
top of the ice of the above-mentioned river, as to
render walking on it not only very troublesome,
but dangerous, so after advancing about five
miles we pitched our tents, and the warm weather being likely to continue, the Indians immedi-

U 2                          ately

1772. ately began to build their canoes, which were
completed with such expedition, that in the after-

May
18th
noon of the eighteenth we again set forward on
our journey. but the day being pretty far spent,
we only walked about four miles, and put up for
the night.

19th  The morning of the nineteenth was fine pleafant weather; and as all the water was drained
off from the top of the ice, it rendered walking
on it both fafe and eafy; accordingly we fet out
pretty early, and that day walked upwards of
twenty miles to the Eaft North Eaft on the above-
mentioned river  The next day proved fo cold,
that after walking about fifteen miles, we were
obliged to put up; for having left Doo-baunt
River, we were frequently obliged to wade above
the knees through fwamps of mud, water,
and wet fnow; which froze to our ftockings and
fhoes in fuch a thick cruft, as not only rendered
walking very laborious, but at the fame time fub-
jected us to the danger of having our legs and
feet frozen.

21  The weather on the twenty-firft was more fevere than on the preceding day, but the fwamps
and ponds being by that time frozen over, it
was tolerable walking: we proceeded therefore
on our journey, but the wind blew fo frefh, that
we had not walked fixteen miles, before we found
that thofe who carried the canoes could not poffibly keep up with us, fo that we put up for
the night.  In the courfe of this day's journey
we

we croffed the North Weft Bay of Wholdyah'd Lake, which, at that part, is called by the Nor- thern Indians A Naw-nee tha'd Whoie. This day feveral of the Indians turned back, not being able to proceed for want of provifions. Game of all kinds indeed were fo fcarce, that, except a few geefe, nothing had been killed by any of our party, from our leaving the women and children on the eleventh inftant, nor had we feen one deer the whole way.

The twenty-fecond proved more moderate, 22d when all our party having joined, we again ad- vanced to the North Faft, and after walking about thirteen miles, the Indians killed four deer. Our number, however, had now fo increafed, that four fmall Northern deer would fcarcely afford us all a fingle meal.

The next day we continued our journey, ge- 2;d nerally walking in the North Eaft quarter; and on the twenty-fifth, croffed the North bay of 25'h They-hole-kye'd Whoie, or Snow-bird Lake; and at night got clear of all woods, and lay on the barren ground. The fame day feveral of the Indians ftruck off another way, not being able to proceed to the Fort for want of ammunition. As we had for fome days paft made good jour- nies, and at the fame time were all heavy-laden, and in great diftrefs for provifions, fome of my companions were fo weak as to be obliged to leave their bundles of furrs*; and many others.

* All the furrs thus left were properly fecured in caves and crevices of

others were fo reduced as to be no longer capable of proceeding with us, having neither guns nor ammunition; fo that their whole dependence for fupport was on the fifh they might be able to catch; and though fifh was pretty plentiful in moft of the rivers and lakes hereabout, yet they were not always to be depended on for fuch an immediate fupply of food as thofe poor people required.

Though I had at this time a fufficient ftock of ammunition to ferve me and all my proper companions to the Fort, yet felf-prefervation being the firft law of Nature, it was thought advifable to referve the greateft part of it for our own ufe; efpecially as geefe and other fmaller birds were the only game now to be met with, and which, in times of fcarcity, bears hard on the articles of powder and fhot. Indeed moft of the Indians who actually accompanied me the whole way to the Factory had fome little ammunition remaining, which enabled them to travel in times of real fcarcity better than thofe whom we left behind; and though we affifted many of them, yet feveral of their women died for want. It is a melancholy truth, and a difgrace to the little humanity of which thofe people are poffeffed, to think, that in times of want the poor women

always

the rocks, fo as to withftand any attempt that might be made on them by beafts of prey, and were well fhielded from the weather, fo that, in all probability, few of them were loft.

always come off fhort; and when real diftrefs approaches, many of them are permitted to ftarve, when the males are amply provided for.

The twenty-fixth was fine and pleafant. In the morning we fet out as ufual, and after walking about five miles, the Indians killed three deer; as our numbers were greatly leffened, thefe ferved us for two or three meals, at a fmall expence of ammunition.

In continuing our courfe to the Eaftward, we croffed Cathawhachaga River, on the thirtieth of May, on the ice, which broke up foon after the laft perfon had croffed it. We had not been long on the Faft fide of the river before we perceived bad weather near at hand, and began to make every preparation for it which our fituation would admit, and that was but very indifferent, being on entire barren ground. It is true, we had complete fets of Summer tent-poles, and fuch tent-cloths as are generally ufed by the Northern Indians in that feafon, thefe were arranged in the beft manner, and in fuch places as were moft likely to afford us fhelter from the threatening ftorm. The rain foon began to defcend in fuch torrents as to make the river overflow to fuch a degree as foon to convert our firft place of retreat into an open fea, and oblige us in the middle of the night to affemble at the top of an adjacent hill, where the violence of the wind would not permit us to pitch a tent, fo that the only fhelter we could obtain was to take the tent-cloth about our fhoulders,

and

and fit with our backs to the wind; and in this
situation we were obliged to remain without
the leaft refreshment, till the morning of the

third of June: in the courfe of which time the
wind shifted all round the compafs, but the
bad weather ftill continued, fo that we were conftantly obliged to shift our pofition as the wind
changed

The weather now became more moderate,
though there was ftill a fresh gale from the North
Weft, with hard froft and frequent showers of
fnow   Early in the morning, however, we proceeded on our journey, but the wet and cold I
had experienced the two preceding days fo benumbed my lower extremities, as to render walking for fome time very troublefome.   In the
courfe of this day's journey we faw great numbers of geefe flying to the Southward, a few of
which we killed; but thefe were very difproportionate to the number of mouths we had to feed,
and to make up for our long fafting

From that time to the eighth we killed every
day as many geefe as were fufficient to perferve
life, but on that day we perceived plenty of deer,
five of which the Indians killed, which put us
all into good fpirits, and the number of deer we
then faw afforded great hopes of more plentiful
times during the remainder of our journey.   It
is almoft needlefs to add, that people in our di-
ftrefled fituation expended a little time in eating,
and flicing fome of the flesh ready for drying,
                                                    but

but the drying it occafioned no delay, as we faftened it on the tops of the women's bundles, and
dried it by the fun and wind while we were
walking; and, ftrange as it may appear, meat
thus prepared is not only very fubftantial food,
but pleafant to the tafte, and generally much
efteemed by the natives. For my own part I
muft acknowledge, that it was not only agreeable
to my palate, but after eating a meal of it, I
have always found that I could travel longer
without victuals, than after any other kind of
food. All the dried meat prepared by the Southern Indians is performed by expofing it to the
heat of a large fire, which foon exhaufts all the
fine juices from it, and when fufficiently dry to
prevent putrefaction, is no more to be compared
with that cured by the Northern Indians in the
Sun, or by the heat of a very flow fire, than
meat that has been boiled down for the fake of
the foup, is to that which is only fufficiently
boiled for eating: the latter has all the juices remaining, which, being eafily diffolved by the
heat and moifture of the ftomach, proves a ftrong
and nourifhing food, whereas the former being
entirely deprived of thofe qualities, can by no
means have an equal claim to that character.
Moft of the Europeans, however, are fonder of it
than they are of that cured by the Northern Indians. The fame may be faid to the lean parts of
the beaft, which are firft dried, and then reduced
into a kind of powder. That done by the Northern

thern Indians is entirely free from fmoke, and quite foft and mellow in the mouth, whereas that which is prepared by the Southern tribes is generally as bitter as foot with fmoke, and is as hard as the fcraps of horn, &c. which are burnt to make hardening for the cutlers. I never knew, that any European was fo fond of this as they are of that made by the Northern Indians.

9ᵗʰ On the ninth, as we were continuing our courfe to the Factory, which then lay in the South Eaft quarter, we faw feveral fmokes to the North Eaft, and the fame day fpoke with many Northern Indians, who were going to Knapp's Bay to meet the Churchill floop. Several of thofe Indians had furrs with them, but having fome time before taken up goods on truft at Prince of Wales's Fort, were taking that method to delay the payment of them. Defrauds of this kind have been practifed by many of thofe people with great fuccefs, ever fince the furr-trade has been eftablifhed with the Northern Indians at Knapp's Bay; by which means debts to a confiderable amount are annually loft to the Company, as well as their Governor in the Bay.

Being defirous of improving every opportunity that the fine weather afforded, we did not lofe much time in converfation with thofe Indians, but proceeded on our courfe to the South Eaft, while they continued theirs to the North Eaft.

For

For many days after leaving thofe people, we had the good fortune to meet with plenty of pro-vifions; and as the weather was for a long time remarkably fine and pleafant, our circumftances were altered fo much for the better, that every thing feemed to contribute to our happinefs, as if defirous to make fome amends for the fevere hunger, cold, and exceffive hardfhips that we had fuffered long before, and which had reduced us to the greateft mifery and want.

Deer was fo plentiful great part of the way, that the Indians killed as many as were wanted, without going out of their road, and every lake and river to which we came feemed willing to give us a change of diet, by affording us plenty of the fineft fifh, which we caught either with hooks or nets. Geefe, partridges, gulls, and many other fowls, which are excellent eating, were alfo in fuch plenty, that it only required ammunition, in fkilful hands, to have procured as many of them as we could defire.

The only inconvenience we now felt was from frequent fhowers of heavy rain; but the intervals between thefe fhowers being very warm, and the Sun fhining bright, that difficulty was eafily overcome, efpecially as the belly was plentifully fupplied with excellent victuals. Indeed the very thoughts of being once more arrived fo near home, made me capable of encountering every difficulty even if it had been hunger itfelf in the moft formidable fhape.

On

1772.

June 10th

On the eighteenth we arrived at Egg River, from which place, at the folicitation of my guide Matonabbee, I fent a letter poft-hafte to the Chief at Prince of Wales's Fort, advifing him of my being fo far advanced on my return. The weather at this time was very bad and rainy, which caufed us to lofe near a whole day ; but upon the fine weather returning, we again proceeded at our ufual rate of eighteen or twenty miles a day, fometimes more or lefs, according as the road, the weather, and other circumftances, would admit.

Deer now began to be not quite fo plentiful as they had been, though we met with enough for prefent ufe, which was all we wanted, each perfon having as much dried meat as he could conveniently carry, befides his furrs and other neceffary baggage.

26th.

Early in the morning of the twenty-fixth we arrived at Seal River*, but the wind blowing right up it, made fo great a fea, that we were

obliged

---

* Mr Jeremie is very incorrect in his account of the fituation of this River, and its courfe It is not eafy to guefs, whether the Copper or Dog ribbed Indians be the nation he calls *Platscotez de Chiens* if it be the former, he is much miftaken, for they have abundance of beaver, and other animals of the furr kind in their country and if the latter, he is equally wrong to affert that they have copper-mines in their country, for neither copper nor any other kind of metal is in ufe among them

Mr Jeremie was not too modeft when he faid, (fee Dobb's Account of Hudfon's bay, p 19) " he could not fay any thing pofitively in going farther

obliged to wait near ten hours before we could
venture to crofs it in our little canoes.  In the
after-

farther " North ," for in my opinion he never was fo far North or Weft as
he pretends, otherwife he would have been more correct in his defcription
of thofe parts

The Strait he mentions is undoubtedly no other than what is now
called Chefterfield's Inlet, which, in fome late and cold feafons, it not clear
of ice the whole Summer  for I will affirm, that no Indian, either Northern or Southern, ever faw either Wager Water or Repulfe Bay, except
the two men who accompanied Captain Middleton , and though thofe
men were felected from fome hundreds for their univerfal knowledge of
thofe parts, yet they knew nothing of the coaft fo far North as Marble
Ifland

As a farther proof, that no Indians, except the Efquimaux, ever frequent fuch high latitudes, unlefs at a great diftance from the fea, I muft
here mention, that fo late as the year 1763, when Captain Chriftopher
went to furvey Chefterfield's Inlet, though he was furnifhed with the
moft intelligent and experienced Northern Indians that could be
found, they did not know an inch of the land to the North of Whale
Cove

Mr Jeremie is alfo as much miftaken in what he fays concerning
Church ll River, as he was in the direction of Seal River, for he fays that
no woods were found but in fome iflands which lie about ten or twelve
miles up the river  At the time he wrote, which was long before a fettlement was made there, wood was in great plenty on both fides the river, and that within five miles of where Prince of Wales's Fort now
ftands  But as to the iflands of which he fpeaks, if they ever exifted,
they have of late years moft affuredly difappeared , for fince the Company have had a fettlement on that river, no one ever faw an ifland in it
that produced timber, or wood of any defcription, within forty miles
of the Fort  But the great number of ftumps now remaining, from which,
in all probability, the trees have been cut for firing, are fufficient to prove
that when Church ll River was firft fettled, wood was then in great plenty, but in the courfe of feventy fix years refidence in one place, it is natural to fuppofe it was much thinned near the Settlement  Indeed for
fome years paft common fewel is fo fcarce near that Factory, that it is the
chief employment of moft of the fervants for upward of feven months in
the year, to procure as much wood as will fupply the fires for a Winter,
and a little timber for neceffary repairs

afternoon the weather grew more moderate, fo
that we were enabled to ferry over the river;
after which we refumed our journey, and at night
pitched our tents in fome tufts of willows in
fight of the woods of Po-co-thee-kis-co River,
at which we arrived early in the morning of the
twenty-eighth; but the wind again blowing very
hard in the North Eaft quarter, it was the afternoon of the twenty-ninth before we could attempt
to crofs it.

Juft at the time we were croffing the South
branch of Po-co-thee kis-co River, the Indians
that were fent from Egg River with a letter to
the Chief at Churchill, joined us on their return,
and brought a little tobacco and fome other articles which I had defired. Though it was late
in the afternoon before we had all croffed the river, yet we walked that evening till after ten
o'clock, and then put up on one of the Goofe-
hunting Iflands, as they are generally called,
about ten miles from the Factory. The next
morning I arrived in good health at Prince of
Wales's Fort, after having been abfent eighteen
months and twenty-three days on this laft expedition, but from my firft fetting out with Captain Chawchinaha, it was two years feven months
and twenty-four days.

Though my difcoveries are not likely to prove
of any material advantage to the Nation at large,
or indeed to the Hudfon's Bay Company, yet I
have the pleafure to think that I have fully complied

plied with the orders of my Mafters, and that it has put a final end to all difputes, concerning a North Weft Paffage through Hudfon's Bay. It will alfo wipe off, in fome meafure, the ill-grounded and unjuft afperfions of Dobbs, Ellis, Robfon, and the American Traveller; who have all taken much pains to condemn the conduct of the Hudfon's Bay Company, as being averfe from difcoveries, and from enlarging their trade.

C H A P.

## C H A P.  IX.

A ſhort Deſcription of the Northern Indians, alſo
a farther Account of their Country, Manufactures, Cuſtoms, &c.

*An account of the perſons and tempers of the Northern*
*Indians —They poſſeſs a great deal of art and cun-*
*ning.—Are very guilty of fraud when in their pow-*
*er, and generally exact more for their furrs than*
*any other tribe of Indians —Always diſſatisfied, yet*
*have their good qualities.—The men in general jea-*
*lous of their wives.—Their marriages —Girls al-*
*ways betrothed when children, and their reaſons for*
*it.—Great care and confinement of young girls from*
*the age of eight or nine years old.—Divorces com-*
*mon among thoſe people.—The women are leſs pro-*
*lific than in warmer countries.—Remarkable piece*
*of ſuperſtition obſerved by the women at particular*
*periods.—Their art in making it an excuſe for a*
*temporary ſeparation from their huſbands on any lit-*
*tle quarrel.—Reckoned very unclean on thoſe occaſi-*
*ons —The Northern Indians frequently, for the*
*want of firing, are obliged to eat their meat raw —*
*Some through neceſſity obliged to boil it in veſſels made*
*of the rind of the birch-tree.—A remarkable diſh*
*among thoſe people.—The young animals always cut*
*out of their dams eaten, and accounted a great deli-*
*cacy.—The parts of generation of all animals eat by*
*the*

*the men and boys.—Manner of paffing their time, and method of killing deer in Summer with bows and arrows.—Their tents, dogs, fledges, &c.— Snow fhoes —Their partiality to domeftic vermin —Utmoft extent of the Northern Indian country.— Face of the country —Species of fifh —A peculiar kind of mofs ufeful for the fupport of man —Northern Indian method of catching fifh, either with hooks or nets.—Ceremony obferved when two parties of thofe people meet —Diverfions in common ufe —A fingular diforder which attacks fome of thofe people —Their fuperftition with refpect to the death of their friends.—Ceremony obferved on thofe occafions —Their ideas of the firft inhabitants of the world. —No form of religion among them.----Remarks on that circumftance —The extreme mifery to which old age is expofed —Their opinion of the Aurora Borealis, &c.—Some account of Matonabbee, and his fervices to his country, as well as to the Hudfon's Bay company*

AS to the perfons of the Northern Indians, they are in general above the middle fize; well-proportioned, ftrong, and robuft, but not corpulent. They do not poffefs that activity of body, and livelinefs of difpofition, which are fo commonly met with among the other tribes of Indians who inhabit the Weft coaft of Hudfon's Bay.

Their complexion is fomewhat of the copper caft, inclining rather toward a dingy brown;

X                              and

and their hair, like all the other tribes in India,
is black, ſtrong, and ſtraight*.   Few of the men
have any beard; this ſeldom makes its appearance till they are arrived at middle-age, and then
is by no means equal in quantity to what is obſerved on the faces of the generality of Europeans, the little they have, however, is exceedingly ſtrong and briſtly.   Some of them take but
little pains to eradicate their beards, though it is
conſidered as very unbecoming; and thoſe who
do, have no other method than that of pulling it
out by the roots between their fingers and the
edge of a blunt knife.   Neither ſex have any
hair under their armpits, and very little on any
other part of the body, particularly the women;
but on the place where Nature plants the hair, I
never knew them attempt to eradicate it.

Their features are peculiar, and different from
any other tribe in thoſe parts; for they have very
low foreheads, ſmall eyes, high cheek-bones, Ro-
man noſes, full cheeks, and in general long broad
chins.   Though few of either ſex are exempt
from this national ſet of features, yet Nature
ſeems to be more ſtrict in her obſervance of it
among the females, as they ſeldom vary ſo much
as the men.   Their ſkins are ſoft, ſmooth, and
poliſhed; and when they are dreſſed in clean
clothing,

* I have ſeen ſeveral of the Southern Indian men who were near ſix feet
high, preſerve a ſingle lock of their hair, that, when let down, would trail
on the ground as they walked.   This, however, is but ſeldom ſeen, and
ſome have ſuſpected it to be falſe   but I have examined the hair of
ſeveral of them and found it to be real

clothing, they are as free from an offenfive fmell as any of the human race.

Every tribe of Northern Indians, as well as the Copper and Dog-ribbed Indians, have three or four parallel black ftrokes marked on each cheek; which is performed by entering an awl or needle under the fkin, and, on drawing it out again, immediately rubbing powdered charcoal into the wound.

Their difpofitions are in general morofe and covetous, and they feem to be entirely unacquainted even with the name of gratitude. They are for ever pleading poverty, even among themfelves, and when they vifit the Factory, there is not one of them who has not a thoufand wants.

When any real diftreffed objects prefent themfelves at the Company's Factory, they are always relieved with victuals, clothes, medicines, and every other neceffary, *gratis*, and in return, they inftruct every one of their countrymen how to behave, in order to obtain the fame charity. Thus it is very common to fee both men and women come to the Fort half-naked, when either the fevere cold in Winter, or the extreme troublefomenefs of the flies in Summer, make it neceffary for every part to be covered. On thofe occafions they are feldom at a lofs for a plaufible ftory, which they relate as the occafion of their diftrefs, (whether real or pretended,) and never fail to interlard their hiftory with plenty of fighs, groans, and tears, fometimes affecting to be lame,

X 2

and

and even blind, in order to excite pity. Indeed,
I know of no people that have more command of
their paffions on fuch occafions; and in thofe refpects the women exceed the men, as I can affirm
with truth I have feen fome of them with one
fide of the face bathed in tears, while the other
has exhibited a fignificant fmile. Falfe pretences
for obtaining charity are fo common among thofe
people, and fo often detected, that the Governor
is frequently obliged to turn a deaf ear to many who apply for relief; for if he did not, he
might give away the whole of the Company's
goods, and by degrees all the Northern tribe
would make a trade of begging, inftead of bringing furrs, to purchafe what they want  It may
truly be faid, that they poffefs a confiderable degree of deceit, and are very complete adepts in
the art of flattery, which they never fpare as
long as they find that it conduces to their intereft, but not a moment longer. They take care
always to feem attached to a new Governor,
and flatter his pride, by telling him that they
look up to him as the father of their tribe, on
whom they can fafely place their dependance;
and they never fail to depreciate the generofity
of his predeceffor, however extenfive that might
have been, however humane or difinterefted his
conduct; and if afperfing the old, and flattering
the new Governor, has not the defired effect in a
reafonable time, they reprefent him as the worft of
characters, and tell him to his face that he is one

of

of the moſt cruel of men ; that he has no feeling for the diſtreſſes of their tribe, and that many have periſhed for want of proper aſſiſtance, (which, if it be true, is only owing to want of humanity among themſelves,) and then they boaſt of having received ten times the favours and preſents from his predeceſſor.  It is remarkable that thoſe are moſt laviſh in their praiſes, who have never either deſerved or received any favours from him  In time, however, this language alſo ceaſes, and they are perfectly reconciled to the man whom they would willingly have made a fool, and ſay, " he " is no child, and not to be deceived by them "

They differ ſo much from the reſt of mankind, that harſh uncourteous uſage ſeems to agree bet- ter with the generality of them, particularly the lower claſs, than mild treatment , for if the leaſt reſpect be ſhown them, it makes them intolera- bly inſolent ; and though ſome of their leaders may be exempt from this imputation, yet there are but few even of them who have ſenſe enough to ſet a proper value on the favours and indul- gences which are granted to them while they re- main at the Company's Factories, or elſewhere within their territories  Experience has con- vinced me, that by keeping a Northern Indian at a diſtance, he may be made ſerviceable both to himſelf and the Company ; but by giving him the leaſt indulgence at the Factory, he will grow indolent, inactive, and troubleſome, and only
                                              contrive

contrive methods to tax the generofity of an Eū-
ropean.

The greateſt part of theſe people never fail to
defraud Europeans whenever it is in their power,
and take every method to over-reach them in the
way of trade. They will diſguiſe their perſons
and change their names, in order to defraud them
of their lawful debts, which they are ſometimes
permitted to contract at the Company's Factory;
and all debts that are outſtanding at the ſucceſſion
of a new Governor are entirely loſt, as they
always declare, and bring plenty of witneſſes to
prove, that they were paid long before, but that
their names had been forgotten to be ſtruck out
of the book.

Notwithſtanding all thoſe bad qualities, they
are the mildeſt tribe of Indians that trade at any
of the Company's ſettlements; and as the greateſt part of them are never heated with liquor, are
always in their fenſes, and never proceed to riot,
or any violence beyond bad language.

The men are in general very jealous of their
wives, and I make no doubt but the ſame ſpirit
reigns among the women; but they are kept ſo
much in awe of their huſbands, that the liberty
of thinking is the greateſt privilege they enjoy.
The preſence of a Northern Indian man ſtrikes
a peculiar awe into his wives, as he always aſſumes
the ſame authority over them that the maſter of
a family in Europe uſually does over his dome-
ſtic ſervants.

Their

Their marriages are not attended with any ceremony; all matches are made by the parents, or next of kin. On thofe occafions the women feem to have no choice, but implicitly obey the will of their parents, who always endeavour to marry their daughters to thofe that feem moft likely to be capable of maintaining them, let their age, perfon, or difpofition be ever fo defpicable.

The girls are always betrothed when children, but never to thofe of equal age, which is doubtlefs found policy with people in their fituation, where the exiftence of a family depends entirely on the abilities and induftry of a fingle man. Children, as they juftly obferve, are fo liable to alter in their manners and difpofition, that it is impoffible to judge from the actions of early youth what abilities they may poffefs when they arrive at puberty. For this reafon the girls are often fo difproportionably matched for age, that it is very common to fee men of thirty-five or forty years old have young girls of no more than ten or twelve, and fometimes much younger. From the early age of eight or nine years, they are prohibited by cuftom from joining in the moft innocent amufements with children of the oppofite fex; fo that when fitting in their tents, or even when travelling, they are watched and guarded with fuch an unremitting attention as cannot be exceeded by the moft rigid difcipline of an Englifh boarding-fchool. Cuftom, however, and conftant example, make fuch uncommon reftraint and

confine-

confinement fit light and eafy even on children,
whofe tender ages feem better adopted to innocent and cheerful amufements, than to be coop-
ed up by the fide of old women, and conftantly
employed in fcraping fkins, mending fhoes, and
learning other domeftic duties neceffary in the
care of a family.

Notwithftanding thofe uncommon reftraints
on the young girls, the conduct of their parents is
by no means uniform or confiftent with this
plan; as they fet no bounds to their converfation, but talk before them, and even to them, on
the moft indelicate fubjects.   As their ears are
accuftomed to fuch language from their earlieft
youth, this has by no means the fame effect on
them, it would have on girls born and educated
in a civilized country, where every care is taken
to prevent their morals from being contaminated
by obfcene converfation.   The Southern Indians
are ftill lefs delicate in converfation, in the prefence of their children.

The women among the Northern Indians are
in general more backward than the Southern
Indian women; and though it is well known
that neither tribe lofe any time, thofe early
connections are feldom productive of children for
fome years.

Divorces are pretty common among the Northern Indians, fometimes for incontinency, but
more frequently for want of what they deem
neceffary accomplifhments, or for bad behaviour.

                                             This

This ceremony, in either cafe, confifts of neither more nor lefs than a good drubbing, and turning the woman out of doors; telling her to go to her paramour, or relations, according to the nature of her crime.

Providence is very kind in caufing thefe people to be lefs prolific than the inhabitants of civilized nations, it is very uncommon to fee one woman have more than five or fix children; and thefe are always born at fuch a diftance from one another, that the youngeft is generally two or three years old before another is brought into the world. Their eafy births, and the ceremonies which take place on thofe occafions, have already been mentioned, I fhall therefore only obferve here, that they make no ufe of cradles, like the Southern Indians, but only tie a lump of mofs between their legs, and always carry their children at their backs, next the fkin, till they are able to walk. Though their method of treating young children is in this refpect the moft uncouth and awkward I ever faw, there are few among them that can be called deformed, and not one in fifty who is not bow-legged.

There are certain periods at which they never permit the women to abide in the fame tent with their hufbands. At fuch times they are obliged to make a fmall hovel for themfelves at fome diftance from the other tents. As this is an univerfal cuftom among all the tribes, it is alfo a piece of policy with the women, upon any difference

with

with their hufbands, to make that an excufe for
a temporary feparation, when, without any ceremony, they creep out (as is their ufual cuftom
on thofe occafions) under the eves of that fide of
the tent at which they happen to be fitting; for
at thofe times they are not permitted to go in or
out through the door.   This cuftom is fo generally prevalent among the women, that I have frequently known fome of the fulky dames leave
their hufbands and tent for four or five days at
a time, and repeat the farce twice or thrice in a
month, while the poor men have never fufpected
the deceit, or if they have, delicacy on their part
has not permitted them to enquire into the matter.
I have known Matonabbee's handfome wife, who
eloped from him in May one thoufand feven
hundred and feventy-one, live thun-nardy, as
they call it, (that is alone,) for feveral weeks together, under this pretence; but as a proof he
had fome fufpicion, fhe was always carefully
watched, to prevent her from giving her company to any other man.   The Southern Indians are
alfo very delicate in this point; for though they
do not force their wives to build a feparate tent,
they never lie under the fame clothes during this
period.   It is, however, equally true, that the
young girls, when thofe fymptoms make their
firft appearance, generally go a little diftance from
the other tents for four or five days, and at their
return wear a kind of veil or curtain, made of
beads, for fome time after, as a mark of modefty;

as

as they are then confidered marriageable, and of courfe are called women, though fome at thofe periods are not more than thirteen, while others at the age of fifteen or fixteen have been reckoned as children, though apparently arrived at nearly their full growth

On thofe occafions a remarkable piece of fuperftition prevails among them; women in this fituation are never permitted to walk on the ice of rivers or lakes, or near the part where the men are hunting beaver, or where a fifhing-net is fet, for fear of averting their fuccefs. They are alfo prohibited at thofe times from partaking of the head of any animal, and even from walking in, or croffing the track where the head of a deer, moofe, beaver, and many other animals, have lately been carried, either on a fledge or on the back. To be guilty of a violation of this cuftom is confidered as of the greateft importance; becaufe they firmly believe that it would be a means of preventing the hunter from having an equal fuccefs in his future excurfions.

Thofe poor people live in fuch an inhofpitable part of the globe, that for want of firing they are frequently obliged to eat their victuals quite raw, particularly in the Summer feafon, while on the barren ground; but early cuftom and frequent neceffity make this practice fo familiar to them, that fo far from finding any inconvenience arife from it, or having the leaft diflike to it, they frequently do it by choice, and particularly in the
article

article of fish ; for when they do make a pretence
of dreffing it, they feldom warm it through. I
have frequently made one of a party who has fat
round a frefh-killed deer, and affifted in picking
the bones quite clean, when I thought that the
raw brains and many other parts were exceedingly good ; and, however ftrange it may appear, I
muft beftow the fame epithet on half-raw fifh :
even to this day I give the preference to trout,
falmon, and the brown tittemeg, when they are
not warm at the bone.

The extreme poverty of thofe Indians in general will not permit one half of them to purchafe
brafs kettles from the Company ; fo that they are
ftill under the neceffity of continuing their original mode of boiling their victuals in large upright
veffels made of birch-rind. As thofe veffels will
not admit of being expofed to the fire, the
Indians, to fupply the defect, heat ftones red-hot
and put them into the water, which foon occafions it to boil; and by having a conftant fucceffion
of hot ftones, they may continue the procefs as
long as it is neceffary. This method of cooking,
though very expeditious, is attended with one
great evil; the victuals which are thus prepared
are full of fand : for the ftones thus heated, and
then immerged in the water, are not only liable
to fhiver to pieces, but many of them being of a
coarfe gritty nature, fall to a mafs of gravel in
the kettle, which cannot be prevented from mixing with the victuals which are boiled in it. Befides

fides this, they have feveral other methods of preparing their food, fuch as roafting it by a ftring, broiling it, &c., but thefe need on farther defcription.

The moft remarkable difh among them, as well as all the other tribes of Indians in thofe parts, both Northern and Southern, is blood mixed with the half-digefted food which is found in the deer's ftomach or paunch, and boiled up with a fufficient quantity of water, to make it of the confiftence of peafe-pottage. Some fat and fcraps of tender flefh are alfo fhred fmall and boiled with it. To render this difh more palatable, they have a method of mixing the blood with the contents of the ftomach in the paunch itfelf, and hanging it up in the heat and fmoke of the fire for feveral days, which puts the whole mafs into a ftate of fermentation, and gives it fuch an agreeable acid tafte, that were it not for prejudice, it might be eaten by thofe who have the niceft palates. It is true, fome people with delicate ftomachs would not be eafily perfuaded to partake of this difh, efpecially if they faw it dreffed; for moft of the fat which is boiled in it is firft chewed by the men and boys, in order to break the globules that contain the fat, by which means it all boils out, and mixes with the broth: whereas, if it were permitted to remain as it came from the knife, it would ftill be in lumps, like fuet. To do juftice, however, to their cleanlinefs in this particular, I muft obferve, that they are very

care-

careful that neither old people with bad teeth,
nor young children, have any hand in preparing
this dish. At first, I must acknowledge that I
was rather shy in partaking of this mess, but when
I was sufficiently convinced of the truth of the
above remark, I no longer made any scruple, but
always thought it exceedingly good.

The stomach of no other large animal beside
the deer is eaten by any of the Indians that border on Hudson's Bay. In Winter, when the deer
feed on fine white moss, the contents of the stomach is so much esteemed by them, that I have
often seen them sit round a deer where it was
killed, and eat it warm out of the paunch. In
Summer the deer feed more coarsely, and therefore this dish, if it deserve that appellation, is then
not so much in favour.

The young calves, fawns, beaver, &c. taken out
of the bellies of their mothers, are reckoned most
delicate food; and I am not the only European
who heartily joins in pronouncing them the greatest dainties that can be eaten. Many gentlemen
who have served with me at Churchill, as well as
at York Fort, and the inland settlements, will
readily agree with me in asserting, that no one
who ever got the better of prejudice so far as to
taste of those young animals, but has immediately become excessively fond of them; and the
same may be said of young geese, ducks, &c. in
the shell. In fact, it is almost become a proverb
in the Northern settlements, that whoever
wishes

wifhes to know what is good, muft live with the
Indians.

The parts of generation belonging to any beaft
they kill, both male and female, are always eat-
en by the men and boys; and though thofe parts,
particularly in the males, are generally very tough,
they are not, on any account, to be cut with an
edge-tool, but torn to pieces with the teeth; and
when any part of them proves too tough to be
mafticated, it is thrown into the fire and burnt.
For the Indians believe firmly, that if a dog fhould
eat any part of them, it would have the fame effect on their fuccefs in hunting, that a woman
croffing their hunting-track at an improper period would have. The fame ill-fuccefs is fuppofed
alfo to attend them if a woman eat any of thofe
parts.

They are alfo remarkably fond of the womb of
the buffalo, elk, deer, &c. which they eagerly
devour without wafhing, or any other procefs
but barely ftroking out the contents. This, in
fome of the larger animals, and efpecially when
they are fome time gone with young, needs, no
defcription to make it fufficiently difgufting;
and yet I have known fome in the Company's
fervice remarkably fond of the difh, though I am
not one of the number. The womb of the beaver and deer is well enough, but that of the moofe
and buffalo is very rank, and truly difgufting*.

Our

* The Indian method of preparing this unaccountable difh is by throwing
the

Our Northern Indians who trade at the Factory, as well as all the Copper tribe, pafs their
whole fummer on the barren ground, where they
generally find plenty of deer; and in fome
of the rivers and lakes, a great abundance of fine
fifh.

Their bows and arrows, though their original
weapons, are, fince the introduction of fire-arms
among them, become of little ufe, except in killing deer as they walk or run through a narrow
pafs

the filthy bag or of a pole directly over the fire, the fmoke of which, they
fay, much improves it, by taking off the original flavour, and when any
of it is to be cooked, a large flake, like as much tripe, is cut off and boiled
for a few minutes, but the many large nodes with which the infide of the
womb is ftudded, make it abominable These nodes are as incapable of
being divefted of moifture as the fkin of a live eel, but when boiled,
much refemble, both in fhape and colour, the yolk of an egg, and are fo
called by the natives, and as eagerly devoured by them

The tripe of the buffalo is exceedingly good, and the Indian method of
cooking it infinitely fuperior to that practifed in Europe When opportunity will permit, they wafh it tolerably clean in cold water, ftrip off all
the honey-comb, and only boil it about half, or three-quarters of an
hour in that time it is fufficiently done for eating, and though rather
tougher than what is prepared in England, yet is exceedingly pleafant to
the tafte, and muft be much more nourifhing than tripe that has been
foked and fcrubbed in many hot waters, and then boiled for ten or twelve
hours

The leffer ftomach, or, as fome call it, the many-folds, either of buffalo, moofe, or deer, are ufually eat raw, and are very good, but that of
the moofe, unlefs great care be taken in wafhing it, is rather bitter, owing to the nature of their food

The kidneys of both moofe and buffalo are ufually eat raw by the Southern Indians, for no fooner is one of thofe beafts killed, than the hunter rips up its belly, thrufts in his arm, fnatches out the kidneys, and eats
them warm, before the animal is quite dead They alfo at times put their
mouths to the wound the ball has made, and fuck the blood, which
they fay quenches thirft, and is very nourifhing

pafs prepared for their reception, where feveral Indians lie concealed for that purpofe. This method of hunting is only practicable in Summer, and on the barren ground, where they have an extenfive profpect, and can fee the herds of deer at a great diftance, as well as difcover the nature of the country, and make every neceffary arrangement for driving them through the narrow defiles. This method of hunting is performed in the following manner:

When the Indians fee a herd of deer, and intend to hunt them with bows and arrows, they obferve which way the wind blows, and always get to leeward, for fear of being fmelled by the deer. The next thing to which they attend, is to fearch for a convenient place to conceal thofe who are appointed to fhoot. This being done, a large bundle of fticks, like large ramrods, (which they carry with them the whole Summer for the purpofe,) are ranged in two ranks, fo as to form the two fides of a very acute angle, and the fticks placed at the diftance of fifteen or twenty yards from each other. When thofe neceffary arrangements are completed, the women and boys feparate into two parties, and go round on both fides, till they form a crefcent at the back of the deer, which are drove right forward; and as each of the fticks has a fmall flag, or more properly a pendant, faftened to it, which is eafily waved to and fro by the wind, and a lump of mofs ftuck on each of their tops, the poor timo-

Y

rous deer, probably taking them for ranks of
people, generally run ftraight forward between
the two ranges of fticks, till they get among the
Indians, who lie concealed in fmall circular fences, made with loofe ftones, mofs, &c. When
the deer approach very near, the Indians who are
thus concealed ftart up and fhoot; but as the
deer generally pafs along at full fpeed, few Indians have time to fhoot more than one or two arrows, unlefs the herd be very large.

This method of hunting is not always attended
with equal fuccefs; for fometimes after the Indians have been at the trouble of making places of
fhelter, and arranging the flag-fticks, &c. the deer
will make off another way, before the women and
children can furround them. At other times I
have feen eleven or twelve of them killed with
one volley of arrows; and if any gun-men attend
on thofe occafions, they are always placed behind
the other Indians, in order to pick up the deer
that efcape the bow-men. By thefe means I
have feen upwards of twenty fine deer killed at
one broadfide, as it may be termed.

Though the Northern Indians may be faid to
kill a great number of deer in this manner during
the Summer, yet they have fo far loft the art of
fhooting with bows and arrows, that I never
knew any of them who could take thofe weapons
only, and kill either deer, moofe, or buffalo, in
the common, wandering, and promifcuous method of hunting. The Southern Indians, though
they

they have been longer ufed to fire-arms, are far
more expert with the bow and arrow, their original weapons

The tents made ufe of by thofe Indians, both
in Summer and Winter, are generally compofed
of deer-fkins in the hair; and for convenience of
carriage, are always made in fmall pieces, feldom
exceeding five buck-fkins in one piece. Thefe
tents, as alfo their kettles, and fome other lumber, are always carried by dogs, which are trained to that fervice, and are very docile and tracta-
ble. Thofe animals are of various fizes and colours, but all of the fox and wolf breed, with fharp
nofes, full bufhy tails, and fharp ears ftanding
erect. They are of great courage when attacked,
and bite fo fharp, that the fmalleft cur among
them will keep feveral of our largeft Englifh dogs
at bay, if he can get up in a corner. Thefe
dogs are equally willing to haul in a fledge, but
as few of the men will be at the trouble of making fledges for them, the poor women are obliged to content themfelves with leffening the bulk
of their load, more than the weight, by making
the dogs carry thefe articles only, which are always lafhed on their backs, much after the fame
manner as packs are, or ufed formerly to be, on
pack-horfes

In the fall of the year, and as the Winter advances, thofe people few the fkins of the deers
legs together in the fhape of long portmanteaus,
which, when hauled on the fnow as the hair lies,

are

are as flippery as an otter, and ferve them as
temporary fledges while on the barren ground;
but when they arrive at any woods, they then
make proper fledges, with thin boards of the
larch-tree, generally known in Hudfon's Bay by
the name of Juniper.

Thofe fledges are of various fizes, according to
the ftrength of the perfons who are to haul them:
fome I have feen were not lefs than twelve or
fourteen feet long, and fifteen or fixteen inches
wide, but in general they do not exceed eight or
nine feet in length, and twelve or fourteen inches
in breadth.

The boards of which thofe fledges are compofed are not more than a quarter of an inch thick,
and feldom exceed five or fix inches in width;
as broader would be very unhandy for the Indians to work, who have no other tools than an ordinary knife, turned up a little at the point,
from which it acquires the name of Bafe-hoth
among the Northern Indians, but among the
Southern tribes it is called Mo co-toggan  The
boards are fewed together with thongs of parchment deer-fkin, and feveral crofs bars of wood
are fewed on the upper fide, which ferves both
to ftrengthen the fledge and fecure the ground-
lafhing, to which the load is always faftened by
other fmaller thongs, or ftripes of leather.  The
head or fore-part of the fledge is turned up fo as to
form a femi-circle, of at leaft fifteen or twenty inches diameter.  This prevents the carriage from
diving into light fnow, and enables it to flide over

the

the inequalities and hard drifts of fnow which are conftantly met with on the open plains and barren grounds. The trace or draught-line to thofe fledges is a double ftring, or flip of leather, made faft to the head; and the bight is put acrofs the fhoulders of the perfon who hauls the fledge, fo as to reft againft the breaft. This contrivance, though fo fimple, cannot be improved by the moft ingenious collar-maker in the world.

Their fnow-fhoes differ from all others made ufe of in thofe parts, for though they are of the galley kind, that is, fharp pointed before, yet they are always to be worn on one foot, and cannot be fhifted from fide to fide, like other fnow-fhoes; for this reafon the inner-fide of the frames are almoft ftraight, and the outer-fide has a very large fweep. The frames are generally made of birch-wood, and the netting is compofed of thongs of deer-fkin; but their mode of filling that compartment where the foot refts, is quite different from that ufed among the Southern Indians.

Their clothing, which chiefly confifts of deer fkins in the hair, makes them very fubject to be loufy, but that is fo far from being thought a difgrace, that the beft among them amufe themfelves with catching and eating thefe vermin; of which they are fo fond, that the produce of a loufy head or garment affords them not only pleafing amufement, but a delicious repaft. My old guide, Matonabbee, was fo remarkably fond of thofe little vermin, that he frequently fet five

or

or fix of his ftrapping wives to work to loufe
their hairy deer-fkin fhifts, the produce of which
being always very confiderable, he eagerly received with both hands, and licked them in as
faft, and with as good a grace, as any European
epicure would the mites in a cheefe.  He often
affured me that fuch amufement was not only
very pleafing, but that the objects of the fearch
were very good; for which I gave him credit,
telling him at the fame time, that though I endeavoured to habituate myfelf to every other part
of their diet, yet as I was but a fojourner
among them, I had no inclination to accuftom
myfelf to fuch dainties as I could not procure in
that part of the world where I was moft inclined
to refide.

The Southern Indians and Ffquimaux are
equally fond of thofe vermin, which are fo de-
teftable in the eyes of an European, nay, the
latter have many other dainties of a fimilar kind
for befide making ufe of train-oil as a cordial and
as fauce to their meat, I have frequently feen
them eat a whole handful of maggots that were
produced in meat by fly-blows.  It is their conftant cuftom to eat the filth that comes from the
nofe; and when their nofes bleed by accident,
tney always lick the blood into their mouths, and
fwallow it

The track of land inhabited by the Northern
Indians is very extenfive, reaching from the fifty-
ninth to the fixty-eighth degree of North latitude,

tude; and from Eaſt to Weſt is upward of five
hundred miles wide. It is bounded by Churchill River on the South; the Athapuſcow Indians'
Country on the Weſt; the Dog-ribbed and Copper Indians' Country on the North; and by Hudſon's Bay on the Eaſt. The land throughout
that whole track of country is ſcarcely any thing
but one ſolid maſs of rocks and ſtones, and in
moſt parts very hilly, particularly to the Weſtward, among the woods. The ſurface, it is very
true, is in moſt places covered with a thin ſod of
moſs, intermixed with the roots of the Wee-ſa-ca-
pucca, cranberries, and a few other inſignificant
ſhrubs and herbage; but under it there is in general a total want of ſoil, capable of producing
any thing except what is peculiar to the climate.
Some of the marſhes, indeed, produce ſeveral
kinds of graſs, the growth of which is amazingly
rapid, but this is dealt out with ſo ſparing a hand
as to be barely ſufficient to ſerve the geeſe, ſwans,
and other birds of paſſage, during their migrations in the Spring, and Fall, while they remain
in a moulting ſtate.

The many lakes and rivers with which this part
of the country abounds, though they do not furniſh the natives with water-carriage, are yet of
infinite advantage to them; as they afford great
numbers of fiſh, both in Summer and Winter.
The only ſpecies caught in thoſe parts are trout,
tittameg, (or tickomeg,) tench, two ſorts of barble, (called by the Southern Indians Na-may-pith,)
burbot,

burbot, pike, and a few perch.   The four former
are caught in all parts of this country, as well the
woody as the barren; but the three latter are only
caught to the Weftward, in fuch lakes and rivers
as are fituated among the woods; and though
fome of thofe rivers lead to the barren ground,
yet the three laft mentioned fpecies of fifh are feldom caught beyond the edge of the woods, not
even in the Summer feafon.

There is a black, hard, crumply mofs, that
grows on the rocks and large ftones in thofe
parts, which is of infinite fervice to the natives,
as it fometimes furnifhes them with a temporary
fubfiftence, when no animal food can be procured.   This mofs, when boiled, turns to a
gummy confiftence, and is more clammy in the
mouth than fago; it may, by adding either mofs
or water, be made to almoft any confiftence.
It is fo palatable, that all who tafte it generally
grow fond of it.   It is remarkably good and
pleafing when ufed to thicken any kind of broth,
but it is generally moft efteemed when boiled in
fifh-liquor.

The only method practifed by thofe people to
catch fifh either in Winter or Summer, is by
angling and fetting nets; both of which methods
is attended with much fuperftition, ceremony, and
unneceffary trouble; but I will endeavour to
defcribe them in as plain and brief a manner as
poffible.

When they make a new fifhing-net, which is
always

always compofed of fmall thongs cut from raw deer-fkins, they take a number of birds bills and feet, and tie them, a little apart from each other, to the head and foot rope of the net, and at the four corners generally faften fome of the toes and jaws of the otters and jackafhes. The birds feet and bills made choice of on fuch occafions are generally thofe of the laughing goofe, wavey, (or white goofe,) gulls, loons, and black-heads; and unlefs fome or all of thefe be faftened to the net, they will not attempt to put it into the water, as they firmly believe it would not catch a fingle fifh.

A net thus accoutred is fit for fetting whenever occafion requires, and opportunity offers, but the firft fifh of whatever fpecies caught in it, are not to be fodden in the water, but broiled whole on the fire, and the flefh carefully taken from the bones without diflocating one joint; after which the bones are laid on the fire at full length and burnt. A ftrict obfervance of thefe rules is fuppofed to be of the utmoft importance in promoting the future fuccefs of the new net; and a neglect of them would render it not worth a farthing*.

When they fifh in rivers, or narrow channels

that

---

* They frequently fell new nets, which have not been wet more than once or twice, becaufe they have not been fuccefsful Thofe nets, when foked in water, are eafily opened, and then make moft excellent heel and toe netting for fnow-fhoes. In general it is far fuperior to the netting cut by the Southern Indian women, and is not larger than common net-twine

that join two lakes together, they could frequently, by tying two, three, or more nets together, spread over the whole breadth of the channel, and intercept every sizable fish that passed; but instead of that, they scatter the nets at a considerable distance from each other, from a superstitious notion, that were they kept close together, one net would be jealous of its neighbour, and by that means not one of them would catch a single fish.

The methods used, and strictly observed, when angling, are equally absurd as those I have mentioned, for when they bait a hook, a composition of four, five, or six articles, by way of charm, is concealed under the bait, which is always sewed round the hook. In fact, the only bait used by those people is in their opinion a composition of charms, inclosed within a bit of fish skin, so as in some measure to resemble a small fish. The things used by way of charm, are bits of beavers tails and fat, otter's vents and teeth, musk-rat's guts and tails, loon's vents, squirrel's testicles, the crudled milk taken out of the stomach of sucking fawns and calves, human hair, and numberless other articles equally absurd.

Every master of a family, and indeed almost every other person, particularly the men, have a small bundle of such trash, which they always carry with them, both in Summer and Winter; and without some of those articles to put under their bait, few of them could be prevailed upon

to

to put a hook into the water, being fully perfuaded that they may as well fit in the tent, as
attempt to angle without fuch affiftance. They
have alfo a notion that fifh of the fame fpecies
inhabiting different parts of the country, are
fond of different things; fo that almoft every
lake and river they arrive at, obliges them to alter the compofition of the charm. The fame
rule is obferved on broiling the firft fruits of a
new hook that is ufed for a new net, an old
hook that has already been fuccefsful in catching large fifh is efteemed of more value, than
a handful of new ones which have never been
tried.

Deer alfo, as well as fifh, are very numerous
in many parts of this country; particularly to
the North of the fixtieth degree of latitude.
Alpine hares are in fome parts of the barren
ground pretty plentiful, where alfo fome herds
of mufk oxen are to be met with, and to the
Weftward, among the woods, there are fome
rabbits and partridges. With all thofe feeming
fources of plenty, however, one half of the inhabitants, and perhaps the other half alfo, are
frequently in danger of being ftarved to death,
owing partly to their want of œconomy, and
moft of thefe fcenes of diftrefs happen during
their journies to and from Prince of Wales's
Fort, the only place at which they trade

When Northern Indians are at the Factory,
they are very liable to fteal any thing they
think

think will be ferviceable; particularly iron hoops, fmall bolts, fpikes, carpenters tools, and, in fhort, all fmall pieces of iron-work which they can turn to advantage, either for their own ufe, or for the purpofe of trading with fuch of their country-men as feldom vifit the Company's Settlement: among themfelves, however, the crime of theft is feldom heard of.

When two parties of thofe Indians meet, the ceremonies which pafs between them are quite different from thofe made ufe of in Europe on fimilar occafions; for when they advance within twenty or thirty yards of each other, they make a full halt, and in general fit or lie down on the ground, and do not fpeak for fome minutes. At length one of them, generally an elderly man, if any be in company, breaks filence, by acquaint-ing the other party with every misfortune that has befallen him and his companions from the laft time they had feen or heard of each other; and alfo of all deaths and other calamities that have befallen any other Indians during the fame period, at leaft as many particulars as have come to his knowledge.

When the firft has finifhed his oration, another aged orator, (if there be any) belonging to the other party relates, in like manner, all the bad news that has come to his knowledge; and both parties never fail to plead poverty and famine on all occafions. If thofe orations contain any news that in the leaft affect the other party, it is not
long

long before fome of them begin to figh and fob, and foon after break out into a loud cry, which is generally accompanied by moft of the grown perfons of both fexes; and fometimes it is common to fee them all, men, women, and children, in one univerfal howl. The young girls, in particular, are often very obliging on thofe occafions; for I never remember to have feen a crying match (as I called it) but the greateft part of the company affifted, although fome of them had no other reafon for it, but that of feeing their companions do the fame. When the firft tranfports of grief fubfide, they advance by degrees, and both parties mix with each other, the men always affociating with the men, and the women with the women. If they have any tobacco among them, the pipes are paffed round pretty freely, and the converfation foon becomes general. As they are on their firft meeting acquainted with all the bad news, they have by this time nothing left but good, which in general has fo far the predominance over the former, that in lefs than half an hour nothing but fmiles and cheerfulnefs are to be feen in every face; and if they be not really in want, fmall prefents of provifions, ammunition, and other articles, often take place; fometimes merely as a gift, but more frequently by way of trying whether they cannot get a greater prefent.

They have but few diverfions; the chief is
shooting

shooting at a mark with bow and arrows, and
another out-door game, called Holl, which in
some measure resembles playing with coits;
only it is done with short clubs, sharp at one end.
They also amuse themselves at times with dancing, which is always performed in the night.   It
is remarkable that those people, though a distinct
nation, have never adopted any mode of dancing
of their own, or any songs to which they can
dance; so that when any thing of this kind is
attempted, which is but seldom, they always endeavour to imitate either the Dog-ribbed or Southern Indians, but more commonly the former, as
few of them are sufficiently acquainted either
with the Southern Indian language, or their manner of dancing.   The Dog-ribbed method is not
very difficult to learn, as it only consists in lifting the feet alternately from the ground in a
very quick succession, and as high as possible,
without moving the body, which should be kept
quite still and motionless; the hands at the same
time being closed, and held close to the breast,
and the head inclining forward.   This diversion
is always performed quite naked, except the
breech-cloth, and at times that is also thrown off,
and the dancers, who seldom exceed three or
four at a time, always stand close to the music.
The music may, by straining a point, be called
both vocal and instrumental, though both are
sufficiently humble.   The former is no more
than

than a frequent repetition of the words hee, hee, hee, ho, ho, ho, &c. which, by a more or lefs frequent repetition, dwelling longer on one word and fhorter on another, and raifing and lowering the voice, produce fomething like a tune, and has the defired effect. This is always accompanied by a drum or tabor; and fometimes a kind of rattle is added, made with a piece of dried buffalo fkin, in fhape exactly like an oil-flafk, into which they put a few fhot or pebbles, which, when fhook about, produces mufic little inferior to the drum, though not fo loud.

This mode of dancing naked is performed only by the men; for when the women are ordered to dance, they always exhibit without the tent, to mufic which is played within it; and though their method of dancing is perfectly decent, yet it has ftill lefs meaning and action than that of the men : for a whole heap of them crowd together in a ftraight line, and juft fhuffle themfelves a little from right to left, and back again in the fame line, without lifting their feet from the ground; and when the mufic ftops, they all give a little bend of the body and knee, fomewhat like an awkward curtfy, and pronounce, in a little fhrill tone, h-e-e, h-o-o-o e.

Befide thefe diverfions, they have another fimple in-door game, which is that of taking a bit of wood, a button, or any other fmall thing, and after fhifting it from hand to hand feveral times,

afking

afking their antagonift, which hand it is in?
When playing at this game, which only admits
of two perfons, each of them have ten, fifteen
or twenty fmall chips of wood, like matches; and
when one of the players gueffes right, he takes
one of his antagonift's fticks, and lays it to his
own; and he that firft gets all the fticks from
the other in that manner is faid to win the game,
which is generally for a fingle load of powder
and fhot, an arrow, or fome other thing of inconfiderable value.

The women never mix in any of their diverfions, not even in dancing; for when that is required of them, they always exhibit without the
tent, as has been already obferved; nor are they
allowed to be prefent at a feaft. Indeed, the
whole courfe of their lives is one continued fcene
of drudgery, *viz.* carrying and hauling heavy
loads, dreffing fkins for clothing, curing their
provifions, and practifing other neceffary domeftic duties which are required in a family, without enjoying the leaft diverfion of any kind, or
relaxation, on any occafion whatever; and except
in the execution of thofe homely duties, in which
they are always inftructed from their infancy,
their fenfes feem almoft as dull and frigid as the
zone they inhabit. There are indeed fome exceptions to be met with among them, and I fuppofe it only requires indulgence and precept to
make fome of them as lofty and infolent as any

women in the world. Though they wear their
hair at full length, and never tie it up, like the
Southern Indians ; and though not one in fifty of
them is ever poffeffed of a comb, yet by a wonderful dexterity of the fingers, and a good deal
of patience, they make fhift to ftroke it out fo as
not to leave two hairs entangled , but when their
heads are infefted with vermin, from which very
few of either fex are free, they mutually affift each
other in keeping them under.

A fcorbutic diforder, refembling the worft ftage
of the itch, confumptions, and fluxes, are their
chief diforders. The firft of thefe, though very
troublefome, is never known to prove fatal, unlefs it be accompanied with fome inward complaint ; but the two latter, with a few accidents,
carries off great numbers of both fexes and all
ages : indeed few of them live to any great age,
probably owing to the great fatigue they undergo from their youth up, in procuring a fubfiftence for themfelves and their offspring.

Though the fcorbutic diforder above mentioned does appear to be infectious, it is rare to fee
one have it without the whole tent's crew being
more or lefs affected with it; but this is by no
means a proof of its being contagious ; I rather
attribute it to the effects of fome bad water, or
the unwholefomenefs of fome fifh they may
catch in particular places, in the courfe of their
wandering manner of life. Were it otherwife,
a fingle family would in a fhort time communi-

Z

cate it to the whole tribe ; but, on the contrary,
the difeafe is never known to fpread.  In the
younger fort it always attacks the hands and feet,
not even fparing the palms and foles   Thofe of
riper years generally have it about the wrifts, in-
fteps, and pofteriors, and in the latter particularly, the blotches, or boils as they may juftly be
called are often as large as the top of a man's
thumb.  This diforder moft frequently makes
its appearance in the Summer,  while the Indians
are out in the barren ground ; and though it is
by no means reckoned dangerous, yet it is fo ob-
ftinate, as not to yield to any medicine that has
ever been applied to it while at the Company's Factory.   And as the natives themfelves never make
ufe of any medicines of their own preparing,
Nature alone works the cure, which is never performed in lefs than twelve or eighteen months ;
and fome of them are troubled with this difagreeable and loathfome diforder for years before they
are perfectly cured, and then a dark livid mark
remains on thofe parts of the fkin which have
been affected, for many years afterwards, and in
fome during life.

When any of the principal Northern Indians
die, it is generally believed that they are conjur-
ed to death, either by fome of their own countrymen, by fome of the Southern Indians, or by
fome of the Efquimaux · too frequently the fufpicion falls on the latter tribe, which is the grand
reafon of their never being at peace with thofe
                                                    poor

poor and diftreffed people. For fome time paft, however, thofe Efquimaux who trade with our floops at Knapp's Bay, Navel's Bay, and Whale Cove, are in perfect peace and friendfhip with the Northern Indians, which is entirely owing to the protection they have for feveral years paft received from the Chiefs at the Company's Fort at Churchill River*. But thofe of that tribe who

Z 2

live

---

* In the Summer of 17,   a party of Northern Indians lay in wait at Knapp's Bay till the floop had failed out of the harbour, when they fell on the poor Efquimaux, and killed every foul   Mr John Bean, then Mafter of the floop, and fince Mafter of the Trinity yacht, with all his crew, heard he guns very plain, but did not know the meaning or reafon of it till the Summer following, when he found the fhocking remains of more than forty Efquimaux, who had been murdered in that cowardly manner; and for no other reafon but becaufe two principal Northern Indians had died in the preceding Winter

No Efquimaux were feen at Knapp's Bay for feveral years after, and thofe who trade there at prefent have undoubtedly been drawn from the Northward, fince the above unhappy tranfaction, for the convenience of being nearer the woods, as well as being in the way of trading with the floop that calls there annually   It is to be hoped that the meafures taken by the Governors at Prince of Wales's Fort of late years, will effectually prevent any fuch calamities happening in future, and by degrees be the means of bringing about a lafting, friendly, and reciprocal intereft between the two nations

Notwithstanding the pacific and friendly terms which begin to dawn between thofe two tribes at Knapp's Bay, Navel's Bay, and Whale Cove, farther North hoftilities continue, and moft barbarous murders are perpetrated   and the only protection the Efquimaux have from the fury of their enemies, is their remote fituation in the Winter, and their refiding chiefly on iflands and peninfulas in Summer, which renders them lefs liable to be furprifed during that feafon   But even this fecluded life does not prevent the Northern Indians from haraffing them greatly, and at times they are fo clofely purfued as to be obliged to leave moft of their goods, and utenfils to be deftroyed by their enemy, which muft be a great lofs, as thefe cannot be replaced but at the expence of much time and labour, and the want of them in the main time muft create much diftrefs both to

them-live so far to the North, as not to have any intercourse with our veffels, very often fall a facrifice to the fury and fuperftition of the Northern Indians, who are by no means a bold or warlike people; nor can I think from experience, that they are particularly guilty of committing acts of wanton cruelty on any other part of the human race befide the Efquimaux. Their hearts, however,

themfelves and their families, as they can feldom procure any part of their livelihood without the afffiftance of a confiderable apparatus

In 1756, the Efquimaux at Knapp's Bay fent two of their youths to Prince of Wales's Fort in the floop, and the Summer following they were carried back to their friends, loaded with prefents and much pleafed with the treatment they received while at the Fort In 1767, they again fent one from Knapp's Bay and one from Whale Cove, and though during their ftay at the Fort they made a confiderable progrefs both in the Southern Indian and the Englifh languages, yet thofe intercourfes have not been any ways fo advantageous to the Company, by increafing the trade from that quarter In fact, the only fatisfaction they have found for the great expence they have from time to time incurred, by introducing thofe ftrangers, is, that through the good conduct of their upper fervants at Churchill River, they have at length fo far humanized the hearts of thofe two tribes, that at prefent they can meet each other in a friendly manner, whereas a few years fince, whenever they met, each party premeditated the deftruction of the other, and what made their war more fhocking, was, they never gave quarter fo that the ftrongeft party always killed the weakeft, without fparing either man, woman, or child

It is but a few years ago that the floop's crew who annually carried them all their wants, durft not venture on fhore among the Efquimaux unarmed, for fear of being murdered, but latterly they are fo civilized, that the Company's fervants vifit their tents with the greateft freedom and fafety, are always welcome, and defired to partake of fuch provifions as they have and knowing now our averfion from train oil, they take every means in their power to convince our people that the victuals prepared for them is entirely free from it But the fmell of their tents, cooking utenfils, and other furniture, is fcarcely lefs offenfive than Greenland Dock However I have eaten both fifh and venifon cooked by them in fo cleanly a manner, that I have relifhed them very much, and partaken of them with a good appetite ever, are in general so unsusceptible of tenderness, that they can view the deepest distress in those who are not immediately related to them, without the least emotion, not even half so much as the generality of mankind feel for the sufferings of the meanest of the brute creation. I have been present when one of them, imitating the groans, distorted features, and contracted position, of a man who had died in the most excruciating pain, put the whole company, except myself, into the most violent fit of laughter.

The Northern Indians never bury their dead, but always leave the bodies where they die, so that they are supposed to be devoured by beasts and birds of prey; for which reason they will not eat foxes, wolves, ravens, &c. unless it be through mere necessity.

The death of a near relation affects them so sensibly, that they rend all their cloths from their backs, and go naked, till some persons less afflicted relieve them. After the death of a father, mother, husband, wife, son, or brother, they mourn, as it may be called, for a whole year, which they measure by the moons and seasons. Those mournful periods are not distinguished by any particular dress, except that of cutting off the hair, and the ceremony consists in almost perpetually crying. Even when walking, as well as at all other intervals from sleep, eating, and conversation, they make an odd howling noise, often repeating the relationship of the deceased. But

as

as this is in a great meafure mere form and cuftom, fome of them have a method of foftening
the harfhnefs of the notes, and bringing them out
in a more mufical tone than that in which they
fing their fongs.     When they reflect ferioufly on
the lofs of a good friend, however, it has fuch an
effect on them for the prefent, that they give an
uncommon loofe to their grief   At thofe times
they feem to fympathife (through cuftom) with
each other's afflictions fo much, that I have often
feen feveral fcores of them crying in concert,
when at the fame time not above half a dozen of
them had any more reafon for fo doing than I
had, unlefs it was to preferve the old cuftom, and
keep the others in countenance.   The women
are remarkably obliging on fuch occafions; and as
no reftriction is laid on them, they may with
truth be faid to cry with all their might and
main ; but in common converfation they are obliged to be very moderate.

   They have a tradition among them, that the
firft perfon upon earth was a woman, who, after
having been fome time alone, in her refearches
for berries, which was then her only food, found
an animal like a dog, which followed her to the
cave where fhe lived, and foon grew fond and
domeftic.   This dog, they fay, had the art of
transforming itfelf into the fhape of a handfome
young man, which it frequently did at night, but
as the day approached, always refumed its former
fhape , fo that the woman looked on all that paffed

ed on thofe occafions as dreams and delufions. Thefe tranformations were foon productive of the confequences which at prefent generally follow fuch intimate connexions between the two fexes, and the mother of the world began to advance in her pregnancy.

Not long after this happened, a man of fuch a furprifing height that his head reached up to the clouds, came to level the land, which at that time was a very rude mafs, and after he had done this, by the help of his walking-ftick he marked out all the lakes, ponds, and rivers, and immediately caufed them to be filled with water. He then took the dog, and tore it to pieces; the guts he threw into the lakes and rivers, commanding them to become the different kinds of fifh; the flefh he difperfed over the land, commanding it to become different kinds of beafts and land-animals; the fkin he alfo tore in fmall pieces, and threw it into the air, commanding it to become all kinds of birds; after which he gave the woman and her offspring full power to kill, eat, and never fpare, for that he had commanded them to multiply for her ufe in abundance. After this injunction, he returned to the place whence he came, and has not been heard of fince.

RELIGION has not as yet begun to dawn among the Northern Indians, for though their conjurors do indeed fing fongs, and make long fpeeches, to fome beafts and birds of prey, as alfo to imaginary beings, which they fay affift them in
peiforming

performing cures on the fick, yet they, as well
as their credulous neighbours, are utterly deftitute of every idea of practical religion. It is
true, fome of them will reprimand their youth
for talking difrefpectfully of particular beafts and
birds, but it is done with fo little energy, as to
be often retorted back in derifion. Neither is
this, nor their cuftom of not killing wolves and
quiquehatches, univerfally obferved, and thofe
who do it can only be viewed with more pity and
contempt than the others, for I always found it
arofe merely from the greater degree of confidence which they had in the fupernatural power
of their conjurors, which induced them to believe,
that talking lightly or difrefpectfully of any thing
they feemed to approve, would materially affect
their health and happinefs in this world: and I
never found any of them that had the leaft idea
of futurity. Matonabbee, without one exception, was a man of as clear ideas in other matters
as any that I ever faw. he was not only a perfect
mafter of the Southern Indian language, and their
belief, but could tell a better ftory of our Savi-
our's birth and life, than one half of thofe who
call themfelves Chriftians, yet he always declared to me, that neither he, nor any of his countrymen, had an idea of a future ftate. Though
he had been taught to look on things of this
kind as ufelefs, his own good fenfe had taught
him to be an advocate for univerfal toleration;
and I have feen him feveral times affift at fome of
                                              the

the moft facred rites performed by the Southern Indians, apparently with as much zeal, as if he had given as much credit to them as they did · and with the fame liberality of fentiment he would, I am perfuaded have affifted at the altar of a Chriftian church, or in a Jewifh fynagogue; not with a view to reap any advantage himfelf, but merely, as he obferved, to affift others who believed in fuch ceremonies.

Being thus deftitute of all religious controul, thefe people have, to ufe Matonabbee's own words, "nothing to do but confult their own intereft, "inclinations, and paffions; and to pafs through "this world with as much eafe and contentment "as poffible, without any hopes of reward, or "painful fear of punifhment in the next" In this ftate of mind they are, when in profperity, the happieft of mortals, for nothing but perfonal or family calamities can difturb their tranquillity, while misfortunes of the leffer kind fit light on them. Like moft other uncivilized people, they bear bodily pain with great fortitude, though in that refpeft I cannot think them equal to the Southern Indians.

Old age is the greateft calamity that can befal a Northern Indian; for when he is paft labour, he is neglected, and treated with great difrefpect, even by his own children They not only ferve him laft at meals, but generally give him the coarfeft and worft of the victuals: and fuch of the fkins as they do not chufe to wear, are made up in

in the clumfieft manner into clothing for their
aged parents; who, as they had, in all probability, treated their fathers and mothers with the
fame neglect, in their turns, fubmitted patiently
to their lot, even without a murmur, knowing
it to be the common misfortune attendant an old
age, fo that they may be faid to wait patiently
for the melancholy hour when, being no longer
capable of walking, they are to be left alone, to
ftarve and perifh for want. This, however,
fhocking and unnatural it may appear, is neverthelefs fo common, that, among thofe people, one
half at leaft of the aged perfons of both fexes abfolutely die in this miferable condition.

The Northern Indians call the *Aurora Borealis*,
Ed-thin; that is, Deer*. and when that meteor is
very bright, they fay that deer is plentiful in that
part of the atmofphere, but they have never yet
extended their ideas fo far as to entertain hopes
of tafting thofe celeftial animals.

Befide this filly notion, they are very fuperftitious with refpect to the exiftence of feveral kinds
of fairies, called by them Nant-e-na, whom they
frequently fay they fee, and who are fuppofed by
them

* Their ideas in this refpect are founded on a principle one would not
imagine. Experience has fhewn them, that when a hairy deer-fkin is
brifkly ftroked with the hand in a dark night, it will emit many fparks of
electrical fire, as the back of a cat will. The idea which the Southern
Indians have of this meteor is equally romantic, though more pleafing, as
they believe it to be the fpirits of their departed friends dancing in the
clouds, and when the *Aurora Borealis* is remarkably bright, at which time
they vary moft in colour, form, and fituation, they fay, their deceafed
friends are very merry.

them to inhabit the different elements of earth, fea, and air, according to their feveral qualities. To one or other of thofe fairies they ufually attribute any change in their circumftances, either for the better or worfe , and as they are led into this way of thinking entirely by the art of the conjurors, there is no fuch thing as any general mode of belief , for thofe jugglers differ fo much from each other in their accounts of thefe beings, that thofe who believe any thing they fay, have little to do but change their opinions according to the will and caprice of the conjuror, who is almoft daily relating fome new whim, or extraordinary event, which, he fays, has been revealed to him ·in a dream, or by fome of his favourite fairies, when on a hunting excurfion.

*Some*

*Some Account of* MATONABBEE, *and of the eminent
Services which he rendered to his Country, as well
as to the Hudson's Bay Company.*

MATONABBEE was the fon of a Northern Indian by a flave woman, who was formerly bought
from fome Southern Indians who came to Prince
of Wales's Fort with furrs, &c. This match was
made by Mr Richard Norton, then Governor,
who detained them at and near the Fort, for the
fame purpofe as he did thofe Indians called Home-
guard.  As to Matonabbee's real age, it is impoffible to be particular; for the natives of thofe
parts being utterly unacquainted with letters, or
the ufe of hieroglyphics, though their memories
are not lefs retentive than thofe of other nations,
cannot preferve and tranfmit to pofterity the exact time when any particular event happens.  Indeed, the utmoft extent of their chronology reaches no farther, than to fay,  My fon, or my daughter, was born in fuch a Governor's time, and
fuch an event happened during fuch a perfon's
life-time (though, perhaps, he or fhe has been
dead many years)  However, according to appearance, and fome corroborating circumftances,
Matonabbee was born about the year one thoufand feven hundred and thirty-fix, or one thoufand feven hundred and thirty-feven; and his
father dying while he was young, the Governor
took

took the boy, and, according to the Indian cuſtom, adopted him as his ſon.

Soon after the death of Matonabbee's father, Mr. Norton went to England, and as the boy did not experience from his ſucceſſor the ſame regard and attention which he had been accuſtomed to receive form Mr. Norton, he was ſoon taken from the Factory by ſome of his father's relations, and continued with the Northern Indians till Mr. Ferdinand Jacobs ſucceeded to the command of Prince of Wales's Fort, in the year one thouſand ſeven hundred and fifty-two, when out of regard to old Mr Norton, (who was then dead,) Mr. Jacobs took the firſt opportunity that offered to detain Matonabbee at the Factory, where he was for ſeveral years employed in the hunting-ſervice with ſome of the Company's ſervants, particularly with the late Mr. Moſes Norton*, (ſon of the late Governor,) and Mr. Magnus Johnſton†.

In the courſe of his long ſtay at and near the Fort, it is no wonder that he ſhould have become perfect maſter of the Southern Indian language, and made ſome progreſs in the Engliſh. It was during this period, that he gained a knowledge of the Chriſtian faith, and he always declared, that it was too deep and intricate for his comprehenſion. Though he was a perfect bigot with

reſpect

---

* Aſterwards Governor
† Maſter of the Churchill ſloop.

respect to the arts and tricks of Indian jugglers,
yet he could by no means be impreſſed with a belief of any part of our religion, nor of the religion of the Southern Indians, who have as firm a
belief in a future ſtate as any people under the
Sun.  He had ſo much natural good ſenſe and
liberality of ſentiment, however, as not to think
that he had a right to ridicule any particular ſect
on account of their religious opinions.   On the
contrary, he declared, that he held them all equally in eſteem, but was determined, as he came into the world, ſo he would go out of it, without
profeſſing any religion at all   Notwithſtanding
his averſion from religion, I have met with few
Chriſtians who poſſeſſed more good moral qualities, or fewer bad ones

   It is impoſſible for any man to have been more
punctual in the performance of a promiſe than he
was; his ſcrupulous adherence to truth and ho-
neſty would have done honour to the moſt enlightened and devout Chriſtian, while his benevolence and univerſal humanity to all the human
race*, according to his abilities and manner of
life,

   * I muſt here obſerve, t'at when we went to war with the Eſqu-
maux at the Copper River in July 17/1, it was by no means his propoſal
on the contrary, he was forced into it by his countrymen  I or I have
heard him ſay, that whe he firſt ted that river, in company with
I dot le-aza, they met w th ſeveral Eſqu maix , and ſo far from killing
them, were very friendly to them, and made them ſmall preſents of ſuch
articles as they could beſt ſpare, and t' at would be of moſt uſe to them
It is more than probable that the two bits of iron found among the plun-
                                                                       der

life, could not be exceeded by the moft illuftri-
ous perfonage now on record; and to add to his
other good qualities, he was the only Indian that
I ever faw, except one, who was not guilty of
backbiting and flandering his neighbours.

In ftature, Matonabbee was above the common
fize, being nearly fix feet high†; and, except that
his neck was rather (though not much) too fhort,
he was one of the fineft and beft proportioned
men that I ever faw. In complexion he was
dark, like the other Northern Indians, but his
face was not disfigured by that ridiculous cuftom
of marking the cheeks with three or four black
lines. His features were ragular and agreeable,
and yet fo ftrongly marked and expreffive, that
they formed a completeindex of his mind; which,
as he never intended to deceive or diffemble,
he never wifhed to conceal. In converfation he was
eafy, lively, and agreeable, but exceedingly modeft; and at table, the noblenefs and elegance of
his manners might have been admired by the firft
perfonages in the world; for to the vivacity of a
Frenchman,

der while I was there, were part of thofe prefents   There were alfo a few
long leads found among thofe people, but quite different from any that
the Hudfon's Bay Company had ever fent to the Bay, fo that the only
probable way they could have come by them, muft have been by an intercourfe with fome of the tribe, who had dealings with the Danes in Davis's Straits   It is very probable, however, they might have paffed
through many hands before they reached this remote place   Had they
had an immediate intercourfe with the Efquimaux in Davis's Straits, it is
natural to fuppofe that iron would not have been fo fcarce among them
as it feemed to be, indeed the diftance is too great to admit of it

†I have feen two Northern Indians who meafured fix feet three inches,
and one, fix feet four inches.

Frenchman, and the fincerity of an Englifhman,
he added the gravity and noblenefs of a Turk; all
fo happily blended, as to render his company and
converfation univerfally pleafing to thofe who
underftood either the Northern or Southern Indian languages, the only languages in which he
could converfe

He was remarkably fond of Spanifh wines,
though he never drank to excefs; and  as he
would not partake of fpirituous liquors, however
fine in quality or plainly mixed, he was always
mafter of himfelt.   As no man is exempt from
frailties, it is natural to fuppofe that as a man he
had his fhare ; but the greateft with which I can
charge him, is jealoufy, and that fometimes carried him beyond the bounds of humanity.

In his early youth he difcovered talents equal
to the greateft tafk that could poffibly be expected from an Indian   Accordingly Mr. Jacobs,
then Governor at Prince of Wales's Fort, engaged him, when but a youth, as an Ambaffador
and Mediator between the Northern Indians and
the Athapufcow Tribe, who till then had always
been at war with each other   In the courfe of
this embaffy Matonabbee not only difcovered
the moft brilliant and folid parts, but fhewed an
extenfive knowledge of every advantage that
could arife to both nations from a total fuppreffi-
on of hoftilities; and at times he difplayed fuch
inftances of perfonal courage and magnanimity,

as

as are rarely to be found among perfons of fuperior condition and rank.

He had not penetrated far into the country of
the Athapufcow Indians, before he came to feveral tents with inhabitants, and there, to his great
furprife, he found Captain Keelfhies, (a perfon
frequently mentioned in this Journal*,) who was
then a prifoner, with all his family and fome of
his friends, the fate of whom was then undeter-
mined, but through the means of Matonabbee,
though young enough to have been his fon, Keelfhies and a few others were releafed, with the
lofs of his effects and all his wives, which were
fix in number. Matonabbee not only kept his
ground after Keelfhies and his fmall party had
been permitted to return, but made his way into
the very heart of the Athapufcow country, in
order to have a perfonal conference with all or
moft of the principal inhabitants. The farther
he advanced, the more occafion he had for intre-
pidity. At one time he came to five tents of
thofe favages, which in the whole contained fixteen men, befides their wives, childern, and fervants, while he himfelf was entirely alone, except
one wife and a fervant boy. The Southern Indians, ever treacherous, and apparently the more
kind when they are premeditating mifchief, feemed to give him a hearty welcome, accepted the
tenders of peace and reconciliation with apparent

A a             fatisfaction,

---

* The fame perfon was at Prince of Wales's Fort when the French arrived on the 8th of Augut 1782, and faw them demolifh the Fort

fatisfaction, and, as a mark of their approbation,
each tent in rotation made a feaft, or entertain-
ment, the fame night, and invited him to partake;·at the laft of which they had concerted a
fcheme to murder him. He was, however, fo
perfect a mafter of the Southern Indian language,
that he foon difcovered their defign, and told
them, he was not come in a hoftile manner, but
if they attempted any thing of the kind he was
determined to fell his life as dear as poffible. On
hearing this, fome of them ordered that his fervant, gun, and fnow-fhoes, (for it was winter,)
fhould be brought into the tent and fecured;
but he fprung from his feat, feized his gun and
fnow-fhoes, and went out of the tent, telling
them, if they had an intention to moleft him,
that was the proper place where he could fee his
enemy, and be under no apprehenfions of being
fhot cowardly through the back. "I am fure
" (faid he) of killing two or three of you, and if
" you chufe to purchafe my life at that price,
" now is the time; but if otherwife, let me de-
" part without any farther moleftation." They
then told him he was at liberty to go, on condition of leaving his fervant; but to this he would
not confent. He then rufhed into the tent and
took his fervant by force from two men; when
finding there was no appearance of farther
danger, he fet out on his return to the frontiers
of his own country, and from thence to the
Factory.

The

The year following he again visited the Athapuscow country, accompanied by a considerable
number of chosen men of his own nation, who
were so far superior to such small parties of the
Southern Indians as they had met, that they
commanded respect wherever they came; and
having traversed the whole country, and convers-
ed with all the principal men, peace and friend-
ship were apparently re-established. Accordingly, when the Spring advanced the Northern Indians began to disperse, and draw out to the East-
ward on the barren ground, but Matonabbee,
and a few others, chose to pass the Summer in the
Athapuscow country. As soon as the Southern
Indians were acquainted with this design, and
found the number of the Northern Indians so reduced, a superior number of them dogged and
harassed them the whole Summer, with a view to
surprise and kill them when asleep, and with
that view twice actually approached so near their
tents as fifty yards  But Matonabbee told them,
as he had done when alone, that though there
were but few of them, they were all determined
to sell their lives as dear as possible: on which the
Southern Indians, without making any reply, retired, for no Indians in this country have the
courage to face their enemies when they find
them apprized of their approach, and on their
guard to receive them.

Notwithstanding all these discouragements and
great dangers, Matonabbee persevered with cou-

rage and refolution to vifit the Athapufcow Indians for feveral years fucceffively; and at length,
by an uniform difplay of his pacific difpofition,
and by rendering a long train of good offices to
thofe Indians, in return for their treachery and
perfidy, he was fo happy as to be the fole inftrument of not only bringing about a lafting peace,
but alfo of eftablifhing a trade and reciprocal intereft between the two nations.

After having performed this great work, he
was prevailed upon to vifit the Copper-mine River, in company with a famous leader, called
I-dat-le-aza, and it was from the report of thofe
two men, that a journey to that part was propofed to the Hudfon's Bay Company by the late Mr.
Mofes Norton, in one thoufand feven hundred
and fixty-nine. In one thoufand feven hundred
and feventy he was engaged as the principal guide
on that expedition; which he performed with
greater punctuality, and more to my fatisfaction,
than perhaps any other Indian in all that country
would have done. At his return to the Fort in
one thoufand feven hundred and feventy-two, he
was made head of all the Northern Indian nation;
and continued to render great fervices to the
Company during his life, by bringing a greater
quantity of furrs to their Factory at Churchill
River, than any other Indian ever did, or
ever will do. His laft vifit to Prince of Wales's
Fort was in the Spring of one thoufand feven
hundred and eighty-two, and he intended to have
repeated

repeated it in the Winter following; but when he heard that the French had deſtroyed the Fort, and carried off all the Company's ſervants, he never afterwards reared his head, but took an opportunity, when no one ſuſpected his intention, to hang himſelf. This is the more to be wondered at, as he is the only Northern Indian who, that I ever heard, put an end to his own exiſtence. The death of this man was a great loſs to the Hudſon's Bay Company, and was attended with a moſt melancholy ſcene; no leſs than the death of ſix of his wives, and four children, all of whom were ſtarved to death the ſame Winter, in one thouſand ſeven hundred and eighty-three.

CHAP.

## C H A P.  X.

*An Account of the principal Quadrupeds found in the*
  *Northern Parts of Hudson's Bay.——The Buffalo,*
  *Moose, Musk-ox, Deer, and Beaver.—A capital*
  *Mistake cleared up respecting the We-was-kish*
    *Animals with Canine Teeth.——The Wolf—*
  *Foxes of various colours—Lynx, or Wild Cat—Po-*
  *lar, or White Bear—Black Bear—Brown Bear—*
  *Wolverene.—Otter—Jackash—Wejack—Skunk—*
  *Pine Martin—Ermine, or Stote.*
    *Animals with cutting Teeth.——The Musk Bea-*
  *ver—Porcupine—Varying Hare—American Hare*
  *—Common Squirrel—Ground Squirrel—Mice of*
  *various Kinds,—and the Castor Beaver.*
    *The Pinnated Quadrupeds with finlike Feet,*
  *found in Hudson's Bay, are but three in number,*
  *viz. the Warlus, or Sea-Horse,——Seal,—and Sea-*
  *Unicorn.*

---

*The Species of Fish found in the Salt Water of Hud-*
  *son's Bay are also few in number ; being the Black*
  *Whale—White Whale—Salmon—and Kepling.*
    *Shell-fish, and empty Shells of several kinds, found*
  *on the Sea Coast near Churchill River.*

---

*Frogs of various sizes and colours ; also a great vari-*
  *ety of Grubbs, and other Insects, always found in a*
  *frozen state during Winter, but when exposed to the*
  *heat of a slow fire, are soon re-animated.*

*An*

*An Account of some of the principal Birds found in the NorthernParts of Hudson's Bay, as well those that only migrate there in Summer, as those that are known to brave the coldest Winters ——Eagles of various kinds—Hawks of various sizes and plumage—White or Snowy Owl——Grey or motled Owl—Cob-a-dee-cooch—Raven—Cinerious Crow—Wood Pecker—Ruffed Grouse—Pheasant—Wood Partridge—Willow Partridge—Rock Partridge---Pigeon—Red-breasted Thrush——Grosbeak—Snow Bunting—White-crowned Bunting—Lapland Finch, two forts—Lark—Titmouse—Swallow—Martin---Hopping Crane—Brown Crane—Bitron—Carlow, two forts—Jack Snipe—Red Godwart—Plover—Black Gullemet—Northern Diver—Black-throated Diver—Red-throated Diver—White Gull- Grey Gull---Black-head---Pellican-- Goosander --Swans of two species---Common Grey Goose---Canada Goose---White or Snow Goose---Blue Goose---Horned Wavy---Laughing Goose---Barren Goose---Brent Goose---Dunter Goose---Bean Goose.*

*The Species of Water-Fowl usually called Duck, that resort to those Parts annually, are in great variety; but those that are most esteemed are, the Mallard Duck,—Long-tailed Duck,---Wigeon, and Teal.*

---

*Of the Vegetable Productions as far North as Church-ill River, particularly the most useful; such as the Berry-bearing Bushes, &c.——Gooseberry---Cranberry----Heathberry---Dewater-berry---Black Currans---Juniper-berry--Partridge berry---Strawberry*

*ry---Eye-berry---Blue-Berry,---and a small species
of Hips.*

*Burridge---Coltsfoot—Sorrel—Dandelion,
Wish-a capucca—Jackashey-puck—Moss of various sorts—Grass of several kinds—and Vetches.*

*The Trees found so far North near the Sea, con-
sist only of Pines—Juniper—Small Poplar—Bush-
willows—and Creeping Birch.*

BEFORE I conclude this work, it may not be
improper to give a short account of the
principal Animals that frequent the high Northern latitudes, though most of them are found also
far to the Southward, and consequently in much
milder climates. The buffalo, musk-ox, deer,
and the moose, have been already described in
this Journal. I shall therefore only make a few
remarks on the latter, in order to rectify a mistake, which, from wrong information, has crept
into Mr. Pennant's Arctic Zoology. In page 21
of that elegant work, he classes the Moose with
the We-was-kish, though it certainly has not any
affinity to it.

The We-was-kish, or as some (though improperly) call it, the Waskesse, is quite a different animal from the moose, being by no means so large
in size. The horns of the We-was-kish are some-
thing similar to those of the common deer, but
are not palmated in any part. They stand more
upright, have fewer branches, and want the brow-
antler  The head of this animal is so far from
being

being like that of the Moose, that the nose is
sharp, like the nose of a sheep: indeed, the whole
external appearance of the head is not very unlike that of an ass  The hair is usually of a sandy
red; and they are frequently called by the English
who visit the interior parts of the country, red
deer. Their flesh is tolerable eating; but the
fat is as hard as tallow, and if eaten as hot as
possible, will yet chill in so short a time, that it
clogs the teeth, and sticks to the roof of the mouth,
in such a manner as to render it very disagreeable.  In the Spring of one thousand seven hundred and seventy-five, I had thirteen sledge-loads
of this meat brought to Cumberland House in one
day, and also two of the heads of this animal un-
skinned, but the horns were chopped off; a proof
of their wearing them the whole Winter.  They
are the most stupid of all the deer kind, and frequently make a shrill whistling, and quivering
noise, not very unlike the braying of an ass, which
directs the hunter to the very spot where they
are.  They generally keep in large herds, and
when they find plenty of pasture, remain a long
time in one place.  Those deer are seldom an
object of chace with the Indians bordering on
Basquiau, except when moose and other game
fail.  Their skins, when dressed, very much resemble that of the moose, though they are much
thinner, and have this peculiar quality, that they
will wash as well as shamoy leather, whereas all
the other leathers and pelts dressed by the Indians,

if

if they get wet, turn quite hard, unlefs great care
be taken to keep conftantly rubbing them while
drying.

The perfon who informed Mr. Pennant that
the we-was-kifh and the moofe are the fame animal, never faw one of them ; and the only reafon
he had to fuppofe it, was the great refemblance of
their fkins : yet it is rather ftrange, that fo inde-
fatigable a collector of Natural Hiftory as the
late Mr. Andrew Graham, fhould have omitted
making particular enquiry about them : for any
foreign Indian, particularly thofe that refide near
Bafquiau, could eafily have convinced him to the
contrary.

### *Animals with Canine Teeth.*

Wolves  WOLVES are frequently met with in the countries Weft of Hudfon's Bay, both on the barren
grounds and among the woods, but they are not
numerous; it is very uncommon to fee more
than three or four of them in a herd.  Thofe
that keep to the Weftward, among the woods,
are generally of the ufual colour, but the greateft
part of thofe that are killed by the Efquimaux
are perfectly white.  All the wolves in Hudfon's
Bay are very fhy of the human race, yet when
fharp fet, they frequently follow the Indians for
feveral days, but always keep at a diftance.
They are great enemies to the Indian dogs, and
                                        frequently

frequently kill and eat thofe that are heavy loaded, and cannot keep up with the main body.
The Northern Indians have formed ftrange ideas
of this animal, as they think it does not eat its
victuals raw ; but by a fingular and wondeiful
fagacity, peculiar to itfelf, has a method of cooking them without fire. The females are much
fwifter than the males ; for which reafon the Indians, both Northern and Southern, are of opinion that they kill the greateft part of the game.
This cannot, however, always be the cafe, for to
the North of Churchill they, in general, live a forlorn life all the Winter, and are feldom feen in
pairs till the Spring, when they begin to couple,
and generally keep in pairs all the Summer.
They always burrow under-ground to bring
forth their yonng; and though it is natural to
fuppofe them very fierce at thofe times, yet I
have frequently feen the Indians go to their dens,
and take out the young ones and play with them.
I never knew a Northern Indian hurt one of
them : on the contrary, they always put them
carefully into the den again ; and I have fometimes feen them paint the faces of the young
Wolves with vermillion, or red ochre.

The ARCTIC FOXES are in fome years remarkably plentiful, but generally moft fo on the barren
ground, near the fea-coaft. Notwithftanding
what has been faid of this animal only vifiting the
fettlements once in five or feven years, I can affirm
there is not one year in twenty that they are not
caught

Foxes of
various co-
lours

caught in greater or lefs numbers at Churchill;
and I have known that for three years running,
not lefs than from two hundred to four hundred
have been caught each year within thirty miles
of the Fort.　They always come from the North
along the coaft, and generally make their appearance at Churchill about the middle of October,
but their fkins are feldom in feafon till November; during that time they are never molefted,
but permitted to feed round the Fort, till by degrees they become almoft domeftic.　The great
numbers of thofe animals that vifit Churchill River in fome years do not all come in a body, as
it would be impoffible for the fourth part of them
to find fubfiftence by the way; but when they
come near the Fort, the carcaffes of dead whales
lying along the fhores, and the fkin and other
offal, after boiling the oil, afford them a plentiful
repaft, and prove the means of keeping them
about the Fort till, by frequent reinforcements
from the Northward, their numbers are fo far increafed as almoft to exceeded credibility.

　　When their fkins are in feafon, a number of
traps and guns are fet, and the greateft part of
them are caught in one month, though fome few
are found during the whole Winter.　I have frequently known near forty killed in one night
within half a mile of Prince of Wales's Fort; but
this feldom happens after the firft or fecond night.
When Churchill River is frozen over near the
mouth, the greateft part of the furviving white
Foxes

Foxes crofs the river, and direct their courfe to the Southward, and in fome years affemble in confiderable numbers at York Fort and Severn River. Whether they are all killed, or what becomes of thofe which efcape, is very uncertain; but it is well known that none of them ever migrate again to the Northward. Befides taking a trap fo freely, they are otherwife fo fimple, that I have feen them fhot off-hand while feeding, the fame as fparrows in a heap of chaff, fometimes two or three at a fhot. This fport is always moft fuccefsful in moon-light nights; for in the day-time they generally keep in their holes among the rocks, and under the hollow ice at high-water-mark.

Thefe animals will prey on each other as readily as on any other animals they find dead in a trap, or wounded by gun; which renders them fo deftructive, that I have known upwards of one hundred and twenty Foxes of different colours eaten, and deftroyed in their traps by their comrades in the courfe of one Winter, within half a mile of the Fort.

The Naturalifts feem ftill at a lofs to know their breeding-places, which are doubtlefs in every part of the coaft they frequent. Several of them breed near Churchill, and I have feen them in confiderable numbers all along the Weft coaft of Hudfon's Bay, particularly at Cape Efquimaux, Navel's Bay, and Whale Cove, alfo on Marble Ifland; fo that with fome degree of confidence

we

we may affirm, that they breed on every part of
the coaſt they inhabit during the Summer ſeaſon.
They generally have from three to five young at
a litter; more I never ſaw with one old one.
When young they are all over almoſt of a footy
black, but as the fall advances, the belly, ſides,
and tail turn to a light aſh-colour; the back,
legs, ſome part of the face, and the tip of the tail,
changes to a lead colour; but when the Winter
ſets in they become perfectly white: the ridge of
the back and the tip of the tail are the laſt places
that change to that colour, and there are few
of them which have not a few dark hairs at the
tip of the tail all the Winter.  If taken young,
they are eaſily domeſticated in ſome degree, but
I never ſaw one that was fond of being careſſed;
and they are always impatient of confinement.

The White Fox    WHITE FOXES, when killed at any conſiderable diſtance from the ſea coaſt, (where they cannot poſſibly get any thing to prey upon, except
rabbits, mice, and partridges,) are far from being
diſagreeable eating.   And on Marble Iſland I have
ſhot them when they were equal in flavour to a
rabbit; probably owing to their feeding entirely
on eggs and young birds, but near Churchill
River they are as rank as train-oil.

The Lynx or WildCat    The LYNX, or WILD CAT, is very ſcarce to
the North of Churchill; but is exactly the ſame
as thoſe which are found in great plenty to the
South Weſt.  I have obſerved the tracks of this
animal at Churchill, and ſeen them killed, and
have

have eaten of their flesh in the neighbourhood
of York Fort. The flesh is white, and nearly as
good as that of a rabbit. They are I think, much
larger than that which is described in the Arctic
Zoology; they never approach near the settlements in Hudson's Bay, and are very destructive
to rabbits; they seldom leave a place which is
frequented by rabbits till they have nearly killed
them all.

The POLAR or WHITE BEAR, though common
on the sea-coast, is seldom found in its Winter
retreats by any of our Northern Indians, except
near Churchill River; nor do I suppose that the
Esquimaux see or kill any of them more frequently during that season; for in the course of
many years residence at Churchill River, I scarcely ever saw a Winter skin brought from the
Northward by the sloop. Probably the Esqi-
maux, if they kill any, may reserve the skins for
their own use; for at that season their hair is
very long, with a thick bed of wool at the bottom, and they are remarkably clean and white.
The Winter is the only season that so oily a skin
as the Bear's can possibly be cleaned and dressed
by those people, without greasing the hair, which
is very unpleasant to them; for though they eat
train-oil, &c yet they are as careful as possible
to keep their clothes from being greased with it.
To dress one of those greasy skins in Winter, as
soon as taken from the beast, it is stretched out
on a smooth patch of snow, and there staked
down,

down, where it foon freezes as hard as a board:
while in that ftate, the women fcrape off all the
fat, till they come to the very roots of the hair.
It is fometimes permitted to remain in that pofition for a confiderable time, and when taken from
the fnow, is hung up in the open air. The more
intenfe the froft, the greater is its drying quality; and by being wafted about by the wind,
with a little fcraping, it in time becomes perfectly fupple, and both pelt and hair beautifully
white. Drying deer, beaver, and otter fkins, in
this manner render their pelts very white, but
not fupple; probably owing to the clofe texture
and thicknefs of their fkins, whereas the fkin of
the bear, though fo large an animal, is remarkably thin and fpungy*.

BLACK

* It is rather fingular that the Polar Bears are feldom found on the land
during the Winter, on which account it is fuppofed they go out on the
ice, and keep near the edge of the water during that feafon, while the females that are pregnant feek fhelter at the fkirts of the woods, and dig
themfelves dens in the deepeft drifts of fnow they can find, where they remain in a ftate of inactivity, and without food, from the latter end of December or January, till the latter end of March; at which time they
leave their dens, and bend their courfe towards the fea with their cubs,
which, in general, are two in number  Notwithftanding the great magnitude of thofe animals when full grown, yet their young are not larger than
rabbits, and when they leave their dens, in March, I have frequently feen
them not larger than a white fox, and their fteps on the fnow not bigger
than a crown-piece, when thofe of their dam meafure near fifteen inches
long and nine inches broad  They propagate when young, or at leaft be
fore they are half grown, for I have killed young females not larger than
a London calf, with milk in their teats, whereas fome of the full grown
ones are heavier than the largeft of our common oxen  Indeed I was once
at the killing of one, when one of its hind feet being cut off at the ankle,
weighed fifty four pounds  The males have a bone in their *penis*, as a dog
has

BLACK BEARS are not very numerous to the North West of Churchill. The manner of life is the fame of the reft of the fpecies, though the face of the country they inhabit, differs widely from the more mild climates. In Summer they proul about in fearch of berries, &c. and as the Winter approaches, retire to their dens, which are always under-ground, and generally, if not always, on the fide of a fmall hillock. The Bears that inhabit the Southern parts of America are faid to take up their winter abode in hollow trees; but I never faw any trees in my Northern travels, that could afford any fuch fhelter.

The places of retreat of thofe Bears that burrow under-ground are eafily difcovered in Winter, by the rime that hangs about the mouth of the den; for let the fnow be ever fo deep, the

The Black Bear

B b heat

---

les, and of courfe unite in copulation, but the time of their courtfh p is I believe, not exactly known probably it may be in July or Auguft, for at thofe times I have often been at the killing them, when the males were fo attached to their miftreffes, that after the female was killed, the male would put his two fore-paws over, and fuffer himfelf to be fhot before he would quit her I have frequently feen and killed thofe animals near twelve leagues from the land, but as the Fall of the year advances, they e taught by inft nct to feek the fhore Though fuch a tremendous animal, they are very fhy of coming near a man, but when clofely purfued in the water, they frequently attack the boat, feize the oars, and wreft them from the hands of the ftrongeft man, feeming defirous to go on board, but the people on thofe occafions are always provided with firearms and hatchets, to prevent fuch an unwelcome vifit The flefh of this animal, when killed in Winter, (if not too old,) is far from being unpleafant eating, and the young cubs, in the Spring, are rather delicate than otherwife The teats of the females are only two in number, and are placed between the fore-legs The beft Drawing of this Animal I have feen, is that done by Mr. Webber, among the Places of Cook's laft Voyage

heat and breath of the animal prevents the mouth
of the den from being entirely cloled up    They
generally retire to their Winter quar ers before
the fnow is of any confiderable depth, and never
come abroad again unlefs difturbed, till the
thaws are confiderable, which in thote high latitudes is feldom till the latter end of March or the
beginning of April; fo that the few black Bears
that inhabit thofe cold regions may be faid to
fubfift for four months at leaft without food.  I
have been prefent at the killing two of them in
Winter; and the Northern Indian method is fimilar to that faid to be in ufe among the Kamtfchat-
kans; for they always blocked up the mouth of
the den with logs of wood, then broke open the
top of it, and killed the animal either with a
fpear or a gun, but the latter method is reckoned both cowardly and wafteful, as it is not
poffible for the  Bear either to make its efcape, or
to do the Indians the leaft injury.  Sometimes
they put a fnare about the Bear's neck, and draw
up his head clofe to the hole, and kill him with a
hatchet.  Though thofe animals are but fcarce to
the North of Churchill, yet they are fo numerous between York Fort and Cumberland Houfe,
that in one thoufand feven hundred and feventy-
four I faw eleven killed in the courfe of one day's
journey, but their flefh was abominable.  This
was in the month of June, long before any fruit
was ripe, for the want of which they then fed
entirely on water infects, which in fome of the

lakes we croffed that day were in aftonifhing multitudes*.

The method by which the Bears catch thofe infects is by fwimming with their mouths open, in the fame manner as the whales do, when feeding on the fea-fpider. There was not one of the Bears killed that day, which had not its ftomach as full of thofe infects (only) as ever a hog's was with grains, and when cut open, the ftench from them was intolerable. I have, however, eaten of fome killed at that early feafon which were very good; but they were found among the woods, far from the places where thofe infects haunt, and had fed on grafs and other herbage. After the middle of July, when the berries begin to ripen, they are excellent eating, and fo continue till January or February following; but late in the Spring they are, by long fafting, very poor and dry eating.

The Southern Indians kill great numbers of thofe Bears at all feafons of the year; but no encouragement can prevent them from fingeing al-

B b 2                                    moft

---

* The infects here fpoken of are of two kinds, the one is nearly black, its fkin hard like a beetle, and not very unlike a grafshopper, and darts through the water with great eafe, and with fome degree of velocity The other fort is brown, has wings, and is as foft as the common cleg-fly The latter are the moft numerous, and in fome of the lakes fuch quantities of them are forced into the bays in gales of wind, and there preffed together in fuch multitudes, that they are killed, and remain there a great nuifance, for I have feveral times, in my inland voyages from York Fort, found it fcarcely poffible to land in fome of thofe bays for the intolerable ftench of thofe infects, which in fome places were lying in putrid maffes to the depth of two or three feet It is more than probable, that the Bears occafionally feed on thefe dead infects.

moft every one that is in good condition : fo that
the few fkins they do fave and bring to the market, are only of thofe which are fo poor that their
flefh is not worth eating*   In fact, the fkinning
of a Bear fpoils the meat thereof, as much as it
would do to fkin a young porker, or a roafting
pig   The fame may be faid of fwans 'the fkins
of which the Company have lately made an aiti-
cle of trade ; otherwife thoufands of their fkins
might be brought to market annually,  by the Indians that trade with the Hudfon's Bay Company's fervants at the different fettlements about
the Bay

The Brown
Bear

BROWN BEARS are, I believe, never found in
the North-Indian territories : but I faw the fkin
of an enormous grizzled Bear at the tents of the
Efquimaux at the Copper River, and many of
them are faid to breed not very remote from that
part

The Wolve-
rene

The WOLVERENE is common in the Northern
regions, as far North as the Copper River, and
perhaps farther.  They are equally the inhabitants
of woods and barren grounds,  for the Efquimaux
to the North of Churchill kill many of them when
their fkins are in excellent feafon: a proof of
                                        their

---

* It is common for the Southern Indians to tame and domefticate the
young cubs, and they are frequently taken fo young that they cannot eat.
On thofe occafions, the Indians oblige their wives who have milk in their
breafts to fuckle them  And one of the Company's fervants, whofe name
is Ifaac Batt, willing to be as great a brute as his Indian companions, abf-
lutely forced one of his wives, who had recently loft her infant, to fuckle a
young Bear.

their being capable of braving the fevereft cold. They are very flow in their pace, but their wonderful fagacity, ftrength, and acute fent, make ample amends for that defect, for they are feldom killed at any feafon when they do not prove very fat: a great proof of their being excellent providers. With refpect to the fiercenefs of this animal which fome affert, I can fay little, but I I know them to be beafts of great courage and refolution, for I once faw one of them take poffeffion of a deer that an Indian had killed, and though the Indian advanced within twenty yards, he would not relinquifh his claim to it, but fuffered himfelf to be fhot ftanding on the deer. I once faw a fimilar inftance of a lynx, or wild cat, which alfo fuffered itfelf, to be killed before it would relinquifh the prize The wolverenes have alfo frequently been feen to take a deer from a wolf before the latter had time to begin his repaft after killing it. Indeed their amazing ftrength, and the length and fharpnefs of their claws, render them capable of making a ftrong refiftance againft any other animal in thofe parts, the Bear not excepted. As a proof of their amazing ftrength, there was one at Churchill fome years fince, that overfet the greateft part of a large pile of wood, (containing a whole Winter's firing, that meafured upwards of feventy yards round,) to get at fome provifions, that had been hid there by the Company's fervants, when going to the Factory to fpend the Chriftmas holidays.

days. The fact was, this animal had been lurk-
ing about in the neighbourhood of their tent
(which was about eight miles from the Factory)
for some weeks, and had committed many depredations on the game caught in their traps and
snares, as well as eaten many foxes that were killed by guns set for that purpose: but the Wolverene was too cunning to take either trap or gun
himself. The people knowing the mischievous
disposition of those animals, took (as they
thought) the most effectual method to secure the
remains of their provisions, which they did not
chuse to carry home, and accordingly tied it up
in bundles and placed it on the top of the wood-
pile, (about two miles from their tent,) little
thinking the Wolverene would find it out; but
to their great surprize, when they returned to
their tent after the holidays, they found the pile
of wood in the state already mentioned, though
some of the trees that composed it were as much
as two men could carry. The only reason the
people could give for the animal doing so much
mischief was, that in his attempting to carry off
the booty, some of the small parcels of provisions
had fallen down into the heart of the pile, and
sooner than lose half his prize, he pursued the
above method till he had accomplished his ends.
The bags of flour, oatmeal, and pease, though of
no use to him, he tore all to pieces, and scattered
the contents about on the snow; but every bit
of animal food, consisting of beef, pork, bacon,
venison,

venison, falt geefe, partridges, &c. to a confiderable amount, he carried away.  Thefe animals
are great enemies to the Beaver, but the manner
of life of the latter prevents them from falling
into their clutches fo frequently as many other
animals, they commit vaft depredations on the
foxes during the Summer, while the young ones
are fmall; their quick fcent directs them to their
dens, and if the entrance be too fmall, their
ftrength enables them to widen it, and go in and
kill the mother and all her cubs.  In fact, they are
the moft deftructive animals in this country*.

OTTERS are pretty plentiful in the rivers to the The Otter.
North of Churchill, as far as latitude 62°, farther
North I do not recollect to have feen any.  In
Winter they generally frequent thofe parts of
rivers where there are falls or rapids, which do
not freeze in the coldeft Winters; becaufe in
fuch fituations they are moft likely to find plenty
of fifh, and the open water gives them a free ad-
miffion to the fhore, where they fometimes go
to eat the fifh they have caught; but moft commonly fit on the ice, or get on a great ftone in the
river.  They are frequently feen in the very
depth of Winter at a confiderable diftance from
any

* Mr Graham fays they take their lodging in the clefts of rocks, or in
hollow trees  The former I acknowledge, but I believe that neither Mr
Graham nor any of the Company's fervants ever faw an inftance of the
latter  In fact, during all my travels in the interior parts of Hudfon's
Bay, I never faw a hollow tree that was capable of affording fhelter to any
larger animal than martins, jackalhes, or wejacks, much lefs the quiquehatch or Bear, as fome have afferted.

any known open water, both in woods and on open plains, as well as on the ice of large lakes; but it is not known what has led them to such places: perhaps merely for amusement, for they are not known to kill any game on the land during that season. If pursued when among the woods in Winter, (where the snow is always light and deep,) they immediately dive, and make considerable way under it, but are easily traced by the motion of the snow above them, and soon overtaken. The Indians kill numbers of them with clubs, by tracing them in the snow; but some of the old ones are so fierce when close pursued, that they turn and fly at their pursuer, and their bite is so severe that it is much dreaded by the Indians. Besides this method of killing them, the Indians have another, which is equally successful, namely, by concealing themselves within a reasonable gun-shot of the Otters usual landing-places, and waiting their coming out of the water. This method is more generally practised in moon light nights. They also shoot many of them as they are sporting in the water, and some few are caught in traps.

The Otters in this, as well as every other part of the bay, vary in size and colour, according to age and season. In Summer, when the hair is very short, they are almost black, but as the Winter advances, they turn to a beautiful dark auburn, except a small spot under the chin, which is of a silver gray. This colour they retain all the Winter;

ter; but late in the Spring (though long before they fhed their coat) they turn to a dull rufty brown, fo that a perfon who is acquainted with thofe changes can tell to a great nicety, by looking at the fkins, (when offered for fale,) the very time they were killed, and pay for them according to their value The number of their young is various, from three to five or fix. They unite in copulation the fame as a dog, and fo do every other animal that has a bone in the *penis*. I will here enumerate all of that defcription that I know of in thofe parts, *viz.* bears of all forts, wolves, wolvereens, foxes, martins, otters wejacks, jackafhes, fkunks, and ermines*

JACKASH. This animal is certainly no other than the leffer Otter of Canada, as its colour, fize, and manner of life entirely correfpond with the defcription of that animal in Mr. Pennant's Arctic Zoology. They, like the larger Otter, are frequently found in Winter feveral miles from any water, and are often caught in traps built for martins. They are fuppofed to prey on mice and partridges, the fame as the martin; but when by the fide of rivers or creeks, they generally feed on fifh. They vary fo much in fize and colour, that it was very eafy for Mr Pennant to have miftaken the fpecimen fent home for another animal. They are the eafieft to tame and domefti-

cate

The Jack-afh

---

* The Otter is very fond of play, and one of their favourite paftimes is, to get on a high ridge of fnow, bend their fore-feet backward, and flide down the fide of it, fometimes to the diftance of twenty yards

cate of any animal I know, except a large fpecies
of field-mice, called the Hair-tailed Moufe, for in
a very fhort time they are fo fond, that it is fcarcely poffible to keep them from climbing up one's
legs and body, and they never feel themfelves
happier than when fitting on the fhoulder ; but
when angry, or frightened, (like the fkunk,) they
emit a very difagreeable fmell. They fleep very
much in the day, but prowl about and feed in the
night ; they are very fierce when at their meals,
not fuffering thofe to whom they are moft attached to take it from them. I have kept feveral of
them, but their over-fondnefs made them troublefome, as they were always in the way ; and
their fo frequently emitting a difagreeable fmell,
rendered them quite difgufting.

The We-
jack, and
Skunk

Though the WEJACK * and SKUNK are never
found in the Northern Indian country, yet I cannot help obferving that the foetid fmell of the
latter has not been much exaggerated by any
Author. When I was at Cumberland Houfe,
in the Fall of one thoufand feven hundred and
feventy-four, fome Indians that were tenting on
the

* Mr Graham afferts that this animal frequents the banks of creeks,
and feeds on fifh ; but thefe are by no means their ufual haunts. I have,
however, no doubt, but when they find fifh on the land, that they may
eat it, like other carnivorous animals, but they are as fhy of taking the
water as a domeftic cat They climb trees, and catch partridges, mice,
and rabbits, with as much eafe as a martin They are eafily tamed and
domefticated, are very fond of tea-leaves, have a pleafant mufky fmell, and
are very playful

the plantation killed two of thofe animals, and made a feaft of them; when the fpot wheie they were finged and gutted was fo impregnated with that naufeous fmell which they emit, that after a whole Winter had elapfed, and the fnow had thawed away in the Spring, the fmell was ftill intolerable. I am told, however, that the flefh is by no means tainted with the fmell, if care be taken in gutting, and taking out the bag that contains this furprifing effluvia, and which they have the power of emitting at pleafure; but I rather doubt their being capable of ejecting their urine fo far as is reported; I do not think it is their urine which contains that peftilential effluvia, for if that was the cafe, all the country where they frequent would be fo fcented with it, that neither man nor beaft could live there with any degree of comfort.

The COMMON PINE MARTIN is found in moft parts of this country, and though very fcarce in what is abfolutely called the Northern Indian territory, yet by the Indians ftrolling toward the borders of the Southern Indian country, are killed in great numbers, and annually traded for at Churchill Factory. *The Pine Martin.*

The ERMINE, or STOTE, is common in thofe parts, but generally more plentiful on the barren ground, and open plains or marfhes, than in the woods, probably owing to the mice being more numerous in the former fituations than in the latter. *The Ermine, or Stote.*

latter. In Summer they are of a tawney brown,
but in Winter of a delicate white all over, except the tip of the tail, which is of a gloffy black.
They are, for their fize, the ftrongeft and moft
courageous animal I know: as they not only
kill partridges, but even attack rabbits with great
fuccefs. They fometimes take up their abode in
the out-offices and provifion-fheds belonging to
the Factories, and though they commit fome depredations, make ample amends by killing great
numbers of mice, which are very numerous and
deftructive at moft of the fettlements in the Bay.
I have taken much pains to tame and domefticate
this beautiful animal, but never could fucceed;
for the longer I kept it the more reftlefs and impatient it became.


### Animals with Cutting Teeth.

The Mufk
Rat.

The MUSK RAT, or MUSQUASH; or, as Naturalifts call it, the MUSK BEAVER; is common in
thofe parts; generally frequenting ponds and
deep fwamps that do not freeze dry in Winter.
The manner of life of this fpecies of animals is
peculiar, and refembles that of the Beaver, as
they are in fome refpects provident, and build
houfes to fhelter themfelves from the inclemency
of the cold in Winter; but inftead of making
thofe houfes on the banks of ponds or fwamps,
like the Beaver, they generally build them on the

ice

ice as foon as it is fkinned over, and at a confiderable diftance from the fhore, always taking care
to keep a hole open in the ice to admit them to
dive for their food, which chiefly confifts of the
roots of grafs: in the Southern parts of the country they feed much on a well known root, call *Ca-*
*lamus Aromaticus.* The materials made ufe of in
building their houfes are mud and grafs, which
they fetch up from the bottom.   It fometimes
happens in very cold Winters, that the holes in
their houfes freeze over, in fpite of all their efforts
to keep them open.   When that is the cafe, and
they have no provifions left in the houfe, the
ftrongeft preys on the weakeft, till by degrees
only one is left out of a whole lodge.   I have
feen feveral inftances fufficient to confirm the
truth of this affertion, for when their houfes
were broke open, the fkeletons of feven or eight
have been found, and only one entire animal.
Though they occafionally eat fifh and other animal food, yet in general they feed very clean, and
when fat are good eating, particularly when nicely finged, fcalded, and boiled.   They are eafily
tamed, and foon grow fond, are very cleanly
and playful, and fmell exceedingly pleafant of
mufk, but their refemblance to a Rat is fo great
that few are partial to them.   Indeed the only
difference between them and a common Rat, exclufive of their fuperior fize, is, that their hind-
feet are large and webbed, and the tail, inftead of
being round, is flat and fcaly.

Though

Though I have before faid, that the Mufk Beaver generally build their houfes on the ice, it is
not always the cafe, for in the Southern parts of
the country, particularly about Cumberland
Houfe, I have feen, in fome of the deep fwamps
that were over-run with rufhes and long grafs,
many fmall iflands that have been raifed by the
induftry of thofe animals, on the tops of which
they had built their houfes, like the beaver, fome
of which were very large  The tops of thofe
houfes are favourite breeding places for the geefe,
which bring forth their young brood there, without the fear of being molefted by foxes, or any
other deftructive animal, except the Eagle.

The Porcu-
pine
     PORCUPINES are fo fcarce to the North of
Churchill River, and I do not recollect to have
feen more than fix during almoft three years refidence among the Northern Indians  Mr Pennant obferves in his Arctic Zoology, that they
always have two at a time, one brought forth
alive and the other ftill-born*; but I never faw
an inftance of this kind, though in different parts
of the country I have feen them killed in all
ftages of pregnancy.  The flefh of the porcupine
is very delicious, and fo much efteemed by the
Indians, that they think it the greateft luxury
that their country affords.  The quills are in
great

* This information was given to Mr Pennant from the authority of Mr.
Graham, but the before-mentioned account of feeing them killed in all
ftages of pregnancy, when no fymptoms of that kind appeared, will I
hope, be fufficient to clear up that miftake

great requeſt among the women; who make
them into a variety of ornaments, ſuch as ſhot-
bags, belts, garters, bracelets, &c. Their mode
of copulation is ſingular, for their quills will not
permit them to perform that office in the uſual
mode, like other quadrupeds. To remedy this inconvenience, they ſometimes lie on their ſides, and
meet in that manner, but the uſual mode is for
the male to lie on his back, and the female to
walk over him, (beginning at his head,) till the
parts of generation come in contact. They are
the moſt forlorn animal I know; for in thoſe
parts of Hudſon's Bay where they are moſt numerous, it is not common to ſee more than one
in a place. They are ſo remarkably ſlow and
ſtupid, that our Indians going with packets from
Fort to Fort often ſee them in the trees, but not
having occaſion for them at that time, leave them
till their return; and ſhould their abſence be a
week or ten days, they are ſure to find them
within a mile of the place where they had ſeen
them before.

Foxes of various colours are not ſcarce in thoſe Foxes of
parts; but the natives living ſuch a wandering various Colours.
life, ſeldom kill many. It is rather ſtrange that
no other ſpecies of Fox, except the white, are
found at any diſtance from the woods on the
barren ground; for ſo long as the trade has been
eſtabliſhed with the Eſquimaux to the North of
Churchill, I do not recollect that Foxes of any
other colour than white were ever received from
them.

The

The VARYING HARES are numerous to the North of Churchill River, and extend as far as latitude 72°, probably farther. They delight most in rocky and stony places, near the borders of woods; though many of them brave the coldest Winters on entire barren ground. In Summer they are nearly the colour of our English wild rabbit; but in Winter assume a most delicate white all over, except the tips of the ears, which are black They are, when full grown and in good condition very large, many of them weighing fourteen or fifteen pounds; and if not too old, are good eating In Winter they feed on long rye grass and the tops of dwarf willows, but in Summer eat berries, and different sorts of small herbage. They are frequently killed on the South side of Churchill River, and several have been known to breed near the settlement at that place. They must multiply very fast, for when we evacuated Prince of Wales's Fort in one thousand seven hundred and eighty-two, it was rare to see one of them within twenty or thirty miles of that place; but at our return, in one thousand seven hundred and eighty-three, we found them in such numbers, that it was common for one man to kill two or three in a day within half a mile of the new settlement. But partly perhaps, from so many being killed, and partly from the survivors being so frequently disturbed, they have shifted their situation, and are at present as scarce near the settlement as ever. The Northern
Indians

Indians purfue a fingular method of fhooting thofe Hares; finding by long experience that thefe animals will not bear a direct approach, when the Indians fee a hare fitting, they walk round it in circles, always drawing nearer at every revolution, till by degrees they get within gun fhot. The middle of the day, if it be clear weather, is the beft time to kill them in this manner; for before and after noon, the Sun's altitude being fo fmall, makes a man's fhadow fo long on the fnow, as to frighten the Hare before he can approach near enough to kill it. The fame may be faid of deer when on open plains, who are frequently more frightened at the long fhadow than at the man himfelf.

The AMERICAN HARES, or, as they are called The American Hare. in Hudfon's Bay, RABBITS, are not plentiful in the Faftern parts of the Northern Indian country, not even in thofe parts that are fituated among the woods; but to the Weftward, bordering on the Southern Indian country, they are in fome places pretty numerous, though by no means equal to what has been reported of them at York Fort, and fome other fettlements in the Bay.

The furr of thofe animals, when killed in the beft part of the feafon, was for many years entirely neglected by the furriers; for fome time paft the Company have ordered as many of their fkins to be fent home as can be procured; they are but of fmall value

The flefh of thofe Hares is generally more

efteemed

efteemed than that of the former.  They are in
feafon all the Winter ; and though they generally feed on the brufh of pine and fir during that
feafon, yet many of the Northern Indians eat the
contents of the ftomach.   They are feldom fought
after in Summer, as in that feafon they are not
efteemed good eating; but as the Fall advances
they are,  by feeding on berries, &c moft excellent   In Spring they fhed their Winter coat, and
during the Summer are  nearly the colour of the
Englifh wild rabbit,  but  as the Winter advances
they become nearly white   In thick weather they
are eafily fhot with the gun; but the moft ufual
method of killing them is by fnares. fet nearly in
the manner defcribed by Dragge in the Firft Volume of his North Weft Paffage.

The Com-
mon Squir-
rel.   The COMMON SQUIRRELS are plentiful in the
woody parts of  this country,  and are caught by
the natives in confiderable numbers with fnares,
while the boys kill many of them with blunt-
headed arrows.   The method of fnaring them is
rather curious, though very fimple, as it confifts
of nothing more than  fetting a number of fnares
all round the body of  the  tree  in which they are
feen, and arranging them in fuch a  manner that
it is fcarcely poffible for the fquirrels to defcend
without being entangled in one  of them.   This
is generally the amufement of the boys.   Though
fmall, and feldom fat, yet they are good eating.

The beauty and delicacy of this animal induced
me to attempt taming and domefticating fome of
them,

them, but without fuccefs, for though feveral of them were fo familiar as to take any thing out of my hand, and fit on the table wheie I was writing, and play with the pens, &c. yet they never would bear to be handled, and were very milchievous; gnawing the chair-bottoms, window curtains, fafhes, &c. to pieces. They are an article of trade in the Company's ftandard, but the greateft part of their fkins, being killed in Summer, are of very little value.

The GROUND SQUIRRELS are never found in the woody parts of North America, but are very plentiful on the barren ground, to the North of Churchill River, as far as the latitude 71°, and probably much farther. In fize they are equal to the American Grey Squirrel, though more beautiful in colour. They generally burrow among the rocks and under great ftones, but fometimes on the fides of fandy ridges, and are fo provident in laying up a Winter's ftock during the Summer, that they are feldom feen on the furface of the fnow in Winter. They generally feed on the tufts of grafs, the tender tops of dwarf willows, &c. and are for the moft part exceedingly fat, and good eating. They are eafily tamed, and foon grow fond; by degrees they will bear handling as well as a cat, are exceeding cleanly, very playful, and by no means fo reftlefs and impatient of confinement as the Common Squirrel.

The Ground Squirrel

Mice are in great plenty and variety in all parts of Hudfon's Bay, the marfhes being inha-

Mice of various kinds.

bited

bited by one fpecies, and the dry ridges by another. The Shrew Moufe is frequently found in
Beaver houfes during Winter, where they not only find a warm habitation, but alfo pick up a
comfortable livelihood from the fcraps left by the
Beaver. Moft of the other fpecies build or make
nefts of dry grafs, of fuch a fize and thicknefs,
that when covered with fnow, they muft be fufficiently warm. They all feed on grafs in general, but will alfo eat animal food when they can
get it. The Hair-tailed Moufe is the largeft in
the Northern parts of the Bay. being little inferi-
or in fize to a common rat. They always burrow
under ftones, on dry ridges, are very inoffenfive,
and fo eafily tamed, that if taken when full-grown,
fome of them will in a day or two be perfectly
reconciled, and are fo fond of being handled,
that they will creep about your neck, or into
your bofom. In Summer they are grey, and in
Winter change to white, but are by no means fo
beautiful as a white ermine  At that feafon they
are infefted with multitudes of fmall lice, not a
fixth part fo large as the mites in a cheefe, in
fact, they are fo fmall, that at firft fight they only
appear like reddifh-brown duft, but on clofer examination are all perceived in motion  In one
large and beautiful animal of this kind, caught
in the depth of Winter, I found thofe little ver
min fo numerous about it, that almoft every hai
was covered with them as thick as ropes wit
onions, and when they approached near the end

C

of the hair they may be faid to change the moufe
from white to a faint brown. At that time I had
an excellent microfcope, and endeavoured to examine them, and to afcertain their form, but the
weather was fo exceedingly cold, that the glaffes
became damp with the moifture of my breath before I could get a fingle fight. The hind-feet of
thefe Mice are exactly like thofe of a Bear, and the
fore-feet are armed with a horny fubftance, (that
I never faw in any other fpecies of the Moufe,)
which is wonderfully adapted for fcraping away
the ground where they wifh to take up their
abode. They are plentiful on fome of the ftony
ridges near Churchill Factory, but never approach
the houfe, or any of the out-offices. From appearances they are very local, and feldom ftray
far from their habitations even in fummer, and in
Winter they are feldom feen on the furface of the
fnow; a great proof of their being provident in
Summer to lay by a ftock for that feafon.

*Pinnated Quadrupeds.*

With refpect to the Pinnated Quadrupeds with
fin-like feet, there are but few fpecies in Hudfon's Bay. The Walrus, or Sea-Horfe, and Seals,
are the only ones that I know.

The WALRUS are numerous about Merry and The Wal
Jones's Iflands, but more fo on a fmall ifland call-
rus
ed Sea-Horfe Ifland, that lies in the fair way going

ing to Whale Cove. In July one thousand seven hundred and sixty-seven, when on my voyage to the North of Churchill River, in passing Sea-Horse Island, we saw such numbers of those animals lying on the shore, that when some swivel guns loaded with ball were fired among them, the whole beach seemed to be in motion. The greatest part of them plunged into the water, and many of them swam round the vessel within musket-shot Every one on board exerted their skill in killing them, but it was attended with so little success, that the few which were killed sunk to the bottom, and those which were mortally wounded made off out of our reach.

With what propriety those animals are called Horses, I cannot see, for there is not the least resemblance in any one part. Their bodies, fins, &c are exactly like those of an enormous Seal, and the head is not very unlike that animal, except that the nose is much broader, to give room for the two large tusks that project from the upper jaw. Those tusks, and their red sparkling eyes, make them have a very fierce and formidable appearance

They are generally found in considerable numbers, which indicate their love of society; and their affection for each other is very apparent, as they always flock round those that are wounded, and when they sink, accompany them to the bottom, but soon rise to the surface, and make a hideous roaring, and of all amphibious animals,
they

they are at times the leaft fenfible of danger from man that I know.

They often attack fmall boats merely through wantonnefs, and not only put the people in great confufion, but fubject them to great danger; for they always aim at ftaving the boat with their tufks, or endeavour to get in, but are never known to hurt the people. In the year one thoufand feven hundred and fixty-fix fome of the floop's crew, who annually fail to the North to trade with the Efquimaux, were attacked by a great number of thofe animals, and notwith-ftanding their utmoft endeavours to keep them off, one more daring than the reft, though a fmall one, got in over the ftern, and after fitting and looking at the people fome time, he again plung-ed into the water to his companions. At that inftant another, of an enormous fize, was getting in over the bow; and every other means proving ineffectual to prevent fuch an unwelcome vifit, the bowman took up a gun, loaded with goofe-fhot, put the muzzle into the Horfe's mouth, and fhot him dead; he immediately funk, and was followed by all his companions. The people then made the beft of their way to the veffel, and juft arrived before the Sea-Horfes were ready to make their fecond attack, which in all probability might have been worfe than the firft, as they feem-ed much enraged at the lofs of their companion

Thofe animals are of various fizes, according to age and other circumftances; fome are not

larger

larger than an old Seal but there are thofe among them that are not lefs than two ton weight.

The fkin and teeth are the moft valuable parts to the natives, for the fat is hard and grifly, and the flefh coarfe, black, and tough.

Thofe animals are feldom found on the conti-nent which borders on Hudfon's Bay, or far up, in bays, rivers, or inlets, but ufually frequent fmall iflands, and fea-girt fhoals, at fome diftance from the main land, but as thofe places are fro-zen over for many miles during Winter, it is natural to think they keep at the edge of the wa-ter among the driving ice during that feafon. They are fuppofed to feed chiefly on marine plants, and perhaps on fhell-fifh, for their excre-ment is exceedingly offenfive.

Seals.

SEALS of various fizes and colours are com-mon in moft parts of Hudfon's Bay, but moft nu-merous to the North. Some of thofe animals are beautifully fpeckled, black and white; others are of a dirty grey. The former are generally fmall, but fome of the latter arrive at an amazing fize, and their fkins are of great ufe to the Efquimaux; as it is of them they cover their canoes, make all their boot-legs and fhoes, befides many other parts of their clothing. The Seal-fkins are alfo of great ufe to thofe people as a fubftitute for cafks, to preferve oil, &c. for Winter ufe, they are alfo blown full of wind and dried, and then ufed as buoys on the whale-fifhery. The flefh and fat of the Seal is alfo more efteemed by the Efqui-

maux

maux than thofe of any other marine animal, falmon not excepted

Befides thefe, the SEA-UNICORN is known to  Sea Uni-
frequent Hudfon's Bay and Straits, but I never  corn.
faw one of them  Their horns are frequently purchafed from our friendly Efquimaux, who probably get them in the way of barter from thofe
tribes that refide more to the North; but I never could be informed by the natives whether
their fkins are like thofe of the Whale, or hairy
like thofe of the Seal; I fuppofe the former.

---

### Species of Fifh.

The Fifh that inhabit the falt water of Hudfon's
Bay are but few:—the Black Whale, White
Whale, Salmon, and a fmall fifh called Kepling,
are the only fpecies of fea-fifh in thofe parts*.

The BLACK WHALE is fometimes found as far  Black
South as Churchill River, and I was prefent at the  Whale
killing of three there, but this was in the courfe
of twenty years.   To the Northward, particularly near Marble Ifland, they are more plentiful;
but notwithftanding the Company carried on a
fifhery

* In the Fall or the year 1768, a fine rock cod was drove on fhore in a
high gale of wind, and v as eaten at the Governor's table, Meffrs William
Wales and Jofeph Dymond, who went out to obferve the tranfit of Venus
which happened on the 3d of June 1769, partook of it, but I never heard
of one being caught with a hook, nor ever faw an entire fifh of that defcription in thofe parts. their jaw bones are, however, frequently found
on the fhores

fishery in that quarter, from the year one thousand seven hundred and sixty-five till one thousand seven hundred and seventy-two, they were
so far from making it answer their expectations,
that they sunk upwards of twenty thousand
pounds; which is the less to be wondered at,
when we consider the great inconveniencies and
expences they laboured under in such an undertaking. For as it was impossible to prosecute it
from England, all the people employed on that
service were obliged to reside at their settlement
all the year at extravagant wages, exclusive of
their maintenance. The harpooners had no less
than fifty pounds *per annum* standing wages, and
none of the crew less than from fifteen to twenty-
five pounds ; which, together with the Captains
salaries, wear and tear of their vessels, and other
contingent expences, made it appear on calculati-
on, that if there were a certainty of loading the
vessels every year, the Company could not clear
themselves. On the contrary, during the seven
years they persevered in that undertaking, only
four Black Whales were taken near Marble Island,
and, except one, they were so small, that they
would not have been deemed payable fish in the
Greenland service*. But the Hudson's Bay Company, with a liberality that does honour to them,

though

---

* I have heard that no Whale caught by our Greenland ships is called a
Pay-fish, that is, that no emolument arises to the harpooner that strikes
it, unless the longest blade of the bone, usually called Whale bone, mea-
sures six feet, whereas those killed in Hudson's Bay, seldom measured more
than five feet and an inch.

though perfectly acquainted with the rules obferved in the Greenland fervice, gave the fame pre-
mium for a fucking fifh, as for one of the greateft
magnitude.

WHITE WHALFS are very plentiful in thofe White
parts, particularly from Chefterfield's Inlet to Whale
York Fort, or Hay's River, on the Weft fide of
the Bay; and from Cape Smith to Slude River
on the Eaft fide.   On the Weft coaft they are generally found in the greateft numbers at the
mouths of the principal rivers; fuch as Seal
River, Churchill, Port Nelfon, and Hay's Rivers.
But the Eaft fide of the Bay not being fo well
known, Whale River is the only part they are
known to frequent in very confiderable numbers.
Some years ago the Company had a fettlement at
this river, called Richmond Fort; but all their endeavours to eftablifh a profitable fifhery here proved ineffectual, and the few Indians who reforted
to it with furrs proving very inadequate to the
expences, the Company determined to evacuate
it. Accordingly, after keeping up this fettlement
for upward of twelve years, and finking many
thoufands of pounds, they ordered it to be burnt,
for the more eafily getting the fpikes and other
iron-work.   This was in the year one thoufand
feven hundred and fifty eight.

At the old eftablifhed Factories on the Weft
fide of the Bay, the Company have been more
fuccefsful in the White Whale fifhery, particularly at Churchill, were fuch of the Company's fervants as cannot be employed during that feafon

to

to more benefit for the Company, are sent on
that duty, and in some successful years they send
home from eight to thirteen tons of fine oil  To
encourage a spirit of industry among those employed on this service, the Company allows a gratuity, not only to the harpooners, but to every
man that sails in the boats , and this gratuity is
so ample as to inspire them with emulation, as
they well know that the more they kill, the greater will be their emolument.

Salmon     SALMON are in some seasons very numerous on
the North West side of Hudson's Bay, particularly at Knapp's Bay and Whale Cove  At the latter I once found them so plentiful, that had we
been provided with a sufficient number of nets,
casks, and salt, we might soon have loaded the
vessel with them.  But this is seldom the case,
for in some years they are so scarce, that it is
with difficulty a few meals of them can be procured during our stay at those harbours.  They
are in some years so plentiful near Churchill
River, that I have known upward of two hundred fine fish taken out of four small nets in one
tide within a quarter of a mile of the Fort , but
in other years they are so scarce, that barely that
number have been taken in upward of twenty
nets during the whole season, which generally
begins the latter end of June, and ends about
the middle or latter end of August.

Kepling     Beside the fish already mentioned, I know of
no other that inhabits the salt water except the
KEPLING,

KEPLING, which is a small fish about the size of a smelt, but most excellent eating. In some years they resort to the shores near Churchill River in such multitudes to spawn, and such numbers of them are left dry among the rocks, as at times to be quite offensive. In other seasons they are so scarce, that hardly a meal can be procured.

The same remark may be made on almost every species of game, which constitutes the greatest part of the fare of the people residing in those parts. For instance, in some years, hundreds of deer may easily be killed within a mile of York Fort; and in others, there is not one to be seen within twenty or thirty miles. One day thousands and tens of thousands of geese are seen, but the next they all raise flight, and go to the North to breed. Salmon, as I have lately observed, is so plentiful in some years at Churchill River, that it might be procured in any quantity, at others, so scarce as to be thought a great delicacy.

In fact, after twenty years residence in this country, I am persuaded that whoever relies much on the produce of the different seasons, will frequently be deceived, and occasionally expose himself and men to great want.

To remedy this evil, it is most prudent for those in command to avail themselves of plentiful seasons, and cure a sufficient quantity of the least perishable food, particularly geese

*Shell*

*Shell Fish.*

SHELL FISH of a variety of kinds are also found
in some parts of Hudson's Bay. Muscles in particular are in great abundance on the rocky shores
near Churchill River, and what is vulgarly called
the Periwincle are very plentiful on the rocks
which dry at low-water. Small Crabs and Star-
fish are frequently thrown on the shore by the
surf in heavy gales of wind; and the empty shells
of Wilks, small Scallops, Cockles, and many other
kinds, are to be found on the beaches in great
plenty. The same may be said of the interior
parts of the country, where the banks of the
lakes and rivers abound with empty shells of various kinds; but the fish themselves have never
been discovered by the natives.

---

*Frogs, Grubs, and other Insects.*

FROGS of various colours are numerous in those
parts as far North as the latitude 61°. They always frequent the margins of lakes, ponds, rivers,
and swamps: and as the Winter approaches, they
burrow under the mofs, at a considerable distance
from the water, where they remain in a frozen
state till the Spring. I have frequently seen
                                                          them

them dug up with the mofs, (when pitching
tents in Winter,) frozen as hard as ice, in which
ftate the legs are as eafily broken off as a pipe-
ftem, without giving the leaft fenfation to the
animal; but by wrapping them up in warm
fkins, and expofing them to a flow fire, they foon
recover life, and the mutilated animal gains its
ufual activity; but if they are permitted to freeze
again, they are paft all recovery, and are never
more known to come to life. The fame may be
faid of the various fpecies of Spiders and all the <sub>Spiders and</sub>
Grub kind, which are very numerous in thofe <sup>Grubs</sup>
parts. I have feen thoufands of them dug up
with the mofs, when we were pitching our tents
in the Winter; all of which were invariably enclofed in a thick web, which Nature teaches them
to fpin on thofe occafions; yet they were apparently all frozen as hard as ice. The Spiders, if
let fall from any height on a hard fubftance,
would rebound like a grey pea, and all the Grub
kind are fo hard frozen as to be as eafily broken
as a piece of ice of the fame fize, yet when expofed to a flow heat, even in the depth of Winter,
they will foon come to life, and in a fhort time
recover their ufual motions.

---

*Birds.*

The feathered creation that refort to thofe parts
in the different feafons are numerous, but fuch
as

as brave the fevere Winter are but few in num.
ber, and fhall be particularly noticed in their
proper places.

EAGLES of feveral forts are found in the coun.
try bordering on Hudfon's Bay during the Sum.
mer; but none, except the common brown Fifhing Eagle, ever frequent the Northern parts.
They always make their appearance in thofe drea-
ry regions about the latter end of March or be.
ginning of April, and build their nefts in lofty
trees, in the crevices of inacceffible rocks near
the banks of rivers. They lay but two eggs,
(which are white,) and frequently bring but one
young. They generally feed on fifh, which they
catch as they are fwimming near the furface;
but they are very deftructive to the mufk rat and
hares, as alfo to geefe and ducks, when in a moulting ftate, and frequently kill young beaver.
Their nefts are very large, frequently fix feet in
diameter; and before their young can fly, are fo
provident, that the Indians frequently take a moft
excellent meal of fifh, flefh, and fowl from their
larder. Though they bring forth their young
fo early as the latter end of May, or the beginning of June, yet they never fly till September,
a little after which they migrate to the Southward. They are the moft ravenous of any bird
I know, for when kept in confinement or in a
tame ftate as it may be called, I have known two
of them eat more than a bufhel of fifh in a day.
They are never known to breed on the barren
grounds

grounds to the North of Churchill River, though many of the lakes and rivers in thofe parts abound with variety of fifh. This is probably owing to the want of trees or high rocks to build in. The Northern Indians are very partial to the quill-feathers of the Eagle, as well as to thofe of the hawk, to wing or plume their arrows with, out of a fuperftitious notion that they have a greater effect than if winged with the feathers of geefe, cranes, crows, or other birds, that in fact would do equally as well. The flefh of the Eagle is ufually eaten by moft of the Indians, but is always black, hard, and fifhy; even the young ones, when in a callow ftate, though the flefh is de-licate white, are fo rank as to render them very unpleafant to fome perfons, except in times of neceffity.

HAWKS of various fizes and plumage frequent the different parts of the country round Hudfon's Bay during Summer. Some of thofe Hawks are fo large as to weigh three pounds, and others fo fmall as not to exceed five or fix ounces. But the weight of thofe, as well as every other fpe-cies of Birds, is no ftandard for the Naturalift to go by; for at different feafons, and when in want of food, they are often fcarcely half the weight they are when fat and in good order. Notwithftanding the variety of Hawks that re-fort to thofe parts in Summer, I know but one fpecies that brave the intenfe cold of the long Winters to the North of Churchill River; and

Hawks of various fizes

D d                    that

that is what Mr. Pennant calls the Sacre Falcon.
They, like the other large fpecies of Hawks, prey
much on the white groufe or partridge, and alfo
on the American hare, ufually called here Rabbits.   They are always found to frequent thofe
parts where partridges are plentiful, and are detefted by the fportfmen, as they generally drive
all the game off the ground near their tents;
but, in return, they often drive thither frefh
flocks of fome hundreds.   Notwithftanding this,
they fo frequently baulk thofe who are employed
on the hunting fervice, that the Governors generally give a reward of a quart of brandy for
each of their heads.   Their flefh is always eaten
by the Indians, and fometimes by the Englifh;
but it is always black, hard, and tough, and
fometimes has a bitter taite

The Indians are fond of taming thofe birds,
and frequently keep them the whole Summer;
but as the Winter approaches they generally take
flight, and provide for themfelves.   When at
Cumberland Houfe I had one of them, of which
my people were remarkably fond, and as it never wanted for food, would in all probability
have remained with us all the Winter, had it not
been killed by an Indian who did not know it
to be tame.

White or Snowy Owl    The beautiful fpecies of WHITE or SNOWY OWL
is common in all parts of Hudfon's Bay, as far
North as the Copper-mine River.   Thefe birds,
when flying or fitting, appear very large, but when
killed,

killed, feldom weigh more than three and a half, or four pounds, and fometimes fcarcely half that weight. They generally feed on mice and par- tridges, and are at times known to kill rabbits. They are, like the hawk, very troublefome to the fportfmen ; and, contrary to any other bird that I know, have a great propenfity to follow the report of a gun, and frequently follow the hun- ters (as they are ufually called in Hudfon's Bay) the whole day. On thofe occafions they ufually perch on high trees, and watch till a bird is killed, when they fkim down and carry it off before the hunter can get near it; but in return, the hunters, when they fee them on the watch, frequently de- coy them within gun-fhot, by throwing up a dead bird, which the Owl feldom refufes to accept; but the fportfman being fully provided for this vifit, and on his guard, generally fhoots them before they can carry off the partridge. They are, however, fo great a hindrance to thofe em- ployed on the hunting fervice, that the fame pre- mium is given for one of their heads as for that of a hawk.

In Winter they are frequently very fat, their flefh delicately white, and generally efteemed good eating, both by Englifh and Indians. Thofe Owls always make their nefts on the ground, ge- nerally lay from three to four eggs, but feldom hatch more than two, and in the extreme North the young ones do not fly till September They never migrate, but brave the coldeft Winters,

even

even on the barren ground, far remote from any
woods ; and in thofe fituations perch on high
rocks and ftones, and watch for their prey.

Grev or
M...t d
Oa'

    The fpecies of GREY or MOTTLED OWL are by
no means fo numerous as the former, are fomething inferior in fize, and always frequent the
woods  They never go in fearch of their prey in
the day time, but perch on the tops of lofty pines,
and are eafily approached and fhot.  Their food
is generally known to be mice and fmall birds,
yet their flefh is delicately white, and nearly as
good as a barn-door fowl , of courfe it is much
efteemed both by the Englifh and Indians.   This
fpecies of Owl is called by the Southern Indians
Ho-Lo, and the former Wap-a-kee-thow.

Cob-a aee-
cooch

    Befides thofe two fpecies of Owls, there is ano-
ther that remains in Hudfon's Bay all the year,
and is called by the Indians COB-A-DEE-COOCH.
It is fo far inferior in fize to the two former,
that it feldom weighs half a pound ; is of a mottled brown, the feathers long, and of a moft delicate foft and filky quality.   In general this fpecies feed on mice, and birds they find dead , and
are fo impudent at times, that they light on a partridge when killed by the hunter, but not being
able to carry it off, are often obliged to relinquifh
the prize.   Like the White Owl, at times though
but feldom, they follow the report of a gun, and
by fo frequently fkimming round the fportfmen,
frighten the game nearly as much as the hawk.
They feldom go far from the woods, build in trees,
                           and

and lay from two to four eggs. They are never fat, and their flesh is eaten only by the Indians.

RAVENS of a moft beautiful gloffy black, richly Ravens tinged with purple and violet colour, are the conftant inhabitants of Hudfon's Bay; but are fo far inferior in fize to the Englifh Raven, that they are ufually called Crows. They build their nefts in lofty pine trees, and generally lay four fpeckled eggs; they bring forth their young fo early as the latter end of May, or the beginning of June. In Summer many of them frequent the barren grounds, feveral hundred miles from any woods; probably invited there by the multitudes of deer and mufk-oxen that are killed by the Northern Indians during that feafon, merely for their fkins, and who leave their flefh to rot, or be devoured by beafts or birds of prey. At thofe times they are very fat, and the flefh of the young ones is delicately white, and good eating. But in Winter they are, through neceffity, obliged to feed on a black mofs that grows on the pine-trees, alfo on deer's dung, and excrements of other animals. It is true, they kill fome mice, which they find in the furface of the fnow, and catch many wounded partridges and hares, in fome parts of the country they are a great nuifance to the hunter, by eating the game that is either caught in fnares or traps. With all this affiftance, they are in general fo poor during the fevere cold in Winter, as to excite wonder how they poffibly can exift.

Their

Their faculty of scent must be very acute; for
in the coldest days in Winter, when every kind
of effluvia is almost instantaneously destroyed by
the frost, I have frequently known buffaloes and
other beasts killed where not one of those birds
were seen; but in a few hours scores of them
would gather about the spot to pick up the
dung, blood, and other offal.   An unarmed man
may approach them very near when feeding, but
they are shy of those that have a gun, a great
proof that they smell the gunpowder.   They
are, however, frequently shot by guns set for
foxes, and sometimes caught in traps built for
martins.   Though, on the whole, they may be
called a shy bird, yet their necessities in Winter
are so great, that, like the White Owl, they frequently follow the report of a gun, keep prudently at a distance from the sportsman, and frequently carry off many wounded birds.   Their quills
make most excellent pens for drawing, or for la-
dies to write with.

Cinereous
Crow

The CINEREOUS CROW, or, as it is called by the
Southern Indians, Whisk-e-jonish, by the English
Whiskey jack, and by the Northern Indians Gee-
za, but as some pronounce it, and that with more
propriety, Jee-za, though classed among the
Crows, is in reality so small, as seldom to weigh
three ounces; the plumage grey, the feathers very
long, soft, and silky, and in general entirely un-
webbed, and in some parts much resembles hair.
This bird is very familiar, and fond of frequenting

ing habitations, either houfes or tents; and fo much given to pilfering, that no kind of provifions it can come at, either frefh or falt, is fafe from its depredation It is fo bold as to come into tents, and fit on the edge of the kettle when hanging over the fire, and fteal victuals out of the difhes. It is very troublefome to the hunters, both Englifh and Indian, frequently following them a whole day, it will perch on a tree while the hunter is baiting his martin-traps, and as foon as his back is turned go and eat the baits. It is a kind of mock bird, and of courfe has a variety of notes, it is eafily tamed, but never lives long in confinement It is well known to be a provident bird, laying up great quantities of berries in Summer for a Winter ftock; but its natural propenfity to pilfer at all feafons makes it much detefted both by the Englifh and Indians. It builds its neft in trees, exactly like that of the blackbird and thrufh, lays four blue eggs, but feldom brings more than three young ones.

I know of only one fort of WOOD-PECKER that Wood-pecker frequents the remote Northern parts of Hudfon's Bay; and this is diftinguifhed by Mr Pennant by the name of the Golden Winged Bird, but to the South Weft that beautiful fpecies of Woodpecker with a fcarlet crown is very frequent. The manner of life of this fpecies is nearly alike, always building their nefts in holes in trees, and feeding on worms and infects. They generally
have

have from four to fix young at a time. They
are faid to be very deftructive to fruit-trees that
are raifed in gardens in the more Southern parts
of America, but the want of thofe luxuries in
Hudfon's Bay renders them very harmlefs and
inoffenfive birds. The red feathers of the larger
fort, which frequent the interior and Southern
parts of the Bay, are much valued by fome of
the Indians, who ornament their pipe-ftems with
them, and at times ufe them as ornaments to their
children's clothing. Neither of the two fpecies
here mentioned ever migrate, but are conftant
inhabitants of the different climates in which
they are found.

Groufe

There are feveral fpecies of GROUSE in the different parts of Hudfon's Bay, but two of the
largeft, and one of them the moft beautiful, never reach fo far North as the latitude 59°: but as
I have feen them in great plenty near Cumberland
Houfe, I fhall take the liberty to defcribe them.

The Ruffed Groufe.

The RUFFED GROUSE. This is the moft beautiful of all that are claffed under that name.
They are of a delicate brown, prettily variegated
with black and white: tail large and long, like
that of a hawk, which is ufually of an orange-
colour, beautifully barred with black, chocolate,
and white; and the tail is frequently expanded
like a fan. To add to their beauty, they have a
ruff of gloffy black feathers, richly tinged with
purple round the neck, which they can erect at
pleafure: this they frequently do, but more particularly

ticulaily fo when they fpread their long tail, which gives them a noble appearance. In fize they exceed a partridge, but are inferior to a pheafant. In Winter they are ufually found perched on the branches of the pine trees; and in that feafon are fo tame as to be eafily approached, and of courfe readily fhot.

They always make their nefts on the ground, generally at the root of a tree, and lay to the number of twelve or fourteen eggs. In fome of the Southern parts of America feveral attempts have been made to tame thofe beautiful birds, by taking their eggs and hatching them under domeftic hens, but it was never crowned with fuccefs, for when but a few days old, they always make their efcape into the woods, where they probably pick up a fubfiftence. Their flefh is delicately white and firm, and though they are feldom fat, they are always good eating, and are generally efteemed beft when larded and roafted, or nicely boiled with a bit of bacon.

There is fomething very remarkable in thofe birds, and I believe peculiar to themfelves, which is that of clapping their wings with fuch a force, that at half a mile diftance it refembles thunder. I have frequently heard them make that noife near Cumberland Houfe in the month of May, but it was always before Sun-rife, and a little after Sun-fet. It is faid by Mr. Barton and Le Hontan, that they never clap in this manner but in the Spring and Fall, and I muft acknowledge
that

that I never heard them in Winter, though I have killed many of them in that feafon. The Indians informed me they never make that noife but when feeding, which is very probable; for it is notorioufly known that all the fpecies of Groufe feed very early in the mornings, and late in the afternoons. This fpecies is called by fome of the Indians bordering on Hudfon's Bay, Pus-pus-kee, and by others Pus-pus-cue.

Sharp-tail-ed Groufe

SHARP-TAILED GROUSE, or as they are called in Hudfon's Bay, Pheafant. Thofe birds are always found in the Southern parts of the Bay, are very plentiful in the interior parts of the country, and in fome Winters a few of them are fhot at York Fort, but never reach fo far North as Churchill. In colour they are not very unlike that of the Englifh hen pheafant; but the tail is fhort and pointed, like that of the common duck; and there is no perceivable difference in plumage between the male and female. When full-grown, and in good condition, they frequently weigh two pounds, and though the flefh is dark, yet it is juicy, and always efteemed good eating, particularly when larded and roafted. In Summer they feed on berries, and in Winter on the tops of the dwarf birch, and the buds of the poplar. In the Fall they are tolerably tame, but in the fevere cold more fhy; frequently perch on the tops of the higheft poplars, out of moderate gun-fhot, and will not fuffer a near approach. They fometimes, when difturbed in this fituati-

on,

on, dive into the fnow; but the fportfman is equally baulked in his expectations, as they force their way fo faft under it as to raife flight many yards diftant from the place they entered, and very frequently in a different direction to that from which the fportfman expects\*. They, like the other fpecies of groufe, make their nefts on the ground, and lay from ten to thirteen eggs. Like the Ruffed Groufe, they are not to be tamed, as many trials have been made at York Fort, but without fuccefs; for though they never made their efcape, yet they always died, probably for the want of proper food; for the hens that hatched them were equally fond of them, as they could poffibly have been had they been the produce of their own eggs This fpecies of Groufe is called by the Southern Indians Aw-kis-cow.

The WOOD PARTRIDGES have acquired that name in Hudfon's Bay from their always frequenting the forefts of pines and fir, and in Winter feeding on the brufh of thofe trees, though they are fondeft of the latter. This fpecies of Groufe is inferior in fize and beauty to the Ruffed, yet may be called a handfome bird; the plumage being of a handfome brown, elegantly fpotted with white and black. The tail is long, and tipped with orange; and the legs are warmly covered with fhort feathers, but the feet are naked. They are generally in the extreme with refpect

Wood Partridge

spect to shyness; sometimes not suffering a man
to come within two gun-shots, and at others so
tame that the sportsman may kill five or six out
of one tree without shifting his station.   They
are seen in some years in considerable numbers
near York Fort.   They are very scarce at Churchill, though numerous in the interior parts, particularly on the borders of the Athapuscow Indians
country, where I have seen my Indian companions kill many of them with blunt-headed
arrows.   In Winter their flesh is black, hard and
bitter, probably owing to the resinous quality of
their food during that season ; but this is not observed in the rabbits, though they feed exactly
in the same manner in Winter : on the contrary,
their flesh is esteemed more delicate than that of
the English rabbit.   The Southern Indians call
this species of Partridge, Mittick a-pethow ; and
the Northern Indians call it, Day.

Willow
Partridge

The WILLOW PARTRIDGES have a strong black
bill, with scarlet eye-brows, very large and beautiful in the male, but less conspicuous in the female.   In Summer they are brown, elegantly
barred and mottled with orange, white, and
black; and at that season the males are very
proud and handsome, but the females are less
beautiful, being of one universal brown   As the
Fall advances they change to a delicate white,
except fourteen black feathers in the tail, which
are also tipped with white; and their legs and
feet, quite down to the nails, are warmly covered
with

with feathers. In the latter end of September
and beginning of October they gather in flocks
of some hundreds, and proceed from the open
plains and barren grounds, (where they usually
breed,) to the woods and brush-willows, where
they hord together in a state of society, till dis-
persed by their common enemies, the hawks, or
hunters They are by far the most numerous of
any of the grouse species that are found in Hudson's Bay; and in some places when permitted to
remain undisturbed for a considerable time, their
number is frequently so great, as almost to exceed credibility. I shall by no means exceed truth,
if I assert that I have seen upward of four hundred in one flock near Churchill River; but the
greatest number I ever saw was on the North side
of Port Nelson River, when returning with a packet in March one thousand seven hundred and
sixty-eight: at that time I saw thousands flying
to the North, and the whole surface of the snow
seemed to be in motion by those that were feeding on the tops of the short willows. Sir Thomas Button mentions, that when he wintered in
Port Nelson River in one thousand six hundred
and twelve, his crew killed eighteen hundred
dozen of those birds, which I have no reason to
doubt; and Mr. Jeremie, formerly Governor at
York Fort, when that place was in the possession
of the French, and then called Fort Bourbon,
asserts, that he and seventy-nine others eat no

It Is

lefs than ninety thoufand partridges and twenty-
five thoufand hares in the courfe of one Winter;
which, confidering the quantity of venifon,
geefe, ducks, &c. enumerated in his account,
that were killed that year, makes the number fo
great, that it is fcarcely poffible to conceive what
eighty men could do with them ; for on calcula-
tion, ninety thoufand partridges and twenty-five
thoufand hares divided by eighty, amounts to no
lefs than one thoufand one hundred and twenty-
five partridges, and three hundred and twelve
hares per man.    This is by far too great a
quantity, particularly when it is confidered that
neither partridges nor hares are in feafon, or can
be procured in any numbers, more than feven
months in the year    Forty thoufand partridges
and five thoufand hares would, I think, be much
nearer the truth, and will be found, on calculati-
on, to be ample provifion for eighty men for feven months, exclufive of any change.    The
common weight of thofe birds is from eighteen
to twenty-two ounces when firft killed ; there
are fome few that are nearly that weight when
fit for the fpit, but they are fo fcarce as by no
means to ferve as a ftandard ; and as they always
hord with the common fize, there is no room to
fufpect them of another fpecies.    As all thofe
over-grown partridges are notorioufly known
to be males, it is more than probable that they
are imperfect, and grow large and fat like capons;
and every one that has had an opportunity of
                                                    tafting

tafting thofe large partridges, will readily allow
that they excel the common fort as much in flavour as they do in fize.  It is remarked in thofe
birds, as well as the Rock Partridge, that they
are provided with additional clothing, as it may
be called ; for every feather, from the largeft to
the fmalleft, except the quills and tail, are all
double.  The under-feather is foft and downy,
fhooting from the fhaft of the larger ; and is
wonderfully adapted to their fituation, as they not
only brave the coldeft Winters, but the fpecies
now under confideration always burrow under
the fnow at nights, and at day light come forth
to feed.  In Winter they are always found to frequent the banks of rivers and creeks, the fides of
lakes and ponds, and the plains which abound
with dwarf willows ; for it is on the buds and
tops of that tree they always feed during the
Winter.  In fummer they eat berries and fmall
herbage.  Their food in Winter being fo dry
and harfh, makes it neceffary for them to fwallow a confiderable quantity of gravel to promote
digeftion ; but the great depth of fnow renders
it very fcarce during that feafon.  The Indians
having confidered this point, invented the method now in ufe among the Englifh, of catching
them in nets by means of that fimple allurement,
a heap of gravel.  The nets for this purpofe are
from eight to twelve feet fquare, and are ftretched in a frame of wood, and ufually fet on the ice
of rivers, creeks, ponds, and lakes, about one
hundred

hundred yards from the willows, but in some
situations not half that distance.   Under the center of the net a heap of snow is thrown up to
the size of one or two bushels, and when well
packed is covered with gravel.   To set the nets,
when thus prepared, requires no other trouble
than lifting up one side of the frame, and supporting it with two small props, about four feet long:
a line is fastened to those props, and the other
end being conveyed to the neighbouring willows,
is always so contrived that a man can get to it
without being seen by the birds under the net.
When every thing is thus prepared, the hunters
have nothing to do but go into the adjacent willows and woods, and when they start game, endeavour to drive them into the net, which at
times is no hard task, as they frequently run before them like chickens; and sometimes require
no driving, for as soon as they see the black heap
of gravel on the white snow they fly straight towards it.   The hunter then goes to the end of
the line to watch their motions, and when he sees
there are as many about the gravel as the net can
cover, or as many as are likely to go under at
that time, with a sudden pull he hauls down the
flakes, and the net falls horizontally on the snow,
and encloses the greatest part of the birds that
are under it.   The hunter then runs to the
net as soon as possible, and kills all the birds by
biting them at the back of the head.  He then sets
up the net, takes away all the dead game, and
repeats

repeats the operation as often as he pleafes, or as long as the birds are in good humour. By this fimple contrivance I have known upwards of three hundred partridges caught in one morning by three perfons, and a much greater number might have been procured had it been thought neceffary. Early in the morning, juft at break of day, and early in the afternoon, is the beft time for this fport   It is common to get from thirty to feventy at one hawl, and in the Winter of one thoufand feven hundred and eighty-fix, Mr. Prince, then Mafter of a floop at Churchill River, actually caught two hundred and four at two hawls. They are by no means equally plentiful every year; for in fome Winters I have known them fo fcarce, that it was impoffible to catch any in nets, and all that could be procured with the gun would hardly afford one day's allowance per week to the men during the feafon; but in the Winter one thoufand feven hundred and eighty-five, they were fo plentiful near Churchill, and fuch numbers were brought to the Factory, that I gave upward of two thoufand to the hogs. In the latter end of March, or the beginning of April, thofe birds begin to change, from white to their beautiful Summer plumage, and the firft brown feathers make their appearance on the neck*, and by degrees fpread over the whole bo-

E e          dy;

* Mr Dragge obferves, in his North Weft Paffage, that when the par-tridges begin to change colour, the firft brown feathers appear in the rump, but

dy, but their Summer dress is seldom complete
till July  The feathers of those birds make excellent beds, and as they are the perquisite of the
hunters, are usually sold to the Captains and
Mates of the Companys' ships, at the easy rate of
three pence per pound.

Rock Pa-
* dges. ROCK PARTRIDGES.  This species of Grouse
are in Winter of the same colour as the former,
but inferior in size; being in general not more
than two-thirds of the weight.  They have a
black line from the bill to the eye, and differ in
nature and manner from the Willow Partridge.
They never frequent the woods or willows, but
brave the severest cold on the open plains.  They
always feed on the buds and tops of the dwarf
birch, and after this repast, generally sit on the
high ridges of snow, with their heads to windward.  They are never caught in nets, like the
Willow Partridge; for when in want of gravel,
their bills are of such an amazing strength, that
they pick a sufficient quantity out of the rocks.
Beside, being so much inferior in size to the former species, their flesh is by no means so good,
being black, hard, and bitter.  They are in general,

but this is so far from being a general rule, that an experienced Hudsonian
must smile at the idea  That Mr Dragge never saw an instance of this
* a I will not say, but when Nature deviates so far from its usual course,
it is undoubtedly owing to some accident; and nothing is more likely
than that the feathers of the bird Mr Dragge had examined, had been
struck off by a haw, and as the usual season for changing their plumage
was near, the Summer feathers supplied their place, for out of the many
hundreds of thousands that I have seen killed, I never saw or heard of a
similar instance

ral, like the Wood Partridge, either exceeding wild - or very tame, and when in the latter humour, I have known one man kill one hundred and twenty in a few hours, for as they ufually keep in large flocks, the fportfman can frequently kill fix or eight at a fhot. Thefe, like the Willow Partridge, change their plumage in Summer to a beautiful fpeckled brown; and at that feafon are fo hardy, that, unlefs fhot in the head or vitals, they will fly away with the greateft quantity of fhot of any bird I know. They difcover great fondnefs for their young; for during the time of incubation, they will frequently fuffer themfelves to be taken by hand off their eggs*. Pigeons of a fmall fize, not larger than a thrufh, are in fome Summers found as far North as Churchill River. The bill is of a flefh-colour, legs red, and the greateft part of the plumage of a light lilac or blufh. In the interior parts of the country they fly in large flocks, and perch on the

E e 2                                           poplar

* Befides the birds already mentioned, which form a conftant difh at our tables in Hudfon's Bay, during their refpective feafons, Mr Jerome afferts, that during the time he was Governor at York Fort, the buftard was common. But fince that Fort was delivered up to the Englifh at the peace of Utrecht in 1713, none of the Company's fervants have ever feen one of thofe birds nor does it appear by all the Journals now in the poffeffion of the Hudfon's Bay Company, that any fuch bird was ever feen in the noft Southern parts of the Bay, much lefs at York Fort, which is in the latitude 57° North, fo that a capital error, or a wilful defign to miflead, muft have taken place Indeed, his account of the country immediately where he refided and the productions of it, are fo erroneoufly ftated as to deferve no notice His colleague, De le Potries, afferts the exiftence of the buftard in thofe parts and with an equal regard to truth

poplar trees in such numbers that I have seen twelve of them killed at one shot. They usually feed on poplar buds, and are good eating, though seldom fat. They build their nests in trees, the same as the Wood Pigeons do; never lay but two eggs, and are very scarce near the sea-coast in the Northern parts of Hudson's Bay.

Red-breast-
ed Thrush. The RED-BREASTED THRUSHES, commonly called in Hudson's Bay the Red Birds, but by some the Black Birds, on account of their note, and by others the American Fieldfares usually make their appearance at Churchill River about the middle of May, build their nests of mud, like the English Thrush, and lay four beautiful blue eggs. They have a very loud and pleasing note, which they generally exercise most in the mornings and evenings, when perched on some lofty tree near their nest; but when the young can fly they are silent, and migrate to the South early in the Fall. They are by no means numerous, and are generally seen in pairs; they are never sought after as an article of food, but when killed by the Indian boys, are esteemed good eating, though they always feed on worms and insects.

Grosbeak GROSBEAK. These gay birds visit Churchill River in some years so early as the latter end of March, but are by no means plentiful; they are always seen in pairs, and generally feed on the buds of the poplar and willow. The male is in most parts of its plumage of a beautiful crimson, but the female of a dull dirty green. In form they

they much refemble the Englifh bullfinch, but
are near double their fize. They build their nefts
in trees, fometimes not far from the ground; lay
four white eggs, and always hatch them in June.
They are faid to have a pleafing note in Spring,
though I never heard it, and are known to retire
to the South early in the Fall. The Englifh refiding in Hudfon's Bay generally call this bird the
American Red Bird.

SNOW BUNTINGS, univerfally known in Hud Snow
fon's Bay by the name of the Snow Birds, and in Bunting
the Ifles of Orkney by the name of Snow Flakes,
from their vifiting thofe parts in fuch numbers
as to devour the grain as foon as fown, in fome
years are fo deftructive as to oblige the farmer to
fow his fields a fecond, and occafionally a third
time. Thefe birds make their appearance at the
Northern fettlements in the Bay about the latter
end of May, or beginning of April, when they
are very fat, and not inferior in flavour to an
ortolan. On their firft arrival they generally
feed on grafs-feeds, and are fond of frequenting
dunghills. At that time they are eafily caught in
great numbers under a net baited with groats or
oatmeal; but as the Summer advances, they feed
much on worms, and are then not fo much
efteemed. They fometimes fly in fuch large
flocks, that I have killed upwards of twenty at
one fhot, and have known others who have killed double that number. In the Spring their plumage is prettily variegated, black and white;
but

but their Summer drefs may be called elegant, though not gay.   They live long in confinement, have naturally a pleafing note, and when in company with Canary birds foon  imitate their fong. I have kept many of them in  cages in the fame room with Canary birds, and always found they fung in Winter as well as in Summer, but even in confinement they change their plumage according to the feafon, the fame as in a wild ftate  This fpecies of bird feem  fond of the coldeft regions, for as the Spring advances  they fly fo far North that their  breeding places are not  known to the inhabitants of Hudfon's Bay.   In Autumn they return to the South in large flocks, and are frequently fhot  in confiderable numbers merely as a delicacy, at that feafon, however, they are by no means fo good as when  they firft  make their appearance in Spring

White-crowned Bunting.   This fpecies is inferior in fize to the former, and feldom make their appearance till June.   They breed in moft parts of the Bay, always make their nefts on the ground, at the root of a dwarf willow or a goofeberry-bufh.   During the time their young are in a callow ftate they have a delightful note, but as foon as they are fledged they become filent, and retire to the South early in September.

Lapland Finch.   This bird is common on Hudfon's Bay, and never migrates Southward in the coldeft Winters.   During that feafon it generally frequents the juniper plains, and feeds on the
                                                              fmall

finall buds of that tree, alfo on grafsfeeds; but
at the approach of Summer it flies ftill farther
North to breed. A variety of this bird is alfo
common, and is beautifully marked with a red
forehead and breaft. It is moft common in the
Spring, and frequently caught in nets fet for the
Snow Bunting; and when kept in cages has a
pleafing note, but feldom lives long in confinement, though it generally dies very fat.

LARKS of a pretty variegated colour frequent Larks
thofe parts in Summer, and always make their
appearance in May; build their nefts on the
ground, ufually by the fide of a ftone at the root
of a fmall bufh, lay four fpeckled eggs, and bring
forth their young in June. At their firft arrival,
and till the young can fly, the male is in full
fong; and, like the fky-lark, foars to a great
height, and generally defcends in a perpendicular direction near their neft. Their note is loud
and agreeable, but confifts of little variety, and
as foon as the young can fly they become filent,
and retire to the Southward early in the Fall.
They are impatient of confinement, never fing in
that ftate, and feldom live long.

The TITMOUSE is ufually called in Hudfon's Titmoufe
Bay, Blackcap. This diminutive bird braves the
coldeft Winter, and during that feafon feeds on
the feeds of long rye-grafs, but in Summer on
infects and berries. The Southern Indians call
this bird Kifs-kifs-hefhis, from a twittering noife
they make, which much refembles that word in
found.

SWALLOWS

Swallows

SWALLOWS vifit thefe parts in confiderable numbers in Summer, and are very domeftic; building their nefts in neceffaries, ftables, and other out-offices that are much frequented. They feldom make their appearance at Churchill River till June, and retire South early in Auguft They, like the European Swallow, gather in large flocks on the day of their departure, make feveral revolutions round the breeding-places, and then take their leave till the next year I do not recollect to have feen any of thofe birds to the North of Seal River.

Martins

MARTINS alfo vifit Hudfon's Bay in great numbers, but feldom fo far North as Churchill River They ufually make their nefts in holes formed in the fteep banks of rivers, and, like the Swallow, lay four or five fpeckled eggs, and retire Southward in Auguft. At the Northern fettlements they are by no means fo domeftic as the Swallow.

Hooping Crane

HOOPING CRANE. This bird vifits Hudfon's Bay in the Spring, though not in great numbers They are generally feen only in pairs, and that not very often. It is a bird of confiderable fize, often equal to that of a good turkey, and the great length of the bill, neck, and legs, makes it meafure, from the bill to the toes, near fix feet in common, and fome much more Its plumage is of a pure white, except the quill feathers, which are black, the crown is covered with a red fkin, thinly befet with black briftles, and the legs are

large

large and black. It ufually frequents open fwamps, the fides of rivers, and the margins of lakes and ponds, feeds on frogs and fmall fifh, and efteemed good eating. The wing-bones of this bird are fo long and large, that I have known them made into flutes with tolerable fuccefs. It feldom has more than two young, and retires Southward early in the fall.

The Brown Crane. This fpecies is far infe-rior in fize to the former, being feldom three feet and a half in length, and on an average not weighing feven pounds. Their haunts and man-ner of life are nearly the fame as that of the Hoop-ing Crane, and they nevei have more than two young, and thofe feldom fly till September. 1 hey are found farther North than the former, for I have killed feveral of them on Marble Ifland, and have feen them on the Continent as high as the latitude 65° They are generally efteemed good eating, and, from the form of the body when fit for the fpit, they acquire the name of the North Weft Turkey. There is a circumftance refpect-ing this bird that is very peculiar, which is, that the gizzard is laiger than that of a fwan, and re-markably fo in the young birds. The Brown Cranes are frequently feen in hot calm days to foar to an amazing height, always flying in circles, till by degrees they are almoft out of fight, yet their note is fo loud, that the fportfman, before he fees their fituation, often fancies they are very near him. They vifit Hudfon's Bay in far

greater

Brown Crane

greater numbers than the former, and are very good eating.

Bitterns.      BITTERNS are common at York Fort in Summer, but are seldom found so far North as Churchill River.   I have seen two species of this bird; some having ash-coloured legs, others with beautiful grass-green legs, and very gay plumage. They always frequent marshes and swamps, also the banks of rivers that abound with reeds and long grass.   They generally feed on insects that are bred in the water, and probably on small frogs; and though seldom fat, they are generally good eating.   They are by no means numerous even at York Fort, nor in fact in the most Southern parts of the Bay that I have visited.

Curlews.      CURLEWS.   There are two species of this bird which frequent the coasts of Hudson's Bay in great numbers during Summer, and breed in all parts of it as far North as the latitude 72°, the largest of this species is distinguished by that great Naturalist Mr. Pennant, by the name of the Esquimaux Curlew.   They always keep near the sea coast; attend the ebbing of the tide, and are frequently found at low-water-mark in great numbers, where they feed on marine insects, which they find by the sides of stones in great plenty; but at high-water they retire to the dry ridges and wait the receding of the tide.   They fly as steady as a woodcock, answer to a whistle that resembles their note, lay long on their wings, and are a most excellent shot, and at times are

delicious

delicious eating. The other fpecies of Curlew are in colour and fhape exactly like the former, though inferior in fize, and differ in their manner of life, as they never frequent the water's-edge, but always keep among the rocks and dry ridges, and feed on berries and fmall infects. The flefh of this bird is generally more efteemed than that of the former, but they are by no means fo numerous. This fpecies of Curlew are feldom found farther North than Egg River.

JACK SNIPES. Thofe birds vifit Hudfon's Bay JackSnipes. in Summer in confiderable numbers, but are feldom feen to the North of Whale Cove. They do not arrive till the ice of the rivers is broke up, and they retire to the South early in the Fall. During their ftay, they always frequent marfhes near the fea coaft, and the fhores of great rivers. In manner and flight they exactly refemble the European Jack Snipe; and when on the wing, fly at fuch a diftance from each other, that it is but feldom the beft fportfman can get more than one or two at a fhot. Their flefh is by no means fo delicate as that of the Englifh Snipe.

RED GODWAITS, ufually called at the Northern Red Godwait fettlements in Hudfon's Bay, Plovers. Thofe birds vifit the fhores of that part in very large flocks, and ufually frequent the marfhes and the margins of ponds. They alfo frequently attend the tide, like the Efquimaux Curlews; fly down to low-water-mark, and feed on a fmall fifh, not much unlike a fhrimp; but as the tide flows,

they

they retire to the marfhes. They fly in fuch large flocks, and fo clofe to each other, that I have often killed upwards of twelve at one fhot; and Mr. Atkinfon, long refident at York Fort, actually killed feventy-two at one fhot, but that was when the birds were fitting. Near Church-ill River they are feldom fat, though tolerably flefhy, and are generally good eating. They ufu-ally weigh from ten to thirteen ounces; the female is always larger than the male, and differs in colour, being of a much lighter brown. They retire to the South long before the froft commen-ces; yet I have feen this bird as far North as the latitude 71° 50.

Spotted
Godwait

SPOTTED GODWAIT, known in Hudfon's Bay by the name of Yellow Legs. This bird alfo vi-fits that country in confiderable numbers, but more fo in the interior parts; and ufually fre-quents the flat muddy banks of rivers. In fum-mer it is generally very poor, but late in the Fall is, as it may be called, one lump of fat. This bird, with many others of the migratory tribe, I faw in confiderable numbers as far North as the lati-tude 71° 54'; and at York Fort I have known them fhot fo late as the latter end of October. at which time they are in the greateft perfection, and moft delicious eating, more particularly fo when put into a bit of pafte, and boiled like an apple dumpling; for in fact they are generally too fat at that feafon to be eaten either roafted or boiled.

HEBRIDAL

HEBRIDAL SANDPIPERS, but more commonly Hebridal Sandpipers
known in Hudfon's Bay by the Name of Whale
Birds, on account of their feeding on the carcafes
of thofe animals which frequently lie on the
fhores, alfo on maggots that are produced in them
by fly-blows. Thefe birds frequent thofe parts
in confiderable numbers, and always keep near
the margin of the fea. They may, in fact, be
called beautiful birds, though not gay in their
plumage; they are ufually very fat, but even
when firft killed they fmell and tafte fo much like
train-oil as to render them by no means pleafing
to the palate, yet they are frequently eaten by
the Company's fervants. As the Summer advances they fly fo far North of Churchill River,
that their breeding-places are not known, though
they remain at that part till the beginning of
July, and return early in the Fall. They are by
no means large birds, as they feldom weigh four
ounces. The bill is black, plumage prettily variegated black and white, and the legs and feet are
of a beautiful orange colour*.

PLOVERS, commonly called Hawk's Eyes, from Plover
their watchfulnefs to prevent a near approach
when fitting. When thefe birds are on the
wing, they fly very fwift and irregular, particularly when fingle or in fmall flocks. At
Churchill River they are by no means numerous,
but

---

* They exactly correfpond with the bird defcribed by Mr. Pennan', except that they are much longer

but I have feen them in fuch large flocks at York
Fort in the Fall of one thoufand feven hundred
and feventy-three, that Mr. Ferdinand Jacobs then
Governor, Mr. Robert Body Surgeon, and myfelf, killed in one afternoon as many as two men
could conveniently carry.   They generally feed
on infeéts, and are at all times good eating, but
late in the Fall are moft excellent.   They are by
no means equally plentiful in all years; and at
the Northern fettlements in the Bay they are not
claffed with thofe fpecies of game that add to the
general ftock of provifions, being only killed as
a luxury; but I am informed that at Albany
Fort, feveral barrels of them are annually falted
for Winter ufe, and are efteemed good eating.
This bird during Summer reforts to the remoteft
Northern parts; for I have feen them at the Copper River, though in thofe dreary regions only
in pairs.   The young of thofe birds  always
leave their nefts as foon as hatched, and when but
a few days old run very faft; at night, or in
rainy weather, the old ones call them together,
and cover them with their wings, in the fame
manner as a hen does her chickens

Black Gul-
lemots.    BLACK GULLFMOTS, known in Hudfon's Bay
by the name of Sea Pigeons.   Thofe birds frequent the fhores of Hudfon's Bay and Straits in
confiderable numbers; but more particularly the
Northern parts, where they fly in large flocks; to
the Southward they are only feen in pairs  They
are of a fine black, but not gloffy, with fcarlet

                                              legs

legs and feet; and the coverets of the wings are
marked with white. They are in weight equal
to a Widgeon, though to appearance not fo
large. They ufually make their nefts in the holes
of rocks, and lay two white eggs, which are delicate eating, but not proportionably large for
the fize of the bird. My friend Mr. Pennant
fays, they brave the coldeft Winters in thofe parts,
by keeping at the edge of the ice near the open
water; but as the fea at that feafon is frozen
over for feveral miles from the fhore, I believe
no one's curiofity ever tempted him to confirm
the truth of this, and it is well known they never make their appearance near the land after the
froft becomes fevere.

NORTHERN DIVERS. Thefe birds, though com- Northern
mon in Hudfon's Bay, are by no means plentiful; Divers.
they are feldom found near the fea coaft, but more
frequently in frefh water lakes, and ufually in
pairs. They build their nefts at the edge of fmall
iflands, or the margins of lakes or ponds; they
lay only two eggs, and it is very common to
find only one pair and their young in one fheet
of water; a great proof of their averfion to fociety. They are known in Hudfon's Bay by the
name of Loons. They differ in fpecies from the
Black and Red throated Divers, having a large
black bill near four inches long; plumage on the
back of a gloffy black, elegantly barred with
white, the belly of a filver white; and they are
fo large as at times to weigh fiftcen or fixteen
pounds.

pounds. Their flesh it always black, hard, and fishy, yet it is generally eaten by the Indians.

BLACK-THROATED DIVERS. This species are more beautiful than the former; having a long white bill, plumage on the back and wings black, elegantly tinged with purple and green, and prettily marked with white spots. In size they are equal to the former; but are so watchful as to dive at the flash of a gun, and of course are seldom killed but when on the wing. Their flesh is equally black and fishy with the former, but it is always eaten by the Indians. The skins of those birds are very thick and strong, and they are frequently dressed with the feathers on, and made into caps for the Indian men. The skins of the Eagle and Raven, with their plumage complete, are also applied to that use, and are far from being an unbecoming head-dress for a savage.

RED-THROATED DIVERS. This species are also called Loons in Hudson's Bay; but they are so far inferior to the two former, that they seldom weigh more than three or four pounds. They, like the other species of Loon, are excellent divers, they always feed on fish, and when in pursuit of their prey, are frequently entangled in fishing-nets, set at the mouths of creeks and small rivers. They are more numerous than either of the former, as they frequently fly in flocks; but like them make their nests at the edge of the water, and only lay two eggs, which, though very rank and fishy, are always eaten by Indians and
                                            English

Englifh. The legs of thofe three fpecies of Loon are placed fo near the rump as to be of no fervice to them on the land, as they are perfectly incapable of walking, and when found in that fituation (which is but feldom) they are eafily taken, though they make a ftrong refiftance with their bill, which is very hard and fharp.

WHITE GULLS. Thefe birds vifit Hudfon's WhiteGulls Bay in great numbers, both on the fea coafts and in the interior parts, and probably extend quite acrofs the continent of America. They generally make their appearance at Churchill River about the middle of May; build their nefts on the iflands in lakes and rivers, lay two fpeckled eggs, and bring forth their young in June Their eggs are generally efteemed good eating, as well as the flefh of thofe in the interior parts of the country, though they feed on fifh and carrion. They make their ftay on Hudfon's Bay as long in the Fall as the froft will permit them to procure a livelihood.

GREY GULLS. Thefe birds, though common, Grey Gulls. are by no means plentiful, and I never knew their breeding places, as they feldom make their appearance at Churchill River till the Fall of the year, and remain there only till the ice begins to be formed about the fhores. They feldom frequent the interior parts of the country. They are not inferior in fize to the former, and in the Fall of the year are generally fat. The flefh is white and very good eating, and, like moft other

F f                              Gulls,

Gulls, they are a moft excellent fhot when on the wing.

Black Gull.  BLACK GULLS, ufually called in Hudfon's Bay, Men of War, from their purfuing and taking the prey from a leffer fpecies of Gull, known in that country by the name of Black head. In fize they are much inferior to the two former fpecies; but, like them, always make their nefts on iflands, or at the margins of lakes or ponds; they lay only two eggs, and are found at a confiderable diftance from the fea coaft. The length of their wings is very great in proportion to the body; the tail is uniform, and the two middle feathers are four or five inches longer than the reft. Their eggs are always eaten, both by the Indians and Englifh; but the bird itfelf is generally rejected, except when other provifions are very fcarce.

Black-heads.  BLACK-HEADS. Thefe are the fmalleft fpecies of Gull that I know. They vifit the fea coaft of Hudfon's Bay in fuch vaft numbers, that they are frequently feen in flocks of feveral hundreds; and I have known bufhels of their eggs taken on an ifland of very fmall circumference. Thefe eggs are very delicate eating, the yolks being equal to that of a young pullet, and the whites of a femi tranfparent azure, but the bird itfelf is always fifhy. Their affection for their young is fo ftrong, that when any perfon attempts to rob their nefts, they fly at him, and fometimes approach fo near as to touch him with their pinions, and when they find their lofs, will frequent-

ly

ly follow the plunderer to a confiderable diftance, and exprefs their grief by making an unufual fcreaming noife

This bird may be ranked with the elegant part of the feathered creation, though it is by no means gay The bill, legs, and feet are of a rich fcarlet, crown black, and the remainder of the plumage of a light afh colour, except the quill-feathers, which are prettily barred, and tipped with black, and the tail much forked. The flight, or extent of wing, in this bird, is very great, in proportion to the body. They are found as far North as has hitherto been vifited, but retire to the South early in the Fall.

PELICANS. Thofe birds are numerous in the Pelicans. interior parts of the country, but never appear near the fea-coaft. They generally frequent large lakes, and always make their nefts on iflands. They are fo provident for their young, that great quantities of fifh lie rotting near their nefts, and emit fuch a horrid ftench as to be fmelt at a confiderable diftance. The flefh of the young Pelican is frequently eaten by the Indians; and as they are always very fat, great quantities of it is melted down, and preferved in bladders for Winter ufe*, to mix with pounded flefh; but by

F f 2 keeping,

* In the Fall of 1774, when I firft fettled at Cumberland Houfe, the Indians impofd on me and my people very much, by felling us Pelican fat for the fat of the black bear Our knowledge of the delicacy of the latter induced us to referve this fat for particular purpofes, but when we came to open the bladders, it was little fuperior to train oil, and was only
ly

keeping, it grows very rank. The Pelicans in
those parts are about the size of a common goose;
their plumage is of a delicate white, except the
quill-feathers, which are black. The bill is near
a foot long; and the bag, which reaches from
the outer-end of the under mandible to the breast,
is capable of containing upwards of three quarts.
The skins of those birds are thick and tough,
and are frequently dressed by the Indians and
converted into bags, but are never made into
clothing, though their feathers are as hard, close,
and durable, as those of a Loon.

Goosanders    GOOSANDERS, usually called in Hudson's Bay,
Shell-drakes. Those birds are very common on
the sea-coast, but in the interior parts fly in very
large flocks, The bill is long and narrow, and
toothed like a saw, and they have a tuft of feathers at the back of the head, which they can
erect at pleasure. They are most excellent divers,
and such great destroyers of fish, that they are
frequently obliged to vomit some of them before
they can take flight. Though not much larger
than the Mallard Duck, they frequently swallow
fish of six or seven inches long and proportionably thick. Those that frequent the interior parts
of the country prey much on crawfish, which
                                                    are

Iv eatable by a few of my crew which at that time consisted only of eight
Englishmen and two of the home Indians from York Fort

Cumberland House was the first inland settlement the Company made
from Hudson's Fort, and though begun on so small a scale, yet upon it
and Hudson's House, which is situated beyond it, upwards of seventy
men were now employed.

are very numerous in fome of the fhallow ftony rivers. In the Fall of the year they are very fat, and though they always feed on fifh, yet their flefh at that feafon is very good; and they remain in thofe parts as long as the froft will permit them to procure a fubfiftence.

Swans. There are two fpecies of this bird that vifit Hudfon's Bay in fummer; and only differ in fize, as the plumage of both are perfectly white, with black bill and legs. The fmaller fort are more frequent near the fea-coaft, but by no means plentiful, and are moft frequently feen in pairs, but fometimes fingle, probably owing to their mates having been killed on their paffage North. Both fpecies ufually breed on the iflands which are in lakes; and the eggs of the larger fpecies are fo big, that one of them is a fufficient meal for a moderate man, without bread, or any other addition. In the interior parts of the country the larger Swan precedes every other fpecies of water-fowl, and in fome years arrive fo early as the month of March, long before the ice of the rivers is broken up. At thofe times they always frequent the open waters of falls and rapids, where they are frequently fhot by the Indians in confiderable numbers. They ufually weigh upwards of thirty pounds, and the leffer fpecies from eighteen to twenty-four. The flefh of both are excellent eating, and when roafted, is equal in flavour to young heifer-beef, and the cygnets are very delicate.

Not-

Notwithstanding the size of this bird, they are so swift on the wing as to make them the most difficult to shoot of any bird I know, it being frequently necessary to take sight ten or twelve feet before their bills  This, however, is only when flying before the wind in a brisk gale, at which time they cannot fly at a less rate than an hundred miles an hour ; but when flying across the wind, or against it, they make but a slow progress, and are then a noble shot.   In their moulting state they are not easily taken, as their large feet, with the assistance of their wings, enables them to run on the surface of the water as fast as an Indian canoe can be paddled, and therefore they are always obliged to be shot, for by diving and other manœuvres they render it impossible to take them by hand.   It has been said that the swans whistle or sing before their death, and I have read some elegant descriptions of it in some of the poets ; but I have never heard any thing of the kind, though I have been at the deaths of several. It is true, in serene evenings, after Sun-set, I have heard them make a noise not very unlike that of a French-horn, but entirely divested of every note that constituted melody, and have often been sorry to find it did not forebode their death.   Mr. Lawson, who, as Mr. Pennant justly remarks, was no inaccurate observer, properly enough calls the largest species Trumpeters, and the lesser, Hoopers.   Some years ago, when I built Cumberland House, the Indians killed those
                                                birds

birds in fuch numbers, that the down and quills
might have been procured in confiderable quantities at a trifling expence, but fince the depopulation of the natives by the fmall pox, which has
alfo driven the few furvivors to frequent other
parts of the country, no advantage can be made
of thofe articles, though of confiderable value in
England*.

GEESE. There are no lefs than ten different Geefe
fpecies of Geefe that frequent the various parts of
Hudfon's Bay during Summer, and are as follow:
Firft, The Common Grey Goofe. Second, The
Canada Goofe. Third, The White, or Snow
Goofe. Fifth, The Blue Goofe. Sixth, The
Laughing Goofe. Seventh, The Barren Goofe.
Eighth, The Brent Goofe. Ninth, The Dunter;
and Tenth, the Bean Goofe.

COMMON GREY GOOSE. This bird precedes Common
Grey Goofe.
every other fpecies of Goofe in thofe parts, and
in fome forward Springs arrives at Churchill
River fo early as the latter end of April, but more
commonly from the eleventh to the fixteenth of
May, and in one year it was the twenty-fixth of

May

---

* Mr Pennant, in treating of the Whiftling Swan, takes notice of the
formation of the Windpipe, but on examination, the windpipes of both
the fpecies which frequent Hudfon's Bay are found to be exactly alike,
though their note is quite different. The breaft bone of this bird is different from any other I have feen, for inftead of being fharp and folid, like
that of a goofe, it is broad and hollow. Into this cavity the windpipe paffes
from the valve, and reaching quite down to the abdomen, returns into the
cheft, and joins the lungs. Neither of the fpecies of Swan that frequent
Hudfon's Bay are mute but the note of the larger is much louder and
harfher than that of the fmaller

May before any Geefe made their appearance,
At their firft arrival they generally come in pairs,
and are fo fond of fociety, that they fly ftreight
to the call that imitates their note; by which
means they are eafily fhot. They breed in great
numbers in the plains and marfhes near Churchill River; and in fome years the young ones can
be taken in confiderable numbers, and are eafily
tamed, but will never learn to eat corn, unlefs
fome of the old ones are taken with them, which
is eafily done when in a moulting ftate. On the
ninth of Auguft one thoufand feven hundred and
eighty-one, when I refided at Prince of Wales's
Fort, I fent fome Indians up Churchill River in
canoes to procure fome of thofe Geefe, and in the
afternoon they were feen coming down the river
with a large flock before them; the young ones
not more than half grown, and the old ones fo
far in a moulting ftate as not to be capable of flying: fo that, with the affiftance of the Englifh and
the Indians then refiding on the plantation, the
whole flock, to the amount of forty-one, was
drove within the ftockade which inclofes the
Fort, where they were fed and fattened for Winter ufe. Wild Geefe taken and fattened in this
manner are much preferable to any tame Geefe
in the world. When this fpecies of Geefe are
full-grown, and in good condition, they often
weigh twelve pounds, but more frequently much
lefs.

Canada
Goofe

CANADA GOOSE, or Pifk-a-fifh, as it is called
by

by the Indians, as well as the Englifh in Hudfon's Bay This fpecies do not differ in plumage from the former, but are inferior in fize; the bill is much fmaller in proportion, and the flefh being much whiter, of courfe is more efteemed. They are by no means fo numerous as the former, and generally fly far North to breed; but fome few of their eggs are found near Churchill River. It is feldom that either of thefe fpecies lay more than four eggs, but if not robbed, they ufually bring them all forth.

WHITE or SNOW GOOSE. Thefe are the moft numerous of all the fpecies of birds that frequent the Northern parts of the Bay, and generally make their appearance about a week or ten days after the Common Grey Goofe. In the firft part of the feafon they come in fmall parties, but in the middle, and toward the latter end, they fly in fuch amazing flocks, that when they fettle in the marfhes to feed, the ground for a confide-rable diftance appears like a field of fnow. When feeding in the fame marfh with the Grey Geefe, they never mix. Like the Grey Geefe, they fly to the call that refembles their note, and in fome years are killed and falted in great numbers for Winter provifion; they are almoft univerfally thought good eating, and will, if proper care be taken in curing them, continue good for eighteen months or two years The Indians are far more expert in killing Geefe, as well as every other fpe-cies of game, than any European I ever faw in Hudfon's

White or Snow Goofe

Hudfon's Bay ; for fome of them frequently kill
upward of a hundred Geefe in a day, whereas
the moft expert of the Englifh think it a good
day's work to kill thirty. Some years back it
was common for an Indian to kill from a thoufand
to twelve hurdred Geefe in one feafon ; but latterly he is reckoned a good hunter that kills three
hundred. This is by no means owing to the de-
generacy of the natives ; for the Geefe of late
years do not frequent thofe parts in fuch numbers as formerly. The general breeding-place
of this bird is not known to any Indian in Hudfon's Bay, not even to the Efquimaux who frequent the remoteft North. The general route
they take in their return to the South in the Fall
of the year, is equally unknown, for though fuch
multitudes of them are feen at Churchill River
in the Spring, and are frequently killed to the
amount of five or fix thoufand ; yet in the Fall
of the year, feven or eight hundred is confidered
a good hunt. At York Fort, though only two
degrees South of Churchill River, the Geefe feafons fluctuate fo much, that in fome Springs they
have falted forty hogfheads, and in others not
more than one or two . and at Albany Fort, the
Spring feafon is by no means to be depended on,
but in the fall they frequently falt fixty hogfheads of Geefe, befides great quantities of Plover.
The retreat of thofe birds in Winter is equally
unknown, as that of their breeding-places. I
obferve in Mr. Pennant's Arctic Zoology, that
                                                        about

about Jakutz, and other parts of Siberia, they are caught in great numbers, both in nets, and by decoying them into hovels; but if thefe are the fame birds, they muft at times vary as much in manner as they do in fituation, for in Hudfon's Bay they are the fhyeft and moft watchful of all the fpecies of Geefe, never fuffering an open approach, not even within two or three gun fhots: yet in fome of the rivers near Cumberland Houfe, and at Bafquiau, the Indians frequently kill twenty at one fhot, but this is only done in moon-light nights, when the Geefe are fitting on the mud, and the fportfmen are perfectly concealed from their view. Though the plumage of thofe Geefe are perfectly white, except the quill-feathers, which are black, the fkin is of a dark lead-colour, and the flefh is excellent eating, either frefh or falt. They are much inferior in fize to the Common Grey Geefe, but equal to the Canada Geefe.

BLUE GEESE. This fpecies are of the fame fize Blue Geefe. as the Snow Geefe; and, like them, the bill and legs are of a deep flefh-colour, but the whole plumage is of a dirty blue, refembling old lead. The fkin, when ftripped of its feathers, is of the fame colour as the Snow Goofe, and they are equally good eating. This fpecies of Geefe are feldom feen to the North of Churchill River, and not very common at York Fort, but at Albany Fort they are more plentiful than the White or Snow Geefe. Their breeding-places are as little

known

known to the most accurate obferver as thofe of
the Snow Geefe, for I never knew any of their
eggs taken and their Winter haunts have hitherto been undifcovered   Thofe birds are frequently feen to lead a flock of the White ones; and, as
they generally fly in angles, it is far from unpleafant to fee a bird of a different colour leading the
van   The leader is generally the object of the
firft fportfman who fires, which throws the whole
flock into fuch confufion, that fome of the other
hunters frequently kill fix or feven at a fhot.

HORNED WAVEY   This delicate and diminutive fpecies of the Goofe is not much larger than
the Mallard Duck   Its plumage is delicately
white, except the quill feathers, which are black
The bill is not more than an inch long, and at the
bafe is ftudded round with little knobs about the
fize of peas, but more remarkably fo in the males.
Both the bill and feet are of the fame colour
with thofe of the Snow Goofe.   This fpecies is
very fcarce at Churchill River, and I believe are
never found at any of the Southern fettlements,
but about two or three hundred miles to the
North Weft of Churchill, I have feen them in as
large flocks as the Common Wavey, or Snow
Goofe   The flefh of this bird is exceedingly delicate, but they are fo fmall, that when I was on
my journey to the North I eat two of them one
night for fupper   I do not find this bird defcribed by my worthy friend Mr Pennant in his Arctic Zoology   Probably a fpecimen of it was not
fent

Horned
Wavey

fent home, for the perfon that commanded at Prince of Wales's Fort* at the time the collection was making, did not pay any attention to it.

LAUGHING GOOSE. This elegant fpecies has a white bill, and the legs and feet are of a fine yellow colour; the upper part of the plumage is brown, the breaft and belly white, the former prettily blotched with black. In fize they are equal to the Snow Goofe, and their fkins, when ftripped of their feathers, are delicately white, and the flefh excellent. They vifit Churchill River in very fmall numbers, but about two hundred miles to the North Weft of that river I have feen them fly in large flocks, like the Common Waveys, or Snow Geefe, and near Cumberland Houfe and Bafquiau they are found in fuch numbers, that the Indians in moon light nights frequently kill upwards of twenty at a fhot. Like the Horned Wavey, they never fly with the lead of the coaft, but are always feen to come from the Weftward Their general breeding places are not known, though fome few of their eggs are occafionally found to the North of Churchill, but I never heard any Indian fay that he had feen any eggs of the Horned Wavey. It is probable they retire to North Greenland to breed, and their route in the Fall of the year, as they return Southward, is equally unknown. They are, I believe, feldom feen on the coaft of Hudfon's Bay to the Southward of latitude 59° North.

BARREN GEESE. Thefe are the largeft of all the

Laughing Goofe

Barren Geefe.

* Mr Mofes Norton.

the fpecies of Geefe that frequent Hudfon's Bay, as they frequently weigh fixteen or feventeen pounds. They differ from the Common Grey Goofe in nothing but in fize, and in the head and breaft being tinged with a rufty brown. They never make their appearance in the Spring till the greateft part of the other fpecies of Gee e are flown Northward to breed, and many of them remain near Churchill River the whole Summer. This large fpecies are generally found to be males, and from the exceeding fmallnefs of their tefti- cles, they are, I fuppofe, incapable of propagating their fpecies I believe I can with truth fay, that I was the firft European who made that remark, though they had always been diftinguifhed by the name of the Barren Geefe ; for no other reafon than that of their not being known to breed. Their flefh is by no means unpleafant, though al- ways hard and tough ; and their plumage is fo thick before they begin to moult, that one bird ufually produces a pound of fine feathers and down, of a furprifing elafticity.

**Brent Geefe.** BRENT GEESE This fpecies certainly breed in the remoteft parts of the North, and feldom make their appearance at Churchill River till late in Auguft or September. The rout they take in Spring is unknown, and their breeding-places have never been difcovered by any Indian in Hudfon's Bay. When they make their appear- ance at Churchill River, they always come from the North, fly near the margin of the coaft, and are never feen in the interior parts of the country.

In

In fize they are larger than a Mallard Duck, but inferior to the Snow Goofe, and though their flefh appears delicate to the eye, it is not much efteemed In fome years they pafs the mouth of Churchill River in prodigious numbers, and many of them are killed and ferved to the Company's fervants as provifions, but, as I have juft obferved, they are not much relifhed. When migrating to the South, they generally avail themfelves of a ftrong North or North Wefterly wind, which makes then fly fo fwift, that when I have killed four or five at a fhot, not one of them fell lefs than from twenty to fifty yards from the perpendicular fpot where they were killed. Like the White, or Snow Geefe, when in large flocks they fly in the fhape of a wedge, and make a great noife. Their flight is very irregular, fometimes being forty or fifty yards above the water, and in an inftant after they fkim clofe to the furface of it, and then rife again to a confiderable height; fo that they may juftly be faid to fly in feftoons

The DUNTER GEESE, as it is called in Hudfon's Bay, but which is certainly the Eider Duck. They are common at the mouth of Churchill River as foon as the ice breaks up, but generally fly far North to breed; and the few that do remain near the fettlement are fo fcattered among fmall iflands, and fea-girt rocks and fhoals, as to render it not worth while to attempt gathering their down. Their eggs, when found, are exceeding good eating; and in the Fall of the year the flefh

*Dunter Goofe*

is

is by no means unpleafant, though they are notoriouſly known to feed on fiſh.

BeanGoofe.    BEAN GOOSE. This ſpecies is feldom found in
any part of Hudſon s Bay, as in all my travels I
have only feen three that were killed. This bird
never came under the infpection of Mr Graham,
or the late Mr. Hutchins, though they both contributed very largely to the collection ſent home
to the Royal Society*.


*Species of Water-Fowl.*


Ducks.    DUCKS of various kinds are found in thoſe
parts during Summer; ſome only frequenting
the ſea-coaſt, while others viſit the interior parts
of the country in aſtoniſhing numbers. The ſpecies of this bird which is found moſt commonly
here are, the King Duck, Black Duck, Mallard
Duck, Long tailed Duck, Widgeon, and Teal.
The two firſt only viſit the ſea-coaſt, feed on fiſh
and

---

* It is, however, no leſs true, that the late Mr Humphry Martin, many
year-Governor of Albany Fort, fent home feveral hundred ſpecimens of
animals and plants to complete that collection, but by ſome miſtake, nothing of the kind was placed to the credit of his account  Even my refpected friend Mr Pennant, who with a candour that does him honour,
has ſo generouſly acknowledged his obligations to all to whom he thought
he was indebted for information when he was writing his Arctic Zoology,
(fee the Advertiſement,) has not mentioned his name, but I am fully perfuaded that it entirely proceeded from a want of knowing the perſon,
and as Mr Hutchins fucceeded him at Albany in the year 1774,
every thing that has been fent over from that part has been placed to his
account

and fish-spawn, and their flesh is by no means esteemed good, though their eggs are not disagreeable. The Mallard and Long tailed Duck visit Hudson's Bay in great numbers, and extend from the sea coast, to the remotest Western parts, and near Cumberland House are found in vast multitudes. At their first arrival on the sea coast, they are exceeding good eating; but when in a moulting state, though very fat, they are in general so rank that few Europeans are fond of them. At those seasons the difference in flavour is easily known by the colour of the fat; for when that is white, the flesh is most assuredly good; but when it is yellow, or of an orange colour, it is very rank and fishy. This difference is only peculiar to those that frequent and breed near the sea-coast; for in the interior parts I never knew them killed but their flesh was very good; and the young Mallard Duck before it can fly is very fat, and most delicate eating. The same may be said of the Long-tailed Duck. Neither of those species lay more than six or eight eggs in common, and frequently bring them all forth,

WIDGEON. This species of Duck is very un- <sup>Widgeon</sup> common in Hudson's Bay; usually keeping in pairs, and being seldom seen in flocks They are by no means so numerous as the two former, and are most frequently seen in rivers and marshes near the sea coast Their flesh is generally esteemed; and the down of those I have examined is little interior in elasticity to that of the

G g                                    Eider,

Fider, though much fhorter. The fame may be faid of feveral other fpecies of Ducks that frequent thofe parts; but the impoffibility of collecting the down in any quantity, prevents it from becoming an article of trade.

Teal     TEAL. Like the Mallard, they are found in confiderable numbers near the fea-coaft; but are more plentiful in the interior parts of the country, and fly in fuch large flocks that I have often killed twelve or fourteen at one fhot, and have feen both Englifh and Indians kill a much greater number  At their firft arrival they are but poor, though generally efteemed good eating. This diminutive Duck is by far the moft prolific of any I know that reforts to Hudfon's Bay; for I have often feen the old ones fwimming at the head of feventeen young, when not much larger than walnuts  This bird remains in thofe parts as long as the feafon will permit, for in the year one thoufand feven hundred and feventy-five, in my paffage from Cumberland Houfe to York Fort, I, as well as my Indian companions, killed them in the rivers we paffed through as late as the twentieth of October  At thofe times they are entirely involved in fat, but delicately white, and may truly be called a great luxury.

Befides the birds already defcribed, there is a great variety of others, both of land and water fowl, that frequent thofe parts in Summer; but thefe came not fo immediately under my infpection as thofe I have already defcribed.

                                              Of

*Of the Vegetable Productions.*

The vegetable productions of this country by no means engaged my attention fo much as the animal creation; which is the lefs to be wondered at, as fo few of them are ufeful for the fupport of man. Yet I will endeavour to enumerate as many of them as I think are worth notice

The GOOSEBERRIES thrive beft in ftony and rocky ground, which lies open and much expofed to the Sun. But in thofe fituations few of the bufhes grow to any height, and fpread along the ground like vines The fruit is always moft plentiful and the fineft on the under-fide of the branches, probably owing to the reflected heat from the ftones and gravel, and from being fheltered from all cold winds and fog by the leaves. I never faw more than one fpecies of Goofeberry in any part of Hudfon's Bay, which is the red one. When green, they make excellent pies or tarts; and when ripe are very pleafant eating, though by no means fo large as thofe produced in England.

Goofe-berries

CRANBERRIES grow in great abundance near Churchill, and are not confined to any particular fituation, for they are as common on open bleak plains and high rocks as among the woods. When carefully gathered in the Fall, in dry weather,

Cranberries

ther, and as carefully packed in casks with moist
sugar, they will keep for years, and are annually
sent to England in confiderable quantities as presents, where they are much esteemed.   When the
ships have remained in the Bay so late that the
Cranberries are ripe, some of the Captains have
carried them home in water with great succefs.

Heath.  The Heathberries are in some years so plen-
berries.  tiful near Churchill, that it is impoffible to walk
in many places without treading on thoufands and
millions of them.   They grow clofe to the ground,
and are a favourite repast of many birds that migrate to thofe parts in Summer, particularly the
Grey Goofe, on which account the Indians di-
finguifh them by the name of Nifhca minnick,
or the Grey Goofeberry.   The juice of this berry
makes an exceeding pleafant Leverage, and the
fruit itfelf would be more pleafing were it not
for the number of fmall feeds it contains

Betha-  Bethago-tominick, as it is called by the Indi-
gotomi-  ans, or the Dewater-berry of Mr. Dragge.   I
nick.  have feen this berry as far North as Marble Ifland,
and that in great abundance   It flourifhes beft,
and is moft productive, in fwampy boggy ground
covered with mofs, and is feldom found among
grafs   The plant itfelf is not very unlike that of
a Strawberry, but the leaves are larger.   Out of
the center of the plant fhoots a fingle ftalk, fometimes to the height of feven or eight inches, and
each plant only produces one berry, which at
fome diftance refembles a Strawberry; but on
                                    exami-

examination they have not that conical form;
and many of them are only compofed of three or
four lobes, while others confift of near twenty.
The flavour of this berry is far from unpleafing,
and it is eaten by our people in confiderable
quantities during the feafon, (which is Auguft,)
and, like all the other fruits in thofe parts, is fuppofed to be wholefome, and a great antifcorbutic.

CURRANS, both red and black, are common Currans
abqut Churchill River, but the latter are far more
plentiful than the former, and are very large and
fine    The bufhes on which thofe currans grow,
frequently exceed three feet in height, and generally thrive beft in thofe parts that are moift
but not fwampy.    Small vallies between the
rocks, at fome little diftance from the woods, are
very favourable to them; and I have frequently
obferved that the fruit produced in thofe fituations is larger and finer than that which is found
in the woods.    Thofe berries have a very great
effect on fome people if eaten in any confiderable
quantities, by acting as a very powerful purgative,
and in fome as an emetic at the fame time;
but if mixed with Cranberries, they never have
that effect.

JUNIPER-BERRIES are frequently found near the Juniper-
berries
new fettlement at Churchill River, but by no
means in fuch plenty as in the more Southern
and interior parts of the country    The bufh
they grew on is fo fimilar to the creeping pine,
that one half of the Company's fervants refiding

in Hudfon's Bay do not know one from the other.
Like the Goofeberry bufhes in thofe parts, the
fruit is always moft plentiful on the under-fide of
the branches.     They are not much efteemed either by the Indians or Englifh, fo that the few
that are made ufe of are generally infufed in brandy, by way of making a cordial, which is far from
unpleafant*.

S raw-
berr es
        STRAWBERRIES †, and thofe of a confiderable
fize and excellent flavour, are found as far North
as Churchill River; and what is moft remarkable, they are frequently known to be more plentiful in fuch places as have formerly been fet on
fire.   This is not peculiar to the Strawberry, but
it is well known that in the interior parts of the
country, as well as at Albany and Moofe Forts,
that after the ground, or more properly the under-
wood and mofs, have been fet on fire, that Rafp-
berry-bufhes and Hips have fhot up in great numbers on fpots where nothing of the kind had
ever been feen before.   This is a phænomenon
that is not eafily accounted for; but it is more
than probable that Nature wanted fome affiftance,
and the mofs being all burnt away, not only admits the fun to act with more power, but the
heat of the fire muft, in fome meafure, loofen the
texture of the foil, fo as to admit the plants to
                                                    fhoot

---

* The Indians call the Juniper berry Caw caw-eue-minick, or the Crow-
berry.

† The O eagh minick of the Indians, is fo called, becaufe it in fome
meafure refembles a heart.

fhoot up, after having been deep-rooted for many years without being able to force their way to
the furface.

Befides the Berries already mentioned, there
are three others found as far North as Churchill;
namely, what the Indians call the Eye-berry, and
the other two are termed Blue-berry and Partridge-berry by the Englifh.

The EYE-BERRY grows much in the fame man- Eye-berry
ner as the Strawberry, and though fmaller, is infinitely fuperior in flavour. This berry is found
in various fituations; but near Churchill River
they are moft plentiful in fmall hollows among
the rocks, which are fituated fome diftance from
the woods; but they are never known to grow
in fwampy ground, and I never faw them fo plentiful in any part of Hudfon's Bay as about
Churchill River.

The BLUE-BERRY is about the fize of a Hur- Blue berry.
tleberry, and grows on bufhes which rife to eighteen inches or two feet, but in general are much
lower. They are feldom ripe till September, at
which time the leaves turn to a beautiful red;
and the fruit, though fmall, have as fine a bloom
as any plum, and are much efteemed for the plea-
fantnefs of their flavour.

The PARTRIDGE-BERRY is nearly as large as the Partridge-berry
Cranberry imported from Newfoundland, and
though of a beautiful tranfparent red, yet has a
difagreeable tafte. Thefe berries are feldom taken, either by the Indians or Englifh; and many
of

of the latter call them Poifon-berries, but feveral birds are fond of them. They grow clofe to the ground, like the Cranberry, and the plant that produces them is not very unlike fmall fage, either in fhape or colour, but has none of its virtues.

I had nearly forgotten another fpecies of Berry, which is found on the dry ridges at Churchill in confiderable numbers. In fize and colour they much refemble the Red Curran, and grow on bufhes fo much like the Creeping Willow, that people of little obfervation fcarcely known the difference, particularly as all the fruit is on the under-fide of the branches, and entirely hid by the leaves. I never knew this Berry eaten but by a frolickfome Indian girl; and as it had no ill effect, it is a proof it is not unwholefome, though exceedingly unpleafant to the palate, and not much lefs fo to the fmell

Hips of a fmall fize, though but few in number, are alfo found on the banks of Churchill River, at fome diftance from the fea. But in the interior parts of the country they are frequently found in fuch vaft quantities, that at a diftance they make the fpots they grow on appear perfect ly red. In the interior parts of Hudfon's Bay they are as large as any I ever remember to have feen, and when ripe, have a moft delightful bloom, but at that feafon there is fcarcely one in ten which has not a worm in it, and they frequently act as a ftrong purgative.

With

With refpe*ct to the fmaller produ*ctions of the vegetable world, I am obliged to be in a great meafure filent, as the nature of my various occupations during my refidence in this country gave me little leifure, and being unacquainted with botany, I viewed with inattention things that were not of immediate ufe: the few which follow are all that particularly engaged my attention.

The WISH-A-CA-PUCCA, which grows in moft parts of this country, is faid by fome Authors to have great medical virtues, applied, either inwardly as an alterative, or outwardly dried and pulverifed, to old fores and gangrenes. The truth, of this I much doubt, and could never think it had the leaft medical quality. It is, however, much ufed by the lower clafs of the Company's feivants as tea; and by fome is thought very pleafant. But the flower is by far the moft delicate, and if gathered at a proper time, and carefully dried in the fhade, will retain its flavour for many years, and make a far more pleafant beverage than the leaves. There are feveral fpecies of this plant, of which fome of the leaves are nearly as large as that of the Creeping Willow, while others are as fmall and narrow as that of the Rofemary, and much refembles it in colour, but all the fpecies have the fame fmell and flavour.

JACKASHEY-PUCK. This herb much refembles Creeping Box; and is only ufed, either by the Indians or Englifh, to mix with tobacco, which makes it fmoke mild and pleafant; and would, I

am

am perfuaded, be very acceptable to many fmo-
kers in England.

Mofs.　　Moss of various forts and colours is plentiful
enough in moft parts of this country, and is what
the deer ufually feed on.

Grafs.　　GRASS of feveral kinds is alfo found in thofe
parts, and fome of it amazingly rapid of growth,
particularly that which is there called Rye-grafs,
and which, in our fhort Summer at Churchill,
frequently grows to the height of three feet.
Another fpecies of Grafs, which is produced in
marfhes, and on the margins of lakes, ponds, and
rivers, is particularly adapted for the fupport of
the multitudes of the feathered creation which
refort to thofe parts in Summer. The Marfh
Grafs at Churchill is of that peculiar nature, that
where it is mowed one year, no crop can be procured the next Summer; whereas at York Fort,
though the climate is not very different, they
can get two crops, or harvefts, from the fame
fpot in one Summer. Vetches are plentiful in
fome parts as far North as Churchill River; and
Burrage, Sorrel, and Coltsfoot, may be ranked
among the ufeful plants. Dandelion is alfo plentiful at Churchill, and makes an early falad, long
before any thing can be produced in the gardens.

In fact, notwithftanding the length of the
Winter, the feverity of the cold, and the great
fcarcity of vegetables at this Northern fettlement
by proper attention to cleanlinefs, and keeping
the people at reafonable exercife, I never had one

mar

man under me who had the leaft fymptoms of the fcurvy; whereas at York Fort, Albany, and Moofe River, there were almoft annual complaints that one half of the people were rendered incapable of duty by that dreadful difforder

I do not wifh to lay claim to any merit on this occafion, but I cannot help obferving that, during ten years I had the command at Churchill River, only two men died of that diftemper, though my complement at times amounted in number to fifty-three

The Foreft Trees that grow on this inhofpita- Trees ble fpot are very few indeed; Pine, Juniper, fmall fcraggy Poplar, Creeping Birch, and Dwarf Willows, compofe the whole catalogue. Farther Weftward the Birch Tree is very plentiful; and in the Athapufcow country, the Pines, Larch, Poplar, and Birch, grow to a great fize; the Alder is alfo found there.

## THE END.

# DIRECTIONS TO THE BINDER.

Fig 1
A Bone

Fig 2 An Arrow

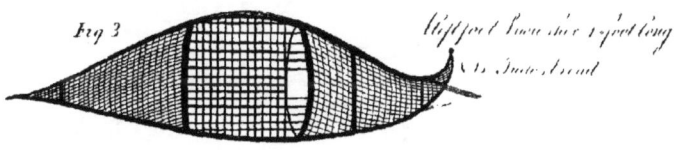

Fig 3 Eight foot from their 3 foot long
As is Snow bread

Fig 4 A Sledge

Fig 5

A Kettle made of Birch rinds

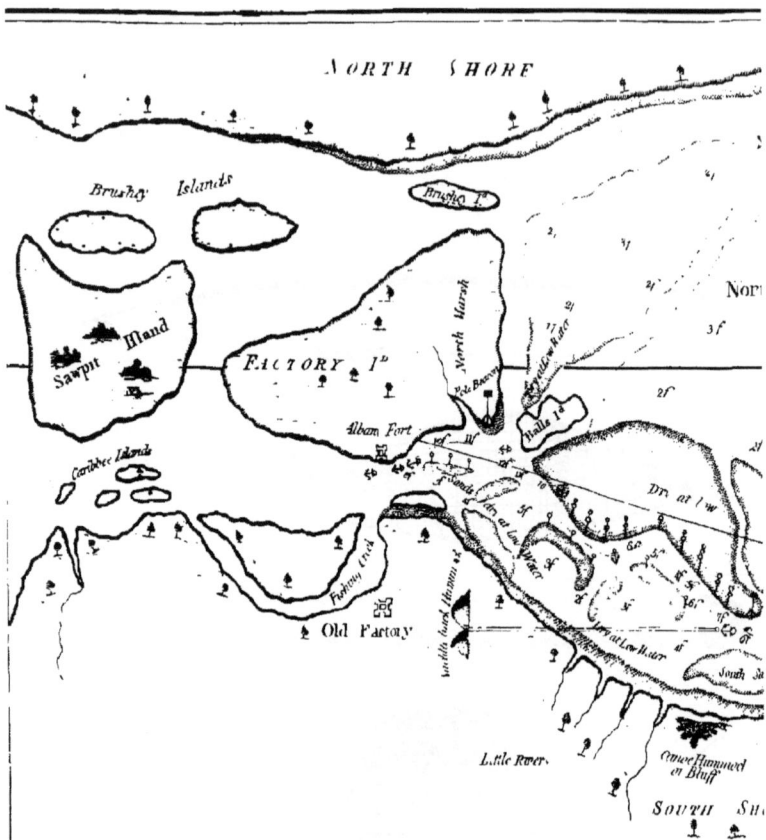

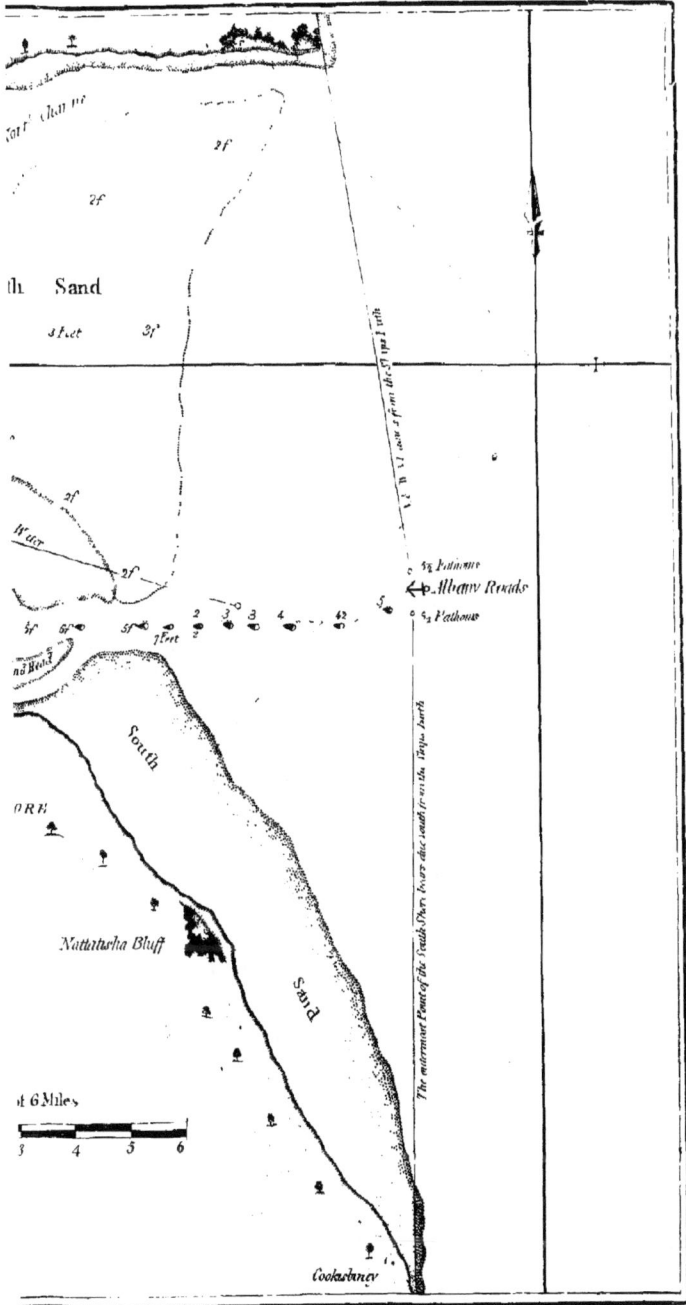

Plan
of
MOOS RIVER
— in —
HUDSONS BAY NORTH AMERICA
Lat 51 N Lon 83 W from London
by S H 1774

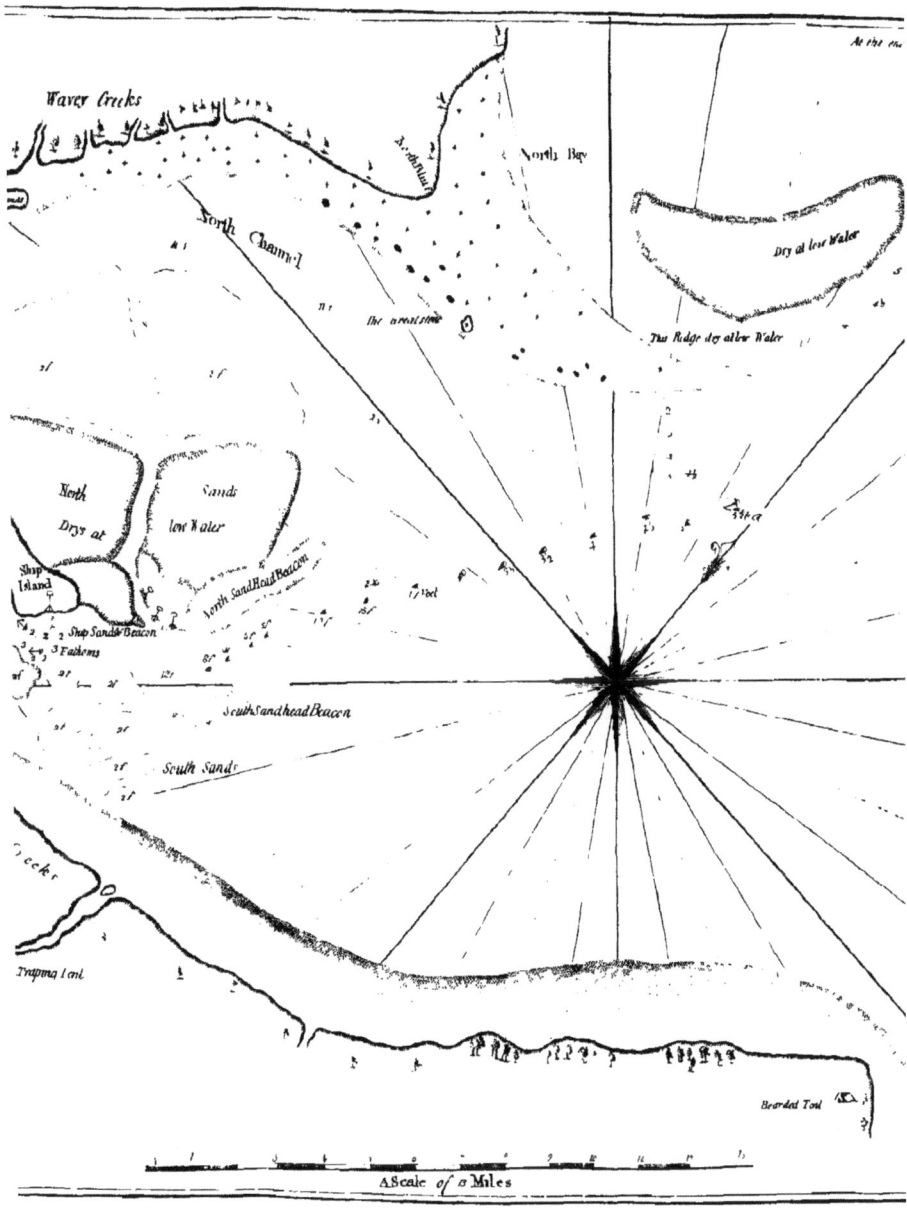

Wavey Creeks

North Bay

North Channel

Dry at low Water

This Ridge dry at low Water

North Sands

Dry at low Water

Ship Island

North Sand head Beacon

Ship Sands Beacon

3 Fathoms

South Sand head Beacon

South Sands

Trapping Point

Bearded Toil

A Scale of 12 Miles

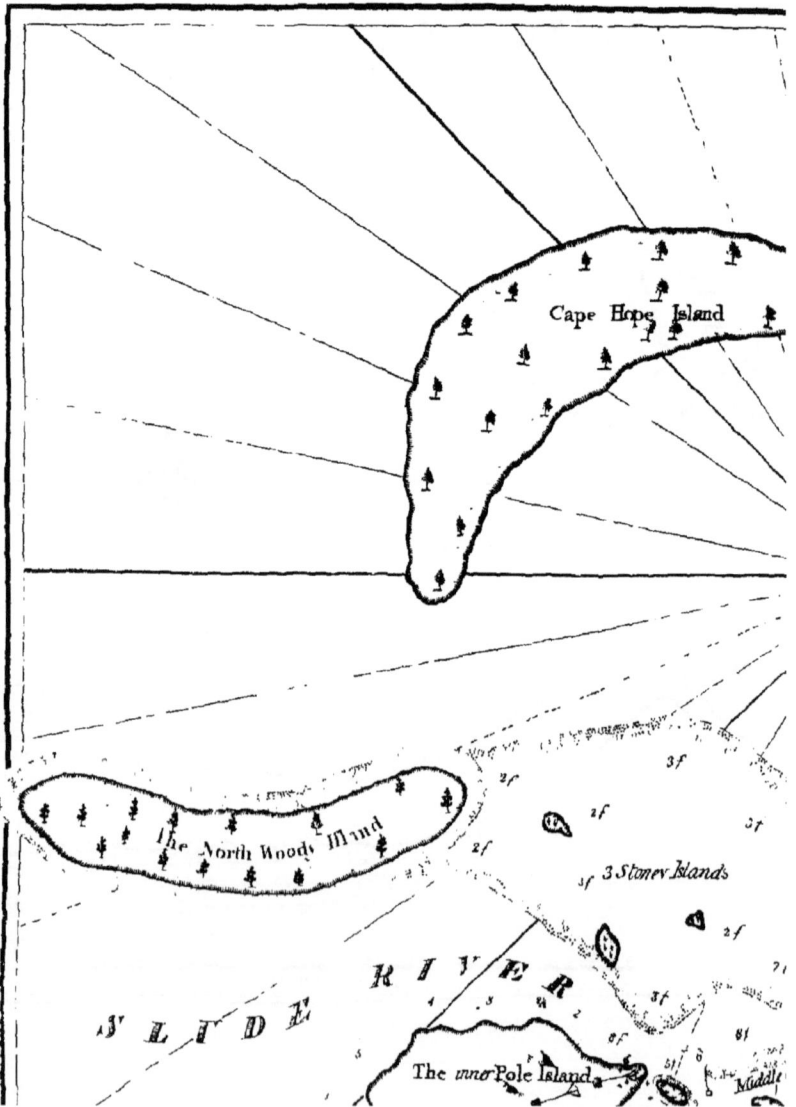

Cape Hope Island

The North Woods Island

S' LIDE RIVER

The inner Pole Island

3 Stoney Islands

Middle

Old Falt Man House

Fishing Creek

North Point

The upper Rock Drie
at low Water

12

10 f    3 f

6 f

3 f

3 f    3 f

ground Drys at low Water

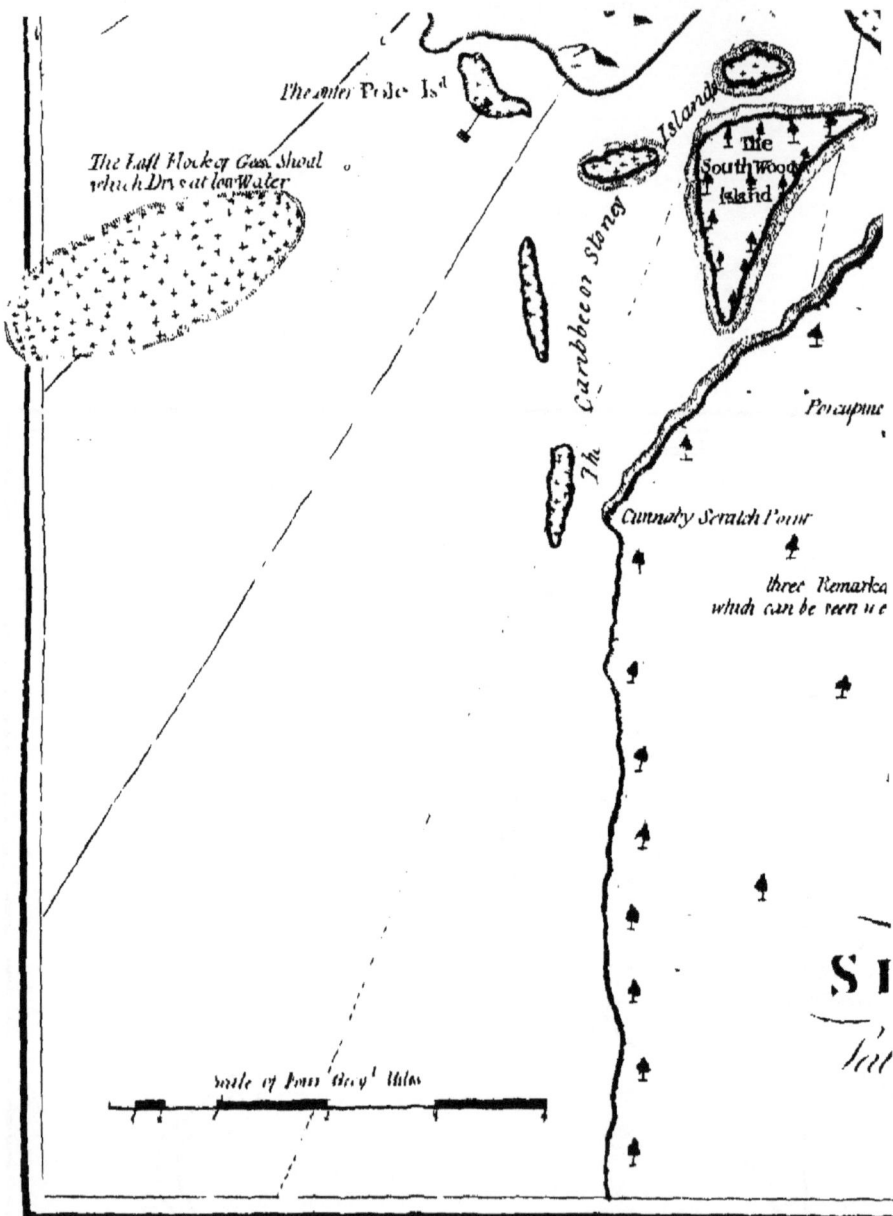

The outer Pole Isd

The Last Flock or Gass Shoal
which Dries at low Water

The Caribbee or Stoney Islands

The
South Wood
Island

Porcupine

Cunnaby Scratch Point

three Remarka
which can be seen u e

S I

scale of Four Geog.l Miles

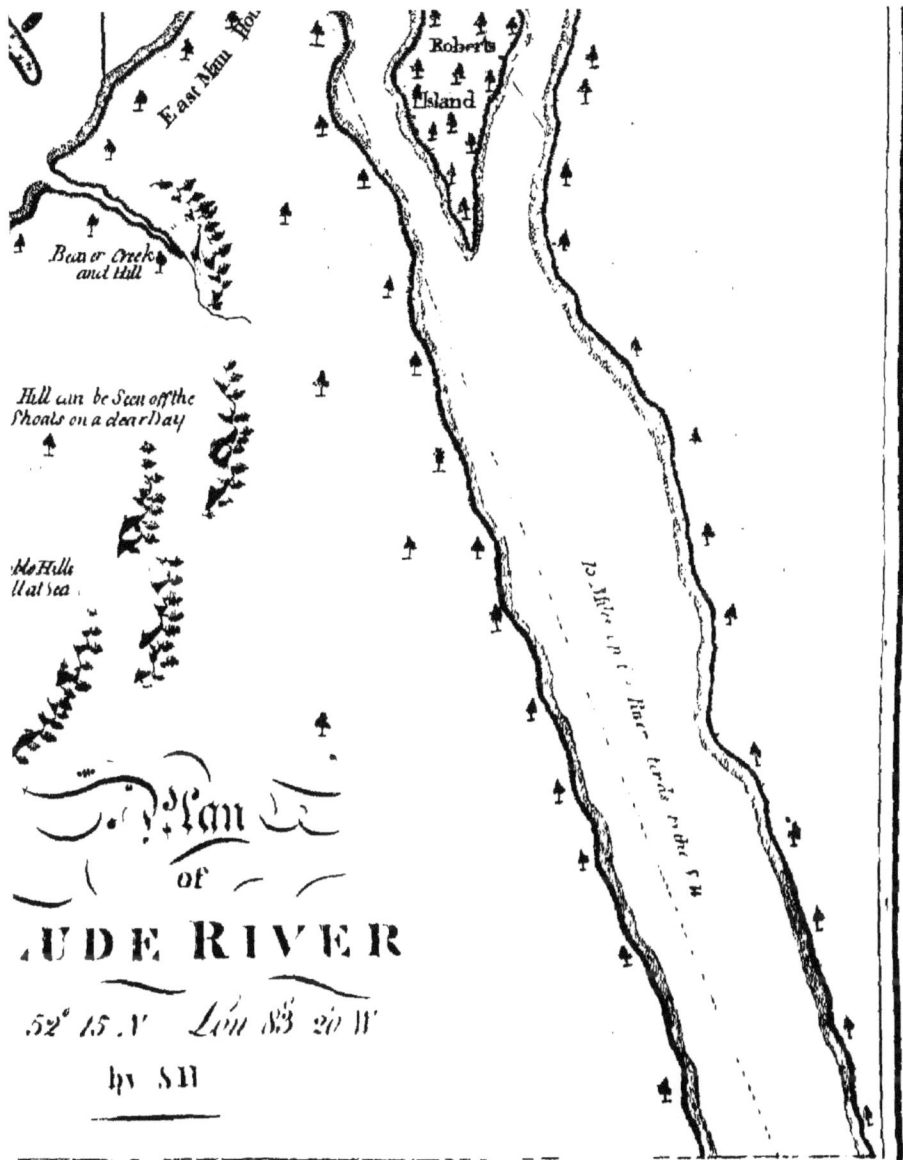

East Man Ho...

Roberts
Island

Beaver Creek
and Hill

Hill can be Seen off the
Shoals on a clear Day

...ble Hills
...ll at Sea

Plan
of
...UDE RIVER

52° 15 N   Lon 83 20 W

by SH

Milton Keynes UK
Ingram Content Group UK Ltd.
UKHW050008060124
435443UK00004BA/73

9 781379 320029